From Idea to Essay

A Rhetoric, Reader, and Handbook

From Idea to Essay

A Rhetoric, Reader, and Handbook

Jo Ray McCuen

Glendale College

and

Anthony C. Winkler

SCIENCE RESEARCH ASSOCIATES, INC.
Chicago, Palo Alto, Toronto, Henley-on-Thames, Sydney, Paris, Stuttgart
A Subsidiary of IBM

Library of Congress Cataloging in Publication Data

McCuen, Jo Ray, 1929–
  From reading to writing.

  Includes index.
  1. English language—Rhetoric.   2. College
readers.   I. Winkler, Anthony C., joint author.
II. Title.
PE1408.M24   808'.0427   76-49669
ISBN 0-574-22030-5

Cover photograph by Larry West

Acknowledgments

WALLACE   Reprinted by permission; © 1950 The New Yorker Magazine, Inc.

ELEVEN   Copyright 1952 by Archibald MacLeish. Reprinted by permission of Houghton Mifflin Company.

A MISERABLE, MERRY CHRISTMAS   From THE AUTOBIOGRAPHY OF LINCOLN STEFFENS, copyright 1931 by Harcourt Brace Jovanovich, Inc.; copyright 1959 by Peter Steffens. Reprinted by permission of the publishers.

MY SECRET PLACE   Reprinted by permission of the author.

THE CODE   Reprinted by permission; © 1957 The New Yorker Magazine, Inc.

Selection from ANNE FRANK: DIARY OF A YOUNG GIRL   Copyright 1952 by Otto H. Frank. Reprinted by permission of Doubleday & Company, Inc. Copyright by Vallentine, Mitchell & Co. Ltd. (for Canada).

THE LAMENT   Public domain.

ELEGY FOR JANE   From *The Collected Poems of Theodore Roethke.* Copyright 1950 by Theodore Roethke. Reprinted by permission of Doubleday & Company, Inc.

ATOMIC BOMBING OF NAGASAKI TOLD BY FLIGHT MEMBER   © 1945 by The New York Times Company. Reprinted by permission.

HANK   Reprinted by permission of the author.

A TURTLE   From THE GRAPES OF WRATH by John Steinbeck. Copyright 1939 by John Steinbeck, Copyright © renewed 1967 by John Steinbeck. Reprinted by permission of The Viking Press.

THE EDGE OF THE SEA   Copyright 1955 by Rachel L. Carson. Reprinted by permission of Houghton Mifflin Company.

THEFT   Copyright, 1935, 1963, by Katherine Anne Porter. Reprinted from her volume, FLOWERING JUDAS AND OTHER STORIES, by permission of Harcourt Brace Jovanovich, Inc.

NOBODY LOSES ALL THE TIME   Copyright 1926 by Horace Liveright; copyright 1954 by E. E. Cummings. Reprinted from COMPLETE POEMS 1913–1962 by E. E. Cummings by permission of Harcourt Brace Jovanovich, Inc.

THE SATISFACTION OF LIFE   Reprinted from ON THE MEANING OF LIFE edited by Will Durant. © 1932 by Will Durant. Published by Robert P. Long. Used by permission of Will Durant.

A GOOD YEAR   Reprinted by permission of the author.

SMALL ECONOMIES   Public domain.

COURTSHIP THROUGH THE AGES   Copr. © 1945 James Thurber, Copr. © 1973 Helen W. Thurber and Rosemary Thurber Sauers. From THE THURBER CARNIVAL, published by Harper & Row, New York. Originally printed in *The New Yorker.*

SOLDIER'S HOME   ''Soldier's Home'' (Copyright 1925 Charles Scribner's Sons) is reprinted by permission of Charles Scribner's Sons from IN OUR TIME by Ernest Hemingway.

THE SOUND OF SILENCE   © 1964 Paul Simon. Used with the permission of the publisher.

THESE ARE THREE OF THE ALIENATED   © 1967 by The New York Times Company. Reprinted by permission.

WHAT IS ALIENATION?   Reprinted by permission of the author.

THE NATURE OF PREJUDICE   Reprinted from READING THE NATURE OF PREJUDICE by Gordon Allport. © 1952 by The Claremont College Curriculum Laboratory. Reprinted by permission.

Preface

The teaching of writing in college traditionally has swung between two polar approaches. The first approach teaches writing by fearlessly prescribing to the student the rhetorical techniques and strategies used by professional writers. Based on the belief that the interested student will automatically write better than the student whose spirit is broken by boredom, the second approach teaches writing by attempting to stimulate the student's interest. The verdict from the field is that each approach suffers from inherent limitations and deficiencies. *From Idea to Essay*—a combined rhetoric, reader, and handbook—is therefore a judicious blend of these two approaches.

From Idea to Essay is unashamedly prescriptive. The student is given thorough instruction in strategies for writing paragraphs and essays. Traditional proven labels are used. Boredom, on the other hand, is exorcised through the inclusion of stimulating stories and poems that generate a specific and different writing assignment for each unit. Before attempting the assignment, the student is treated to specific, sensible instructions on how to do it; moreover, he has the opportunity of reading two essays on the assignment—one by a professional writer, the other by a student. Each chapter closes with two additional essays and numerous alternate writing assignments. In short, the student is instructed, stimulated, and given models to follow.

From Idea to Essay is broad in the scope of its instruction and coverage. While emphasizing the essay, it also instructs the student in writing the paragraph and the research paper. Its coverage includes nine stories, nine poems, twenty-seven professional essays, nine student essays, one research paper, countless exercises, and innumerable illustrative paragraphs, making the book adaptable to a variety of quarter, semester, and trimester writing courses.

Contents

Unit 9
Process

First of all, keep your dream journal in a notebook small enough to carry with you all the time.

Unit 10
Classification

Love is divisible into four types.

Unit 11
Causal Analysis

Unit 12
Argumentation

Part III   Revising the Essay: a brief handbook

Unit 13
Grammar Fundamentals (with Exercises)

Unit 14
Correcting Common Errors (with Exercises)

Appendix: the research paper

Part I

Fundamentals

1

Elements of an Essay

Essay is a middle-aged term, not quite 400 years old. From the French *essai* meaning "attempt," the word was used by the sixteenth-century French writer Montaigne to name the new literary form he had invented. The essay is well named, for without doubt, it is difficult to write, requiring concentration, focus, and effort.

The 500-word theme has evolved as the most common form of the essay taught in the classroom. Short enough to be written in a single class period, yet long enough to accommodate fairly complex topics, the 500-word theme forces the student to pay attention to structure and to choose his words carefully. It also is about as long as the typical office memo, and thus requires writing skills the student will find useful in the business world. We shall begin our discussion of the essay with a paragraph from a student's 500-word theme.

Assignment: *Write a 500-word theme about a relative.*

Student title: "My Father"

My father is my favorite relative. I like him a lot. He grew up in Iowa and wanted to be a doctor. Instead, he became a farmer because his parents couldn't afford to send him to medical school. They couldn't afford to because they were poor and because medical school is expensive. I read someplace that the reason medical school is so expensive is because the AMA keeps the number of students low so there will be few doctors who can therefore charge high fees. Farmers, no matter what you read, don't make much money. They have to endure a lot of hardships and get little in return. Doctors, on the other hand, have an easy life. They work for themselves, make a sure income, and are looked up to by everyone in the community. Farmers, however, are just as important to any country as doctors, yet are paid less. But my father wanted to become a doctor and ended up being a farmer, just like his father. I think I want to be a farmer, too, but my Dad wants me to be a doctor. However, I don't hold this against him.

Even to the casual reader, this paragraph would appear muddled. It is glaringly disorganized, with its sentences pulling in different directions as if the writer could not make up his mind which way to go. We may compare this paragraph to an orchestra in which each musician is playing a different tune. No matter how accurately each member of the orchestra renders the tune he is playing, the total effect will still be horribly discordant. Similarly, the individual sentences in this paragraph may be grammatical, but the paragraph as a whole is not.

There is, in fact, a grammar of the paragraph and of the essay just as there is a grammar of the sentence. *Grammar* refers to rules governing customary usage and practice in language. The "grammar" of the paragraph and the essay is a collection of commonsense guidelines and practices, generally grouped under the heading of *rhetoric*, that writers observe and English teachers struggle to impart. This unit deals with some guidelines for writing the essay; Units 2 and 3 examine the guidelines for preparing an outline and writing a paragraph.

A. Purpose

Every essay must have a *purpose*. This guideline seems simple enough, but it bristles with complications. The down-to-earth student might object that the purpose of writing any essay in Freshman English is to pass the course. Granting this as a sort of long-range aim, we have something quite different in mind. Purpose refers to the goal of an essay: the effect it hopes to achieve, the information or impression it intends to impart, the sentiment it wishes to arouse. With a clear purpose in mind, a writer is less likely to be seduced by irrelevant concepts and details. The student paragraph, for instance, began with the assertion "my father is my favorite relative." It then meandered to an analysis of why medical school is expensive, drifted off into a contrast between doctors and farmers, and finally petered out with an expression of the writer's ambition to become a farmer. It is difficult to discern the writer's purpose. He probably started out with no definite purpose, intending simply to pile sentence upon sentence and hope for the best. Some professional writers can and do work this way, but it is a skill acquired after reams of written work. Few beginning writers can write a good essay without having a definite purpose. Usually, such essays end up sounding as muddled as the student paragraph.

B. Strategy

Having formulated a definite purpose, the writer can plan his essay before beginning to write. He can choose a *strategy* for implementing his purpose, gather relevant facts and detail, and construct an outline. In effect, a writer's purpose imposes limits on his essay, while his strategy enables him to achieve his purpose within the imposed limits.

There are nine common strategies for developing an essay, each of which is covered in a separate unit in Part II. These strategies are: narration, description, example, definition, comparison/contrast, process, classification, causal analysis, and argumentation. An essay assignment may be broadly worded to allow the student to choose his own strategy for developing it—for example, "Write an essay on a favorite relative." Or it may be specifically worded to include the strategy of development that must be used—for example, "Compare and contrast your mother and father." In either case, the strategy is a means to an end—a technique for developing the essay.

Here are some possible strategies for developing a 500-word essay about a favorite relative, each based on a different purpose:

Purpose	*Strategy*
To explain why my father has become so bitter and frustrated in his middle years.	Write a *causal analysis* of why my father has become bitter.
To give the reader a vivid picture of what my father is like.	Write an essay *describing* my father—his physical looks, his personality, his habits.
To illustrate to the reader the effect of the generation gap on my relationship with my father.	Begin by *defining* the generation gap. Support this definition with specific *examples* of generation differences that have cropped up between me and my father.

In the first example, the writer has decided on the strategy of *causal analysis*. His essay will be limited to analyzing the cause of his father's bitterness. The essay in the second example will be limited to a *description;* in the third example, the essay will *define* generation gap and give *examples* of the generation gap in the writer's relationship with his father. In each case, the writer has made the assignment easier by limiting the essay he has to write.

Some students believe that what they are taught in English courses has little usefulness in the outside world. To dismiss this myth, we have selected some examples of real-world applications of the writing strategies discussed in this book. All examples were compiled from experiences either reported to the authors or lived by them.

1. You have applied for a job with a large multinational corporation and have gone successfully through a battery of screening tests. The candidates have been narrowed to a field of five. As a basis for final selection, the personnel psychologist has asked each applicant to write an essay about his or her greatest personal success. You sit down and try to think. Then you begin to write.

   Purpose: To persuade the personnel psychologist that you are the person for the job.
   Strategy: Narration.

2. You are a social worker responsible for supervising the living conditions in some state-supported nursing homes for the elderly. You find unsanitary living conditions at one nursing home and file a stop-payment order against it to cut off its state funding. Your supervisor asks you to write a description of the conditions at this nursing home in support of your action.

   Purpose: To convince the state to withdraw aid from this nursing home.
   Strategy: *Description*.

3. As a vocal member of your PTA group, you listen with horror as the school district officials propose curriculum changes that you are convinced will lower the standard of education. You are opposed to the changes because you have read of other districts in which such changes have not been beneficial. You meet with other parents who share your view and a committee is formed. You are asked to find examples of other districts where similar changes have produced no advantages.

   Purpose: To persuade the school district not to make the proposed changes in the curriculum.
   Strategy: *Example*.

4. You work as a textbook salesperson for a college publisher. A sociology book published by your company is being criticized by the professors using it because it lacks a section on "deviance." You report this to your editor, who fires back a memo asking you to find out exactly what the professors mean by "deviance."

   Purpose: To acquaint the editor with the professors' complaint about the text.
   Strategy: *Definition*.

5. You are employed in the accounting division of a major department store. An employee has made a suggestion for changing the method of reporting daily income. Your boss likes the idea but is uncertain that it would be enough of an improvement over the existing method to justify the change. He asks you to write a comparison of this new method with the existing one.

   Purpose: To persuade the boss to adopt the new reporting method.
   Strategy: *Comparison/contrast*.

6. Mad about creamy chocolate pudding, you have perfected the ideal recipe. Neither riches nor fame can tempt you to share it. Love, however, does. You sit down to write out the recipe for your beloved.

   Purpose: To share your recipe for perfect chocolate pudding with a friend.
   Strategy: *Process*.

7. You work in the counseling office of a major university where entering freshmen are required to take an English test. The university is planning new English classes for its freshmen, and you are assigned to write a report dividing and classifying the incoming freshmen according to their English placement scores.

   Purpose: To gather data to help with curriculum planning.
   Strategy: *Classification*.

8. Your firm specializes in the manufacture of household brushes. Sales of one

particular item—a plastic brush designed as a bathroom grout cleaner—have slumped badly. Your boss assigns you to find out why.

Purpose: To find out why sales of this brush have fallen.
Strategy: *Causal analysis*.

9. You and eleven other jurors have listened for two weeks to a procession of witnesses. Finally, closeted with the other jury members, you begin the painstaking evaluation of evidence. Along with four other jurors, you become convinced of the defendant's guilt, but to your amazement and dismay, the rest of the jurors have come to the exact opposite view. Undecided himself, the foreman asks each group to prepare a written argument outlining its reasons for believing in the defendant's guilt or innocence. Your group assigns you to argue their viewpoint.

Purpose: To persuade your fellow jurors to vote in favor of a guilty verdict.
Strategy: *Argument*.

C. The Controlling Idea

Every essay must have a *controlling idea*. Also called a *thesis,* the controlling idea is simply a statement of what the author intends to do in the essay—what the essay will demonstrate, exemplify, prove, or implement. The controlling idea is usually placed in the first paragraph, most often as the final sentence in the first paragraph, early enough to serve both the writer and reader. The writer is served by knowing what he has to do, the reader by knowing what to expect. Here are three controlling ideas taken from different essays:

> The biggest piece of claptrap about the Press is that it deals almost exclusively, or even mainly with news.
>
> T. S. Matthews, *The Power of the Press*

> While I was still a boy, I came to the conclusion that there were three grades of thinking; and since I was later to claim thinking as my hobby, I came to an even stronger conclusion—namely, that I myself could not think at all.
>
> William Golding, *Thinking as a Hobby*

> Although Boswell and Johnson belonged to the same literary club, were close friends, held the same views on the Monarchy, and the English class system, there are significant differences in their literary opinions and preferences.
>
> Student essay: *A Contrast on the Literary Opinions of Boswell and Johnson*

In the first essay, we expect the author to tell us why it is claptrap to say that the Press deals with the news. We expect the second essay to catalog and explain the three grades of thinking; we expect the third to contrast the literary opinions and preferences of Boswell and Johnson.

How do you find the controlling idea? Sometimes it is implied in the way an assignment is worded. For instance, if your assignment is to write an essay comparing and contrasting the lives of two acquaintances from different social classes, the controlling idea of the assignment is clear: You must do a comparison/contrast. The broader wording of other assignments, however, may force you to find your own controlling idea and impose your own structure on the material. Suppose you are asked to write about your activities over the past year. How do you find a controlling idea?

First, begin by asking yourself some questions about the past year, "What have my activities consisted of?" "What was my state of mind most of the time?" "Did my activities repeat themselves, or did I play different roles every day?" "Have I suffered constant big upheavals, or have I led a calm existence?" "Has my family approved of me or not?" After playing with these questions and others, you hit on the following crudely worded ideas:

1. Most of the time I have been hassled with money worries.
2. Basically, it's been deadly dull of which I can't stand, making me so bored day in and day out.
3. The last year being a series of compromises.
4. Major upheavals have caused me to sink or swim as I met various Waterloos.
5. Why have I felt so guilty all year?
6. The first six months were misery. The second six months were ecstasy.

Each item contains a kernel idea for an essay, but each idea needs a better focus, a sharper edge, a smoother shape.

From the outset of an essay, the reader wants a clear picture of what to expect. The controlling idea obligates the writer to move in a specific direction and allows the reader to see that direction from the start. Consider the following improvements:

1. Meeting my monthly expenses on a budget of $300 has kept me anxious and depressed all year.

    (The word *hassled* has been refined to "anxious and depressed." "Money worries" have been more specifically identified as "monthly expenses." The phrase "on a budget of $300" helps explain the writer's anxiety and worry. Develop by *examples*.)

2. Because of the deadly routine of my studies and work, the past year has been unbearably boring.

    (The main problem with the original version is incoherence. The words do not add up to a comprehensible thought. The reader gets the general meaning but has to guess where it is leading. The revision is more pointed and purposeful. Develop by *causal analysis*.)

3. The last year has been a series of compromises.

    (The original version is a sentence fragment. By replacing the participle *being* with *has been*, we turn the fragment into a complete thought. Develop by *examples*.)

4. Major upheavals required difficult decisions from me this past year.

   (The original version misuses a figure of speech. In the first place, one cannot sink or swim as one faces a Waterloo because Waterloo was a famous field battle. Furthermore, the saying, "to meet one's Waterloo" implies one's destruction, just as the Battle of Waterloo caused Napoleon's final downfall. Figures of speech tend to blur the issue and should be avoided in the wording of a controlling idea. Develop by *examples*.)

5. Because of several serious errors in judgment, I have felt guilt-ridden during most of last year.

   (Our new version simply turns a question into an answer, thereby giving better direction to the content of the essay. Develop by *causal analysis*.)

6. In contrast to my misery during the first six months of the year, I spent the second six months in a glorious, ecstatic mood.

   (The original version suggests two unrelated controlling ideas that tend to tug the reader in separate directions. The term *in contrast* links the two ideas—misery in the first six months and ecstasy in the second six months. Develop by *comparison/contrast*.)

We now can propose six guidelines on the writing of good controlling ideas:

1. Your controlling idea must predict the content of your essay as specifically as possible and without a waste of words.
2. Your controlling idea must make sense—it must have coherence.
3. Your controlling idea must be stated in one complete sentence.
4. Your controlling idea must not be obscured by figures of speech.
5. Your controlling idea must be a statement, not a question.
6. Your controlling idea must move toward a single point, not diverge toward two or more.

D. Effective Supporting Detail

A controlling idea, once expressed on paper, thereafter convinces or bores the reader according to the quality of the *supporting detail*. If the detail is vague, the controlling idea will bore; if the detail is crisp, the controlling idea will invariably convince. Consider, for instance, this paragraph:

> At the turn of the century, many diseases shortened mankind's life. Man did not live very long; what life he had was miserable. If disease did not kill him off, poor hygiene did. However, through improvement in medicine and public hygiene, man now lives many years longer.

Convinced? Probably not. We need more detail. What diseases killed off man? How was medicine improved? What improvements were made in public hygiene? How much longer do people now live? A writer doesn't need to be a genius to amass this sort of detail—all he needs to do is scour his sources more thoroughly for specifics. Consider now this paragraph:

> At the turn of this century, infectious diseases were the primary health menace to this nation. Acute respiratory conditions such as pneumonia and influenza were the major killers. Tuberculosis, too, drained the nation's vitality. Gastrointestinal infections decimated the child population. A great era of environmental control helped change all this. Water and milk supplies were made safe. Engineers constructed systems to handle and treat perilous human wastes and to render them safe. Food sanitation and personal hygiene became a way of life. Continual labors of public health workers diminished death rates of mothers and their infants. Countless children were vaccinated. Tuberculosis was brought under control. True, new environmental hazards replaced the old. But people survived to suffer them. In 1900, the average person in the United States rarely eked out fifty years of life. Some twenty years have since been added to this life expectancy.
>
> Benjamin A. Kogan, *Health: Man in a Changing Environment*

By the time the final sentence is read, we are convinced simply because of the writer's generous use of detail.

Fiction writers have always known that detail is an absolute necessity in storytelling. A writer of westerns dreaming up a story about a gunfighter in Abilene will spend most of his time inventing convincing details about guns, horses, the surroundings, tombstones, outlaws, and hostile Indians.

The skillful use of detail will even make a lie sound convincing. In 1917, H. L. Mencken published a bogus history of the bathtub. Mencken's tale was so widely believed that it was reprinted by numerous newspapers. Mencken claimed that the bathtub was invented by "a man named Adam Thompson, a dealer in cotton and grain," who lived in Cincinnati and "later devised the machine that is still used for bagging hams and bacon." Here is a sample from Mencken's history of the bathtub, which demonstrates his ingenious use of convincing, if invented, detail:

> The bathtub was then still a novelty in England. It had been introduced in 1828 by Lord John Russell and its use was yet confined to a small class of enthusiasts. Moreover, the English bathtub, then as now, was a puny and inconvenient contrivance—little more, in fact, than a glorified dishpan—and filling and emptying it required the attendance of a servant. Taking a bath, indeed, was a rather heavy ceremony, and Lord John in 1835 was said to be the only man in England who had yet come to doing it every day.
>
> Thompson, who was of inventive fancy—he later devised the machine that is still used for bagging hams and bacon—conceived the notion that the English bathtub would be much improved if it were made large enough to admit the whole body of an adult man, and if its supply of water, instead of being hauled to the scene by a maid, were admitted by pipes from a central reservoir and run off by the same means. Ac-

cordingly, early in 1842 he set about building the first modern bathroom in his Cincinnati home—a large house with Doric pillars, standing near what is now the corner of Monastery and Oregon streets. . . .

The tub itself was of new design and became the grandfather of all the bathtubs of today. Thompson had it made by James Guiness, the leading Cincinnati cabinet maker of those days, and its material was Nicaragua mahogany. It was nearly seven feet long and fully four feet wide. To make it watertight the interior was lined with sheet lead, carefully soldered at the joints. The whole contraption weighed about 1,750 pounds, and the floor of the room in which it was placed had to be reinforced to support it. The exterior was elaborately polished.

In this luxurious tub Thompson took two baths on December 20, 1842— a cold one at 8 A.M. and a warm one some time during the afternoon. The warm water, heated by the kitchen fire, reached a temperature of 105 degrees. On Christmas day, having a party of gentlemen to dinner, he exhibited the new marvel to them and gave an exhibition of its use, and four of them, including a French visitor, Col. Duchanel, risked plunges into it. The next day all Cincinnati—then a town of about 100,000 people—had heard of it, and the local newspapers described it at length and opened their columns to violent discussions of it.

The history sounds authentic because Mencken inserts the kind of specific detail one would expect to find in a real history of the bathtub. Thompson's house had "Doric" pillars in front and "stood near what is now the corner of Monastery and Oregon streets"; the first bathtub weighed 1,750 pounds; Thompson took the first bath, in cold water, on December 20th, 1842, at 8 A.M.

Take a cue from the pros. If you have to write an essay on the controlling idea, "Meeting my monthly expenses on a budget of $300 kept me anxious and depressed all year," pack the page with details of your budgetary woes. Don't just ho-hum and say, "My cat got sick and cost me a lot of money to get well." Tell how your cat got sick. Did the vet have to perform an emergency operation on her? Was an anesthetic necessary? Was she in the hospital? How much a day did it cost? What exactly was the vet's fee? Perhaps, you'll end up with something like this:

My female cat, a Persian with the personality of a Hollywood floozie, developed female troubles and had to have an emergency operation on her private organs. She required anesthetic and antibotics (the penicillin shots alone came to $15.48), and convalesced in a private room at Happy Valley Cat Hospital (she was too finicky to go public with all the other sickies) where she devoured $13.98 worth of cat food in four days. By the time she felt well enough to come back to Mama, she'd cost me $54.87— more than twice my monthly mad money which I usually splurge on movies and candy for myself. The rest of that month a heated can of Hunt's baked beans was my most lavish meal.

Shakespeare was better, no doubt, but this paragraph illustrates how details may be used in support of a controlling idea.

E. Unity

Stick to the point of your essay. If your controlling idea is a comparison of cows and goats, write about that and nothing else. If your controlling idea is to define love, then you must define love. Good writing does not beat about the bush; it approaches the subject directly. The writer moves in the direction of his point without being distracted. This straightforward progression, called *unity*, means that every statement in the essay supports or proves the controlling idea. You introduce only material related to your controlling idea, suppressing the urge to bring up matters that are irrelevant. An essay crowded with irrelevant facts, anecdotes, or illustrations is like a quart of hearty beef soup diluted with a gallon of water.

The following excerpt is an example of writing that does not stick to the point. Notice the pieces of irrelevant information, set in italics, that are thrown in here and there, destroying the unity of the essay. Read the essay without them, and you will see how the writing is strengthened.

The deadly routine of my studies and work turned the past year into unbearable boredom. Each day proceeded with unerring predictability, from sunrise to sunset. If I were to use a symbol to reflect my life this past year, it would be one gigantic yawn—so dull was the schedule by which I was tyrannized. *Of course, there were always a few bright accidents that invaded the boredom, but they were rare.* Every morning at 7:00 A.M. the alarm dragged me out of bed so that I could race to school in time to answer Prof. Huber's Western Civilization roll call at 8:07 A.M. For the next 50 minutes I listened to the prof drone through his battered and stained lecture notes on the meaning of *civitas*, the First Triumvirate, or the Barbarian Invasion. I took plenty of notes so that I could quote verbatim on the next test. Then I moved on to the next class, Introduction to Psychology, where the instructor always got hung up on "standard deviations," "chi square," and "correlation" because those were his graduate work specialities. Then I moved on the the next class, and to the next—all equally numbing to my senses.

At 1:00 P.M. it was time to report to my job as cashier of the Arco self-service gas station, located one block from where I live. *I should probably mention that I live in Bakersfield, a town whose reputation is cruelly maligned. I have found that most people think of Bakersfield as the garbage dump of creation. "How can you stand to live in that ugly place?" they often ask. "Nothing but Oakies, fog and cow dung there," they insist. But I'm defensive of my hometown, so I stick up for it.* Anyway, at the Arco station, I sat in a cage, like a monkey at the zoo, collecting money through a barred window from citizens whose lives must have been duller than mine judging by the way their feet dragged and their faces drooped. "That will be $2.50. Thank you, ma'am." "That will be $3.00. Thank you, sir." "No, you will have to work the pump yourself. This is self-service." I repeated myself over and over again— endlessly until I felt that my voice was floating out in the air somewhere, separate from my body. Sometimes I almost wished for a robbery to inject a moment of excitement into my life. *My friend Jimmy Davenport, who works for a posh liquor store, was held up once, and the robbers handcuffed him in the men's toilet, along with the manager of the store and two customers. He told me that he was never so scared in his life as when he looked down the barrel of that big black pistol one of the robbers stuck in his face.* But for me the most exciting event of the job was when I opened by sandwich bag to see if I was having salami or cream cheese.

At night my routine involved first propping up fat textbooks on my desk and then propping up my eyelids to keep from falling asleep as I doggedly underlined the significant passages with a thick yellow pen. *I recommend these pens to all my friends because they really make the print stand out.* For example, in English Lit, we studied poems like Shelley's "Hymn to Intellectual Beauty," a long rambling piece about shadows, unseen powers, and shrieks of ecstasy; but I never understood a word that I read, so gradually I would nod and nap. Then I would raise up, startled, and slap my face to keep awake. As I underlined steadily, tome after tome, I eventually allowed myself the luxury of crawling into bed, where I would fall asleep, knowing that the next day would repeat that day's petty pace.

F. Coherence

If you flub a sentence while speaking, you can hastily backtrack with an apologetic, "I mean," correct yourself, then resume with a smooth, "Now, as I was saying." Once an essay is written and turned in, however, you may have numerous reasons for remorse, but no opportunities for correction. Helpless and alone on the page, your words glorify or brutalize the instructor's image of you. It is essential, therefore, that you write, rewrite, and rewrite again until your sentences say clearly what your inner self intends.

An essay that is clear and logical has *coherence*. Not only must its sentences be clear, logical, and grammatically correct, they must be arranged so that the reader understands the flow of thought and the relationships among sentences and words. Perhaps the best way to achieve coherence is to think of your essay as a unit rather than as individual bits and pieces. The focal point of the unit, of course, is your controlling idea. You carefully build your essay so that each sentence follows in logical sequence and so that the essay as a whole hits the reader with a clear and definite impact, as if he had been led to an address through many streets by a well-designed map.

We occasionally receive essays that sound like this:

In the past year it's been through times of extreme highs and lows in my emotional outlook on life. The trend of any life seems to follow this general pattern. Some of the high moments were meeting new people that turned out to be much more than mere acquaintances, having the newly met person turn into a friend a person could know for the rest of their life. Also meeting and going out with a few special girls, which in our relationship between each other bloomed into a kind of affection for ourselves. Then, too, I gave top performances in the area of athletics, track and field, and also in baseball were most gratifying.

The low points in my life one of them was the splitting up of my parents, watching both of them lose a little youthfulness from inside like a plant that has been cut with a sharp object, the plant will heal and continue to live but forever will be scarred. And, too, breaking up with one girl I was extremely close to. There were other low moments in my life. It occurred at times when least needed. My injuries in the sports in which I competed compounded my feelings of despair.

The cycle of my life in the past year would be for me of course totally and completely unique, but in reality it probably compares to people in everyday life.

Frustrating reading, isn't it? This student's writing is *garbled*—muddled, illogical, or downright unintelligible. It reminds us of a child forcing pieces of a puzzle into the wrong spaces, creating a topsy-turvy picture. Much of this kind of writing is the result of laziness. Some students simply dash off an essay and turn it in without a second glance. They do not try out their sentences by speaking them aloud or by reading through a first draft of the essay to see how it sounds. If one of your sentences sounds choppy or senseless, strike it out and start all over again. Rewrite until the words say what you want them to say, even if it means writing in simpler sentences. As a matter of fact, if you are a chronic garbler, you should avoid embroidered, complex sentences until you have mastered simple, clear sentences.

Incoherence has numerous causes. The following rules and examples will help you to avoid the most common errors.

RULE 1: *Avoid mixed constructions.* Here are examples of mixed constructions:

Mixed: Whereas parents insist on stifling their children's independence, they encourage rebellion.

Improved: When parents insist on stifling their children's independence, they encourage rebellion.

Mixed: With every new service on the part of government suggests that our taxes are going to be raised.

Improved: Every new service on the part of government suggests that our taxes are going to be raised.

Mixed: My mind was filled with horror at the sight of so many hungry people, which they made me feel guilty for being part of a society that neglects its poor.

Improved: My mind was filled with horror at the sight of so many hungry people. They made me feel guilty for being part of a society that neglects its poor.

Mixed constructions are confusing because they force the reader into quick mental adjustments for which he isn't prepared. The writer begins with one pattern of expression but then quickly switches to another, forcing the reader to correct the sentence in his mind in order to give it some coherence.

RULE 2: *Use pronouns that refer only to identifiable antecedents.** Here is an example of incoherence resulting from poor pronoun reference:

> Everybody today wants psychological advice so that *they* will tell *them* what to do. But *that's* a way of avoiding *your* problems and losing *one's* sense of responsibility, *which* is the only healthy way to survive.

A careless and inconsistent use of pronouns jumbles the ideas. The passage simply does not stick together properly. To whom do *they* and *them* refer? What does *that's* stand for? Why is there a sudden shift from *everybody* to *your* and yet another shift to *one's?* Finally, *which* seems to refer to "responsibility," creating further confusion. Now observe the revision:

> Everybody today wants psychological advice from a counselor who will tell him what to do. But relying on counseling is a way of avoiding problems and losing one's sense of responsibility; without responsibility a happy life is impossible.

RULE 3: *Use similar grammatical structures to achieve balance in a sentence.* This is called *parallelism.*† The use of parallelism could improve the following sentence:

> Walking a beat, riding patrol cars, and the work of an undercover agent are all dangerous aspects of police work.

Walking and *riding* are similar verb forms, but "the work of an undercover agent" breaks the pattern. The following is an improvement:

> Walking a beat, riding patrol cars, and doing undercover work are all dangerous aspects of police work.

RULE 4: *Use transition words to help the reader move easily through your writing.* Transition words identify the logical connection between two parts of a sentence. They help the reader to move smoothly from one idea to another. For example:

Too abrupt: She searched and searched for her purse. She could not find it.

Improved: She searched and searched for her purse, *but* she could not find it.

Too abrupt: Romance may express itself in a variety of ways. A man may send a woman a dozen long-stemmed roses. A husband may wax the kitchen floor.

Improved: Romance may express itself in a variety of ways. *For example,* a man may send a woman a dozen long-stemmed roses. *Or, as a romantic gesture,* a husband may wax the kitchen floor.

---

*For an explanation of antecedent, see pages 262–263.
†For a fuller explanation of parallelism, see page 269.

When choosing a transition word, be certain of the type of signal you wish to send the reader—addition, contrast, specification, or conclusion.

RULE 5: *Repeat key words to attract and hold your reader's attention.* Notice the effective repetition of the word *dance* in the following excerpt from Hans Christian Andersen's *The Red Shoes:*

> The shoes would not let her do what she liked: when she wanted to go to the right, they *danced* to the left. When she wanted to *dance* up the room, the shoes *danced* down the room, and then down the stairs, through the streets and out of the town gate. Away she *danced,* and away she had to *dance,* right into the dark forest. Something shone up above the trees and she thought it was the moon, for it was a face, but it was the old soldier with the red beard. He nodded and said, "See what pretty *dancing* shoes!"
>
> This frightened her terribly and she wanted to throw off the red shoes, but they stuck fast. She tore off her stockings, but the shoes had grown fast to her feet. So off she *danced,* and off she had to *dance,* over fields and meadows, in rain and sunshine, by day and by night, but at night it was fearful.

The repetition of the word *dance* holds the reader's attention and reinforces the point of the fairy tale—that the red shoes were magical.

2

The Outline

A. Planning and Organization

Some writers need to organize an essay before writing it; others do not and would only be inhibited by such advance planning. Advance organization of an essay has the advantage of giving the writer an overall plan to survey at a glance. Defects in structure and emphasis are highlighted and easy to detect. This is especially true of organizing by an *outline,* the method discussed in this unit.

An outline condenses and lays out the major elements of an essay in the sequence they will be dealt with, providing a quick bird's eye view of the whole essay. It lets you see at a glance whether your organization is logical and complete, or whether it is choppy and full of gaps. An outline should not become a straight jacket, however, forcing you into a pattern that will result in a stilted, wooden essay. It should remain flexible enough to allow your essay to be influenced by divine inspiration.

B. Form and Elements of the Outline

An outline subdivides the controlling idea of the essay into smaller ideas, which are then developed in separate paragraphs. The currently accepted form of outlining uses numbers and letters to identify and order ideas according to their importance. Consider this sample outline:

Controlling idea

  I. Main idea
    A. Sub-idea
    B. Sub-idea
      1. Supporting detail
      2. Supporting detail
 II. Main idea
    A. Sub-idea
    B. Sub-idea
      1. Supporting detail
      2. Supporting detail

You can write either a *sentence outline* or a *topic outline*. All entries in a sentence outline are full sentences, whereas the entries in a topic outline consist of single words or phrases. The following excerpts will illustrate the difference.

TOPIC OUTLINE

Controlling idea: Two primary problems of adolescent youth

I. Extreme dependence on family
  A. Financial
  B. Emotional

II. Search for personal identity
  A. Between childhood and adulthood
  B. Difficulty of finding self in today's world
  C. Blurred social standards
  D. No official rites of passage to adulthood

SENTENCE OUTLINE

Controlling idea: Adolescent youths in our society face two primary problems.

I. Adolescents are extremely dependent on their families.
  A. Because jobs for the young don't pay well, adolescents have to depend on parents for financial support.
  B. Since parents have always provided emotional stability, adolescents feel lost without parental support.

II. Adolescents are perplexed by their search for an identity in a changing world.
  A. They are torn between acting as children and acting as adults.
  B. It is difficult for adolescents to form ideals or goals when the world is in an upheaval.
  C. Blurred social standards cause frustration and consequent insecurity in adolescents.
  D. Without official rites of passage to adulthood, adolescents in American society must establish their own rites to account for their emerging identities.

The advantage of the topic outline is that it is brief, giving an instant overview of the entire essay. A sentence outline, on the other hand, provides a complete and detailed plan of the essay. The rule of thumb is: Use topic outlines for simple subjects; use sentence outlines for complex subjects.

C. Use of the Outline

In effect, the outline is a map of what you will cover. It should tell you whether you are developing your controlling idea logically and should indicate the supporting points you need to supply. It may even suggest some details. The most important function of the outline, however, is to prevent the essay from dwelling on some topics while failing to develop others.

Consider the following student essay, which was written without an outline:

Because of its practical uses as well as its psychological effects, my backpack is my most valuable possession. It is difficult to describe, but it resembles a chair that one places on one's hips and piles with things like sleeping bag, canteen, pots, underwear, and mosquito poison.

My backpack gives me a sense of independence because it represents perseverance and self-reliance as I climb trail after trail. I know, when I set out on a trail, that for the next three or four days, my backpack and I will be challenged by the mountain, as were the old mountaineers of our country. So I fill it carefully and methodically with all the equipment I will need—from food to clothing.

Campfire time is the nicest part about camping, but sitting around the campfire I sometimes wish I had a transistor radio, which is what I thought I was getting when I got my backpack.

It's been a tradition in our family to go backpacking every summer, so each member of my family has his own backpack and each of us has to carry his own load up the mountain trails. As we climb, we sing, watch the beautiful scenery, and occasionally munch on some food. My favorite climb is Mt. Whitney although once I had a terrible case of altitude sickness when I reached the top. I hope that never happens again because I really suffered.

I wish I had a Kelty backpack because it is the best. Mine is just a plain orange nylon polyester backpack of some minor brand, but it will do until I can afford the Kelty. My Dad surprised me with the backpack my last birthday. I had expected a transistor radio, but instead I received the backpack, which pleased me enormously. I plan to use it frequently.

Here is a sketchy outline of this effort:

Controlling idea: Because of its practical uses as well as its psychological effects, my backpack is my most valuable possession.

I. My backpack gives me a sense of independence.
   A. It represents perseverance.
   B. I feel like a mountaineer with it.

II. Campfire time is the nicest part about camping.
   A. Sometimes I wish I had a transistor radio.
   B. I got a backpack instead.

III. It's a tradition in our family to camp.
   A. We have a good time climbing and singing.
   B. I got sick at Mt. Whitney, my favorite climbing spot.

IV. I wish I had a Kelty backpack.
   A. Mine is just a plain orange polyester backpack.
   B. I had expected a transistor radio.

One glance at this outline would have been enough to convince most writers that trouble loomed ahead. The student writer, however, plunged into the topic without an outline, and was thereafter blown and scattered over the page by uncontrollable gusts of inspiration.

We subdivided the controlling idea into smaller ideas, assembled them into an outline, and added a statement specifying the purpose of the essay and a suggested strategy for implementing it:

Controlling idea: Because of its practical uses as well as its psychological effects, my backpack is my most valuable possession.

I. Description of my backpack
    A. It is made of nylon polyester.
    B. It resembles a chair.

II. My father gave me my backpack.
    A. It was a surprise birthday present.
    B. Backpacking is a family tradition.

III. My backpack has practical uses.
    A. It serves as a portable restaurant.
    B. I can use it as a folding motel.

IV. My backpack has important psychological effects.
    A. It gives me a feeling of strength and self-reliance.
    B. It gives me a feeling of independence.

Purpose: To acquaint the reader with the reasons that the backpack is your most valuable possession.

Strategy: Analysis of the reasons you value your backpack: *causal analysis.*

We gave the writer the outline and asked him to rewrite his essay. He now knew why he was writing the essay, what subtopics to cover, and which strategy to use. Limited by a definite purpose and strategy, the writer produced a revised essay improved in focus, content, and detail:

Because of its practical uses as well as its psychological effects, my backpack is my most valuable possession. Made of bright orange waterproof nylon polyester tied to a light aluminum frame, my backpack resembles a chair that I tie to my back and pile high with camping necessities.

My Dad surprised me with this pack on my eighteenth birthday. I had expected a transistor radio, but instead I received the backpack, which pleased me enormously since backpacking is a tradition in our family and everyone except me had his own personal backpack.

I value my backpack for its practical uses. It is really a portable restaurant capable of carrying sixty pounds of food tucked away in its various compartments. When properly filled, my backpack will feed me for ten days in comfort and style. Whenever I get to a particularly beautiful spot, after climbing for two or three hours, I can simply set down my pack, open the food compartment, spread out a picnic of dried and canned foods and dine on a meal washed down with the tang of a mountain stream.

Out in the crisp blue mountain air, the fare tastes better than that of a four-star Michelin bistro. Once the sun has disappeared and night has fallen, I can check in without a reservation, for my backpack is also a folding motel. It contains all I need: insect repellent, a propane lantern, a sleeping bag, and a portable tent. The rains can pour and the winds can howl, but I remain immune to the elements and to the mountain.

I value my backpack also because of its psychological effect on me. When I am carrying it on my back, slowly inching up the mountains, one steady step at a time, I feel strong and self-reliant. In liberating me from restaurants, motels, grocery stores, my backpack helps me overcome the timidity in myself, making me feel independent and free. Sometimes I imagine myself an early American mountaineer—tough, strong, and weatherbeaten. I don't have to rely on expensive tourist traps because my backpack supplies everything I will need during the time that I will be camping out. For both its practical uses and its psychological effects, my backpack is truly my most valuable possession.

The outline for the improved essay indicates that the practical uses of the backpack and its psychological effects are roughly equal in importance, and this equality is reflected in the wording of the controlling idea: "Because of its practical uses as well as its psychological effects, my backpack is my most valuable possession." The writer has therefore attempted to give approximately equal time and space to both aspects of his subject. Having written the essay, he can then check to be sure that both ideas have been emphasized in the essay according to their importance in the outline. If he discovers that he has written five paragraphs on the practical uses of the backpack but dismissed its psychological effects in one skimpy sentence, the essay is obviously lopsided and needs to be rewritten.

Not all outlines will reflect a symmetrical and equal development of all sub-ideas. The outline on the problems of adolescent youth, for example, lists two points that need to be developed under the first sub-idea, "Adolescents are extremely dependent on their families," and four points under the second sub-idea, "Adolescents are perplexed by their search for an identity in a changing world." Common sense tells us that more space is required to develop four points under one sub-idea than two points under another. If, however, the sub-idea with the larger number of points ends up being only a skimpy paragraph, the writer has probably muddled his train of thought and produced a lopsided essay.

Exercises

1. Break down the following controlling ideas into their logical major divisions:

   a. The major strokes in tennis can be grouped into five types: the service, the the topspin shot, the chop, the full volley, and the smash.
   b. Secretion of digestive juices in the stomach, constriction of the circulatory system, and an elevated heartbeat, are some of the effects of smoking.

c. *Hardhat*—used in the singular—is a term that designates a member of the working class who is usually union affiliated and politically conservative.

d. I am an impossible spendthrift at rummage sales and estate auctions.

2. Rewrite the following outlines, correcting any defects.

a. *Controlling idea:* A manual portable typewriter is less expensive, less distracting, and more convenient than an electric portable.

    I. The manual portable typewriter is less expensive than an electric portable.
       A. The manual typewriter has no motor or electrical wiring.
       B. The electric typewriter has an expensive motor, drive chain, and electrical grounding system.
    II. The manual portable typewriter is less distracting than an electric portable.
       A. The manual typewriter makes only the noise of its keys striking against the platen.
       B. The motor of an electric typewriter makes a constant whirring noise.
    III. The new electric portable with cartridge ribbons is troublesome to use.
       A. The cartridge ribbon feature makes a big job out of correcting a simple mistake.
       B. The cartridge ribbons are more expensive than ordinary ribbons.
    IV. The manual portable is more convenient than an electric portable.
       A. The manual is lighter, smaller, and requires no electrical outlet.
       B. The electric typewriter is heavier, bulkier, and requires an electrical outlet.

b. *Controlling idea:* Buying a used car is risky because dealers sometimes falsify background information on the car; odometer readings are sometimes inaccurate; and mechanical difficulties are sometimes impossible to detect.

    I. Dealers sometimes falsify background information on the car.
       A. Background information is useful assessing the probable condition of a used car.
       B. Most dealers seem to sell only used cars that were owned by little old ladies.
    II. Foreign car dealers usually have good buys on domestic makes.
       A. The foreign car dealer is interested in selling his brand.
       B. The bluebook on domestic cars is traditionally lower than on foreign cars.
    III. Odometer readings are sometimes inaccurate.
       A. The owner may have backed the odometer before trading in the car.
       B. An overzealous salesman may have backed the odometer.
    IV. Mechanical defects are sometimes impossible to detect.
       A. The warranty on a used car is usually limited and short.
       B. Serious mechanical problems can be easily disguised.

3

The Paragraph

A. The Topic Sentence

Once the outline for an essay has been prepared, its individual entries—the main ideas—must be developed into paragraphs. Most paragraphs consist of three parts: a topic sentence, supporting detail, and a summary sentence. Often, but not always, a paragraph begins with its topic sentence, which states the main idea. The main idea is then developed through supporting details—examples, arguments, and other particulars. The summary sentence restates the main idea, usually by extending it slightly from its original presentation in the topic sentence. Here is an example:

Topic sentence: *By a strange perversity in the cosmic plan, the biologically good die young.* Species are not destroyed for their shortcomings but for their achievements. The tribes that slumber in the graveyards of the past were not the most simple and undistinguished of their day, but the most complicated and con-

Supporting detail: spicuous. The magnificent sharks of the Devonian period passed with the passing of the period, but certain contemporaneous genera of primitive shellfish are still on earth. Similarly, the lizards of the Mesozoic era have long outlived the dinosaurs who were immeasurably their biologic betters.

Summary sentence: Illustrations such as these could be endlessly increased. *The price of distinction is death.*

John Hodgdon Bradley, "Is Man an Absurdity?"
Harper's Magazine, October 1936

This paragraph opens with the topic sentence, the main idea that "the biologically good die young." Supporting detail and examples are found in sentences 2 through 5, while the final sentence rephrases the main idea and slightly extends it. A paragraph organized in this manner is said to move from the *general* to the *particular.*

Some paragraphs, however, reverse this organization, proceeding from the *particular* to the *general,* from supporting detail to the main idea. Here is an example:

Supporting detail: When we watch a person walk away from us, his image shrinks in size. But since we know for a fact that he is not shrinking, we make an unconscious correcting and "see" him as retaining his full stature. Past experience tells us what his true stature is with respect to our own. Any sane and dependable expectation of the future requires that he have the same *Topic* true stature when we next encounter him. *Our perception is thus a prediction;* *sentence:* *it embraces the past and the future as well as the present.*

Warren J. Wittreich, Visual Perception and Personality

Sometimes the idea in a topic sentence is too complex to be developed in a single paragraph. In the following example, a single topic sentence, "There are many types of poetical obscurity," is developed in two paragraphs:

There are many types of poetical obscurity. There is the obscurity that results from the poet's being mad. This is rare. Madness in poets is as uncommon as madness in dogs. A discouraging number of reputable poets are sane beyond recall. There is also the obscurity that is the result of the poet's wishing to appear mad, even if only a little mad. This is rather common and rather dreadful. I know of nothing more distasteful than the work of a poet who has taken leave of his reason deliberately, as a commuter might of his wife.

Then there is the unintentional obscurity or muddiness that comes from the inability of some writers to express even a simple idea without stirring up the bottom. And there is the obscurity that results when a fairly large thought is crammed into a three- or four-foot line. The function of poetry is to concentrate; but sometimes over-concentration occurs, and there is no more comfort in such a poem than there is in the subway at the peak hour.

E. B. White, "Types of Poetical Obscurity"

There are no rules governing the length of an adequately developed paragraph. The topic sentence must guide you. When you have supported and developed it to your satisfaction, you have completed your paragraph. Often, students fall into the error of writing thin, emaciated paragraphs. Look over your finished essay; if your paragraphs are all three or four lines long, something is wrong. Most likely your supportive detail is inadequate, and you are probably writing empty paragraphs that sound like this:

The defensive backfielders of footballs are disciplined men. They are tenacious and controlled. They must be tough and defend aggressively.

This paragraph is so empty it could float a balloon. Sentences 2 and 3 simply parrot back the content of sentence 1 without adding any detail, substantiation, examples, or proof. Here is an example of a well-developed paragraph on the same topic:

In the defensive backfield the aggression gets buried under more and more inhibition and discipline. These men are like long-distance runners: They are loners, but they are nowhere near as hungry for glory as are the wide receivers.

In place of the vanity and fantasies of the wide receivers, the defensive backs experience depression and rage. They have traits that can be found in offensive linemen, wide receivers, and linebackers. They are tenacious. They must learn zone and man-on-man pass-defense patterns that require incredible self-discipline in the furor of battle. They must not be led by their natural inclination, which is to follow receivers out of their zone before the quarterback releases the ball on a pass play. They must execute patterns precisely. To counter running plays, however, they must move up fast and, though lighter and weaker than the running backs they are trying to stop, hit very hard. So they need controlled and timed brutality and anger.

Arnold J. Mandell, "In Pro Football They Play
Best Who Play What They Are," *Saturday Review/World*

The topic sentence "A pig is ugly" could probably be adequately supported in 100 words; on the other hand, "Poverty is ugly" might require at least 300 words. The more restricted the topic sentence, the shorter the paragraph. Your duty is to make sure the paragraph fully supports its topic sentence.

C. Developmental Strategies

With considerable justification, the paragraph has frequently been called a miniature essay. Just as an essay must develop its controlling idea, so must a paragraph develop its topic sentence—in both cases, through the use of supporting detail. Both essay and paragraph are subjected to demands of unity and coherence. Clinching the comparison, however, is the fact that both the essay and the paragraph use the same developmental strategies—narration, description, example, definition, comparison/contrast, process, classification, causal analysis, and argumentation.

Later in this book, separate units are devoted to specific instruction in the use of each strategy in writing an essay. For now, we will discuss the application of each strategy to paragraph writing.

1. Narration

To narrate means to tell a story. A paragraph developed by narration therefore tells a story, sometimes from the personal point of view and sometimes from the third person point of view. Narrative writing convinces the reader by using specific detail, by following a clear and understandable sequence, and by recounting the story in terms a reader may have experienced in his own life. Here is an example of a paragraph developed by narration:

Every morning I lay on the floor in the front parlour watching her door. The blind was pulled down to within an inch of the sash so that I could not be seen. When she came out on the doorstep my heart leaped. I ran to the hall, seized my books and followed her. I kept her brown figure always in my eye and, when we came near the point at which our ways diverged, I quickened my pace and passed her. This happened morning after morning. I had never spoken to her, except for a few casual words, and yet her name was like a summons to all my foolish blood.

James Joyce, Araby

The detail is specific and the sequence fast-paced and clear. Furthermore, the event recounted—of young unrequited love—is one with which most readers can identify. Unit 4 teaches how to develop an entire essay by narration.

2. Description

If narration means to tell, *description* means to show. A paragraph developed by description uses a dominant impression as a central theme to unify its descriptive detail. In the following passage, the dominant impression of Braggioni is of an expensively dressed, grossly fat man. We have italicized specific words that support this impression.

> Braggioni catches her glance solidly as if he had been waiting for it, leans forward, *balancing his paunch* between his spread knees, and sings with tremendous emphasis, weighing his words. He has, the song relates, no father and no mother, nor even a friend to console him; lonely as a wave of the sea he comes and goes, lonely as a wave. His *mouth opens round* and yearns sideways, his *balloon cheeks* grow oily with the labor of song. He *bulges* marvelously in his expensive garments. Over his lavender collar, crushed upon a purple necktie, held by a diamond hoop: over his ammunition belt of tooled leather worked in silver, buckled cruelly around his *gasping middle:* over the tops of his glossy yellow shoes Braggioni *swells* with *ominous ripeness,* his mauve silk hose *stretched taut,* his ankles bound with the stout leather thongs of his shoes.

Katherine Anne Porter, Flowering Judas

Without a dominant impression, a passage of description runs the risk of becoming overwhelmed by irrelevant detail. Unit 5 teaches the use of a dominant impression in writing a descriptive essay.

3. Example

A paragraph developed by *example* begins with a generalization, which it then supports with specific examples. The example must be to the point, vivid, supportive of the generalization, and clearly connected to it by an introductory phrase such as "for example," or "for instance." Here is an example:

> In man there are certain innate feelings which progress cannot suppress. Take, *for example,* the sense of sin and the feeling of guilt. Today's sexual freedom does not do away with the sense of sin altogether, but causes it rather to turn in another direction. The hippies, *for example,* have a

guilt complex about the war in Vietnam, the colour problem and the pollution of nature. In the same way, I think asceticism is perhaps reappearing in America, with regard not to sex but to money: students are deliberately refusing to go into business, rejecting the attractive propositions of the biggest firms, and opting for more humanitarian careers, such as medicine.

Arnold Toynbee, The Sexual Revolution

The generalization occurs in the first sentence, which also introduces the main idea the paragraph intends to document. The overuse of generalizations without supporting examples is a common failing of student writing. Unit 6 takes up the use of examples as a strategy in the writing of essays.

4. Definition

A *definition* says what something is and what it is not. A paragraph developed by definition therefore focuses on specifying the characteristics of the subject—first by showing the general category it belongs to, and then by distinguishing it from other items in the same category. Here is an example:

Chemistry is that branch of science which has the task of investigating the materials out of which the universe is made. It is not concerned with the forms into which they may be fashioned. Such objects as chairs, tables, vases, bottles, or wires are of no significance in chemistry; but such substances as glass, wool, iron, sulfur, and clay, as the materials out of which they are made, are what it studies. Chemistry is concerned not only with the composition of such substances, but also with their inner structure.

John Arrend Timm, General Chemistry

The writer first places chemistry in the category of science and then differentiates it from other scientific disciplines by the nature and content of its study. This definition is short and to the point. Definitions of more abstract and complex terms such as *love* and *justice,* on the other hand, can consume several paragraphs or entire essays. Unit 7 teaches the development of an essay by definition.

5. Comparison/Contrast

Comparison/contrast paragraphs examine items for similarities and differences. The items are compared on certain specific bases, and the paragraph alternates from one to the other indicating either similarities or differences through the use of appropriate phrases such as *on the other hand, likewise, similarly,* and *but.* In the following example; terms indicating comparison/contrast are in italics:

The way in which culture affects language becomes clear by *comparing* how the English and Hopi languages refer to H_2O in its liquid state. English, like most other European languages, has only one word—"water"— and it pays no attention to what the substance is used for or its quantity.

The Hopi of Arizona, *on the other hand,* use "pahe" to mean the large amounts of water present in natural lakes or rivers, and "keyi" for the small amounts in domestic jugs and canteens. English, *though,* makes other distinctions that Hopi does not. The speaker of English is careful to distinguish between a lake and a stream, between a waterfall and a geyser; *but* "pahe" makes no distinction among lakes, ponds, rivers, streams, waterfalls, and springs.

Peter Farb, *Man at the Mercy of His Language*

The basis of this comparison/contrast between English and Hopi—the way these languages refer to water—is given early in the paragraph. Having announced his intention to compare and the basis of the comparison, the writer then catalogs the similarities and differences between the English and Hopi languages on this one item.

Two common weaknesses in student essays based on comparison/contrast are: (1) failure to fairly examine both items on the same basis, thus favoring one item over another, and (2) failure to use appropriate comparison/contrast expressions, thus disguising the intent of the paragraph. Be alert to these pitfalls when writing your own comparison/contrast paragraphs. Unit 8 discusses the comparison/contrast as it applies to the development of an entire essay.

6. Process

Process refers to any "how-to-do-it" writing that gives step-by-step instructions. Generally considered to be the easiest strategy for developing a paragraph or an essay, a process might give instructions on how to bake a cake, how to tune a bicycle wheel, or how to play the recorder. The example we have chosen instructs the reader in how to sharpen a knife:

The sharpening stone must be fixed in place on the table, so that it will not move around. You can do this by placing a piece of rubber inner tube or a thin piece of foam rubber under it. Or you can tack four strips of wood, if you have a rough worktable, to frame the stone and hold it in place. Put a generous puddle of oil in the stone—this will soon disappear into the surface of a new stone, and you will need to keep adding more oil. Press the knife blade flat against the stone in the puddle of oil, using your index finger. Whichever way the cutting edge of the knife faces is the side of the blade that should get a little more pressure. Move the blade around three or four times in a narrow oval about the size of your fingernail, going *counterclockwise* when the sharp edge is facing right. Now turn the blade over in the same spot on the stone, press hard, and move it around the small oval *clockwise,* with more pressure on the cutting edge that faces left. Repeat the ovals, flipping the knife blade over six or seven times, and applying lighter pressure to the blade the last two times.

Florence H. Pettit, "How to Sharpen Your Knife,"
How to Make Whirligigs and Whimmy Diddles

Writing a process is usually straightforward and considered so easy that many teachers will not allow the student to submit a process essay for a final exam. Other than the occasional muddling of the sequence, students generally have no trouble writing process paragraphs or essays. For further instruction on this strategy, see Unit 9.

7. Classification

Classification means to divide something and group its elements into major categories and types. For a classification to be useful it must be based on a single principle and must be complete. For instance, say you had to write a paragraph classifying students according to their year in college. If your classification included only freshmen, sophomores, and seniors, it would violate the requirement of completeness by omitting all juniors. On the other hand, if your scheme included freshmen, sophomores, juniors, seniors, fraternity members, and non-fraternity members, it would no longer be based on a single principle. The first four categories refer to the student's year in college, while the fifth and sixth refers to membership or nonmembership in campus organizations.

Here is an example of a paragraph developed by classification:

> A few words about the world's reaction to the concentration camps: the terrors committed in them were experienced as uncanny by most civilized persons. It came as a shock to their pride that supposedly civilized nations could stoop to such inhuman acts. The implication that modern man has such inadequate control over his cruelty was felt as a threat. Three different psychological mechanisms were most frequently used for dealing with the phenomenon of the concentration camp: (a) its applicability to man in general was denied by asserting (contrary to available evidence) that the acts of torture were committed by a small group of insane or perverted persons; (b) the truth of the reports were denied by ascribing them to deliberate propaganda. This method was favored by the German government which called all reports on terror in the camps horror propaganda. (Greuelpropaganda); (c) the reports were believed, but the knowledge of the terror was repressed as soon as possible.
>
> Bruno Bettelheim, *The Informed Heart*

The author first specifies the principle of the classifications—the psychological mechanisms used to deny man's control over his cruelty. He then completes the classification by listing the mechanisms. Unit 10 teaches how to develop an entire essay by classification.

8. Causal Analysis

Causal analysis attempts to relate two events by asserting the occurrence of one event to be the reason for the occurrence of the other: A car engine blew up because it lacked oil. A woman slipped and fell because the pavement was slippery. A dog got rabies because it was bitten by a squirrel. Each of these statements asserts a causal relationship between two events.

Cause always refers to an event in the past. First, the engine lacked oil, then it blew up; first, the pavement was slippery, then the woman fell; first, the dog was bitten, then it got rabies. *Effect,* on the other hand, always refers to an event in the future. If a car engine is run without oil, it will blow up; if a well-used pavement is slippery, someone will probably fall; if a dog is bitten by a rabid squirrel, it will probably get rabies.

While cause relates two events by asserting one event as the *reason* for the other, effect relates two events by asserting one event as the *result* of another. If you write an essay giving as a reason for your father's bitterness his failure to fulfill his ambition to be a doctor, you are analyzing cause. If you write an essay analyzing what happens to a person who fails to fulfill his lifelong career ambition, you are analyzing effect. Both essays nevertheless would be considered as examples of causal analysis.

Consider this paragraph, which analyzes why our age has no "great" men:

> Why have giants vanished from our midst? One must never neglect the role of accident in history; and accident no doubt plays a part here. But too many accidents of the same sort cease to be wholly accidental. One must inquire further. Why should our age not only be without great men but even seem actively hostile to them? Surely one reason we have so few heroes now is precisely that we had so many a generation ago. Greatness is hard for common humanity to bear. As Emerson said, "Heroism means difficulty, postponement of praise, postponement of ease, introduction of the world into the private apartment, introduction of eternity into the hours measured by the sitting-room clock." A world of heroes keeps people from living their own private lives.
>
> Arthur M. Schlesinger, Jr., *The Decline of Heroes*

The following paragraph analyzes the effects of changes in the sun's nuclear balance:

> Inevitably, the solar nuclear balances will change. The hydrogen will be used up, converted into helium. The sun's core will start to burn helium in a struggle for life. The heat will increase, the sun will grow redder and swell, on the way to being a red giant star. As it expands it will bring biblical fire and brimstone to the inner planets. Mercury, Venus will melt and drop into the expanding plasma; on earth, all life will be gone long before the oceans boil and vaporize and the rocks are smelted down.
>
> Lennard Bickel, *Our Sun: The Star We Live In*

Student-written causal analyses sometimes suffer from *dogmatism*—an authoritative stating of opinion as fact without sufficient evidence. Cause and effect often have a complex and frail association, which the student should assert with caution. For more on how to write a causal analysis, see Unit 11.

9. Argumentation

Argumentation, the final strategy for developing a paragraph or an essay, involves the persuasion of someone else to the writer's viewpoint. Such a paragraph will often be a combination of the strategies discussed so far, simultaneously analyzing cause, describing, comparing/contrasting, and defining. Unlike a paragraph developed by comparison/contrast, the argumentative paragraph has no definite structure but is recognizable instead by its intent. Here, for example, is a paragraph that argues that the Bible is a human document:

Description: Can any rational person believe that the Bible is anything but a human document? We now know pretty well where the various books came from, and about when they were written. We know that they were written by human beings who had no knowledge of science, little knowledge of life, and were influenced by the barbarous morality of primitive times, and were grossly ignorant of most things that men know today. *For instance,*

Example: Genesis says that God made the earth, and he made the sun to light the day and the moon to light the night, and in one clause disposes of the stars by saying that "he made the stars also." This was plainly written by someone who had no conception of the stars. Man, by the aid of his telescope, has looked out into the heavens and found stars whose diameter is as great as the distance between the earth and the sun. We know that the universe is filled with stars and suns and planets and systems. Every new telescope looking further into the heavens only discovers more and more worlds and suns and systems in the endless reaches of space. The men who

Causal analysis: wrote Genesis believed, of course, that this tiny speck of mud that we call the earth was the center of the universe, the only world in space, and made for man, who was the only being worth considering. These men believed that the stars were only a little way above the earth, and were set in the firmament for man to look at, and for nothing else. Everyone today knows that this conception is not true.

Clarence Darrow, Why I Am an Agnostic

In presenting his argument, the writer resorts to a variety of strategies: he describes the men who wrote the Bible, gives an example of its misconception, and analyzes the probable causes of it. An argument involves the complex formulation of ideas and facts; a paragraph developed by argumentation will therefore frequently employ more than one strategy.

We do not wish to leave you with a purist's impression of paragraph development. Many paragraphs do more or less exactly conform to one strategy of development or another, but more complex paragraphs, especially those involved in the formulation of argument, will blend several strategies:

Example: We are a long, long way from understanding the complexities of individual motivation. We understand very imperfectly, *for example,* the inner pressures to excel which are present in some children and absent in others.

Contrast: We don't really know why, from earliest years, some individuals seem

Causal analysis: indomitable, while others are tossed about by events like the bird in a badminton game. Differences in energy and other physiological traits are partially responsible. Even more important may be the role of early experiences—relations with brothers and sisters, early successes and failures.

Example: We know, *for example,* that high standards may be a means of challenging and stimulating the child or, depending on the circumstances, a means of frightening and intimidating him.

John W. Gardner, Excellence

Observable in the work of many writers, the strategies of development outlined here are ideal techniques, not inviolable laws. The student writer is advised to follow them closely until he is thoroughly familiar with them. After that, he is as free to experiment, combine, blend, and modify as any other writer who has ever set words and sentences on a page.

D. Transitions between Paragraphs

Clear transitions between paragraphs are necessary if an essay is to read smoothly. If the gap between the idea at the end of one paragraph and that at the beginning of another is too wide, the reader will lose the line of thought. Paragraphs must therefore be carefully bridged, as in the following example:

The police relationship with the community served is the most important and difficult law enforcement problem of the 1970's. Effective law enforcement depends not only on the respect and confidence of the police but on close, direct and continuous communication between the police and every segment of the population. Indeed, one is not possible without the other. Strong *community ties* provide the base for police prevention, deterrence, detection and control.

Only where *such ties* exist do police have the chance to work effectively. School authorities can then learn how to watch for, identify and report the presence of narcotics peddlers and student addicts. Students are more likely to understand the risks of LSD and refuse to joy-ride with friends in a stolen car. Slum dwellers, who know police, can complain of consumer fraud in the hope that action may result. Addicts, alcoholics and the mentally ill may find treatment through police who are in *contact* with friends, family or those in need themselves. The thief and the dangerously violent, frequently unrestrained in the ghetto, will be identified and apprehended *when the people trust the police.*

Strong police ties with residents in every block of densely populated slum areas are the only opportunity for law enforcement to measure the dimension and the nature of our vast unreported ghetto crime. Police presence can cool rather than heat angry street crowds where officers are known and respected. On campus, police can placate rather than provoke. Organized crime cannot reap the profits of gambling, narcotics traffic, loansharking and prostitution, which account for most of its income, where *police-*

community relations are strong and there is law enforcement commitment to eliminate such activity. Extortion, blackmail and strong-arm tactics cannot then be safely used.

Ramsey Clark, Crime in America

The train of thought runs smoothly through these paragraphs, connected through the linking key words denoting police-community ties.

For major transitions, as from one main section of a long paper to the next, a special transitional paragraph can prepare the reader for the next section. Here is an example:

> There was, however, a darker and more sinister side to the Irish character. "They are," said a land agent on the eve of the famine, "a very desperate people, with all this degree of courtesy, hospitality, and cleverness amongst them."
>
> *Transitional paragraph:* To understand the Irish of the nineteenth century and their blend of courage and evasiveness, tenacity and inertia, loyalty and double-dealing, it is necessary to go back to the Penal Laws.
>
> *New topic:* The Penal Laws, dating from 1695, and not repealed in their entirety until Catholic emancipation in 1829, aimed at the destruction of Catholicism in Ireland by a series of ferocious enactments. . . .

Cecil Woodham-Smith, The Great Hunger: Ireland, 1845–1849

E. Beginning and Ending Paragraphs

1. Openings That Command Attention

The opening paragraph often makes or breaks an essay. If a reader isn't grabbed by your beginning, he may never linger to read your brilliant middle. To get off to a good start, begin with a snappy introduction—a funny anecdote, a memorable personal experience. The following is an intriguing opening paragraph:

> A pickup truck drives slowly down the street. The truck stops as it comes abreast of a man sitting on a cast-iron porch and the white driver calls out, asking if the man wants a day's work. The man shakes his head and the truck moves on up the block, stopping again whenever idling men come within calling distance of the driver. At the Carry-out corner, five men debate the question briefly and shake their heads no to the truck. The truck turns the corner and repeats the same performance up the next street. In the distance, one can see one man, then another, climb into the back of the truck and sit down. It starts and stops, the truck finally disappears.

Elliot Liebow, Source

Avoid beginnings that start with an apology or complaint, a big, broad, abstract passage, or a trite and obvious statement.

2. Endings That Clinch

Take leave from your audience with an emphatic exit. Don't bolt or fade. Use the final paragraph to clinch the point of the essay. Here are two final paragraphs that clinch the author's case against frivolity in American education:

> If by some miracle the creative intelligence could be made as glamorous as Pat Boone, it would not be long, for example, before we ceased appointing ambassadors who know nothing of the language or the history of the country to which they are accredited. We might even go so far as to modify our idea of representative government and insist that our more important public servants be well-educated men. We might teach our children that all the material miracles that surround them are only incidentally the consequence of our extraordinary system of production and distribution, and that we wear such fine stockings only because Wallace H. Carothers, of the Du Pont Company, happened to come across Nylon while he was making a purely scientific investigation of the molecular structure of certain chemical compounds.
>
> The prestige symbols must be changed. Somehow or other the child will have to be taught the stark, chilly truth—that the intellectual is and always has been the most valuable man in the world, the one on whom we all live, the one whose ideas and discoveries and inventions afford us the opportunity for a livelihood and show us how interesting life can be. It is only when he is convinced that this is so, and that Mickey Mantle and Elvis Presley and Rock Hudson, while doubtless estimable creatures, are mere specks of thin icing on a very large and solid cake—it is only when he deeply feels the truth of this that his natural desire to know will express itself freely, and he will learn what it is now difficult to teach him—how to read, write, calculate, speak, listen, and think.
>
> Clifton Fadiman, *Why We Must Improve Our Minds*

Convince your reader that you have ended your essay not because you are tired of writing or have run out of ideas, but because nothing more needs to be said. Avoid endings that apologize for your shortcomings, insert an afterthought or trivial detail, or peter out with inconclusive or contradictory statements.

Exercises

1. Identify the topic sentence in each of the following paragraphs, and state whether the material moves from the particular to the general or from the general to the particular.

   a. Everyone who makes money in the mechanical city uses the money that he makes there to escape, as far and as frequently as he can, from the inferno that is the source of his wealth. As soon as he can afford it, he moves his home out from within the city-limits into suburbia; he takes his holidays in what is still left of genuinely rural country; and, when he retires, he withdraws to die on the French Riviera or in

Southern California or at Montreux or Vevey. This is not surprising, considering that the mechanized city is as repulsively ugly as the mass-produced manufactures that it pours out. It is, however, a spiritual misfortune for a worker to be alienated emotionally from the place in which he has done his work, has earned his living, and has made his mark, for good or for evil, on the history of the human race.

Arnold Toynbee, Cities on the Move

b. If you enjoy working out the strategy of games, tit-tat-toe or poker or chess; if you are interested in the frog who jumped up three feet and fell back two in getting out of a well, or in the fly buzzing between the noses of two approaching cyclists, or in the farmer who left land to his three sons; if you have been captivated by codes and ciphers or are interested in crossword puzzles; if you like to fool around with numbers; if music appeals to you by the sense of form which it expresses—then you will enjoy logic. You ought to be warned, perhaps. Those who take up logic get glassy-eyed and absentminded. They join a fanatical cult. But they have a good time. Theirs is one of the most durable, absorbing and inexpensive of pleasures. Logic is fun.

Roger W. Holmes, The Rhyme of Reason

c. Two dark spots in this otherwise bright picture must be noted.

America's affluent society does not adequately care for its old people. The elderly have a sharply declining place in the family compared with the grandparents of a simpler age. The average "home for the aged" can hardly be called an asset to the human condition.

And secondly, this affluent society is built on an exceedingly shaky foundation of natural resources. Here we connect with the liability of a degenerating environment. The United States with only some 6 percent of the world's population uses up some 40 percent of the world's annual production of raw materials. If all the world enjoyed American affluence, there would be about twelve times the current demand for raw materials—an impossible drain on the resources of this planet.

Stuart Chase, Two Cheers for Technology

d. She was a lonesome, passionate woman of dalliance, a castoff of five men and living unmarried with a sixth. But she had wit, insight and a longing for a better way. It was to her that Jesus made the first outright declaration of His universal messiahship.

She also became His first massively persuasive evangelist and the first to convey His mission beyond His Jewish homeland.

Not only did He give this extraordinary role to a woman in an age when that sex was regarded as of secondary value, but He did so to a socially tainted woman of a scorned, segregated race—a woman of Samaria.

It was a strikingly revolutionary action which shocked His disapproving male disciples and which was part of His consistent practice of defying sexist prejudices to give women equal status, a pattern that marked Him as the first and foremost champion of women's liberation.

He "vigorously promoted the dignity and equality of women in a very male-dominated society," writes theologian Leonard Swidler. "Jesus was a feminist and a very radical one."

George W. Cornell, Jesus Viewed as a Women's Liberationist

2. Identify the pattern of development used in the following paragraphs.

a. The "human condition" may be defined as a measure of the extent to which the potential for living is realized under the limitations of the inborn genes and of the environment of the Earth. Full potential means adequate food, shelter, clothing, education, and health care, plus useful and creative work and leisure for every normal baby born. The slums of Calcutta or Rio, the ghettos of the West, represent a potential close to zero.

Stuart Chase, Two Cheers for Technology

b. I have said that a scientific answer must be practical as well as sensible. This really rules out at once the panaceas which also tend to run the argument into a blind alley at this stage; the panaceas which say summarily "Get rid of them." Naturally, it does not seem to me to be sensible to get rid of scientists; but in any case, it plainly is not practical. And whatever we do with our own scientists, it very plainly is not practical to get rid of the scientists of rival nations; because if there existed the conditions for agreement among nations on this far-reaching scheme, then the conditions for war would already have disappeared. If there existed the conditions for international agreement, say to suspend all scientific research, or to abandon warlike research, or in any other way to forgo science as an instrument of nationalism—if such agreements could be reached, then they would already be superfluous; because the conditions for war would already have disappeared. So, however we might sigh for Samuel Butler's panacea in *Erewhon*, simply to give up all machines, there is no point in talking about it. I believe it would be a disaster for mankind like the coming of the Dark Ages. But there is no point in arguing this. It just is not practical, nationally or internationally.

Jacob Bronowski, Science, the Destroyer or Creator

c. Of course, humor is often more than a laughing matter. In its more potent guises, it has a Trojan-horse nature: no one goes on guard against a gag; we let it in because it looks like a little wooden toy. Once inside, however, it can turn a city to reform, to rebellion, to resistance. Some believe, for instance, that, next to the heroic British RAF, British humor did the most to fend off German takeover in World War II. One sample will suffice: that famous story of the woman who was finally extracted from the rubble of her house during the London blitz. Asked, "Where is your husband?" she brushed brick dust off her head and arms and answered, "Fighting in Libya, the bloody coward!"

William D. Ellis, Solve That Problem—with Humor

Writing Assignments

1. Write a paragraph in which you state your pet peeve and give an example of it.

2. Define *vasectomy* in one paragraph.

3. Write a paragraph comparing a ten-speed bicycle with an ordinary bicycle.

4. Write a paragraph classifying the houses of the zodiac under the four elements: earth, air, fire, and water.

5. In a paragraph, state some probable reasons for the popularity of newspaper lovelorn columns.

6. Narrate a love-at-first-sight episode in a single paragraph.

7. Argue for or against the Equal Rights Amendment in a paragraph.

8. In one paragraph, state the effect inflation has had on your income.

9. In a single paragraph, outline the steps involved in any process with which you're familiar.

10. In a paragraph, describe the best teacher you've ever had.

Part II

Writing the Essay

4

Narration

*As I flew, I gazed up into the sky and imagined
that I was flying among the clouds.*

A. Reading for Ideas

The following story, "Wallace," tells of a memorable childhood friendship. As you
read the story, notice the author's selection and combination of events into an
uninterrupted narrative. Notice also the pace of the narrative—the glossing over of
some scenes and events and the highlighting of others. Allow the story to trigger
some memories of your own youth, and ask yourself the following questions: What
is my favorite childhood memory? What did this memory teach me about life?
How did it affect my growing up?

Wallace
Richard H. Rovere

1   As a schoolboy, my relations with teachers were almost always tense and hostile.
I disliked my studies and did very badly in them. There are, I have heard, inept students
who bring out the best in teachers, who challenge their skill and move them to sympathy
and affection. I seemed to bring out the worst in them. I think my personality had more
to do with this than my poor classroom work. Anyway, something about me was deeply
offensive to the pedagogic temperament.

2   Often, it took a teacher no more than a few minutes to conceive a raging dislike for
me. I recall an instructor in elementary French who shied a textbook at my head the very
first day I attended his class. We had never laid eyes on each other until fifteen or twenty
minutes before he assaulted me. I no longer remember what, if anything, provoked him
to violence. It is possible that I said something that was either insolent or intolerably
stupid. I guess I often did. It is also possible that I said nothing at all. Even my silence,
my humility, my acquiescence, could annoy my teachers. The very sight of me, the mere
awareness of my existence on earth, could be unendurably irritating to them.

3   This was the case with my fourth-grade teacher, Miss Purdy. In order to make the
acquaintance of her new students on the opening day of school, she had each one rise
and give his name and address as she called the roll. Her voice was soft and gentle,

her manner sympathetic, until she came to me. Indeed, up to then I had been dreamily entertaining the hope that I was at last about to enjoy a happy association with a teacher. When Miss Purdy's eyes fell on me, however, her face suddenly twisted and darkened with revulsion. She hesitated for a few moments while she looked me up and down and thought of a suitable comment on what she saw. "Aha!" she finally said, addressing not me but my new classmates, in a voice that was now coarse and cruel. "I don't have to ask *his* name. There, boys and girls, is Mr. J. Pierpont Morgan, lounging back in his mahogany-lined office." She held each syllable of the financier's name on her lips as long as she was able to, so that my fellow-students could savor the full irony of it. I imagine my posture was a bit relaxed for the occasion, but I know well that she would not have resented anyone else's sprawl as much as she did mine. I can even hear her making some friendly, schoolmarmish quip about too much summer vacation to any other pupil. Friendly quips were never for me. In some unfortunate and mysterious fashion, my entire being rubbed Miss Purdy and all her breed the wrong way. Throughout the fourth grade, she persisted in tormenting me with her idiotic Morgan joke. "And perhaps Mr. J. P. Revere can tell us all about Vasco da Gama this morning," she would say, throwing in a little added insult by mispronouncing my surname.

4   The aversion I inspired in teachers might under certain circumstances have been turned to good account. It might have stimulated me to industry; it might have made me get high marks, just so I could prove to the world that my persecutors were motivated by prejudice and perhaps by a touch of envy; or it might have bred a monumental rebelliousness in me, a contempt for all authority, that could have become the foundation of a career as the leader of some great movement against all tyranny and oppression.

5   It did none of these things. Instead, I became, so far as my school life was concerned, a thoroughly browbeaten boy, and I accepted the hostility of my teachers as an inescapable condition of life. In fact, I took the absolutely disastrous view that my teachers were unquestionably right in their estimate of me as a dense and altogether noxious creature who deserved, if anything, worse than he got. These teachers were, after all, men and women who had mastered the parts of speech, the multiplication tables, and a simply staggering number of imports and exports in a staggering number of countries. They could add up columns of figures the very sight of which made me dizzy and sick to the stomach. They could read "As You Like It" with pleasure—so they said, anyway, and I believed everything they said. I felt that if such knowledgeable people told me that I was stupid, they certainly must know what they were talking about. In consequence, my grades sank lower and lower, my face became more noticeably blank, my manner more mulish, and my presence in the classroom more aggravating to whoever presided over it. To be sure, I hated my teachers for their hatred of me, and I missed no chance to abuse them behind their backs, but fundamentally I shared with them the view that I was a worthless and despicable boy, as undeserving of an education as I was incapable of absorbing one. Often, on school days, I wished that I were dead.

6   This was my attitude, at least, until my second year in preparatory school, when, at fourteen, I fell under the exhilarating, regenerative influence of my friend Wallace Duckworth. Wallace changed my whole outlook on life. It was he who freed me from my terrible awe of teachers; it was he who showed me that they could be brought to book and made fools of as easily as I could be; it was he who showed me that the gap between their knowledge and mine was not unbridgeable. Sometimes I think that I should like to become a famous man, a United States Senator or something of that sort, just to be able to repay my debt to Wallace. I should like to be so important that people would inquire into the early influences on my life and I would be able to tell them about Wallace.

7   I was freshly reminded of my debt to Wallace not long ago when my mother happened

to come across a packet of letters I had written to her and my father during my first two years in a boarding school on Long Island. In one of these, I reported that "There's a new kid in school who's supposed to be a scientifical genius." Wallace was this genius. In a series of intelligence and aptitude tests we all took in the opening week, he achieved some incredible score, a mark that, according to the people who made up the tests, certified him as a genius and absolutely guaranteed that in later life he would join the company of Einstein, Steinmetz, and Edison. Naturally, his teachers were thrilled—but not for long.

8   Within a matter of weeks it became clear that although Wallace was unquestionably a genius, or at least an exceptionally bright boy, he was disposed to use his considerable gifts not to equip himself for a career in the service of mankind but for purely antisocial undertakings. Far from making the distinguished scholastic record everyone expected of him, he made an altogether deplorable one. He never did a lick of school work. He had picked up his scientific knowledge somewhere but evidently not from teachers. I am not sure about this, but I think Wallace's record, as long as he was in school, was even worse than mine. In my mind's eye there is a picture of the sheet of monthly averages thumbtacked to the bulletin board across the hall from the school post office; my name is one from the bottom, the bottom name being Wallace's.

9   As a matter of fact, one look at Wallace should have been enough to tell the teachers what sort of genius he was. At fourteen, he was somewhat shorter than he should have been and a good deal stouter. His face was round, owlish, and dirty. He had big, dark eyes, and his black hair, which hardly ever got cut, was arranged on his head as the four winds wanted it. He had been outfitted with attractive and fairly expensive clothes, but he changed from one suit to another only when his parents came to call on him and ordered him to get out of what he had on.

10   The two most impressive things about him were his mouth and the pockets of his jacket. By looking at his mouth, one could tell whether he was plotting evil or had recently accomplished it. If he was bent upon malevolence, his lips were all puckered up, like those of a billiard player about to make a difficult shot. After the deed was done, the pucker was replaced by a delicate, unearthly smile. How a teacher who knew anything about boys could miss the fact that both expressions were masks of Satan I'm sure I don't know. Wallace's pockets were less interesting than his mouth, perhaps, but more spectacular in a way. The side pockets of his jacket bulged out over his pudgy haunches like burro hampers. They were filled with tools—screwdrivers, pliers, files, wrenches, wire cutters, nail sets, and I don't know what else. In addition to all this, one pocket always contained a rolled-up copy of *Popular Mechanics,* while from the top of the other protruded *Scientific American* or some other such magazine. His breast pocket contained, besides a large collection of fountain pens and mechanical pencils, a picket fence of drill bits, gimlets, kitchen knives, and other pointed instruments. When he walked, he clinked and jangled and pealed.

11   Wallace lived just down the hall from me, and I got to know him one afternoon, a week or so after school started, when I was wrestling with an algebra lesson. I was really trying to get good marks at the time, for my father had threatened me with unpleasant reprisals if my grades did not show early improvement. I could make no sense of the algebra, though, and I thought that the scientific genius, who had not as yet been unmasked, might be generous enough to lend me a hand.

12   It was a study period, but I found Wallace stretched out on the floor working away at something he was learning to make from *Popular Mechanics.* He received me with courtesy, but after hearing my request he went immediately back to his tinkering. "I could do that algebra all right," he said, "but I can't be bothered with it. Got to get this dingbat going this afternoon. Anyway, I don't care about algebra. It's too twitchy. Real

engineers never do any of that stuff. It's too twitchy for them.'' I soon learned that "twitch'' was an all-purpose word of Wallace's. It turned up in one form or another, in about every third sentence he spoke. It did duty as a noun, an adjective, a verb, and an adverb.

13   I was disappointed by his refusal of help but was fascinated by what he was doing. I stayed on and watched him as he deftly cut and spliced wires, removed and replaced screws, referring, every so often, to his magazine for further instruction. He worked silently, lips fiendishly puckered, for some time, then looked up at me and said, "Say, you know anything about that organ in the chapel?''

14   "What about it?'' I asked.
"I mean do you know anything about how it works?''
"No,'' I said. "I don't know anything about that.''

15   "Too bad,'' Wallace said, reaching for a pair of pliers. "I had a really twitchy idea.'' He worked at his wires and screws for quite a while. After perhaps ten minutes, he looked up again, "Well, anyhow,'' he said, "maybe you know how to get in the chapel and have a look at the organ?''

16   "Sure, that's easy,'' I said. "Just walk in. The chapel's always open. They keep it open so you can go in and pray if you want to, and things like that.''
"Oh'' was Wallace's only comment.

17   I didn't at all grasp what he had in mind until church time the following Sunday. At about six o'clock that morning, several hours before the service, he tip-toed into my room and shook me from sleep. "Hey, get dressed,'' he said. "Let's you and I twitch over to the chapel and have a look at the organ.''

18   Game for any form of amusement, I got up and went along. In the bright, not quite frosty October morning, we scurried over the lawns to the handsome Georgian chapel. It was an hour before the rising bell.

19   Wallace had brought along a flashlight as well as his usual collection of hardware. We went to the rear of the chancel, where the organ was, and he poked the light underneath the thing and inside it for a few minutes. Then he got out his pliers and screwdrivers and performed some operations that I could neither see nor understand. We were in the chapel for only a few minutes. "There,'' Wallace said as he came up from under the keyboard. "I guess I got her twitched up just about right. Let's go.'' Back in my room, we talked softly until the rest of the school began to stir. I asked Wallace what, precisely, he had done to the organ. "You'll see,'' he said, with that faint, faraway smile where the pucker had been. Using my commonplace imagination, I guessed that he had fixed the organ so it would give out peculiar noises or something like that. I didn't realize then that Wallace's tricks were seldom commonplace.

20   Church began as usual that Sunday morning. The headmaster delivered the invocation and then announced the number and title of the first hymn. He held up his hymnal and gave the genteel, throat-clearing cough that was his customary signal to the organist to get going. The organist came down on the keys but not a peep sounded from the pipes. He tried again. Nothing but a click.

21   When the headmaster realized that the organ wasn't working, he walked quickly to the rear and consulted in whispers with the organist. Together they made a hurried inspection of the instrument, peering inside it, snapping the electric switch back and forth, and reaching to the base plug to make certain the juice was on. Everything seemed all right, yet the organ wouldn't sound a note.

22   "Something appears to be wrong with our organ,'' the headmaster said when he returned to the lectern. "I regret to say that for this morning's services we shall have to—''

23   At the first word of the announcement, Wallace, who was next to me in one of the rear pews, slid out of his seat and bustled noisily down the middle aisle. It was highly unusual conduct, and every eye was on him. His gaudy magazines flapped from his pockets, his portable workshop clattered and clanked as he strode importantly to the chancel and rose on tiptoe to reach the ear of the astonished headmaster. He spoke in a stage whisper that could be heard everywhere in the chapel. "Worked around organs quite a bit, sir," he said. "Think I can get this one going in a jiffy."

24   Given the chance, the headmaster would undoubtedly have declined Wallace's kind offer. Wallace didn't give him the chance. He scooted for the organ. For perhaps a minute, he worked on it, hands flying, tools tinkling.

25   Then, stuffing the tools back into his pockets, he returned to the headmaster. "There you are, sir," he said, smiling up at him. "Think she'll go all right now." The headmaster, with great doubt in his heart, I am sure, nodded to the organist to try again. Wallace stood by, looked rather like the inventor of a new kind of airplane waiting to see his brain child take flight. He faked a look of deep anxiety, which, when a fine, clear swell came from the pipes, was replaced by a faint smile of relief, also faked. On the second or third chord, he bustled back down the aisle, looking very solemn and businesslike and ready for serious worship.

26   It was a fine performance, particularly brilliant in its timing. If Wallace had had to stay at the organ even a few seconds longer—that is if he had done a slightly more elaborate job of twitching it in the first place—he would have been ordered back to his pew before he had got done with the repairs. Moreover, someone would probably have guessed that it was he who had put it on the fritz in the first place. But no one did guess it. Not then, anyway. For weeks after that, Wallace's prestige in the school was enormous. Everyone had had from the beginning a sense of honor and pride at having a genius around, but no one up to then had realized how useful a genius could be. Wallace let on after church that Sunday that he was well up on the working not merely of organs but also of heating and plumbing systems, automobiles, radios, washing machines, and just about everything else. He said he would be pleased to help out in any emergency. Everyone thought he was wonderful.

27   "That was a real good twitch, wasn't it?" he said to me when we were by ourselves. I said that it certainly was.

28   From that time on, I was proud and happy to be Wallace's cupbearer. I find it hard now to explain exactly what his victory with the organ, and all his later victories over authority, meant to me, but I do know that they meant a very great deal. Partly, I guess, it was just the knowledge that he enjoyed my company. I was an authentic, certified dunce and he was an acknowledged genius, yet he liked being with me. Better yet was my discovery that this super-brain disliked schoolwork every bit as much as I did. He was bored silly, as I was, by "Il Penseroso" and completely unable to stir up any enthusiasm for "Silas Marner" and all the foolish goings on over Eppie. Finally, and this perhaps was what made me love him most, he had it in his power to humiliate and bring low the very people who had so often humiliated me and brought me low.

29   As I spent the long fall and winter afternoons with Wallace, being introduced by him to the early novels of H. G. Wells, which he admired extravagantly, and watching him make crystal sets, window-cleaning machines, automatic chair-rockers, and miniature steam turbines from plans in *Popular Mechanics,* I gradually absorbed bits of his liberating philosophy. "If I were you," he used to say, "I wouldn't be scared by those teachers. They don't know anything. They're twitches, those teachers, real twerpy, twitchy twitches." "Twerpy" was an adjective often used by Wallace to modify "twitch." It added several degrees of twitchiness to anything twitchy.

30   Although Wallace had refused at first to help me with my lessons, he later gave freely of his assistance. I explained to him that my father was greatly distressed about my work and that I really wanted to make him happier. Wallace was moved by this. He would read along in my Latin grammar, study out algebra problems with me, and explain things in language that seemed a lot more lucid than that of my teachers. Before long, I began to understand that half my trouble lay in my fear of my studies, my teachers, and my-self. "Don't know why you get so twitched up over this stuff," Wallace would say a trifle impatiently as he helped me get the gist of a speech in "As You Like It." "There isn't anything hard about this. Fact, it's pretty good right in here. It's just those teachers who twitch it all up. I wish they'd all go soak their heads."

31   Wallace rode along for quite a while on the strength of his intelligence tests and his organ-fixing, but in time it became obvious that his disappointing classroom performance was not so much the result of failure to adjust to a new environment (as a genius, he received more tolerance in this respect than non-geniuses) as of out-and-out refusal to coöperate with the efforts being made to educate him. Even when he had learned a lesson in the course of helping me with it, he wouldn't give the teachers the satisfaction of thinking he had learned anything in their classes. Then, too, his pranks began to catch up with him. Some of them, he made no effort to conceal.

32   He was easily the greatest teacher-baiter I have ever known. His masterpiece, I think, was one he thought up for our algebra class. "Hey, you twitch," he called to me one day as I was passing his room on my way to the daily ordeal of "x"'s and "y"'s. "I got a good one for old twitch Potter." I went into his room, and he took down from his closet shelf a spool of shiny copper wire. "Now, watch this," he said. He took the free end of the wire and drew it up through the left sleeve of his shirt. Then he brought it across his chest, underneath the shirt, and ran it down the right sleeve. He closed his left fist over the spool and held the free end of the wire between right thumb and forefinger. "Let's get over to that dopey class," he said, and we went.

33   When the lesson was well started, Wallace leaned back in his seat and began to play in a languorous but ostentatious manner with the wire. It glistened brightly in the strong classroom light, and it took Mr. Potter, the teacher, only a few seconds to notice that Wallace was paying no mind to the blackboard equations but was, instead, completely absorbed in the business of fingering the wire.

34   "Wallace Duckworth, what's that you're fiddling with?" Mr. Potter said.
"Piece of wire, sir."
"Give it to me this instant."
"Yes, sir," Wallace said, extending his hand.

35   Mr. Potter had, no doubt, bargained on getting a stray piece of wire that he could unceremoniously pitch into the wastebasket. Wallace handed him about eighteen inches of it. As Mr. Potter took it, Wallace released several inches more.
"I want *all* that wire, Wallace," Mr. Potter said.

36   "I'm giving it to you, sir," Wallace answered. He let go of about two feet more. Mr. Potter kept pulling. His rage so far overcame his reason that he couldn't figure out what Wallace was doing. As he pulled, Wallace fed him more and more wire, and the stuff began to coil up on the floor around his feet. Guiding the wire with the fingers of his right hand, Wallace created quite a bit of tension, so that eventually Mr. Potter was pulling hand over hand, like a sailor tightening lines in a high sea. When he thought the tension was great enough, Wallace let two or three feet slip quickly through his hands, and Mr. Potter toppled to the floor, landing in a terrible tangle of wire.

37   I no longer remember all of Wallace's inventions in detail. Once, I recall, he made, in the chemistry laboratory, some kind of invisible paint—a sort of shellac, I suppose—and

covered every blackboard in the school with it. The next day, chalk skidded along the slate and left about as much impression as it would have made on a cake of ice. The dormitory he and I lived in was an old one of frame construction, and when we had fire drills, we had to climb down outside fire escapes. One night, Wallace tied a piece of flypaper securely around each rung of each ladder in the building, then rang the fire alarm. Still another time, he went back to his first love, the organ, and put several pounds of flour in the pipes, so that when the organist turned on the pumps, a cloud of flour filled the chapel. One of his favorite tricks was to take the dust jacket from a novel and wrap it around a textbook. In a Latin class, then, he would appear to be reading "Black April" when he should have been reading about the campaigns in Gaul. After several of his teachers had discovered that he had the right book in the wrong cover (he piously explained that he put the covers on to keep his books clean), he felt free to remove the textbook and really read a novel in class.

38   Wallace was expelled shortly before the Easter vacation. As the winter had drawn on, life had become duller and duller for him, and to brighten things up he had resorted to pranks of larger conception and of an increasingly anti-social character. He poured five pounds of sugar into the gasoline tank of the basketball coach's car just before the coach was to start out, with two or three of the team's best players in his car, for a game with a school about twenty-five miles away. The engine functioned adequately until the car hit an isolated spot on the highway, miles from any service place. Then it gummed up completely. The coach and the players riding with him came close to frost-bite, and the game had to be called off. The adventure cost Wallace's parents a couple of hundred dollars for automobile repairs. Accused of the prank, which clearly bore his trademark, Wallace had freely admitted his guilt. It was explained to his parents that he would be given one more chance in school; another trick of any sort and he would be packed off on the first train.

39   Later, trying to justify himself to me, he said, "You don't like that coach either, do you? He's the twerpiest twitch here. All teachers are twitchy, but coaches are the worst ones of all."

40   I don't recall what I said. Wallace had not consulted me about several of his recent escapades, and although I was still loyal to him, I was beginning to have misgivings about some of them.

41   As I recall it, the affair that led directly to his expulsion was a relatively trifling one, something to do with blown fuses or short circuits. At any rate, Wallace's parents had to come and fetch him home. It was a sad occasion for me, for Wallace had built in me the foundations for a sense of security. My marks were improving, my father was happier, and I no longer cringed at the sight of a teacher. I feared, though, that without Wallace standing behind me and giving me courage, I might slip back into the old ways. I was very near to tears as I helped him pack up his turbines, his tools, and his stacks of magazines. He, however, was quite cheerful. "I suppose my Pop will put me in another one of these places, and I'll have to twitch my way out of it all over again," he said.

42   "Just remember how dumb all those teachers are," he said to me a few moments before he got into his parents' car. "They're so twitchy dumb they can't even tell if any-one else is dumb." It was rather a sweeping generalization, I later learned, but it served me well for a number of years. Whenever I was belabored by a teacher, I remembered my grimy genius friend and his reassurances. I got through school somehow or other. I still cower a bit when I find that someone I've met is a schoolteacher, but things aren't too bad and I am on reasonably civil terms with a number of teachers, and even a few professors.

4,640 words

Questions

1. What typical characteristics of youth does this story bring to light?
2. How do you explain the teachers' hostility toward the narrator?
3. How would you evaluate Wallace's influence on the narrator? Was he good or bad for him?
4. What do Wallace's tricks have in common?
5. Where in the story is there some clear indication that the narrator has matured?
6. Where in the narration, if anywhere, is there a tone of sadness?
7. What is the organization of the narration? Write an outline of it.
8. How is Wallace's use of the word *twitchy* related to the inventiveness of youth? Comment on the effectiveness of Wallace's use of this word.
9. How would you have handled Wallace, if you had been his teacher?
10. What is Wallace's opinion of teachers? What generalization have you made about teachers?

Eleven

Archibald MacLeish

And summer mornings the mute child, rebellious,
Stupid, hating the words, the meanings, hating
The Think now, Think, the O but Think! would leave
On tiptoe the three chairs on the verandah
And crossing tree by tree the empty lawn
Push back the shed door and upon the sill
Stand pressing out the sunlight from his eyes
And enter and with outstretched fingers feel
The grindstone and behind it the bare wall
10 And turn and in the corner on the cool
Hard earth sit listening. And one by one,
Out of the dazzled shadow in the room
The shapes would gather, the brown plowshare, spades,
Mattocks, the polished helves of picks, a scythe
Hung from the rafters, shovels, slender tines
Glinting across the curve of sickles—shapes
Older than men were, the wise tools, the iron
Friendly with earth. And sit there quiet, breathing
The harsh dry smell of withered bulbs, the faint
20 Odor of dung, the silence. And outside
Beyond the half-shut door the blind leaves
And the corn moving. And at noon would come,
Up from the garden, his hard crooked hands
Gentle with earth, his knees still earth-stained, smelling
Of sun, of summer, the old gardener, like
A priest, like an interpreter, and bend
Over his baskets.

            And they would not speak:

They would say nothing. And the child would sit there
30   Happy as though he had no name, as though
He had been no one: like a leaf, a stem,
Like a root growing—

Questions

1. Why would the child leave the veranda? What was he trying to escape?
2. The first two lines of the poem refer to the child as "rebellious, Stupid." Whose attitude toward the child do these words reflect?
3. What is the significance of the tools in the shed? What meanings do they hold for the child?
4. By implication, with whom does the poem contrast the gardener?
5. To what figures does the poem liken the gardener? Why?
6. The poem says that the "child would sit there/Happy as though he had no name." What does this line mean? Why would having no name make a child happy?
7. What value can physical contact with the earth have for a child?

B. How to Write a Narration

Narration tells what happened. A storyteller who begins with "Once upon a time. . . ." is introducing the first step in what will probably become a bending, tortuous progression of happenings. Narration, in its widest sense, includes history, biography, personal experience, travel, and fiction—in short, any writing that recounts the events of a story in a dramatic and climactic order.

Writing Assignment

Narrate a childhood memory that is especially vivid to you—for example, re-create your first day at school, or the worst punishment from your parents, or an encounter that helped you to mature. Re-create it on paper exactly as you remember it. Keep the events in the order in which they occurred. As you narrate, try to remember what it was like to be a child; try to liberate yourself from your present adult sense of propriety and values so that you can relive the incident and your childhood feelings about it.

Specific Instructions

1. NARRATIVE WRITING MUST HAVE A CONSISTENT POINT OF VIEW. You must decide early who you are in the story, take on the voice of your assumed character, and remain faithful to him or her for the duration of the story. For instance, if you are relating an incident from the point of view of a young boy, the language of the story should reflect his youthfulness. It would seem incongruous if, having indicated to the reader that the story is to be told from a boy's point of view, you then make him sound like an elderly college professor.

Writers resort to a variety of techniques and devices to make their prose reflect the character they have assumed as the narrator. The most common technique is playacting: the writer simply pretends to be the person who is narrating the story and tries to write the way that person would write.

This passage is taken from a story narrated from the point of view of an uneducated slave. Notice how the language is wrenched to reflect his character:

> A long time ago, in times gone by, in slavery times, there was a man named Cue. I want you to think about him. I've got a reason.
>
> He got born like the cotton in the boll or the rabbit in the pea patch. There wasn't any fine doings when he got born, but his mammy was glad to have him. Yes. He didn't get born in the Big House, or the overseer's house, or any place where the bearing was easy or the work light. No, Lord. He came out of his mammy in a field hand's cabin one sharp winter, and about the first thing he remembered was his mammy's face and the taste of a piece of bacon rind and the light and shine of the pitch-pine fire up the chimney. Well, now, he got born and there he was.
>
> Stephen Vincent Benét, *Freedom's a Hard-Bought Thing*

Whatever character you choose to hide behind—innocent young boy, lonely middle-aged man, or wise old woman—you must remain with him or her throughout your narrative. Don't be one character in one paragraph, only to shift suddenly to another in the next. Such an abrupt change makes the point of view choppy and inconsistent. Here is an example of the sort of shift to avoid:

> Jessica and me hated all grownups. We'd climb onto my parents' four-story apartment roof, and you can bet that we were up to no good. Gosh, sometimes we'd spit down on old lady Gunther cause she was such a grouch about us playing on her lawn. I find it rather nostalgic to reflect on those budding days of my youth, when life was free and easy and time held me golden at the mercy of its means.

Notice the sudden shift from mischievous child to reflective adult in line 4.

2. THE NARRATION MUST HAVE A THEME.   We have already pointed out that good writing must have unity—it must be centered on a controlling idea. Narration is no exception. In narrative writing, however, the controlling idea is called the "theme" and is supported by incidents rather than by "sub-ideas." For example, the theme of "Wallace"—the healthy effects of friendship on a young boy's confidence—is supported by various incidents connecting the narrator with Wallace. The incidents are united by the theme to form a complete action with a beginning, middle, and end:

Beginning: The narrator is rejected by his teachers. He meets Wallace.

Middle: The narrator admires Wallace. Wallace expresses friendship for the narrator.

End: The narrator's self-confidence rises because of the friendship to the point that he is on the verge of rejecting Wallace's disruptive tactics.

Narration establishes its theme by first raising, then resolving, conflict. The conflict gives rise to events that will determine a resolution from which the reader may infer a theme. For instance, the conflict in "Wallace" between the narrator and his teachers is raised at the very outset of the narrative. The character of Wallace is then introduced and the narrative focuses on his friendship with the narrator. Because of this friendship with the school genius, the narrator loses his fear of teachers, acquires greater self-confidence, and is on the verge of questioning his friend's pranks when Wallace is summarily expelled from school. This resolution leads us to infer the theme of the narrative—that friendship can have a healthy effect on the self-confidence of a young boy. Had the resolution of the conflict been otherwise, the reader would have inferred a different theme.

3. PACE YOUR NARRATION TO FOCUS ON IMPORTANT SCENES.   Every reader of fiction has encountered passages that read like this:

> The first time I saw her she was chasing a schnauzer in the park. Her hair was wind-blown and wild as she dodged pedestrians and bicyclists and ran screaming after the runaway schnauzer. Her calico frock billowed in furls as she tried to run in floppy leather-tonged sandals. She was as lissome and lovely as ever a woman could be. *I didn't see her for three weeks after that.* Then one Tuesday morning, as I was taking a postdigestive jog along the elm-lined footpath, I saw her again.

Three sentences are devoted to a description of the encounter between the narrator and the girl in the park; then three weeks are dismissed in a single, brief sentence. Obviously, life was not suspended during those three weeks, but because that intervening period is unimportant to the narrative, it is quickly passed over.

This is an example of *pacing*, an important and commonsense principle of narrative writing. Unimportant time, events, and scenes are dismissed as the narrative focuses on and develops in detail only what is important to its theme. A narrative about a favorite hiding place, for example, should develop the hiding place in detail, glossing over everything else as secondary or unrelated. Common sense must guide you in selecting the scenes and events to be developed, but the ultimate rule of thumb is the relevance of the material to your theme.

4. USE DETAILS TO MAKE VIVID PEOPLE AND PLACES IN YOUR NARRATIVE.   People and places are the lifeblood of your narration. Make them real and imaginable through the use of detail (see Unit 5, Description). Notice how Wallace is brought to life through details:

> As a matter of fact, one look at Wallace should have been enough to tell the teachers what sort of genius he was. At fourteen, he was somewhat shorter than he should have been and a good deal stouter. His face was round, owlish and dirty. He had big, dark eyes, and his black hair, which hardly ever got cut, was arranged on his head as the four winds wanted it. He has been outfitted with attractive and fairly expensive clothes, but he changed from one suit to another only when his parents came to call on him and ordered him to get out of what he had on.

Detailed dialogue is another technique that narration uses to infuse life in a character. In "The Code" (p. 57), dialogue reveals the father as a man who will not tolerate emotional, irrational beliefs. For example, when the aunts go into hysterics over the death of the author's younger brother, calling him "a perfect baby," "a saint." "too perfect to live," the father angrily reacts:

> His face was very pale, and his eyes flashed almost feverishly. "Don't talk like that, Agnes!" he exclaimed, with a strange violence that was not anger but something much deeper. "I won't have you talking like that any more. I don't want anybody talking like that!" His whole body seemed to tremble. I had never seen him so worked up before. "Of course he was a bad boy at times!" he cried. "Every boy's bad once in a while. What do you have to change him for? Why don't you leave him as he was?"

A vivid narrative requires careful observation of people and their environment, and the inclusion of details that contribute most efficiently to a clear, vigorous, and interesting story.

In this selection, Lincoln Steffens (1866–1936), U.S. journalist and author, relates a memorable Christmas of his childhood. The selection is taken from *The Autobiography of Lincoln Steffens*.

Professional Model

A Miserable, Merry Christmas
Lincoln Steffens

1   My father's business seems to have been one of slow but steady growth. He and his local partner, Llewelen Tozer, had no vices. They were devoted to their families and to "the store," which grew with the town, which, in turn, grew and changed with the State from a gambling, mining, and ranching community to one of farming, fruit-raising, and building. Immigration poured in, not gold-seekers now, but farmers, business men and home-builders, who settled, planted, reaped, and traded in the natural riches of the State, which prospered greatly, "making" the people who will tell you that they "made the State."

2   As the store made money and I was getting through the primary school, my father bought a lot uptown, at Sixteenth and K Streets, and built us a "big" house. It was off the line of the city's growth, but it was near a new grammar school for me and my sisters, who were coming along fast after me. This interested the family, not me. They were always talking about school; they had not had much of it themselves, and they thought they had missed something. My father used to write speeches, my mother verses, and their theory seems to have been that they had talents which a school would have brought to flower. They agreed, therefore, that their children's gifts should have

all the schooling there was. My view, then, was that I had had a good deal of it already, and I was not interested at all. It interfered with my own business, with my own education.

3   And indeed I remember very little of the primary school. I learned to read, write, spell, and count, and reading was all right. I had a practical use for books, which I searched for ideas and parts to play with, characters to be, lives to live. The primary school was probably a good one, but I cannot remember learning anything except to read aloud "perfectly" from a teacher whom I adored and who was fond of me. She used to embrace me before the whole class and she favored me openly to the scandal of the other pupils, who called me "teacher's pet." Their scorn did not trouble me; I saw and I said that they envied me. I paid for her favor, however. When she married I had queer, unhappy feelings of resentment; I didn't want to meet her husband, and when I had to I wouldn't speak to him. He laughed, and she kissed me—happily for her, to me offensively. I never would see her again. Through with her, I fell in love immediately with Miss Kay, another grown young woman who wore glasses and had a fine, clear skin. I did not know her, I only saw her in the street, but once I followed her, found out where she lived, and used to pass her house, hoping to see her, and yet choking with embarrassment if I did. This fascination lasted for years; it was still a sort of super-romance to me when later I was "going with" another girl nearer my own age.

4   What interested me in our new neighborhood was not the school, nor the room I was to have in the house all to myself, but the stable which was built back of the house. My father let me direct the making of a stall, a little smaller than the other stalls, for my pony, and I prayed and hoped and my sister Lou believed that that meant that I would get the pony, perhaps for Christmas. I pointed out to her that there were three other stalls and no horses at all. This I said in order that she should answer it. She could not. My father, sounded, said that some day we might have horses and a cow; meanwhile a stable added to the value of a house. "Some day" is a pain to a boy who lives in and knows only "now." My good little sisters, to comfort me, remarked that Christmas was coming, but Christmas was always coming and grown-ups were always talking about it, asking you what you wanted and then giving you what they wanted you to have. Though everybody knew what I wanted, I told them all again. My mother knew that I told God, too, every night. I wanted a pony, and to make sure that they understood, I declared that I wanted nothing else.

5   "Nothing but a pony?" my father asked.

6   "Nothing," I said.

7   "Not even a pair of high boots?"

8   That was hard. I did want boots, but I stuck to the pony. "No, not even boots."

9   "Nor candy? There ought to be something to fill your stocking with, and Santa Claus can't put a pony into a stocking."

10   That was true, and he couldn't lead a pony down the chimney either. But no. "All I want is a pony," I said. "If I can't have a pony, give me nothing, nothing."

11   Now I had been looking myself for the pony I wanted, going to sales stables, inquiring of horsemen, and I had seen several that would do. My father let me "try" them. I tried so many ponies that I was learning fast to sit a horse. I chose several, but my father always found some fault with them. I was in despair. When Christmas was at hand I had given up all hope of a pony, and on Christmas Eve I hung up my stocking along with my sisters', of whom, by the way, I now had three. I haven't mentioned them or their coming because, you understand, they were girls, and girls, young girls, counted for nothing in my manly life. They did not mind me either; they were so happy that Christmas Eve that I caught some of their merriment. I speculated on what I'd get: I hung up the biggest stocking I had, and we all went reluctantly to bed to wait till morning. Not to sleep; not right away. We were told that we must not only sleep promptly, we

must not wake up till seven-thirty the next morning—or if we did, we must not go to the fireplace for our Christmas. Impossible.

12   We did sleep that night, but we woke up at six A.M. We lay in our beds and debated through the open doors whether to obey till, say, half-past six. Then we bolted. I don't know who started it, but there was a rush. We all disobeyed; we raced to disobey and get first to the fireplace in the front room downstairs. And there they were, the gifts, all sorts of wonderful things, mixed-up piles of presents; only, as I disentangled the mess, I saw that my stocking was empty; it hung limp; not a thing in it; and under and around it—nothing. My sisters had knelt down, each by her pile of gifts; they were squealing with delight, till they looked up and saw me standing there in my nightgown with nothing. They left their piles to come to me and look with me at my empty place. Nothing. They felt my stocking: nothing.

13   I don't remember whether I cried at that moment, but my sisters did. They ran with me back to my bed, and there we all cried till I became indignant. That helped some. I got up, dressed, and driving my sisters away, I went alone out into the yard, down to the stable, and there, all by myself, I wept. My mother came out to me by and by; she found me in my pony stall, sobbing on the floor, and she tried to comfort me. But I heard my father outside; he had come part way with her, and she was having some sort of angry quarrel with him. She tried to comfort me; besought me to come to breakfast. I could not; I wanted no comfort and no breakfast. She left me and went on into the house with sharp words for my father.

14   I don't know what kind of breakfast the family had. My sisters said it was "awful." They were ashamed to enjoy their own toys. They came to me, and I was rude. I ran away from them. I went around to the front of the house, sat down on the steps, and the crying over, I ached. I was wronged, I was hurt—I can feel now what I felt then, and I am sure that if one could see the wounds upon our hearts, there would be found still upon mine a scar from that terrible Christmas morning. And my father, the practical joker, he must have been hurt, too, a little. I saw him looking out of the window. He was watching me or something for an hour or two, drawing back the curtain ever so little lest I catch him, but I saw his face, and I think I can see now the anxiety upon it, the worried impatience.

15   After—I don't know how long—surely an hour or two—I was brought to the climax of my agony by the sight of a man riding a pony down the street, a pony and a brand-new saddle; the most beautiful saddle I ever saw, and it was a boy's saddle; the man's feet were not in the stirrups; his legs were too long. The outfit was perfect; it was the realization of all my dreams, the answer to all my prayers. A fine new bridle, with a light curb bit. And the pony! As he drew near, I saw that the pony was really a small horse, what we called an Indian pony, a bay, with black mane and tail, and one white foot and a white star on his forehead. For such a horse as that I would have given, I could have forgiven, anything.

16   But the man, a disheveled fellow with a blackened eye and a fresh-cut face, came along, reading the numbers on the houses, and as my hopes—my impossible hopes— rose, he looked at our door and passed by, he and the pony, and the saddle and the bridle. Too much. I fell upon the steps, and having wept before, I broke now into such a flood of tears that I was a floating wreck when I heard a voice.

17   "Say, kid," it said, "do you know a boy named Lennie Steffens?"

18   I looked up. It was the man on the pony, back again, at our horse block.

19   "Yes," I spluttered through my tears. "That's me."

20   "Well," he said, "then this is your horse. I've been looking all over for you and your house. Why don't you put your number where it can be seen?"

21   "Get down," I said, running out to him.

22   He went on saying something about "ought to have got here at seven o'clock; told me to bring the nag here and tie him to your post and leave him for you. But, hell, I got into a drunk—and a fight—and a hospital, and—."

23   "Get down," I said.

24   He got down, and he boosted me up to the saddle. He offered to fit the stirrups to me, but I didn't want him to. I wanted to ride.

25   "What's the matter with you?" he said, angrily. "What you crying for? Don't you like the horse? He's a dandy, this horse. I know him of old. He's fine at cattle; he'll drive'em alone."

26   I hardly heard, I could scarcely wait, but he persisted. He adjusted the stirrups, and then, finally, off I rode, slowly, at a walk, so happy, so thrilled, that I did not know what I was doing. I did not look back at the house or the man, I rode off up the street, taking note of everything—of the reins, of the pony's long mane, of the carved leather saddle. I had never seen anything so beautiful. And mine! I was going to ride up past Miss Kay's house. But I noticed on the horn of the saddle some stains like rain-drops, so I turned and trotted home, not to the house but to the stable. There was the family, father, mother, sisters, all working for me, all happy. They had been putting in place the tools of my new business: blankets, currycomb, brush, pitchfork—everything, and there was hay in the loft.

27   "What did you come back so soon for?" somebody asked. "Why didn't you go on riding?"

28   I pointed to the stains. "I wasn't going to get my new saddle rained on," I said. And my father laughed. "It isn't raining," he said "Those are not rain-drops."

29   "They are tears," my mother gasped, and she gave my father a look which sent him off to the house. Worse still, my mother offered to wipe away the tears still running out of my eyes. I gave her such a look as she had given him, and she went off after my father, drying her own tears. My sisters remained and we all unsaddled the pony, put on his halter, led him to his stall, tied and fed him. It began really to rain; so all the rest of that memorable day we curried and combed that pony. The girls plaited his mane, fore-lock, and tail, while I pitch-forked hay to him and curried and brushed, curried and brushed. For a change we brought him out to drink; we led him up and down, blanketed like a race-horse; we took turns at that. But the best, the most inexhaustible fun, was to clean him. When we went reluctantly to our midday Christmas dinner, we all smelt of horse, and my sisters had to wash their faces and hands. I was asked to, but I wouldn't, till my mother bade me look in the mirror. Then I washed up—quick. My face was caked with the muddy lines of tears that had coursed over my cheeks to my mouth. Having washed away that shame, I ate my dinner, and as I ate I grew hungrier and hungrier. It was my first meal that day, and as I filled up on the turkey and the stuffing, the cran-berries and the pies, the fruit and the nuts—as I swelled, I could laugh. My mother said I still choked and sobbed now and then, but I laughed, too; I saw and enjoyed my sisters' presents till—I had to go out and attend to my pony, who was there, really and truly there, the promise, the beginning, of a happy double life. And—I went and looked to make sure—there was the saddle, too, and the bridle.

30   But that Christmas, which my father had planned so carefully, was it the best or the worst I ever knew? He often asked me that; I never could answer as a boy. I think now that it was both. It covered the whole distance from broken-hearted misery to bursting happiness—too fast. A grown-up could hardly have stood it.

2,490 words

Questions

1. Conflict is at the heart of good narrative writing. In this selection, where is the reader first given an inkling of the conflict it will depict?
2. Paragraphs 1 and 2 include some unimportant details. What are the details and what purpose do they serve?
3. What does paragraph 3 tell us about the author's personality as a child?
4. The incident narrated takes place in the author's boyhood, when he was still in primary school. How does the author's style of writing reflect this youthfulness?
5. In paragraph 11, the author casually mentions that he had three sisters and then dismisses them. Why? What is this intended to reflect? His chauvinism?
6. Why did the author's parents instruct their children not to rise before 7:30 A.M.?
7. What explanation probably occurred to the author when he found nothing in his stocking?
8. Why didn't the father tell the boy that he had bought him a pony, but it had not yet been delivered?
9. Whose fault was it that the pony didn't arrive when it was supposed to?
10. In paragraph 29, the author describes the pony as "the promise, the beginning, of a happy double life." What does the term *double life* mean?

In *My Secret Place*, Doug Lencki narrates an especially vivid memory of his childhood love—flying. The weakness of this essay is its abrupt, anticlimatic ending. The title is also a misnomer. Vivid diction and colorful details are its strengths.

Student Model

My Secret Place
Doug Lencki

As a child I would look to the sky in utter amazement of anything that flew. I was enchanted by things that could glide on the wind or storm through the sky. At night I would dream of flying over my neighborhood, seeing everything from the air as a bird or a person in a plane would. I would get a crystal-clear picture of all that surrounded me as I lived entrapped on the earth. I would soar high into the sky and plummet to earth at speeds obtainable only in dreams. Faster, faster I would go, feeling the air rush by me, feeling the strain of the speed on my body—going faster than any bird, plane, or jet could possibly go. I would cruise over the treetops and the roofs of the homes in my neighborhood, sailing ever so close to objects that were blurred by my intense speed.

I would construct model airplanes and watch them fly and picture myself flying in them. But mere observation didn't seem to fulfill my dream of actually flying.

At that time, I had a nextdoor neighbor who was always building things. He helped me out if I had trouble putting together any of my model airplanes. One day I climbed over our fence into his backyard, and there I spied a gigantic kite. It had to be seven feet long and three to four feet wide. From my little boy's point of view, it seemed as big as any plane that flew. My neighbor had made the kite out of bamboo poles and bed sheets.

56

To my utter and boundless joy he gave it to me because it was too large for him to fly like a regular kite. Immediately I decided to test the kite to see if it could support my weight when I jumped off a small hill. I took the kite up to a knoll in back of our house, expecting very little, I jumped off the hill. To my great surprise and utter elation, I glided over the slope of the hill. The kite supported my weight perfectly, and I actually flew twenty to thirty feet.

I spent the whole day riding on my kite, holding onto the bamboo poles, which were supporting the bed sheets of the kite.

As I flew, I gazed up into the sky and imagined that I was flying among the clouds. I would see them forming into ice cream castles, feather cannons, cotton candy Ferris wheels, and a lot of other magical things. And always I was flying in and out of them. I would take an occasional nose dive straight into the hill, but the ivy on the hill would break my fall and I would escape unscathed.

At the end of the day I was exhausted; still, I couldn't wait until daylight of the next day. However, it rained that night and the rain turned my kite into a limp, wet, distorted mess of bamboo and bed linen. But my childhood dreams of flying had been fulfilled.

In "The Code," an old understanding between a young man and his father turns out to be a source of suffering for both of them.

Alternate Reading

The Code
Richard T. Gill

1   I remember, almost to the hour, when I first began to question my religion. I don't mean that my ideas changed radically just at that time. I was only twelve, and I continued to go to church faithfully and to say something that could pass for prayers each night before I went to sleep. But I never again felt quite the same. For the first time in my life, it had occurred to me that when I grew up I might actually leave the Methodist faith.

2   It all happened just a few days after my brother died. He was five years old, and his illness was so brief and his death so unexpected that my whole family was almost crazed with grief. My three aunts, each of whom lived within a few blocks of our house, and my mother were all firm believers in religion, and they turned in unison, and without reservation, to this last support. For about a week, a kind of religious frenzy seized our household. We would all sit in the living room—my mother, my aunts, my two sisters, and I, and sometimes Mr. Dodds, the Methodist minister, too—saying prayers in low voices, comforting one another, staying together for hours at a time, until someone remembered that we had not had dinner or that it was time for my sisters and me to be in bed.

3   I was quite swept up by the mood that had come over the house. When I went to bed, I would say the most elaborate, intricate prayers. In the past, when I had finished my "Now I lay me down to sleep," I would bless individually all the members of my immediate family and then my aunts, and let it go at that. Now, however, I felt that I had to bless everyone in the world whose name I could remember. I would go through all my friends at school, including the teachers, the principal, and the janitor, and then through the names of people I had heard my mother and father mention, some of whom I had

never even met. I did not quite know what to do about my brother, whom I wanted to pray for more than for anyone else. I hesitated to take his name out of its regular order, for fear I would be committed to believing that he had really died. But then I *knew* that he had died, so at the end of my prayers, having just barely mentioned his name as I went along, I would start blessing him over and over again, until I finally fell asleep.

4   The only one of us who was unmoved by this religious fervor was my father. Oddly enough, considering what a close family we were and how strongly my mother and aunts felt about religion, my father had never shown the least interest in it. In fact, I do not think that he had ever gone to church. Partly for this reason, partly because he was a rather brusque, impatient man, I always felt that he was something of a stranger in our home. He spent a great deal of time with us children, but through it all he seemed curiously unapproachable. I think we all felt constrained when he played with us and relieved when, at last, we were left to ourselves.

5   At the time of my brother's death, he was more of a stranger than ever. Except for one occasion, he took no part in the almost constant gatherings of the family in the living room. He was not going to his office that week—we lived in a small town outside Boston —and he was always around the house, but no one ever seemed to know exactly where. One of my aunts—Sarah, my mother's eldest sister—felt very definitely that my father should not be left to himself, and she was continually saying to me, "Jack, go upstairs and see if you can find him and talk to him." I remember going timidly along the hallway of the second floor and peeking into the bedrooms, not knowing what I should say if I found him and half afraid that he would scold me for going around looking into other people's rooms. One afternoon, not finding him in any of the bedrooms, I went up into the attic, where we had a sort of playroom. I remember discovering him there by the window. He was sitting absolutely motionless in an old wicker chair, an empty pipe in his hands, staring out fixedly over the treetops. I stood in the doorway for several minutes before he was aware of me. He turned as if to say something, but then, looking at me or just above my head—I was not sure which—he seemed to lose himself in his thoughts. Finally, he gave me a strangely awkward salute with his right hand and turned again to the window.

6   About the only times my father was with the rest of us were when we had meals or when, in the days immediately following the funeral, we all went out to the cemetery, taking fresh flowers or wreaths. But even at the cemetery he always stood slightly apart —a tall, lonely figure. Once, when we were at the grave and I was nearest him, he reached over and squeezed me around the shoulders. It made me feel almost embarrassed as though he were breaking through some inviolable barrier between us. He must have felt as I did, because he at once removed his arm and looked away, as though he had never actually embraced me at all.

7   It was the one occasion when my father was sitting in the living room with us that started me to wondering about my religion. We had just returned from the cemetery —two carloads of us. It was three or four days after the funeral and just at the time when, the shock having worn off, we were all experiencing our first clear realization of what had happened. Even I, young as I was, sensed that there was a new air of desolation in our home.

8   For a long time, we all sat there in silence. Then my aunts, their eyes moist, began talking about my brother, and soon my mother joined in. They started off softly, telling of little things he had done in the days before his illness. Then they fell silent and dried their eyes, and then quickly remembered some other incident and began speaking again. Slowly the emotion mounted, and before long the words were flooding out. "God

will take care of him!'' my Aunt Sarah cried, almost ecstatically, ''Oh, yes, He will! He will!'' Presently, they were all talking in chorus—saying that my brother was happy at last and that they would all be with him again one day.

9   I believed what they were saying and I could barely hold back my tears. But swept up as I was, I had the feeling that they should not be talking that way while my father was there. The feeling was one that I did not understand at all at the moment. It was just that when I looked over to the corner where he was sitting and saw the deep, rigid lines of his face, saw him sitting there silently, all alone, I felt guilty. I wanted everyone to stop for a while—at least until he had gone upstairs. But there was no stopping the torrent once it had started.

10   ''Oh, he was too perfect to live!'' Aunt Agnes, my mother's youngest sister, cried. ''He was never a bad boy. I've never seen a boy like that. I mean he was never even naughty. He was just too perfect.''

''Oh, yes. Oh, yes,'' my mother sighed.

''It's true,'' Aunt Sarah said. ''Even when he was a baby, he never really cried. There was never a baby like him. He was a saint.''

''He *was* a saint!'' Aunt Agnes cried. ''That's why he was taken from us!''

''He was a perfect baby,'' my mother said.

''He was taken from us,'' Aunt Agnes went on, ''because he was too perfect to live.''

11   All through this conversation, my father's expression has been growing more and more tense. At last, while Aunt Agnes was speaking, he rose from his chair. His face was very pale, and his eyes flashed almost feverishly. ''Don't talk like that, Agnes!'' he exclaimed, with a strange violence that was not anger but something much deeper. ''I won't have you talking like that any more. I don't want anybody talking like that!'' His whole body seemed to tremble. I had never seen him so worked up before. ''Of course he was a bad boy at times!'' he cried. ''Every boy's bad once in a while. What do you have to change him for? Why don't you leave him as he was?''

12   ''But he was such a perfect baby,'' Aunt Sarah said.

''He *wasn't* perfect!'' my father almost shouted, clenching his fist. ''He was no more perfect than Jack here or Betty or Ellen. He was just an ordinary little boy. He wasn't perfect. And he wasn't a saint. He was just a little boy, and I won't have you making him over into something he wasn't!''

13   He looked as though he were going to go on talking like this, but just then he closed his eyes and ran his hand up over his forehead and through his hair. When he spoke again, his voice was subdued. ''I just wish you wouldn't talk that way,'' he said. ''That's all I mean.'' And then, after standing there silently for a minute, he left the living room and walked upstairs.

14   I sat watching the doorway through which he had gone. Suddenly, I had no feeling for what my mother and my aunts had been saying. It was all a mist, a dream. Out of the many words that had been spoken that day, it was those few sentences of my father's that explained to me how I felt about my brother. I wanted to be with my father to tell him so.

15   I went upstairs and found him once again in the playroom in the attic. As before, he was silent and staring out the window when I entered, and we sat without speaking for what seemed to me like half an hour or more. But I felt that he knew why I was there, and I was not uncomfortable with him.

16   Finally, he turned to me and shook his head. ''I don't know what I can tell you, Jack,'' he said, raising his hands and letting them drop into his lap. ''That's the worst part of it. There's just nothing I can say that will make it any better.''

17   Though I only half understood him then, I see now that he was telling me of a draw-back—that he had no refuge, no comfort, no support. He was telling me that you were

all alone if you took the path that he had taken. Listening to him, I did not care about the drawback. I had begun to see what a noble thing it was for a man to bear the full loss of someone he had loved.

II

18   By the time I was thirteen or fourteen I was so thoroughly committed to my father's way of thinking that I considered it a great weakness in a man to believe in religion. I wanted to grow up to face life as he did—truthfully, without comfort, without support.

19   My attitude was never one of rebellion. Despite the early regimen of Sunday school and church that my mother had encouraged, she was wonderfully gentle with me, particularly when I began to express my doubts. She would come into my room each night after the light was out and ask me to say my prayers. Determined to be honest with her, I would explain that I could not say them sincerely, and therefore should not say them at all. "Now, Jack," she would reply, very quietly and calmly, "you mustn't talk like that. You'll really feel much better if you say them." I could tell from the tone of her voice that she was hurt, but she never tried to force me in any way. Indeed, it might have been easier for me if she *had* tried to oppose my decision strenuously. As it was, I felt so bad at having wounded her that I was continually trying to make things up—running errands, surprising her by doing the dishes when she went out shopping —behaving, in short, in the most conscientious, considerate fashion. But all this never brought me any closer to her religion. On the contrary, it only served to free me for my decision *not* to believe. And for that decision, as I say, my father was responsible.

20   Part of his influence, I suppose, was in his physical quality. Even at that time—when he was in his late forties and in only moderately good health—he was a most impressive figure. He was tall and heavychested, with leathery, rough-cast features and with an easy, relaxed rhythm in his walk. He had been an athlete in his youth, and, needless to say, I was enormously proud of his various feats and told about them, with due exaggeration, all over our neighborhood. Still, the physical thing had relatively little to do with the matter. My father, by that time, regarded athletes and athletics with contempt. Now and again, he would take me into the back yard to fool around with boxing gloves, but when it came to something serious, such as my going out for football in high school, he invariably put his foot down. "It takes too much time," he would tell me. "You ought to be thinking of college and your studies. It's nonsense what they make of sports nowadays!" I always wanted to remind him of *his* school days, but I knew it was no use. He had often told me what an unforgivable waste of time he considered his youth to have been.

21   Thus, although the physical thing was there, it was very much in the background— little more, really, than the simple assumption that a man ought to know how to take care of himself. The real bond between us was spiritual, in the sense that courage, as opposed to strength, is spiritual. It was this intangible quality of courage that I wanted desperately to possess and that, it seemed to me, captured everything that was essential about my father.

22   We never talked of this quality directly. The nearest we came to it was on certain occasions during the early part of the Second World War, just before I went off to college. We would sit in the living room listening to a speech by Winston Churchill, and my father would suddenly clap his fist against his palm. "My God!" he would exclaim, fairly beaming with admiration. "That man's got the heart of a tiger!" And I would listen to the rest of the speech, thrilling to every word, and then, thinking of my father, really, I would say aloud that, of all men in the world, the one I would most like to be was Churchill.

23   Nor did we often talk about religion. Yet our religion—our rejection of religion—was the deepest statement of the bond between us. My father, perhaps our of deference to my mother and my sisters and aunts, always put his own case very mildly. "It's certainly a great philosophy," he would say of Christianity. "No one could question that. But for the rèst . . ." Here he would throw up his hands and cock his head to one side, as if to say that he had tried, but simply could not manage the hurdle of divinity. This view, however mildly it may have been expressed, became mine with absolute clarity and certainty. I concluded that religion was a refuge, without the least foundation in fact. More than that, I positively objected to those—I should say those *men,* for to me it was a peculiarly masculine matter—who turned to religion for support. As I saw it, a man ought to face life as it really is, on his own two feet, without a crutch, as my father did. That was the heart of the matter. By the time I left home for college, I was so deeply committed to this view that I would have considered it a disloyalty to him, to myself, to the code we had lived by, to alter my position in the least.

24   I did not see much of my father during the next four years or so. I was home during the summer vacation after my freshman year, but then, in the middle of the next year, I went into the Army. I was shipped to the Far East for the tail end of the war, and was in Japan at the start of the Occupation. I saw my father only once or twice during my entire training period, and, naturally, during the time I was overseas I did not see him at all.

25   While I was away, his health failed badly. In 1940, before I went off to college, he had taken a job at a defense plant. The plant was only forty miles from our home, but he was working on the night shift, and commuting was extremely complicated and tiresome. And, of course, he was always willing to overexert himself out of a sense of pride. The result was that late in 1942 he had a heart attack. He came through it quite well, but he made no effort to cut down on his work and, as a consequence, suffered a second, and more serious, attack, two years later. From that time on, he was almost completely bedridden.

26   I was on my way overseas at the time of the second attack, and I learned of it in a letter from my mother. I think she was trying to spare me, or perhaps it was simply that I could not imagine so robust a man as my father being seriously ill. In any event, I had only the haziest notion of what his real condition was, so when, many months later, I finally did realize what had been going on, I was terribly surprised and shaken. One day, some time after my arrival at an American Army post in Japan, I was called to the orderly room and told that my father was critically ill and that I was to be sent home immediately. Within forty-eight hours, I was standing in the early-morning light outside my father's bedroom, with my mother and sisters at my side. They had told me, as gently as they could, that he was not very well, that he had had another attack. But it was impossible to shield me then. I no sooner stepped into the room and saw him than I realized that he would not live more than a day or two longer.

27   From that moment on, I did not want to leave him for a second. Even that night, during the periods when he was sleeping and I was of no help being there, I could not get myself to go out of the room for more than a few minutes. A practical nurse had come to sit up with him, but since I was at the bedside, she finally spent the night in the hallway. I was really quite tired, and late that night my mother and my aunts begged me to go to my room and rest for a while, but I barely heard them. I was sure he would wake up soon, and when he did, I wanted to be there to talk to him.

28   We did talk a great deal that first day and night. It was difficult for both of us. Every once in a while, my father would shift position in the bed, and I would catch a glimpse of his wasted body. It was a knife in my heart. Even worse were the times when he would

reach out for my hand, his eyes misted, and begin to tell me how he felt about me. I tried to look at him, but in the end I always looked down. And, knowing that he was dying, and feeling desperately guilty, I would keep repeating to myself that he knew how I felt, that he would understand why I looked away.

29   There was another thing, too. While we talked that day, I had a vague feeling that my father was on the verge of making some sort of confession to me. It was, as I say, only the vaguest impression, and I thought very little about it. The next morning, however, I began to sense what was in the air. Apparently, Mr. Dodds, the minister, whom I barely knew, had been coming to the house lately to talk to my father. My father had not said anything about this, and I learned it only indirectly, from something my mother said to my eldest sister at the breakfast table. At the moment, I brushed the matter aside. I told myself it was natural that Mother would want my father to see the minister at the last. Nevertheless, the very mention of the minister's name caused something to tighten inside me.

30   Later that day, the matter was further complicated. After lunch, I finally did go to my room for a nap, and when I returned to my father's room, I found him and my mother talking about Mr. Dodds. The conversation ended almost as soon as I entered, but I was left with the distinct impression that they were expecting the minister to pay a visit that day, whether very shortly or at suppertime or later in the evening, I could not tell. I did not ask. In fact, I made a great effort not to think of the matter at all.

31   Then, early that evening, my father spoke to me. I knew before he said a word that the minister *was* coming. My mother had straightened up the bedroom, and fluffed up my father's pillows so that he was half sitting in the bed. No one had told me anything, but I was sure what the preparations meant. "I guess you probably know," my father said to me when we were alone, "we're having a visitor tonight. It's—ah—Mr. Dodds. You know, the minister from your mother's church."

32   I nodded, half shrugging, as if I saw nothing the least unusual in the news.
"He's come here before once or twice," my father said. "Have I mentioned that? I can't remember if I've mentioned that."

"Yes, I know. I think Mother said something, or perhaps you did. I don't remember."

"I just thought I'd let you know. You see, your mother wanted me to talk to him. I—I've talked to him more for her sake than anything else."

"Sure. I can understand that."

33   "I think it makes her feel a little better. I think—" Here he broke off, seeming dissatisfied with what he was saying. His eyes turned to the ceiling, and he shook his head slightly, as if to erase the memory of his words. He studied the ceiling for a long time before he spoke again. "I don't mean it was all your mother exactly," he said. "Well, what I mean is he's really quite an interesting man. I think you'd probably like him a good deal."

"I know Mother has always liked him," I replied. "From what I gather most people seem to like him very much."

"Well, he's that sort," my father went on, with quickening interest. "I mean, he isn't what you'd imagine at all. To tell the truth, I wish you'd talk to him a little. I wish you'd talk things over with him right from scratch." My father was looking directly at me now, his eyes flashing.

"I'd be happy to talk with him sometime," I said. "As I say, everybody seems to think very well of him."

34   "Well, I wish you would. You see, when you're lying here day after day, you get to thinking about things. I mean, it's good to have someone to talk to." He paused for a moment. "Tell me," he said, "have you ever . . . have you ever wondered if there wasn't some truth in it? Have you ever thought about it that way at all?"

35   I made a faint gesture with my hand. ''Of course, it's always possible to wonder,'' I replied. ''I don't suppose you can ever be completely certain one way or the other.''

''I know, I know,'' he said, almost impatiently. ''But have you ever felt—well, all in a sort of flash—that is *was* true? I mean, have you ever had that feeling?

36   He was half raised up from the pillow now, his eyes staring into me with a feverish concentration. Suddenly, I could not look at him any longer. I lowered my head.

''I don't mean permanently or anything like that,'' he went on. ''But just for a few seconds. The feeling that you've been wrong all along. Have you had that feeling—ever?''

37   I could not look up. I could not move. I felt that every muscle in my body had suddenly frozen. Finally, after what seemed an eternity, I heard him sink back into the pillows. When I glanced up a moment later, he was lying there silent, his eyes closed, his lips parted, conveying somehow the image of the death that awaited him.

38   Presently, my mother came to the door. She called me into the hall to tell me that Mr. Dodds had arrived. I said that I thought my father had fallen asleep but that I would go back and see.

It was strangely disheartening to me to discover that he was awake. He was sitting there, his eyes open, staring grimly into the gathering shadows of the evening.

''Mr. Dodds is downstairs,'' I said matter-of-factly. ''Mother wanted to know if you felt up to seeing him tonight.''

39   For a moment, I thought he had not heard me; he gave no sign of recognition whatever. I went to the foot of the bed and repeated myself. He nodded, not answering the question but simply indicating that he had heard me. At length, he shook his head. ''Tell your mother I'm a little tired tonight,'' he said. ''Perhaps—well, perhaps some other time.''

''I could ask him to come back later, if you'd like.''

''No, no, don't bother. I—I could probably use the rest.''

I waited a few seconds. ''Are you sure?'' I asked. ''I'm certain he could come back in an hour or so.''

40   Then, suddenly, my father was looking at me. I shall never forget his face at that moment and the expression burning in his eyes. He was pleading with me to speak. And all I could say was that I would be happy to ask Mr. Dodds to come back later, if he wanted it that way. It was not enough. I knew, instinctively, at that moment that it was not enough. But I could not say anything more.

41   As quickly as it had come, the burning flickered and went out. He sank back into the pillows again. ''No, you can tell him I won't be needing him tonight,'' he said, without interest. ''Tell him not to bother waiting around.'' Then he turned on his side, away from me, and said no more.

42   So my father did not see Mr. Dodds that night. Nor did he ever see him again. Shortly after midnight, just after my mother and sisters had gone to bed, he died. I was at his side then, but I could not have said exactly when it occurred. He must have gone off in his sleep, painlessly, while I sat there awake beside him.

43   In the days that followed, our family was together almost constantly. Curiously enough, I did not think much about my father just then. For some reason, I felt the strongest sense of responsibility toward the family. I found myself making the arrangements for the funeral, protecting Mother from the stream of people who came to the house, speaking words of consolation to my sisters and even to my aunts. I was never alone except at night, when a kind of oblivion seized me almost as soon as my head touched the pillow. My sleep was dreamless, numb.

44   Then, two weeks after the funeral, I left for Fort Devens, where I was to be discharged

from the Army. I had been there three days when I was told that my terminal leave would begin immediately and that I was free to return home. I had half expected that when I was at the Fort, separated from the family, something would break inside me. But still no emotion came. I thought of my father often during that time, but, search as I would, I could find no sign of feeling.

45   Then, when I had boarded the train for home, it happened. Suddenly, for no reason whatever, I was thinking of the expression on my father's face that last night in the bedroom. I saw him as he lay there pleading with me to speak. And I knew then what he had wanted me to say to him—that it was really all right with me, that it wouldn't change anything between us if he gave way. And then I was thinking of myself and what I had said and what I had *not* said. Not a word to help! Not a word!

46   I wanted to beg his forgiveness. I wanted to cry out aloud to him. But I was in a crowded train, sitting with three elderly women just returning from a shopping tour. I turned my face to the window. There, silent, unnoticed, I thought of what I might have said.

4,960 words

Vocabulary

unison (2)	inviolable (6)
brusque (4)	intangible (21)
constrained (4)	deference (23)

Questions

1. What was the author's childhood faith? How old was he when he thought he might give it up?
2. Why, after the death of his brother, did the narrator feel he had to bless everyone, even people whose names he had heard mentioned but whom he really didn't know?
3. What was the value of religion to the narrator's mother and aunts? Where is this stated?
4. What did the past athletic prowess of the father have to do with the code that developed between him and the narrator? How was the code related to "masculinity"?
5. What "intangible quality" drew the author to his father?
6. Examine paragraphs 24 and 26 and identify at least two examples of the author's use of pacing.
7. In paragraph 40, the narrator says of his father, "He was pleading with me to speak" and that he, the narrator, knew that his answer "was not enough." What did the narrator's father want him to say? Why didn't the narrator say it?
8. What does "The Code" have to say about role-playing and about rigid beliefs in "masculinity"?
9. How would you characterize the father's deathbed behavior? Was he courageous? Cowardly?
10. What is the significance of the final scene and the three elderly women in the train?

Anne Frank was born to wealthy Jewish parents in Frankfurt, Germany on June 12, 1929, and died three months before her sixteenth birthday in the Nazi concentration camp at Bergen Belsen. Her family moved from Frankfurt to Amsterdam where they went into hiding during the war to escape persecution by the Nazis. While hiding out in cramped living quarters behind her father's former office, Anne kept a diary of the family's confinement in which she recorded daily incidents, squabbles, her ambitions to become a writer, and her daydreams. The diary, which she addressed as "Kitty," was discovered after her death. From it, the following selection was excerpted.

Alternate Reading

Selection from Diary of a Young Girl
Anne Frank

Saturday, 7 November, 1942

Dear Kitty,

1   Mummy is frightfully irritable and that always seems to herald unpleasantness for me. Is it just chance that Daddy and Mummy never rebuke Margot and that they always drop on me for everything? Yesterday evening, for instance: Margot was reading a book with lovely drawings in it; she got up and went upstairs, put the book down ready to go on with it later. I wasn't doing anything, so picked up the book and started looking at the pictures. Margot came back, saw "her" book in my hands, wrinkled her forehead and asked for the book back. Just because I wanted to look a little further on, Margot got more and more angry. Then Mummy joined in: "Give the book to Margot; she was reading it," she said. Daddy came into the room. He didn't even know what it was all about, but saw the injured look on Margot's face and promptly dropped on me: "I'd like to see what you'd say if Margot ever started looking at one of your books!" I gave way at once, laid the book down, and left the room—offended, as they thought. It so happened I was neither offended nor cross, just miserable. It wasn't right of Daddy to judge without knowing what the squabble was about. I would have given Margot the book myself, and much more quickly, if Mummy and Daddy hadn't interfered. They took Margot's part at once, as though she were the victim of some great injustice.

2   It's obvious that Mummy would stick up for Margot; she and Margot always do back each other up. I'm so used to that that I'm utterly indifferent to both Mummy's jawing and Margot's moods.

3   I love them; but only because they are Mummy and Margot. With Daddy it's different. If he holds Margot up as an example, approves of what she does, praises and caresses her, then something gnaws at me inside, because I adore Daddy. He is the one I look up to. I don't love anyone in the world but him. He doesn't notice that he treats Margot differently from me. Now Margot is just the prettiest, sweetest, most beautiful girl in the world. But all the same I feel I have some right to be taken seriously too. I have always been the dunce, the ne'er-do-well of the family, I've always had to pay double for my deeds, first with the scolding and then again because of the way my feelings are hurt. Now I'm not satisfied with this apparent favoritism any more. I want something from Daddy that he is not able to give me.

4   I'm not jealous of Margot, never have been. I don't envy her good looks or her beauty. It is only that I long for Daddy's real love: not only as his child, but for me—Anne, myself.

5   I cling to Daddy because it is only through him that I am able to retain the remnant of family feeling. Daddy doesn't understand that I need to give vent to my feelings over Mummy sometimes. He doesn't want to talk about it; he simply avoids anything which might lead to remarks about Mummy's failings. Just the same, Mummy and her failings are something I find harder to bear than anything else. I don't know how to keep it all to myself. I can't always be drawing attention to her untidiness, her sarcasm, and her lack of sweetness, neither can I believe that I'm always in the wrong.

6   We are exact opposites in everything; so naturally we are bound to run up against each other. I don't pronounce judgment on Mummy's character, for that is something I can't judge. I only look at her as a mother, and she just doesn't succeed in being that to me; I have to be my own mother. I've drawn myself apart from them all; I am my own skipper and later on I shall see where I come to land. All this comes about particularly because I have in my mind's eye an image of what a perfect mother and wife should be; and in her whom I must call "Mother" I find no trace of that image.

7   I am always making resolutions not to notice Mummy's bad example. I want to see only the good side of her and to seek in myself what I cannot find in her. But it doesn't work; and the worst of it is that neither Daddy nor Mummy understands this gap in my life, and I blame them for it. I wonder if anyone can ever succeed in making their children absolutely content.

8   Sometimes I believe that God wants to try me, both now and later on; I must become good through my own efforts, without examples and without good advice. Then later on I shall be all the stronger. Who besides me will ever read these letters? From whom but myself shall I get comfort? As I need comforting often, I frequently feel weak, and dissatisfied with myself; my shortcomings are too great. I know this, and every day I try to improve myself, again and again.

9   My treatment varies so much. One day Anne is so sensible and is allowed to know everything; and the next day I hear that Anne is just a silly little goat who doesn't know anything at all and imagines that she's learned a wonderful lot from books. I'm not a baby or a spoiled darling any more, to be laughed at, whatever she does. I have my own views, plans, and ideas, though I can't put them into words yet. Oh, so many things bubble up inside me as I lie in bed, having to put up with people I'm fed up with, who always misinterpret my intentions. That's why in the end I always come back to my diary. That is where I start and finish, because Kitty is always patient. I'll promise her that I shall persevere, in spite of everything, and find my own way through it all, and swallow my tears. I only wish I could see the results already or occasionally receive encouragement from someone who loves me.

10   Don't condemn me; remember rather that sometimes I too can reach the bursting point.

Yours, Anne

1,050 words

Questions

1. Anne was 13 years old when she wrote this entry in her diary. What characteristics of her writing point to her youthfulness?
2. What was the cause of the squabble between Anne and Margot?
3. How does Anne feel about her mother?
4. According to paragraph 3, how does Anne feel about herself? About Margot?

5. What does Anne say she has in her "mind's eye"?
6. What does Anne accuse her father of?
7. How would you characterize Anne's attitude toward her father and mother? Does she have an unusual or strange attitude toward them?
8. What resolution does Anne express at the end of the entry?
9. What does this episode suggest is the value of keep a diary?

Additional Writing Assignments

1. Narrate any incident in your life in which you were forced by a role to suppress your true feelings.
2. Narrate the story of your most memorable Christmas.
3. Tell a story illustrating how you feel about your mother and your father.
4. Tell the story of the day when "everything went wrong."
5. Write a story titled "Trapped."
6. Write a story titled "My Jealousy."
7. Write a story that illustrates the way you feel about religion.
8. Narrate a story about an episode with an animal.
9. Narrate a story of how you repulsed an aggressive salesperson.
10. Write a story on a close call with death.

5

Description

He is an old man now, as gnarled and twisted as a
cypress on a cliff above the sea.

A. Reading for Ideas

"Lament" is the story of a poor Russian cabdriver who is overwhelmed by the grief of losing his only son. Read the story for a dominant impression—a central theme that unifies the descriptive details. Observe carefully the accumulation of details and how they fit into the narrative. What does the story tell you about grief, about society, and about man's capacity for suffering? What is the conflict in the story? How is it finally resolved? What feelings does the story arouse in you?

The Lament
Anton Chekhov

1   It is twilight. A thick wet snow is twirling around the newly lighted street lamps, and lying in soft thin layers on roofs, on horses' backs, on people's shoulders and hats. The cabdriver Iona Potapov is quite white, and looks like a phantom; he is bent double as far as a human body can bend double; he is seated on his box; he never makes a move. If a whole snowdrift fell on him, it seems as if he would not find it necessary to shake it off. His little horse is also quite white, and remains motionless; its immobility, its angularity, and its straight wooden-looking legs, even close by, give it the appearance of a gingerbread horse worth a *kopek*. It is, no doubt, plunged in deep thought. If you were snatched from the plow, from your usual gray surroundings, and were thrown into this slough full of monstrous lights, unceasing noise, and hurrying people, you too would find it difficult not to think.

2   Iona and his little horse have not moved from their place for a long while. They left their yard before dinner, and up to now, not a fare. The evening mist is descending over the town, the white lights of the lamps replacing brighter rays, and the hubbub of the street getting louder. "Cabby for Viborg way!" suddenly hears Iona, "Cabby!"

3   Iona jumps, and through his snow-covered eyelashes sees an officer in a greatcoat, with his hood over his head.

68

"Viborg way!" the officer repeats. "Are you asleep, eh? Viborg way!"

4   With a nod of assent Iona picks up the reins, in consequence of which layers of snow slip off the horses's back and neck. The officer seats himself in the sleigh, the cabdriver smacks his lips to encourage his horse, stretches out his neck like a swan, sits up, and, more from habit than necessity, brandishes his whip. The little horse also stretches its neck, bends its wooden-looking legs, and makes a move undecidedly.

5   "What are you doing, werewolf!" is the exclamation Iona hears from the dark mass moving to and fro, as soon as they have started.

"Where the devil are you going? To the r-r-right!"

"You do not know how to drive. Keep to the right!" calls the officer angrily.

6   A coachman from a private carriage swears at him; a passerby, who has run across the road and rubbed his shoulder against the horse's nose, looks at him furiously as he sweeps the snow from his sleeve. Iona shifts about on his seat as if he were on needles, moves his elbows as if he were trying to keep his equilibrium, and gapes about like someone suffocating, who does not understand why and wherefore he is there.

7   "What scoundrels they all are!" jokes the officer; "one would think they had all entered into an agreement to jostle you or fall under your horse."

Iona looks round at the officer, and moves his lips. He evidently wants to say something, but the only sound that issues is a snuffle.

"What?" asks the officer.

8   Iona twists his mouth into a smile, and with an effort says hoarsely:

"My son, *barin*, died this week."

"Hm! What did he die of?"

Iona turns with his whole body toward his fare, and says:

"And who knows! They say high fever. He was three days in the hospital, and then died. . . . God's will be done."

"Turn round! The devil!" sounds from the darkness. "Have you popped off, old doggie, eh? Use your eyes!"

"Go on, go on," says the officer, "otherwise we shall not get there by tomorrow. Hurry up a bit!"

9   The cabdriver again stretches his neck, sits up, and, with a bad grace, brandishes his whip. Several times again he turns to look at his fare, but the latter has closed his eyes, and apparently is not disposed to listen. Having deposited the officer in the Viborg, he stops by the tavern, doubles himself up on his seat, and again remains motionless, while the snow once more begins to cover him and his horse. An hour, and another. . . . Then, along the footpath, with a squeak of galoshes, and quarreling, come three young men, two of them tall and lanky, the third one short and humpbacked.

"Caby, the the Police Bridge!" in a cracked voice calls the humpback. "The three of us for two *griveniks!*"

10   Iona picks up his reins, and smacks his lips. Two *griveniks* is not a fair price, but he does not mind whether it is a *rouble* or five *kopeks*—to him it is all the same now, so long as they are fares. The young men, jostling each other and using bad language, approach the sleigh, and all three at once try to get onto the seat; then begins a discussion as to which two shall sit and who shall be the one to stand. After wrangling, abusing each other, and much petulance, it is at last decided that the humpback shall stand, as he is the smallest.

11   "Now then, hurry up!" says the humpback in a twanging voice, as he takes his place and breathes on Iona's neck. "Old furry! Here, mate, what a cap you have! There is not a worse one to be found in all Petersburg! . . ."

"He-he!—he-he!" giggles Iona. "Such a . . . ."

"Now you, 'such a,' hurry up, are you going the whole way at this pace? Are you?

. . . Do you want it in the neck?''

"My head feels like bursting," says one of the lanky ones. "Last night at the Donk-masovs, Vaska and I drank the whole of four bottles of cognac."

12   "I don't understand what you lie for," says the other lanky one angrily; "you lie like a brute."

"God strike me, it's the truth!"

"It's as much the truth as that a louse coughs!"

"He, he," grins Iona, "what gay young gentlemen!"

"Pshaw, go to the devil!" says the humpback indignantly.

"Are you going to get on or not, you old pest? Is that the way to drive? Use the whip a bit! Go on, devil, go on, give it to him well!"

13   Iona feels at his back the little man wriggling, and the tremble in his voice. He listens to the insults hurled at him, sees the people, and little by little the feeling of loneliness leaves him. The humpback goes on swearing until he gets mixed up in some elaborate six-foot oath, or chokes with coughing. The lankies begin to talk about a certain Nadejda Petrovna. Iona looks round at them several times; he waits for a temporary silence, then, turning round again, he murmurs:

"My son . . . died this week."

14   "We must all die," sighs the humpback, wiping his lips after an attack of coughing. "Now, hurry up, hurry up! Gentlemen, I really cannot go any farther like this! When will he get us there?"

"Well, just you stimulate him a little in the neck!"

"You old pest, do you hear, I'll bone your neck for you! If one treated the like of you with ceremony one would have to go on foot! Do you hear, old serpent Gorinytch! Or do you not care a spit?"

15   Iona hears rather than feels the blows they deal him.

"He, he," he laughs. "They are gay young gentlemen, God bless 'em!"

"Cabby, are you married?" asks a lanky one.

"I? He, he, gay young gentlemen? Now I have only a wife and the moist ground. . . . He, ho, ho . . . that is to say, the grave. My son has died, and I am alive. . . . A wonderful thing, death mistook the door . . . instead of coming to me, it went to my son. . . ."

16   Iona turns round to tell them how his son died, but at this moment, the humpback, giving a little sigh, announces, "Thank God, we have at least reached our destination," and Iona watches them disappear through the dark entrance. Once more he is alone, and again surrounded by silence. . . . His grief, which has abated for a short while, returns and rends his heart with greater force. With an anxious and hurried look, he searches among the crowds passing on either side of the street to find whether there may be just one person who will listen to him. But the crowds hurry by without noticing him or his trouble. Yet it is such an immense, illimitable grief. Should his heart break and the grief pour out, it would flow over the whole earth, so it seems, and yet no one sees it. It has managed to conceal itself in such an insignificant shell that no one can see it even by day and with a light.

17   Iona sees a hall porter with some sacking, and decides to talk to him.

"Friend, what sort of time is it?" he asks.

"Past nine. What are you standing here for? Move on."

18   Iona moves on a few steps, doubles himself up, and abandons himself to his grief. He sees it is useless to turn to people for help. In less than five minutes he straightens himself, holds up his head as if he felt some sharp pain, and gives a tug at the reins; he can bear it no longer. "The stables," he thinks, and the little horse, as if it understood, starts off at a trot.

19   About an hour and a half later Iona is seated by a large dirty stove. Around the stove, on the floor, on the benches, people are snoring; the air is thick and suffocatingly hot. Iona looks at the sleepers, scratches himself, and regrets having returned so early.

20   "I have not even earned my fodder," he thinks. "That's what's my trouble. A man who knows his job, who has had enough to eat, and his horse too, can always sleep peacefully."

21   A young cabdriver in one of the corners half gets up, grunts sleepily, and stretches toward a bucket of water.

"Do you want a drink?" Iona asks him.

"Don't I want a drink!"

"That's so? Your good health! But listen, mate—you know, my son is dead. . . . Did you hear? This week, in the hospital. . . . It's a long story."

22   Iona looks to see what effect his words have, but sees none—the young man has hidden his face and is fast asleep again. The old man sighs, and scratches his head. Just as much as the young one wants to drink, the old man wants to talk. It will soon be a week since his son died, and he has not been able to speak about it properly to anyone. One must tell it slowly and carefully; how his son fell ill, how he suffered, what he said before he died, how he died. One must describe every detail of the funeral, and the journey to the hospital to fetch the dead son's clothes. His daughter Anissia has remained in the village—one must talk about her too. Is it nothing he has to tell? Surely the listener would gasp and sigh, and sympathize with him? It is better, too, to talk to women; although they are stupid, two words are enough to make them sob.

23   "I'll go and look after my horse," thinks Iona, "there's always time to sleep. No fear of that!"

24   He puts on his coat, and goes to the stables to his horse; he thinks of the corn, the hay, the weather. When he is alone, he dares not think of his son; he can speak about him to anyone, but to think of him, and picture him to himself, is unbearably painful.

25   "Are you tucking in?" Iona asks his horse, looking at its bright eyes; "go on, tuck in, though we've not earned our corn, we can eat hay. Yes! I am too old to drive—my son could have, not I. He was a first-rate cabdriver. If only he had lived!"

26   Iona is silent for a moment, then continues:

"That's how it is, my old horse. There's no more Kuzina Ionitch. He has left us to live, and he went off pop. Now let's say, you had a foal, you were the foal's mother, and suddenly, let's say, that foal went and left you to live after him. It would be sad, wouldn't it?"

27   The little horse munches, listens, and breathes over its master's hand. . . . Iona's feelings are too much for him, and he tells the little horse the whole story.

2,048 words

Vocabulary

angularity (1)	brandishes (4)
slough (1)	petulance (10)

Questions

1. How does the title "Lament" relate to the content of this story?
2. Death of a loved one is not the only loss probed in the story. What other sorrows are examined?

3. What is Iona's overwhelming desire throughout the story? Why does he have this desire?
4. What do all of Iona's passengers have in common?
5. In what paragraph does Iona think about the exact steps he should take in expressing his grief?
6. Examine paragraph 1, and point out some details suggesting that the story will involve some kind of grief, sadness, or loss.
7. What details create the dominant impression of a father grieving for his son? Point to specific paragraphs.
8. What is the conflict of the story? How is it resolved?

Elegy for Jane

(My student, thrown by a horse)
Theodore Roethke

I remember the neckcurls, limp and damp as tendrils;
And her quick look, a sidelong pickerel smile;
And how, once startled into talk, the light syllables leaped for her.
And she balanced in the delight of her thought,
A wren, happy, tail into the wind,
Her song trembling the twigs and small branches.
The shade sang with her;
The leaves, their whispers turned to kissing,
And the mould sang in the bleached valleys under the rose.

Oh, when she was sad, she cast herself down into such a pure depth,
Even a father could not find her:
Scraping her cheek against straw,
Stirring the clearest water.

My sparrow, you are not here,
Waiting like a fern, making a spiney shadow.
The sides of wet stones cannot console me,
Nor the moss, wound with the last light.

If only I could nudge you from this sleep,
My maimed darling, my skittery pigeon.
Over this damp grave I speak the words of my love:
I, with no rights in this matter,
Neither father nor lover.

Questions

1. What characteristic is shared by this poem and "Lament?"
2. What is the poet's dominant impression of Jane?
3. What details support the dominant impression? Refer to specific passages.

4. What kind of person was Jane? What were her personality traits? Supply examples from the poem.
5. What do you think is the meaning of the ambiguous line "I, with no rights in this matter,/neither father nor lover"?

B. How to Write a Description

A vivid description supports a dominant impression with specific details. The dominant impression of a description is its central and unifying theme. In *The Godfather,* for instance, Mario Puzo bases his description of Don Corleone's sons on the dominant impression of their resemblance to Cupid. This impression is introduced in the description of Sonny and applied to all the other sons of Don Corleone:

> Sonny Corleone was tall for a first generation American of Italian parentage, almost six feet, and his crop of bushy, curly hair made him look even taller. *His face was that of a gross Cupid, the features even but the bowshaped lips thickly sensual, the dimpled cleft chin in some curious way obscene.*

With slightly varying details, this dominant impression accommodates a description of the Don's second son, Frederico Corleone:

> He was short and burly, not handsome but with the same Cupid head of the family, the curly helmet of hair over the round face and the sensual bow-shaped lips. Only, in Fred, these lips were not sensual but granitelike.

A contrast to this dominant impression is provided in the description of Michael Corleone, the third son:

> Michael Corleone was the youngest son of the Don and the only child who had refused the great man's direction. He did not have the heavy, Cupid-shaped face of the other children, and his jet black hair was straight rather than curly. His skin was a clear olive-brown that would have been called beautiful in a girl. He was handsome in a delicate way.

Writing Assignment

Describe as vividly as you can a person, a place, or an event. Begin by picking a subject that strikes you with force. If possible, accumulate details and impressions by observing your subject up close. Next, find the dominant impression created by the person, place, or event, and state it in one sentence. The dominant impression of a place might be, "Ben's cafe is a dingy hole in the wall." Of a person, it might be "Alicia has a delicate beauty." Support this dominant impression with details, omitting anything irrelevant that might break the unity of the impression. Develop the dominant impression and selected supporting details into a well-shaped essay.

Specific Instructions

1. ESTABLISH THE DOMINANT IMPRESSION.   To begin, you should establish the dominant impression of whatever you wish to describe. If you are assigned to describe a place, visit the place and spend some time observing it. The details observed will often suggest a suitable dominant impression. Once chosen, this dominant impression in turn will influence your selection of details.

For example, suppose you are assigned to write a description of your local airport lobby. You visit the airport and observe the following details:

1. A man's hat falls off as he lurches down the hall to catch his plane.
2. A sailor passionately kissing a girl suddenly looks at his watch and abruptly heads toward the escalator.
3. A little girl shrieks as an elderly woman—probably her grandmother—jerks her out of the arms of her mother to rush along toward Gate 31.
4. A fat executive takes a last hurried drag from his cigar before huffing and puffing his way to the ticket counter.
5. People of all sizes, ages, and races scramble across the lobby, bumping into each other then resuming their frantic journeys.
6. A well manicured woman sits casually on a bench reading *Cosmopolitan* and looking bored.
7. Two uniformed porters belly-laugh over a joke during a lull in foot traffic.

Most of these details suggest a dominant impression of the airport as a place where people are *rushed.* You formulate the following controlling idea, which includes this dominant impression: "At certain hours the International Airport lobby is a throughfare for people who are *rushed.*"

The function of the dominant impression at this stage of the essay is to provide a standard for judging the relevance of details. Details that support the dominant impression are relevant; those that contradict it are irrelevant. Details 1 through 5, for instance, can be included because they support this dominant impression, but details 6 and 7 must be omitted because they contradict it. The dominant impression therefore acts as a pattern that unifies the description, preventing your essay from being mercilessly pulled in two or three different directions by irrelevant details.

2. FOCUS THE DOMINANT IMPRESSION.   The dominant impression in a description is the equivalent of the controlling idea in an essay. Like the controlling idea, it must have a focus. The following dominant impressions lack focus:

Unfocused: Toward evening the meadow becomes eerie in its forsaken barrenness as the magpies chatter happily.

Better: Toward evening the meadow becomes eerie in its forsaken barrenness as the wind howls and groans.

(Happily chattering magpies destroy the idea of "forsaken barrenness.")

Unfocused: A translucent fragility was the outstanding feature of this husky old lady.

Better: A translucent fragility gave beauty to the face of this aristocratic old lady.

("Husky" ruins the impression of fragility.)

3. SELECT SPECIFIC AND SENSORY DETAILS.   A good dominant impression will attract details the way a whirlpool sucks water toward its center. You must not only avoid irrelevant details that will obscure the dominant impression of your description, but also you must select details that are specific and appeal to the senses.

Lack of *specific details* is the biggest mistake in student descriptions. The overwhelming tendency is to fill the page with mushy generalizations—for example:

> One could tell at a look that Chaim Sachar was poor. He was always hungry, and as a result he would wander about with a hungry attitude. His continual poverty caused him to become stingy to the point where he would collect garbage to use as fuel for his stove, and he cooked poor meals.

The description never comes to life because the supporting evidence is so vague. Contrast the above with another account:

> Two small eyes, starved and frightened, peered from beneath his dishevelled eyebrows; the red rims about his eyes were reminiscent of the time when he could wash down a dish of fried liver and hard-boiled eggs with a pint of vodka every morning after prayer. Now, all day long, he wandered through the marketplace, inhaling butcher-shop odors and those from restaurants, sniffing like a dog, and occasionally napping on porters' carts. With the refuse he had collected in a basket, he fed his kitchen stove at night; then, rolling the sleeves over his hairy arms, he would grate turnips on a grater.
>
> Isaac Bashevis Singer, *"The Old Man"*

Now the portrait leaps at you, punctuated by specific details, including "dishevelled eyebrows," "red rims about his eyes," and "hairy arms." The first description seems to present a shadowy figure in a darkened room, while the second reveals that same figure after the lights have been turned on.

Remember too that you can appeal to your reader through all the *senses*. You can make a reader see, taste, smell, touch, and hear what you are describing:

> The winter was difficult. There was no coal, and since several tiles were missing from the stove, the apartment was filled with thick black smoke each time the old man made a fire. A crust of blue ice and snow covered the window panes by November, making the rooms constantly dark or dusky. Overnight, the water on his night table froze in the pot. No matter how many clothes he piled over him in bed, he never felt warm; his feet remained stiff, and as soon as he began to doze, the entire pile of clothes would fall off, and he would have to climb out naked to make his bed once more. There was no kerosene; even matches were at a premium. Although he recited chapter upon chapter of the Psalms, he could not fall asleep. The wind, freely roaming about the rooms, banged the doors; even the mice left. When he hung up his shirt to dry, it would grow brittle and break, like glass.
>
> Isaac Bashevis Singer, *"The Old Man"*

The passage uses details that appeal to the reader's senses:

Visual: "crust of *blue ice* and snow covered the window panes"

Auditory: "the wind, freely roaming about the rooms, *banged* the door"

Tactile: "No matter how many clothes he piled over him in bed, he never *felt warm.*"

3. USE FIGURES OF SPEECH. To add vividness to a description, a writer will often use words and expressions lifted out of their exact sense. These expressions usually involve some kind of comparison, as when Washington Irving compares Ichabod Crane's head with its big nose to "a weathercock perched upon his spindle neck to tell which way the wind blew." Here is an example of a passage containing figures of speech:

> She was a little woman, with brown, dull hair very elaborately arranged, and she had prominent blue eyes behind invisible pince-nez. Her face was long, *like a sheep's;* but she gave no impression of foolishness, rather of extreme alertness; *she had the quick movements of a bird.* The most remarkable thing about her was her voice, high, metallic, and without inflection; it fell on the ear with a hard monotony, irritating to the nerves *like the pitiless clamour of the pneumatic drill.*
>
> W. Somerset Maugham, "Rain"

A caution: avoid the obvious, trite figures of speech, such as "busy as a bee," "white as a sheet," "big as a bear." Worn and ineffective, such figures hit the reader in the face *like a truck,* and could possibly render him or her *dead as a doornail.* If you use figures of speech, make them *as fresh as a daisy.* Get the idea?

In this Pulitzer Prize-winning account, William L. Laurence, who flew the mission aboard one of the B-29 Superforts, describes the bombing of Nagasaki on August 9th, 1945. Just three days earlier, 100,000 people had been killed by an atomic bomb dropped on Hiroshima.

Professional Model

Atomic Bombing of Nagasaki Told by Flight Member
William L. Laurence

1   With the atomic-bomb mission to Japan, August 9 (Delayed)—We are on our way to bomb the mainland of Japan. Our flying contingent consists of three specially designed B-29 Superforts, and two of these carry no bombs. But our lead plane is on its way with another atomic bomb, the second in three days, concentrating in its active substance an explosive energy equivalent to twenty thousand and, under favorable conditions, forty thousand tons of TNT.

2   Somewhere beyond these vast mountains of white clouds ahead of me there lies Japan, the land of our enemy. In about four hours from now one of its cities, making weapons of war for use against us, will be wiped off the map by the greatest weapon ever made by man: In one tenth of a millionth of a second, a fraction of time immeasurable by any clock, a whirlwind from the skies will pulverize thousands of its buildings and tens of thousands of its inhabitants.

3   But at this moment no one yet knows which one of the several cities chosen as targets is to be annihilated. The final choice lies with destiny. The winds over Japan will make the decision. If they carry heavy clouds over our primary target, that city will be saved, at least for the time being. None of its inhabitants will ever know that the wind of a benevolent destiny had passed over their heads. But that same wind will doom another city.

4   Our weather planes ahead of us are on their way to find out where the wind blows. Half an hour before target time we will know what the winds have decided.

5   Does one feel any pity or compassion for the poor devils about to die? Not when one thinks of Pearl Harbor and of the Death March on Bataan.

6   Captain Bock informs me that we are about to start our climb to bombing altitude.

7   He manipulates a few knobs on his control panel to the right of him, and I alternately watch the white clouds and ocean below me and the altimeter on the bombardier's panel. We reached our altitude at nine o'clock. We were then over Japanese waters, close to their mainland. Lieutenant Godfrey motioned to me to look through his radar scope. Before me was the outline of our assembly point. We shall soon meet our lead ship and proceed to the final stage of our journey.

8   We reached Yakushima at 9:12 and there, about four thousand feet ahead of us, was *The Great Artiste* with its precious load. I saw Lieutenant Godfrey and Sergeant Curry strap on their parachutes and I decided to do likewise.

9   We started circling. We saw little towns on the coastline, heedless of our presence. We kept on circling, waiting for the third ship in our formation.

10   It was 9:56 when we began heading for the coastline. Our weather scouts had sent us code messages, deciphered by Sergeant Curry, informing us that both the primary target as well as the secondary were clearly visible.

11   The winds of destiny seemed to favor certain Japanese cities that must remain nameless. We circled about them again and again and found no opening in the thick umbrella of clouds that covered them. Destiny chose Nagasaki as the ultimate target.

12   We had been circling for some time when we noticed black puffs of smoke coming through the white clouds directly at us. There were fifteen bursts of flak in rapid succession, all too low. Captain Bock changed his course. There soon followed eight more bursts of flak, right up to our altitude, but by this time they were too far to the left.

13   We flew southward down the channel and at 11:33 crossed the coastline and headed straight for Nagasaki, about one hundred miles to the west. Here again we circled until we found an opening in the clouds. It was 12:01 and the goal of our mission had arrived.

14   We heard the prearranged signal on our radio, put on our arc welder's glasses, and watched tensely the maneuverings of the strike ship about half a mile in front of us.

15   "There she goes!" someone said.

16   Out of the belly of *The Great Ariste* what looked like a black object went downward.

17   Captain Bock swung around to get out of range; but even though we were turning away in the opposite direction, and despite the fact that it was broad daylight in our cabin, all of us became aware of a giant flash that broke through the dark barrier of our arc welder's lenses and flooded our cabin with intense light.

18   We removed our glasses after the first flash, but the light still lingered on, a bluish-green light that illuminated the entire sky all around. A tremendous blast wave struck

our ship and made it tremble from nose to tail. This was followed by four more blasts in rapid succession, each resounding like the boom of cannon fire hitting our plane from all directions.

19   Observers in the tail of our ship saw a giant ball of fire rise as though from the bowels of the earth, belching forth enormous white smoke rings. Next they saw a giant pillar of purple fire, ten thousand feet high, shooting skyward with enormous speed.

20   By the time our ship had made another turn in the direction of the atomic explosion the pillar of purple fire had reached the level of our altitude. Only about forty-five seconds had passed. Awe-struck, we watched it shoot upward like a meteor coming from the earth instead of from outer space, becoming ever more alive as it climbed skyward through the white clouds. It was no longer smoke, or dust, or even a cloud of fire. It was a living thing, a new species of being, born right before our incredulous eyes.

21   At one stage of its evolution, covering millions of years in terms of seconds, the entity assumed the form of a giant square totem pole, with its base about three miles long, tapering off to about a mile at the top. Its bottom was brown, its center was amber, its top white. But it was a living totem pole, carved with many grotesque masks grimacing at the earth.

22   Then, just when it appeared as though the thing had settled down into a state of permanence, there came shooting out of the top a giant mushroom that increased the height of the pillar to a total of forty-five thousand feet. The mushroom top was even more alive than the pillar, seething and boiling in a white fury of creamy foam, sizzling upward and then descending earthward, a thousand Old Faithful geysers rolled into one.

23   It kept struggling in an elemental fury, like a creature in the act of breaking the bonds that held it down. In a few seconds it had freed itself from its gigantic stem and floated upward with tremendous speed, its momentum carrying it into the stratosphere to a height of about sixty thousand feet.

24   But no sooner did this happen when another mushroom, smaller in size than the first one, began emerging out of the pillar. It was as though the decapitated monster was growing a new head.

25   As the first mushroom floated off into the blue it changed its shape into a flowerlike form, its giant petals curving downward, creamy white outside, rose-colored inside. It still retained that shape when we last gazed at it from a distance of about two hundred miles. The boiling pillar of many colors could also be seen at that distance, a giant mountain of jumbled rainbows, in travail. Much living substance had gone into those rainbows. The quivering top of the pillar was protruding to a great height through the white clouds, giving the appearance of a monstrous prehistoric creature with a ruff around its neck, a fleecy ruff extending in all directions, as far as the eye could see.

1,322 words

Vocabulary

pulverize (2)	maneuverings (14)	elemental (23)
annihilated (3)	illuminated (18)	stratosphere (23)
benevolent (3)	entity (21)	decapitated (24)
heedless (9)	totem pole (21)	ruff (25)
flak (12)	grotesque (21)	

Questions

1. What dominant impression does the author use to de~~~~
   over Nagasaki? How does the author achieve this~~~~
2. How does the author achieve a sense of climact~~~~
3. What is the effect of the image in the last line~~~~
4. What is the effect of comparing the explosion t~~~~
5. What are the three varied images suggested in ~~~~
6. What other phenomena can you name that comb~~~~

Beginning with a dominant impression of Hank as an enduring and stubbor~~~~
man, this essay supports the portrait with appropriate details. Good use of detai~~~~
is its primary strength. See, for instance, the inclusion of an anecdote, purportedly
told by Hank, which also helps to characterize his spirit. A cryptic and abrupt
ending is its weakness.

Student Model

Hank

Brian Peterman

The ocean, hard work, and time have shaped him. He is an old man now, as gnarled
and twisted as a cypress on a cliff above the sea. For seventy years he has been a
fisherman, as he will continue to be one until he dies. His name is Hank and he lives in
the small town of Wrangell in Southeast Alaska, where thousands of islands, covered
with evergreens and lavishly carpeted with mosses and ferns, create a maze of channels,
straights, bays, and passages. During the summer months when salmon make their
yearly appearance, Hank makes his in an old sturdy seiner, the *Tiny Boy II*. All the fisher-
men in the Southeast know him and those who know him well respectfully call him the
''Old Man.''

I first saw Hank on the city dock. He and a few of his crewmen were working on their
nets, mending tears and adding a few new corks. Having heard stories about him all
my life, I felt as if I were staring at a museum piece—a Winslow Homer painting of an
old salt come to life.

Years of hardship and toil had carved deep furrows into his brow. The many lines
on his face gave him a permanent look of sadness. Eyes, once sharp and piercing, had
acquired a painful, tired expression, as if he had gazed at the sunset once too often.
Yellow, rotten teeth were the result of careless diet and an ever-present cigarette. And
he had a hacking cough that shook his whole body.

I watched Hank's leathery hands as he mended the net. Knotted, bony fingers did the
work with ease. As he laced the large needle through the web, Hank told a story about
an eagle that had been killed by a fish. The eagle had sunk its talons into a large sea
bass that was much too heavy. Instead of being grasped from the sea, the fish dove
down, and the eagle, unable to loosen its powerful grip, was pulled down with the fish.
In a desperate attempt to keep afloat, the eagle spread its wings on the water. But the
bass went down just the same and the eagle's wings made a loud crack as they broke

disappeared. Hank swore he heard them snap from his boat a quarter mile away—
the engine on.

Everyone laughed and Hank laughed the loudest and then took to wheezing. When
he coughing attack died down, he pulled out another unfiltered cigarette, lit it, and
walked to the outhouse on the end of the dock. He had a small limp that made his baggy
brown pants slip down so that every few steps he had to pull them up.

While he was gone I asked a crewman what kept the old man going. "Hell, I don't
know," he said. "No one really does. This boat's all he lives for. Last year him an' his
son was on the freeway in Seattle. They was goin' down the harbor an' were about
10 miles away when the old man starts to have a heart attack! His son tells him to pull
the car over so's he can drive him to the hospital. Hank just grabs the wheel tighter an
says 'Gotta get to my boat.' An' he did too."

The old man was walking back, his hard shoes thumping on the dock. I watched him
return and asked myself, "What is it inside that man that makes him keep going?" I tried
to be profound and come up with some kind of transcendental reason, such as "a fierce,
passionate love for the sea" or some other dramatic phrase. But somehow it sounded
funny.

However, Hank's grandson, a close friend of mine, came perhaps closest to some
logical explanation. It so happens that Hank spends the winter months in an apartment
in Seattle. Every summer Hank and another old fisherman have a contest to see who
can catch the most salmon. The loser must treat the winner to a pair of season tickets
to the Washington Huskies football games.

And Hank hates to lose bets.

Taken from John Steinbeck's masterpiece, *The Grapes of Wrath* (1939), this excerpt
exemplifies a sustained, vivid description of an animal through the use of a dominant impression.

Alternate Reading

A Turtle
John Steinbeck

1   The sun lay on the grass and warmed it, and in the shade under the grass the insects
moved, ants and ant lions to set traps for them, grasshoppers to jump into the air and
flick their yellow wings for a second, sow bugs like little armadillos, plodding restlessly
on many tender feet. And over the grass at the roadside a land turtle crawled, turning
aside for nothing, dragging his high-domed shell over the grass. His hard legs and
yellow-nailed feet threshed slowly through the grass, not really walking, but boosting
and dragging his shell along. The barley beards slid off his shell, and the clover burrs
fell on him and rolled to the ground. His horny beak was partly open, and his fierce,
humorous eyes, under brows like fingernails, stared straight ahead. He came over the
grass leaving a beaten trail behind him, and the hill, which was the highway embankment, reared up ahead of him. For a moment he stopped, his head held high. He blinked
and looked up and down. At last he started to climb the embankment. Front clawed feet
reached forward but did not touch. The hind feet kicked his shell along, and it scraped
on the grass, and on the gravel. As the embankment grew steeper and steeper, the
more frantic were the efforts of the land turtle. Pushing hind legs strained and slipped,

boosting the shell along, and the horny head protruded as far as the neck could stretch. Little by little the shell slid up the embankment until at last a parapet cut straight across its line of march, the shoulder of the road, a concrete wall four inches high. As though they worked independently the hind legs pushed the shell against the wall. The head upraised and peered over the wall to the broad smooth plain of cement. Now the hands, braced on top of the wall, strained and lifted, and the shell came slowly up and rested its front end on the wall. For a moment the turtle rested. A red ant ran into the shell, into the soft skin inside the shell, and suddenly head and legs snapped in, and the armored tail clamped in sideways. The red ant was crushed between body and legs. And one head of wild oats was clamped into the shell by a front leg. For a long moment the turtle lay still, and then the neck crept out and the old humorous frowning eyes looked about and the legs and tail came out. The back legs went to work, straining like elephant legs, and the shell tipped to an angle so that the front legs could not reach the level cement plain. But higher and higher the hind legs boosted it, until at last the center of balance was reached, the front tipped down, the front legs scratched at the pavement, and it was up. But the head of wild oats was held by its stem around the front legs.

2   Now the going was easy, and all the legs worked, and the shell boosted along, waggling from side to side. A sedan driven by a forty-year old woman approached. She saw the turtle and swung to the right, off the highway, the wheels screamed and a cloud of dust boiled up. Two wheels lifted for a moment and then settled. The car skidded back onto the road, and went on, but more slowly. The turtle had jerked into its shell, but now it hurried on, for the highway was burning hot.

3   And now a light truck approached, and as it came near, the driver saw the turtle and swerved to hit it. His front wheel struck the edge of the shell, flipped the turtle like a tiddly-wink, spun it like a coin, and rolled it off the highway. The truck went back to its course along the right side. Lying on its back, the turtle was tight in its shell for a long time. But at last its legs waved in the air, reaching for something to pull it over. Its front foot caught a piece of quartz and little by little the shell pulled over and flopped upright. The wild oat head fell out and three of the spearhead seeds stuck in the ground. And as the turtle crawled on down the embankment, its shell dragged dirt over the seeds. The turtle entered a dust road and jerked itself along, drawing a wavy shallow trench in the dust with its shell. The old humorous eyes looked ahead, and the horny beak opened a little. His yellow toe nails slipped a fraction in the dust.

675 words

Questions

1. In beginning the description of the turtle, the author writes that the turtle turned aside for nothing. What subsequent details support this statement about the turtle?
2. What was the first obstacle in the turtle's path?
3. What was the second obstacle blocking the way of the turtle?
4. When the red ant ran inside the turtle's shell, how did the turtle kill it?
5. What was the reaction of the woman when she saw the turtle crawling in front of her moving car?
6. How did the truck driver react to the presence of the turtle?
7. What did the truck do to the turtle?
8. What adjective does the author repeatedly use in describing the eyes of the turtle? What effect does this achieve?
9. How would you describe the response of the turtle to the various obstacles in its path? Is there any consistency to the turtle's response?

An excerpt from the book, *The Edge of the Sea,* by U.S. biologist and science writer Rachael Carson (1907–1964), this selection exemplifies the vivid use of language in the description of a place.

Alternate Reading

At the Edge of the Sea
Rachel Carson

1   The shore is an ancient world, for as long as there has been an earth and sea there has been this place of the meeting of land and water. Yet it is a world that keeps alive the sense of continuing creation and of the relentless drive of life. Each time that I enter it, I gain some new awareness of its beauty and its deeper meanings, sensing that intricate fabric of life by which one creature is linked with another, and each with its surroundings.

2   In my thoughts of the shore, one place stands apart for its revelation of exquisite beauty. It is a pool hidden within a cave that one can visit only rarely and briefly when the lowest of the year's low tides fall below it, and perhaps from that very fact it acquires some of its special beauty. Choosing such a tide, I hoped for a glimpse of the pool. The ebb was to fall early in the morning. I knew that if the wind held from the northwest and no interfering swell ran in from a distant storm the level of the sea should drop below the entrance to the pool. There had been sudden ominous showers in the night, with rain like handfuls of gravel flung on the roof. When I looked out into the early morning the sky was full of a gray dawn light but the sun had not yet risen. Water and air were pallid. Across the bay the moon was a luminous disc in the western sky, suspended above the dim line of distant shore—the full August moon, drawing the tide to the low, low levels of the threshold of the alien sea world. As I watched, a gull flew by, above the spruces. Its breast was rosy with the light of the unrisen sun. The day was, after all, to be fair.

3   Later, as I stood above the tide near the entrance to the pool, the promise of that rosy light was sustained. From the base of the steep wall of rock on which I stood, a moss-covered ledge jutted seaward into deep water. In the surge at the rim of the ledge the dark fronds of oarweeds swayed, smooth and gleaming as leather. The projecting ledge was the path to the small hidden cave and its pool. Occasionally a swell, stronger than the rest, rolled smoothly over the rim and broke in foam against the cliff. But the intervals between such swells were long enough to admit me to the ledge and long enough for a glimpse of that fairy pool, so seldom and so briefly exposed.

4   And so I knelt on the wet carpet of sea moss and looked back into the dark cavern that held the pool in a shallow basin. The floor of the cave was only a few inches below the roof, and a mirror had been created in which all that grew on the ceiling was reflected in the still water below.

5   Under water that was clear as glass the pool was carpeted with green sponge. Gray patches of sea squirts glistened on the ceiling and colonies of soft coral were a pale apricot color. In the moment when I looked into the cave a little elfin starfish hung down, suspended by the merest thread, perhaps by only a single tube foot. It reached down to touch its own reflection, so perfectly delineated that there might have been, not one starfish, but two. The beauty of the reflected images and of the limpid pool itself was the poignant beauty of things that are ephemeral, existing only until the sea should return to fill the little cave.

615 words

Vocabulary

exquisite (2)   delineated (5)
pallid (2)   limpid (5)
elfin (5)   ephemeral (5)

Questions

1. The author begins by telling us that in the shore she senses the intricate fabric linking a creature with its surroundings. How is this generality demonstrated at the end of the description?
2. Why is the shore such an ancient place?
3. In paragraph 2, the author says that "one place stands apart." What impression of this place does the description then proceed to support with details?
4. In what month did the author make her journey to the hidden pool?
5. From what fact does the pool acquire "some of its special beauty"?
6. What ominous event occurred during the night?
7. What distance separated the floor of the cave from its ceiling?
8. Point out some terms in paragraphs 3 and 5 that indicate the author's familiarity with marine biology. What effect does this sort of detail achieve?
9. To emphasize the rare, hidden, and special beauty of the pool, what other-worldly term does the author attach to it?
10. Point out an especially effective figure of speech in paragraph 2.

C. Additional Writing Assignments

1. Based on a dominant impression, write a description of your latest family dinner.
2. Using "dingy" as your dominant impression, write a description of an imaginary place. Support the impression with details.
3. Write an essay describing in detail the most *restful* spot you know.
4. Go to your local supermarket, notebook in hand. Observe the scene around you, and reduce it to a single dominant impression. Write the dominant impression and some details that support it. From these notes, develop a descriptive essay.
5. Describe the looks of your closest friend. Begin with a dominant impression and develop details to support it.
6. Describe your most valued possession, beginning with a dominant impression and supplying details.
7. Develop a descriptive essay comparing your lover (real or imaginary) to a flower, animal, or object.
8. Using sensory details, write a description of a garden in spring.
9. Go to a public park or some other place where you can observe an old person. Study his or her face, dress, and movements, and write a description of this person.
10. Write an essay fully describing your favorite television personality.

6

Example

*The best example of why the year has been a good one
took place during the last quarter.*

A. Reading for Ideas

Read the story "Theft" to see if you can discover a pattern emerging from the narrator's encounters. Ask yourself the following questions: What do the encounters have in common? Does the narrator repeat any action or attitude? What personality trait does she display in all these encounters? You will discover that the encounters described provide examples of a pattern in her behavior, which in turn is a clue to the story's meaning. After reading the story, ask yourself what pattern has emerged from your own life during the past year. Try to state that pattern as a controlling idea for an essay.

Theft

Katherine Anne Porter

1   She had the purse in her hand when she came in. Standing in the middle of the floor, holding her bathrobe around her and trailing a damp towel in one hand, she surveyed the immediate past and remembered everything clearly. Yes, she had opened the flap and spread it out on the bench after she had dried the purse with her handkerchief.

2   She had intended to take the Elevated, and naturally she looked in her purse to make certain she had the fare, and was pleased to find forty cents in the coin envelope. She was going to pay her own fare, too, even if Camilo did have the habit of seeing her up the steps and dropping a nickel in the machine before he gave the turnstile a little push and sent her through it with a bow. Camilo by a series of compromises had managed to make effective a fairly complete set of smaller courtesies, ignoring the larger and more troublesome ones. She had walked with him to the station in a pouring rain, because she knew he was almost as poor as she was, and when he insisted on a taxi, she was firm and said, "You know it simply will not do." He was wearing a new hat of a pretty biscuit shade, for it never occurred to him to buy anything of a practical color; he had put it on for the first time and the rain was spoiling it. She kept thinking,

84

"But this is dreadful, where will he get another?" She compared it with Eddie's hats that always seemed to be precisely seven years old and as if they had been quite purposely left out in the rain, and yet they sat with a careless and incidental rightness on Eddie. But Camilo was far different; if he wore a shabby hat it would be merely shabby on him, and he would lose his spirits over it. If she had not feared Camilo would take it badly, for he insisted on the practice of his little ceremonies up to the point he had fixed for them, she would have said to him as they left Thora's house, "Do go home. I can surely reach the station by myself."

3   "It is written that we must be rained upon tonight," said Camilo, "so let it be together."

4   At the end of the platform stairway she staggered slightly—they were both nicely set up on Thora's cocktails—and said: "At least, Camilo, do me the favor not to climb these stairs in your present state, since for you it is only a matter of coming down again at once, and you'll certainly break your neck."

5   He made three quick bows, he was Spanish, and leaped off through the rainy darkness. She stood watching him, for he was a very graceful young man, thinking that tomorrow morning he would gaze soberly at his spoiled hat and soggy shoes and possibly associate her with his misery. As she watched, he stopped at the far corner and took off his hat and hid it under his overcoat. She felt she had betrayed him by seeing, because he would have been humiliated if he thought she even suspected him of trying to save his hat.

6   Roger's voice sounded over her shoulder above the clang of the rain falling on the stairway shed, wanting to know what she was doing out in the rain at this time of night, and did she take herself for a duck? His long, imperturbable face was steaming with water, and he tapped a bulging spot on the breast of his buttoned-up overcoat: "Hat," he said, "Come on, let's take a taxi."

7   She settled back against Roger's arm which he laid around her shoulders, and with the gesture they exchanged a glance full of long amiable associations, then she looked through the window at the rain changing the shapes of everything, and the colors. The taxi dodged in and out between the pillars of the Elevated, skidding slightly on every curve, and she said: "The more it skids the calmer I feel, so I really must be drunk."

8   "You must be," said Roger. "This bird is a homicidal maniac, and I could do with a cocktail myself this minute."

9   They waited on the traffic at Fortieth Street and Sixth Avenue, and three boys walked before the nose of the taxi. Under the globes of light they were cheerful scarecrows, all very thin and all wearing very seedy snappy-cut suits and gay neckties. They were not very sober either, and they stood for a moment wobbling in front of the car, and there was an argument going on among them. They leaned toward each other as if they were getting ready to sing, and the first one said: "When I get married it won't be jus' for getting married, I'm gonna marry for *love,* see?" and the second one said, "Aw, gwan and tell that stuff to *her,* why n't yuh?" and the third one gave a kind of hoot, and said, "Hell, dis guy? Wot the hell's he got?" and the first one said: "Aaah, shurrup yuh mush, I got plenty." Then they all squealed and scrambled across the street beating the first one on the back and pushing him around.

10   "Nuts," commented Roger, "pure nuts."

Two girls went skittering by in short transparent raincoats, one green, one red, their heads tucked against the drive of the rain. One of them was saying to the other, "Yes, I know all about *that*. But what about me? You're always so sorry for *him* . . ." and they ran on with their little pelican legs flashing back and forth.

11   The taxi backed up suddenly and leaped forward again, and after a while Roger said: "I had a letter from Stella today, and she'll be home on the twenty-sixth, so I suppose she's made up her mind and it's all settled."

"I had a sort of letter today too," she said, "making up my mind for me. I think it is time for you and Stella to do something definite."

12   When the taxi stopped on the corner of West Fifty-third Street, Roger said, "I've just enough if you'll add ten cents," so she opened her purse and gave him a dime, and he said, "That's beautiful, that purse."

"It's a birthday present," she told him, "and I like it. How's your show coming?"

"Oh, still hanging on, I guess. I don't go near the place. Nothing sold yet. I mean to keep right on the way I'm going and they can take it or leave it. I'm through with the argument."

"It's absolutely a matter of holding out, isn't it?"

"Holding out's the tough part."

"Good night, Roger."

"Good night, you should take aspirin and push yourself into a tub of hot water, you look as though you're catching cold."

"I will."

13   With the purse under her arm she went upstairs, and on the first landing Bill heard her step and poked his head out with his hair tumbled and his eyes red, and he said: "For Christ's sake, come in and have a drink with me. I've had some bad news."

14   "You're perfectly sopping," said Bill, looking at her drenched feet. They had two drinks, while Bill told how the director had thrown his play out after the cast had been picked over twice, and had gone through three rehearsals. "I said to him, 'I didn't say it was a masterpiece, I said it would make a good show.' And he said, 'It just doesn't play, do you see? It needs a doctor.' So I'm stuck, absolutely stuck," said Bill, on the edge of weeping again. "I've been crying," he told her, "in my cups." And he went on to ask her if she realized his wife was ruining him with her extravagance. "I send her ten dollars every week of my unhappy life, and I don't really have to. She threatens to jail me if I don't, but she can't do it. God, let her try it after the way she treated me! She's no right to alimony and she knows it. She keeps on saying she's got to have it for the baby and I keep on sending it because I can't bear to see anybody suffer. So I'm way behind on the piano and the victrola, both—"

"Well, this is a pretty rug, anyhow," she said.

15   Bill stared at it and blew his nose. "I got it at Ricci's for ninety-five dollars," he said. "Ricci told me it once belonged to Marie Dressler, and cost fifteen hundred dollars, but there's a burnt place on it, under the divan. Can you beat that?"

"No," she said. She was thinking about her empty purse and that she could not possibly expect a check for her latest review for another three days, and her arrangement with the basement restaurant could not last much longer if she did not pay something on account. "It's no time to speak of it," she said, "but I've been hoping you would have by now that fifty dollars you promised for my scene in the third act. Even if it doesn't play. You were to pay me for the work anyhow out of your advance."

16   "Weeping Jesus," said Bill, "you, too?" He gave a loud sob, or hiccough, in his moist handkerchief. "Your stuff was no better than mine, after all. Think of that."

"But you got something for it," she said. "Seven hundred dollars."

17   Bill said, "Do me a favor, will you? Have another drink and forget about it. I can't, you know I can't, I would if I could, but you know the fix I'm in."

"Let it go, then," she found herself saying almost in spite of herself. She had meant to be quite firm about it. They drank again without speaking, and she went to her apartment on the floor above.

18   There, she now remembered distinctly, she had taken the letter out of the purse before she spread the purse out to dry.

19   She had sat down and read the letter over again: but there were phrases that insisted

on being read many times, they had a life of their own separate from the others, and when she tried to read past and around them, they moved with the movement of her eyes, and she could not escape them . . . "thinking about you more than I mean to . . . yes, I even talk about you . . . why were you so anxious to destroy . . . even if I could see you now I would not . . . not worth all this abominable . . . the end . . ."

20 Carefully she tore the letter into narrow strips and touched a lighted match to them in the coal grate.

21 Early the next morning she was in the bathtub when the janitress knocked and then came in, calling out that she wished to examine the radiators before she started the furnace going for the winter. After moving about the room for a few minutes, the janitress went out, closing the door very sharply.

22 She came out of the bathroom to get a cigarette from the package in the purse. The purse was gone. She dressed and made coffee, and sat by the window while she drank it. Certainly the janitress had taken the purse, and certainly it would be impossible to get it back without a great deal of ridiculous excitement. Then let it go. With this decision of her mind, there rose coincidentally in her blood a deep almost murderous anger. She set the cup carefully in the center of the table, and walked steadily downstairs, three long flights and a short hall and a steep short flight into the basement, where the janitress, her face streaked with dust, was shaking up the furnace. "Will you please give me back my purse? There isn't any money in it. It was a present, and I don't want to lose it."

23 The janitress turned without straightening up and peered at her with hot flickering eyes, a red light from the furnace reflected in them. "What do you mean, your purse?"

"The gold cloth purse you took from the wooden bench in my room," she said. "I must have it back."

"Before God I never laid eyes on your purse, and that's the holy truth," said the janitress.

"Oh, well then, keep it," she said, but in a very bitter voice; "keep it if you want it so much." And she walked away.

24 She remembered how she had never locked a door in her life, on some principle of rejection in her that made her uncomfortable in the ownership of things, and her paradoxical boast before the warnings of her friends, that she had never lost a penny by theft; and she had been pleased with the bleak humility of this concrete example designed to illustrate and justify a certain fixed, otherwise baseless and general faith which ordered the movements of her life without regard to her will in the matter.

25 In this moment she felt that she had been robbed of an enormous number of valuable things, whether material or intangible: things lost or broken by her own fault, things she had forgotten and left in houses when she moved: books borrowed from her and not returned, journeys she had planned and had not made, words she had waited to hear spoken to her and had not heard, and the words she had meant to answer with; bitter alternatives and intolerable substitutes worse than nothing, and yet inescapable: the long patient suffering of dying friendships and the dark inexplicable death of love— all that she had had, and all that she had missed, were lost together, and were twice lost in this landslide of remembered losses.

26 The janitress was following her upstairs with the purse in her hand and the same deep red flickering in her eyes. The janitress thrust the purse towards her while they were still a half dozen steps apart, and said: "Don't never tell on me. I musta been crazy. I get crazy in the head sometimes, I swear I do. My son can tell you."

27 She took the purse after a moment, and the janitress went on: "I got a niece who is going on seventeen, and she's a nice girl and I thought I'd give it to her. She needs a pretty purse. I musta been crazy; I thought maybe you wouldn't mind, you leave things

around and don't seem to notice much.''

28   She said: ''I missed this because it was a present to me from someone . . .''

The janitress said: ''He'd get you another if you lost this one. My niece is young and needs pretty things, we oughta give the young ones a chance. She's got young men after her maybe will want to marry her. She oughta have nice things. She needs them bad right now. You're a grown woman, you've had your chance, you ought to know how it is!''

29   She held the purse out to the janitress saying: ''You don't know what you're talking about. Here, take it, I've changed my mind. I really don't want it.''

30   The janitress looked up at her with hatred and said: ''I don't want it either now. My niece is young and pretty, she don't need fixin' up to be pretty, she's young and pretty anyhow! I guess you need it worse than she does!''

''It wasn't really yours in the first place,'' she said, turning away. ''You mustn't talk as if I had stolen it from you.''

''It's not from me, it's from her you're stealing it,'' said the janitress, and went back downstairs.

31   She laid the purse on the table and sat down with a cup of chilled coffee, and thought: I was right not to be afraid of any thief but myself, who will end by leaving me nothing.

2,638 words

Questions

1. What is the marked pattern that emerges from the accumulation of actions and relationships in the narrator's life? State this pattern in the form of a single sentence that could serve as a controlling idea for the story. Which lines in the story best summarize this pattern?
2. What bearing does the title have on the story?
3. What is the crux of the narrator's relationship with Camilo?
4. What is the crux of the narrator's relationship with Roger?
5. What is the crux of the narrator's relationship with Bill?
6. How does the letter mentioned in paragraph 19 clarify the pattern in the narrator's life?
7. What does the incident with the cleaning lady add to the story?
8. What is the narrator's state of mind? Is she happy? Unhappy? Indifferent? See paragraph 25.

---

nobody loses all the time
e. e. cummings

nobody loses all the time

i had an uncle named
Sol who was a born failure and
nearly everybody said he should have gone
into vaudeville perhaps because my Uncle Sol could
sing McCann He Was a Diver on Xmas Eve like Hell Itself which
may or may not account for the fact that my Uncle

Sol indulged in that possibly most inexcusable
of all to use a highfalootin phrase
luxuries that is or to
wit farming and be
it needlessly
added

my Uncle Sol's farm
failed because the chickens
ate the vegetables so
my Uncle Sol had a
chicken farm till the
skunks ate the chickens when

my Uncle Sol
had a skunk farm but
the skunks caught cold and
died and so
my Uncle Sol imitated the
skunks in a subtle manner

or by drowning himself in the watertank
but somebody who'd given my Uncle Sol a Victor
Victrola and records while he lived presented to
him upon the auspicious occasion of his decease a
scrumptious not to mention splendiferous funeral with
tall boys in black gloves and flowers and everything and

i remember we all cried like the Missouri
when my Uncle Sol's coffin lurched because
somebody pressed a button
(and down went
my Uncle
Sol

and started a worm farm)

Questions

1. What is the dominant pattern in Uncle Sol's life? What are some examples of this pattern?
2. How is the title "nobody loses all the time" related to the main pattern of failure?
3. The speaker suggests that Uncle Sol should have gone into vaudeville. What does this imply about Uncle Sol's personality?
4. How does the type of funeral given Uncle Sol fit into the general picture of the poem?
5. How does the structure, word choice, and grammar of the poem affect its content?
6. In your view, what is the overall tone of the poem?

B. How to Write with Examples

An example is an illustration that unmistakably clarifies and enforces the point you are making. During the Middle Ages, most sermons ended with an *exemplum*, a little story that illustrated some important religious truth. Knowing that these stories would awaken dozing audiences and instill them with zeal or fear, the church priests told vivid tales about the evils of money and the dangers of disobedience. The example is still favored in prose writing as a means of proving a point or explaining an idea.

Writing Assignment

Write an essay in which you describe a pattern in your life during this past year and support it with examples. First, think about how your life has been this last year, trying to characterize it in one word. Has the past year been *successful? Frustrating? Exhilarating? Boring?* Next, express this pattern in a single sentence that can function as the controlling idea of an essay—for example,

1. My last year has been characterized by many *successful* enterprises.
2. *Frustration* has filled this past year of my life.
3. Never have I spent a more *exhilarating* year than the year just past.
4. The year just past has been a deadly *bore*.

Having formulated a controlling idea on how you spent this last year, you must now support it with examples.

Specific Instructions

1. USE EXAMPLES THAT ARE RELEVANT.   An example has failed if it does not help your reader to see the general truth of what you are saying. The following example misses the point:

> As the Bible says, there is a right time for everything—even for being born and for dying. For example, the other day I failed my social science test. The day before had been beastly hot—90 degrees in the shade—and I just didn't feel like studying, so I stretched out on the couch, fanning myself and watching TV. I guess it was my time to die intellectually because when the exam was handed back, it was decorated with a big fat F.

The example used is too trivial to illustrate such a somber philosophic truth. The biblical reference deserves a more significant example. The following passage, on the other hand, uses an example that is exactly to the point:

> Some people will do the strangest things to gain fame. For example, there are those who go in for various kinds of marathons, dancing or kissing or blowing bubble gum for days at a time, to get their names in the paper or in a record book of some kind. Then there are people who sit on flag-

poles or who perch on the ledges of skyscrapers for a week or more, apparently enjoying the attention they receive from the crowd below. There are people who hope to be remembered by someone because they ate the most cream pies or because they collected the most bottle tops. And there are even people who seek public notice by way of setting a record for the number of articles of clothing they can put on at one time or the number they can take off. Of course, there are a few mentally twisted individuals who seek fame at the expense of other people's property or even lives, but fortunately the great majority of people satisfy their urge to be remembered in ways that produce little more damage than tired lips or a bad case of indigestion.

Shiela Y. Graham, Writingcraft

These examples do a good job of illustrating the idea that "Some people will do the strangest things to gain fame."

2. USE DETAIL TO MAKE YOUR EXAMPLE VIVID.   The reader should be able to visualize the actual circumstances described in your example. Many student examples are ineffective because they are vague rather than vivid. Consider the vague and consequently boring example in this passage:

There is no control over memory. Sometimes one remembers the most trivial details. For example, I remember trivial things about my father, about pieces of furniture in our house, and about insignificant places that I once visited. I even remember a particular shopping spree that took place a long time ago.

Now observe how the same passage comes to life through the use of detailed examples:

There is no control over memory. Soon you find yourself being vague about an event which seemed so important at the time that you thought you'd never forget it. Or unable to recall the face of someone who you could have sworn was there forever. On the other hand, trivial and meaningless memories may stay with you for life. I can still shut my eyes and see Victoria grinding coffee on the pantry steps, the glass bookcase and the books in it, my father's pipe rack, the leaves of the sandbox tree, the wallpaper of the bedroom in some shabby hotel, the hairdresser in Antibes. It's in this way that I remember buying the pink Milanese-silk underclothes, the assistant who sold them to me, and coming into Bond Street holding the parcel.

Jean Rhys, The New Yorker,
April 26, 1976

Vividness is the basic difference between the first and second passages. The first passage lacks details while the second bristles with them.

3. WHEN NECESSARY, ESTABLISH A CLEAR CONNECTION BETWEEN YOUR EXAMPLE AND THE POINT YOU ARE MAKING. This device is particularly important when you begin an essay or a paragraph with an illustration. Consider the following:

> A 13-year-old girl has had one leg amputated, but three times a week she is put through the humiliation of being forced to change into gym shorts. Says the teacher, "Those are the rules and there's no reason you can't keep score while the other girls play."
>
> A high-school teacher accidentally bumps into the upraised hand of a girl who wants to ask a question. The teacher cries out that the girl is trying to strike her and that if it happens again she'll call the police.
>
> A first-grade teacher forces a boy to sit all day in a wastepaper basket as punishment for being noisy. When an assistant principal orders the boy's release after 2½ hours, it is some minutes before he can stand up straight. He can barely limp to his seat.

Without a connecting comment, these examples are puzzling. The reader wonders what they are intended to illustrate. The sequel makes clear the connection between the examples and the point they illustrate:

> These are all documented cases of teacher ineptitude, insensitivity or brutishness. While the overwhelming majority of America's teachers are professionally competent and sensitive to children's needs, there are enough who are unfit to cause concern among both parents and school administrators.
>
> Bernard Bard, "Unfeeling Teachers?"
> *Ladies Home Journal,* March 1976

Connective expressions commonly used to introduce an example are: *for example, to illustrate, for instance,* and *a case in point is.* Frequently, however, a writer will omit a formal connective in introducing his examples provided the context makes clear what is being illustrated:

> People who sneer at "fancy theories" and prefer to rely on common sense and everyday experience are often in fact the victims of extremely vague and sweeping hypotheses. This morning's newspaper contains a letter from a young person in Pennsylvania who was once "one of a group of teenage pot smokers. Then a girl in the crowd got pregnant. Her baby was premature and deformed and needed two operations." The newspaper's adviser to the teenage lovelorn printed that letter approvingly, as evidence that the price of smoking marijuana is high.
>
> Paul Heyne and Thomas Johnson,
> *Toward Economic Understanding*

This passage clearly illustrates what is meant by "victims of . . . vague and sweeping hypotheses." No connective phrase is necessary; the connection is established by the context.

H. L. Mencken (1880–1956) was one of America's great author/editors. The letter printed below was prompted by a request from the historian Will Durant, who asked Mencken (among others) to explain what meaning life held for him.

Professional Model

The Satisfaction of Life
H. L. Mencken

1   You ask me, in brief, what satisfaction I get out of life, and why I go on working. I go on working for the same reason that a hen goes on laying eggs. There is in every living creature an obscure but powerful impulse to active functioning. Life demands to be lived. Inaction, save as a measure of recuperation between bursts of activity, is painful and dangerous to the healthy organism—in fact, it is almost impossible. Only the dying can be really idle.

2   The precise form of an individual's activity is determined, of course, by the equipment with which he came into the world. In other words, it is determined by his heredity. I do not lay eggs, as a hen does, because I was born without any equipment for it. For the same reason I do not get myself elected to Congress, or play the violoncello, or teach metaphysics in a college, or work in a steel mill. What I do is simply what lies easiest to my hand. It happens that I was born with an intense and insatiable interest in ideas, and thus like to play with them. It happens also that I was born with rather more than the average facility for putting them into words. In consequence, I am a writer and editor, which is to say, a dealer in them and concoctor of them.

3   There is very little conscious volition in all this. What I do was ordained by the inscrutable fates, not chosen by me. In my boyhood, yielding to a powerful but still subordinate interest in exact facts, I wanted to be a chemist, and at the same time my poor father tried to make me a business man. At other times, like any other relatively poor man, I have longed to make a lot of money by some easy swindle. But I became a writer all the same, and shall remain one until the end of the chapter, just as a cow goes on giving milk all her life, even though what appears to be her self-interest urges her to give gin.

4   I am far luckier than most men, for I have been able since boyhood to make a good living doing precisely what I have wanted to do—what I would have done for nothing, and very gladly, if there had been no reward for it. Not many men, I believe, are so fortunate. Millions of them have to make their livings at tasks which really do not interest them. As for me, I have had an extraordinarily pleasant life, despite the fact that I have had the usual share of woes. For in the midst of those woes I still enjoyed the immense satisfaction which goes with free activity. I have done, in the main, exactly what I wanted to do. Its possible effects upon other people have interested me very little. I have not written and published to please other people, but to satisfy myself, just as a cow gives milk, not to profit the dairyman, but to satisfy herself. I like to think that most of my ideas have been sound ones, but I really don't care. The world may take them or leave them. I have had my fun hatching them.

5   Next to agreeable work as a means of attaining happiness I put what Huxley called the domestic affections—the day to day intercourse with family and friends. My home has seen bitter sorrow, but it has never seen any serious disputes, and it has never seen poverty. I was completely happy with my mother and sister, and I am completely happy with my wife. Most of the men I commonly associate with are friends of very old standing. I have known some of them for more than thirty years. I seldom see anyone, intimately, whom I have known for less than ten years. These friends delight me. I turn to them when

work is done with unfailing eagerness. We have the same general tastes, and see the world much alike. Most of them are interested in music, as I am. It has given me more pleasure in this life than any other external thing. I love it more every year.

6   As for religion, I am quite devoid of it. Never in my adult life have I experienced anything that could be plausibly called a religious impulse. My father and grandfather were agnostics before me, and though I was sent to Sunday-school as a boy and exposed to the Christian theology I was never taught to believe it. My father thought that I should learn what it was, but it apparently never occurred to him that I would accept it. He was a good psychologist. What I got in Sunday-school—beside a wide acquaintance with Christian hymnology—was simply a firm conviction that the Christian faith was full of palpable absurdities, and the Christian God preposterous. Since that time I have read a great deal in theology—perhaps much more than the average clergyman—but I have never discovered any reason to change my mind.

7   The act of worship, as carried on by Christians, seems to me to be debasing rather than ennobling. It involves grovelling before a Being who, if He really exists, deserves to be denounced instead of respected. I see little evidence in this world of the so-called goodness of God. On the contrary, it seems to me that, on the strength of His daily acts, He must be set down a most stupid, cruel and villainous fellow. I can say this with a clear conscience, for He has treated me very well—in fact, with vast politeness. But I can't help thinking of his barbaric torture of most of the rest of humanity. I simply can't imagine revering the God of war and politics, theology and cancer.

8   I do not believe in immortality, and have no desire for it. The belief in it issues from the puerile egos of inferior men. In its Christian form it is little more than a device for getting revenge upon those who are having a better time on this earth. What the meaning of human life may be I don't know: I incline to suspect that it has none. All I know about it is that, to me at least, it is very amusing while it lasts. Even its troubles, indeed, can be amusing. Moreover, they tend to foster the human qualities that I admire most—courage and its analogues. The noblest man, I think, is that one who fights God, and triumphs over Him. I have had little of this to do. When I die I shall be content to vanish into nothingness. No show, however good, could conceivably be good forever.

1,116 words

Vocabulary

recuperation (1)	devoid (6)	debasing (7)	puerile (8)
insatiable (2)	agnostics (6)	grovelling (7)	analogues (8)
volition (3)	palpable (6)	revering (8)	

Questions

1. What is the pattern that emerges from Mencken's view of his own life? For him, what is life all about?
2. What examples does Mencken use in paragraph 2 to illustrate his point that man's activity is determined by his heredity?
3. What example does Mencken use in paragraph 3 to prove that what he does "was ordained by the inscrutable fates"?
4. What examples does Mencken use to prove that he has had an extraordinarily pleasant life?
5. What role does God play in Mencken's view of life?
6. Why does Mencken consider the act of worship debasing?
7. How does Mencken feel about the pattern of his life?

This essay begins with a weak and thin opening paragraph, but what follows is systematic and clear. The final paragraph is a somewhat dry and weak summary. The author is conscientious in citing specific details of the "high and low points" of the year.

Student Model

A Good Year
Robert Parker

The last school year had its high and low points, but overall it was a good year. Three examples illustrate why. These involve my biology teacher, the "interim" classes, and our special silent movie assembly.

My biology teacher contributed much toward my enjoyment of this year. Biology always has been one of my greatest interests, so I expected this class would be good from the start. Unfortunately, our text, one of those ponderous tomes burdened with technical language, did not measure up to expectations. However, our teacher managed to make the class snappy despite the book's tedium. He would bring in extra materials just for our edification, and would hold the class spellbound by lecturing on the complex aspects of a biological process in his own inimitable witty style. Some days he would be so good that when he finished, I felt we should have applauded him. Often, while lecturing, he would inject little tidbits of fascinating information about the habits of lizards or the politics of apes; then, if he saw that there was enough interest, he would explain further, and that was usually far more interesting than what was in the textbook. This teacher whetted my appetite for knowledge by turning dry biological facts into fascinating curiosities.

Our "interim" classes—a two-week series of mini-courses offered in addition to the regular curriculum—also contributed to my enjoyment of the year. My mini-courses not only relieved the regimen of normal studies, they also aroused my interest. Two of my classes, psychology and biologics, provided an insight into those topics without the rigorous work demanded from a regular course. Psychology briefly covered the history and basic theories of psychology, providing a useful overview of a complex field. Biologics consisted of two weeks of lectures on topics ranging from cardiovascular surgery to basic first aid. My third class, stained glass technique, taught me how to make a small ornament with my hands as well as the basic theory behind larger art creations.

The best example of why the year has been a good one took place during the last quarter. At the end of the year a few of us put together a special bicentennial assembly —a silent movie, *The Birth of a Nation,* for which I provided the organ accompaniment. I spent several weeks in preparation for the performance, not only in doing research on the producer's intentions and the theme behind the picture, but also in reviewing the three-hour film several times to become accustomed to its plot and emotional action. Furthermore, I had to compose all the musical score for the picture, except for a few short segments, and prepare themes for each character and for each important single scene. I loved this project because it relieved some of the tension around exam time and gave me a chance to "test my wings" in a theatrical performance.

And so when I muse over the year, from its higher points—the biology class, the interim program, and the silent film—to its lowest point—final exam—and weigh them together, it seems to me to have been a very good year.

The selection below is an excerpt from a novel, published in 1851, delineating the misery suffered by English laborers during the Industrial Revolution. Mrs. Gaskell fills her novel with little sketches about humble provincial people.

Alternate Reading

Small Economies
Elizabeth Cleghorn Gaskell

1   I have often noticed that almost everyone has his own individual small economies —careful habits of saving fractions of pennies in some one peculiar direction—any disturbance of which annoys him more than spending shillings or pounds on some real extravagance. An old gentleman of my acquaintance, who took the intelligence of the failure of a joint-stock bank, in which some of his money was invested, with stoical mildness, worried his family all through a long summer's day because one of them had torn (instead of cutting) out the written leaves of his now useless bank-book; of course, the corresponding pages at the other end came out as well, and this little unneccessary waste of paper (his private economy) chafed him more than all the loss of his money. Envelopes fretted his soul terribly when they first came in; the only way in which he could reconcile himself to such waste of his cherished article was by patiently turning inside out all that were sent to him, and so making them serve again. Even now, though tamed by age, I see him casting wistful glances at his daughters when they send a whole inside of a half-sheet of notepaper with three lines of acceptance to an invitation, written on only one of the sides. I am not above owning that I have this human weakness myself. String is my foible. My pockets get full of little hanks of it, picked up and twisted together, ready for uses that never come. I am seriously annoyed if any one cuts the string of a parcel instead of patiently and faithfully undoing it fold by fold. How people can bring themselves to use india-rubber rings,* which are a sort of deification of string, as lightly as they do, I cannot imagine. To me an india-rubber ring is a precious treasure. I have one which is not, new—one that I picked up off the floor nearly six years ago. I have really tried to use it, but my heart failed me, and I could not commit the extravagance.

2   Small pieces of butter grieve others. They cannot attend to the conversation because of the annoyance occasioned by the habit which some people have of invariably taking more butter than they want. Have you not seen the anxious look (almost mesmeric) which such persons fix on the article? They would feel it a relief if they might bury it out of their sight by popping it into their own mouths and swallowing it down; and they are really made happy if the person on whose plate it lies unused suddenly breaks off a piece of toast (which he does not want at all) and eats up his butter. They think that this is not waste.

3   Now, Miss Matty Jenkyns was chary of candles. We had many devices to use as few as possible. In the winter afternoons she would sit knitting for two or three hours—she could do this in the dark, or by firelight—and when I asked her if I might not ring for candles to finish stitching my wristbands, she told me to "keep blind man's holiday." They were usually brought in with tea; but we burnt only one at a time. As we lived in constant preparation for a friend who might come in any evening (but who never did), it required some contrivance to keep our two candles of the same length, ready to be lighted, and to look as if we burnt two always. The candles took it in turns; and, whatever we might be talking about or doing, Miss Matty's eyes were habitually fixed upon the

---

*Rubber bands.

candle, ready to jump up and extinguish it and to light the other before they had become too uneven in length to be restored to equality in the course of the evening.

4   One night I remember this candle economy particularly annoyed me. I had been very much tired of my compulsory "blind man's holiday," especially as Miss Matty had fallen asleep, and I did not like to stir the fire and run the risk of awakening her; so I could not even sit on the rug and scorch myself with sewing by firelight according to my usual custom. I fancied Miss Matty must be dreaming of her early life; for she spoke one or two words in her uneasy sleep bearing reference to persons who were dead long before. When Martha brought in the lighted candle and tea, Miss Matty started into wakefulness with a strange, bewildered look around as if we were not the people she expected to see about her. There was a little sad expression that shadowed her face as she recognized me, but immediately afterwards she tried to give me her usual smile. All through tea-time her talk ran upon the days of her childhood and youth. Perhaps this reminded her of the desirableness of looking over all the old family letters and destroying such as ought not to be allowed to fall into the hands of strangers; for she had often spoken of the necessity of this task, but had always shrunk from it with a timid dread of something painful. Tonight, however, she rose up after tea and went for them—in the dark; for she prided herself on the precise neatness of all her chamber arrangements, and used to look uneasily at me when I lighted a bed-candle to go to another room for anything. When she returned there was a faint, pleasant smell of Tonquin beans in the room. I have always noticed this scent about any of the things which had belonged to her mother; and many of the letters were addressed to her—yellow bundles of love-letters, sixty or seventy years old.

5   Miss Matty undid the packet with a sigh; but she stifled it directly, as if it were hardly right to regret the flight of time, or of life either. We agreed to look them over separately, each taking a different letter out of the same bundle and describing its contents to the other before destroying it. I never knew what sad work the reading of old letters was before that evening, though I could hardly tell why. The letters were as happy as letters could be—at least those early letters were. There was in them a vivid and intense sense of the present time, which seemed strong and full, as if it could never pass away, and as if the warm, living hearts that so expressed themselves could never die, and be as nothing to the sunny earth. I should have felt less melancholy, I believe, if the letters had been more so. I saw the tears stealing down the well-worn furrows of Miss Matty's cheeks, and her spectacles often wanted wiping. I trusted at last that she would light the other candle, for my own eyes were rather dim, and I wanted more light to see the pale, faded ink; but no, even through her tears, she saw and remembered her little economical ways.

1,175 words

Vocabulary

jointstock (1)	hanks (1)	chary (3)	piqued (4)
foible (1)	mesmeric (2)	contrivance (3)	Tonquin (4)

Questions

1. How does the author define "small economies" in paragraph 1?
2. What is the first example given of someone who made "small economies"?
3. What is the author's private "small economy"?
4. What does the author mean when she states that india-rubber rings are "a sort of deification of string"?
5. According to the author, what is it that a person who treats butter as his "small economy" cannot tolerate?

6. What is Miss Matty Jenkyn's small economy"? How is it revealed?
7. In paragraph 5, why does the author say that she would have felt less melancholy if the letters had been more melancholy?
8. What facts in this sketch indicate that the setting is not contemporary?
9. What are some examples of "small economies" with which you are familiar? Can you trace the reasons for these attempts at being thrifty?
10. What examples does the author give in support of her controlling idea that "everyone has his own individual small economies"? What do the examples contribute to the writing?

The following selection was first published by *The New Yorker* in 1939. It is among many of the essays of James Thurber that appeared in the magazine while he was on its staff. The essay is typical of the ironic humor that made this writer famous and well-loved all over America.

Alternate Reading

Courtship through the Ages
James Thurber

1   Surely nothing in the astonishing scheme of life can have nonplussed Nature so much as the fact that none of the females of any of the species she created really cared very much for the male, as such. For the past ten million years Nature has been busily inventing ways to make the male attractive to the female, but the whole business of courtship, from the marine annelids up to man, still lumbers heavily along, like a complicated musical comedy. I have been reading the sad and absorbing story in Volume 6 (Cole to Dama) of the *Encyclopaedia Britannica.* In this volume you can learn all about cricket, cotton, costume designing, crocodiles, crown jewels, and Coleridge, but none of these subjects is so interesting as the Courtship of Animals, which recounts the sorrowful lengths to which all males must go to arouse the interest of a lady.

2   We all know, I think, that Nature gave man whiskers and a mustache with the quaint idea in mind that these would prove attractive to the female. We all know that, far from attracting her, whiskers and mustaches only made her nervous and gloomy, so that man had to go in for somersaults, tilting with lances, and performing feats of parlor magic to win her attention; he also had to bring her candy, flowers, and the furs of animals. It is common knowledge that in spite of all these "love displays" the male is constantly being turned down, insulted, or thrown out of the house. It is rather comforting, then, to discover that the peacock, for all his gorgeous plumage, does not have a particularly easy time in courtship; none of the males in the world do. The first peahen, it turned out, was only faintly stirred by her suitor's beautiful train. She would often go quietly to sleep while he was whisking it around. The *Britannica* tells us that the peacock actually had to learn a certain little trick to wake her up and revive her interest: he had to learn to vibrate his quills so as to make a rustling sound. In ancient times man himself, observing the ways of the peacock, probably tried vibrating his whiskers to make a rustling sound; if so, it didn't get him anywhere. He had to go in for something else;

so, among other things, he went in for gifts. It is not unlikely that he got this idea from certain flies and birds who were making no headway at all with rustling sounds.

3   One of the flies of the family Empidae, who had tried everything, finally hit on something pretty special. He contrived to make a glistening transparent balloon which was even larger than himself. Into this he would put sweetmeats and tidbits and he would carry the whole elaborate envelope through the air to the lady of his choice. This amused her for a time, but she finally got bored with it. She demanded silly little colorful presents, something that you couldn't eat but that would look nice around the house. So the male Empis had to go around gathering flower petals and pieces of bright paper to put into his balloon. On a courtship flight a male Empis cuts quite a figure now, but he can hardly be said to be happy. He never knows how soon the female will demand heavier presents, such as Roman coins and gold collar buttons. It seems probable that one day the courtship of the Empidae will fall down, as man's occasionally does, of its own weight.

4   The bowerbird is another creature that spends so much time courting the female that he never gets any work done. If all the male bowerbirds became nervous wrecks within the next ten or fifteen years, it would not surprise me. The female bowerbird insists that a playground be built for her with a specially constructed bower at the entrance. This bower is much more elaborate than an ordinary nest and is harder to build; it costs a lot more, too. The female will not come to the playground until the male has filled it up with a great many gifts: silvery leaves, red leaves, rose petals, shells, beads, berries, bones, dice, buttons, cigar bands, Christmas seals, and the Lord knows what else. When the female finally condescends to visit the playground, she is in a coy and silly mood and has to be chased in and out of the bower and up and down the playground before she will quit giggling and stand still long enough even to shake hands. The male bird is, of course, pretty well done in before the chase starts, because he has worn himself out hunting for eyeglass lenses and begonia blossoms. I imagine that many a bowerbird, after chasing a female for two or three hours, says the hell with it and goes home to bed. Next day, of course, he telephones someone else and the same trying ritual is gone through again. A male bowerbird is as exhausted as a night-club habitué before he is out of his twenties.

5   The male fiddler crab has a somewhat easier time, but it can hardly be said that he is sitting pretty. He has one enormously large and powerful claw, usually brilliantly colored, and you might suppose that all he had to do was reach out and grab some passing cutie. The very earliest fiddler crabs may have tried this, but, if so, they got slapped for their pains. A female crab will not tolerate any caveman stuff; she never has and she doesn't intend to start now. To attract a female, a fiddler crab has to stand on tiptoe and brandish his claw in the air. If any female in the neighborhood is interested—and you'd be surprised how many are not—she comes over and engages him in light badinage, for which he is not in the mood. As many as a hundred females may pass the time of day with him and go on about their business. By nightfall of an average courting day, a fiddler crab who has been standing on tiptoe for eight or ten hours waving a heavy claw in the air is in pretty sad shape. As in the case of the males of all species, however, he gets out of bed next morning, dashes some water on his face, and tries again.

6   The next time you encounter a male web-spinning spider, stop and reflect that he is too busy worrying about his love life to have any desire to bite you. Male web-spinning spiders have a tougher life than any other males in the animal kingdom. This is because the female web-spinning spiders have very poor eyesight. If a male lands on a female's web, she kills him before he has time to lay down his cane and gloves, mistaking him for a fly or a bumblebee who has tumbled into her trap. Before the species figured out what to do about this, millions of males were murdered by ladies they called on. It is the nature of spiders to perform a little dance in front of the female, but before a male spin-

ner could get near enough for the female to see who he was and what he was up to, she would lash out at him with a flat-iron or a pair of garden shears. One night, nobody knows when, a very bright male spinner lay awake worrying about calling on a lady who had been killing suitors right and left. It came to him that this business of dancing as a love display wasn't getting anybody anywhere except the grave. He decided to go in for web-twitching, or strand-vibrating. The next day he tried it on one of the near-sighted girls. Instead of dropping in on her suddenly, he stayed outside the web and began monkeying with one of its strands. He twitched it up and down and in and out with such a lilting rhythm that the female was charmed. The serenade worked beautifully; the female let him live. The *Britannica's* spider-watchers, however, report that this system is not always successful. Once in a while, even now, a female will fire three bullets into a suitor or run him through with a kitchen knife. She keeps threatening him from the moment he strikes the first low notes on the outside strings, but usually by the time he has got up to the high notes played around the center of the web, he is going to town and she spares his life.

7   Even the butterfly, as handsome a fellow as he is, can't always win a mate merely by fluttering around and showing off. Many butterflies have to have scent scales on their wings. Hepialus carries a powder puff in a perfumed pouch. He throws perfume at the ladies when they pass. The male tree cricket, Oecanthus, goes Hepialus one better by carrying a tiny bottle of wine with him and giving drinks to such doxies as he has designs on. One of the male snails throws darts to entertain the girls. So it goes, through the long list of animals, from the bristle worm and his rudimentary dance steps to man and his gift of diamonds and sapphires. The golden-eye drake raises a jet of water with his feet as he flies over a lake; Hepialus has his powder puff, Oecanthus his wine bottle, man his etchings. It is a bright and melancholy story, the age-old desire of the male for the female, the age-old desire of the female to be amused and entertained. Of all the creatures on earth, the only males who could be figured as putting any irony into their courtship are the grebes and certain other diving birds. Every now and then a courting grebe slips quietly down to the bottom of a lake and then, with a mighty "Whoosh!," pops out suddenly a few feet from his girl friend, splashing water all over her. She seems to be persuaded that this is a purely loving display, but I like to think that the grebe always has a faint hope of drowning her or scaring her to death.

8   I will close this investigation into the mournful burdens of the male with the *Britannica's* story about a certain Argus pheasant. It appears that the Argus displays himself in front of a female who stands perfectly still without moving a feather. . . . The male Argus the *Britannica* tells about was confined in a cage with a female of another species, a female who kept moving around, emptying ashtrays and fussing with lampshades all the time the male was showing off his talents. Finally, in disgust, he stalked away and began displaying in front of his water trough. He reminds me of a certain male (Homo sapiens) of my acquaintance who one night after dinner asked his wife to put down her detective magazine so that he could read her a poem of which he was very fond. She sat quietly enough until he was well into the middle of the thing, intoning with great ardor and intensity. Then suddenly there came a sharp, disconcerting *slap!* It turned out that all during the male's display, the female had been intent on a circling mosquito and had finally trapped it between the palms of her hands. The male in this case did not stalk away and display in front of a water trough; he went over to Tim's and had a flock of drinks and recited the poem to the fellas. I an sure they all told bitter stories of their own about how their displays had been interrupted by females. I am also sure that they all ended up singing "Honey, Honey, Bless Your Heart."

1,950 words

Vocabulary

annelids (1)   doxies (7)

habitué (4)   intoning (8)

badinage (5)

Questions

1. What is the controlling idea of the essay? Where is it stated?
2. Which of the examples cited is most closely allied to the human situation? What does the example reveal?
3. What does the courting grebe of paragraph 7 signify?
4. According to the essay, what is the only successful technique in courting the female? What is not enough?
5. What is ironic about the essay? How does Thurber achieve this irony?
6. Thurber's essay is a mixture of slang and scholarly language. What are some examples of both extremes? What is the effect of this mixture?
7. How does the title relate to the essay?
8. Can you think of instances in nature that would demonstrate a point of view opposite to that expressed by Thurber?
9. Does the *Encyclopaedia Britannica* really contain a section on the courtship of animals, or is this a fictional account?
10. What are the conventional courtesies men offer women today? How do they differ from courtesies of, say, the Renaissance?

Additional Writing Assignments

Illustrate the following assertions with appropriate *examples:*

1. The salaries of professional athletes are too high.
2. American cars are equipped with needless and expensive options.
3. Astrological forecasting is (is not) accurate.
4. The hubbub over the possibility of shark attack that followed the novel and movie *Jaws* is (is not) justified by the facts.
5. The worst part about falling in love is breaking up.
6. Not all the old are fuddy-duddy, conservative, and timid.
7. Baseball games range from being tense thrillers to being slumberous bores.
8. Lovelorn columns sometimes give clever, sensible advice.
9. Some gameshows are vulgar and tasteless.
10. I have fallen in love at first sight many times.

7

Definition

*Alienation entails a sense of removal from established
social values with a subsequent loss of consistent
purpose or meaning.*

A. Reading for Ideas

"Soldier's Home" is about an alienated person. Read this story, asking yourself in
what sense soldier Krebs was alienated. What is alienation? What are its symptoms?
How does it affect people? What causes Krebs to be alienated? From your own
experience, what are some examples of alienation? Be prepared to give a one-
sentence definition of *alienation*.

Soldier's Home
Ernest Hemingway

1 Krebs went to the war from a Methodist college in Kansas. There is a picture which
shows him among his fraternity brothers, all of them wearing exactly the same height
and style collar. He enlisted in the Marines in 1917 and did not return to the United
States until the second division returned from the Rhine in the summer of 1919.

2 There is a picture which shows him on the Rhine with two German girls and another
corporal. Krebs and the corporal look too big for their uniforms. The German girls are
not beautiful. The Rhine does not show in the picture.

3 By the time Krebs returned to his home town in Oklahoma the greeting of heroes was
over. He came back much too late. The men from the town who had been drafted had
all been welcomed elaborately on their return. There had been a great deal of hysteria.
Now the reaction had set in. People seemed to think it was rather ridiculous for Krebs
to be getting back so late, years after the war was over.

4 At first Krebs, who had been at Belleau Wood, Soissons, the Champagne, St. Mihiel
and in the Argonne, did not want to talk about the war at all. Later he felt the need to
talk but no one wanted to hear about it. His town had heard too many atrocity stories
to be thrilled by actualities. Krebs found that to be listened to at all he had to lie, and
after he had done this twice he, too, had a reaction against the war and against talking

about it. A distaste for everything that had happened to him in the war set in because of the lies he had told. All of the times that had been able to make him feel cool and clear inside himself when he thought of them; the times so long back when he had done the one thing, the only thing for a man to do, easily and naturally, when he might have done something else, now lost their cool, valuable quality and then were lost themselves.

5   His lies were quite unimportant lies and consisted in attributing to himself things other men had seen, done or heard of, and stating as facts certain apocryphal incidents familiar to all soldiers. Even his lies were not sensational at the pool room. His acquaintances, who had heard detailed accounts of German women found chained to machine guns in the Argonne forest and who could not comprehend, or were barred by their patriotism from interest in, any German machine gunners who were not chained, were not thrilled by his stories.

6   Krebs acquired the nausea in regard to experience that is the result of untruth or exaggeration, and when he occasionally met another man who had really been a soldier and they talked a few minutes in the dressing room at a dance he fell into the easy pose of the old soldier among other soldiers: that he had been badly, sickeningly frightened all the time. In this way he lost everything.

7   During this time, it was late summer, he was sleeping late in bed, getting up to walk down town to the library to get a book, eating lunch at home, reading on the front porch until he became bored and then walking down through the town to spend the hottest hours of the day in the cool dark of the pool room. He loved to play pool.

8   In the evening he practiced on his clarinet, strolled down town, read and went to bed. He was still a hero to his two young sisters. His mother would have given him breakfast in bed if he had wanted it. She often came in when he was in bed and asked him to tell her about the war, but her attention always wandered. His father was non-committal.

9   Before Krebs went away to the war he had never been allowed to drive the family motor car. His father was in the real estate business and always wanted the car to be at his command when he required it to take clients out into the country to show them a piece of farm property. The car always stood outside the First National Bank building where his father had an office on the second floor. Now, after the war, it was still the same car.

10   Nothing was changed in the town except that the young girls had grown up. But they lived in such a complicated world of already defined alliances and shifting feuds that Krebs did not feel the energy or the courage to break into it. He liked to look at them, though. There were so many good-looking young girls. Most of them had their hair cut short. When he went away only little girls wore their hair like that or girls that were fast. They all wore sweaters and shirt waists with round Dutch collars. It was a pattern. He liked to look at them from the front porch as they walked on the other side of the street. He liked to watch them walking under the shade of the trees. He liked the round Dutch collars above their sweaters. He liked their silk stockings and flat shoes. He liked their bobbed hair and the way they walked.

11   When he was in town their appeal to him was not very strong. He did not like them when he saw them in the Greek's ice cream parlor. He did not want them themselves really. They were too complicated. There was something else. Vaguely he wanted a girl but he did not want to have to work to get her. He would have liked to have a girl but he did not want to have to spend a long time getting her. He did not want to get into the intrigue and the politics. He did not want to have to do any courting. He did not want to tell any more lies. It wasn't worth it.

12   He did not want any consequences. He did not want any consequences ever again. He wanted to live along without consequences. Besides he did not really need a girl.

The army had taught him that. It was all right to pose as though you had to have a girl. Nearly everybody did that. But it wasn't true. You did not need a girl. That was the funny thing. First a fellow boasted how girls mean nothing to him, that he never thought of them, that they could not touch him. Then a fellow boasted that he could not get along without girls, that he had to have them all the time, that he could not go to sleep without them.

13   That was all a lie. It was all a lie both ways. You did not need a girl unless you thought about them. He learned that in the army. Then sooner or later you always got one. When you were really ripe for a girl you always got one. You did not have to think about it. Sooner or later it would come. He had learned that in the army.

14   Now he would have liked a girl if she had come to him and not wanted to talk. But here at home it was all too complicated. He knew he could never get through it all again. It was not worth the trouble. That was the thing about French girls and German girls. There was not all this talking. You couldn't talk much and you did not need to talk. It was simple and you were friends. He thought about France and then he began to think about Germany. On the whole he had liked Germany better. He did not want to leave Germany. He did not want to come home. Still, he had come home. He sat on the front porch.

15   He liked the girls that were walking along the other side of the street. He liked the look of them much better than the French girls or the German girls. But the world they were in was not the world he was in. He would like to have one of them. But is was not worth it. They were such a nice pattern. He liked the pattern. It was exciting. But he would not go through all the talking. He did not want one badly enough. He liked to look at them all, though. It was not worth it. Not now when things were getting good again.

16   He sat there on the porch reading a book on the war. It was a history and he was reading about all the engagements he had been in. It was the most interesting reading he had ever done. He wished there were more maps. He looked forward with a good feeling to reading all the really good histories when they would come out with good detail maps. Now he was really learning about the war. He had been a good soldier. That made a difference.

17   One morning after he had been home about a month his mother came into his bed-room and sat on the bed. She smoothed her apron.

18   "I had a talk with your father last night, Harold," she said, "and he is willing for you to take the car out in the evenings."

"Yeah?" said Krebs, who was not fully awake. "Take the car out? Yeah?"

"Yes. Your father has felt for some time that you should be able to take the car out in the evenings whenever you wished but we only talked it over last night."

"I'll bet you made him," Krebs said.

"No. It was your father's suggestion that we talk the matter over."

"Yeah. I'll bet you made him." Krebs sat up in bed.

"Will you come down to breakfast, Harold?" his mother said.

"As soon as I get my clothes on," Krebs said.

19   His mother went out of the room and he could hear her frying something downstairs while he washed, shaved and dressed to go down into the dining-room for breakfast. While he was eating breakfast his sister brought in the mail.

20   "Well, Hare," she said. "You old sleepy-head. What do you ever get up for?"

21   Krebs looked at her. He liked her. She was his best sister.

"Have you got the paper?" he asked.

22   She handed him *The Kansas City Star* and he shucked off its brown wrapper and opened it to the sporting page. He folded *The Star* open and propped it against the water pitcher with his cereal dish to steady it, so he could read while he ate.

23   "Harold," his mother stood in the kitchen doorway. "Harold, please don't muss up

the paper. Your father can't read his *Star* if it's been mussed."

"I won't muss it," Krebs said.

24   His sister sat down at the table and watched him while he read.

"We're playing indoor over at school this afternoon," she said. "I'm going to pitch."

"Good," said Krebs. "How's the old wing?"

"I can pitch better than lots of the boys. I tell them all you taught me. The other girls aren't much good."

"Yeah?" said Krebs.

"I tell them all you're my beau. Aren't you my beau, Hare?"

"You bet."

"Couldn't your brother really be your beau just because he's your brother?"

"I don't know."

"Sure you know. Couldn't you be my beau, Hare, if I was old enough and if you wanted to?"

"Sure. You're my girl now."

"Am I really your girl?"

"Sure."

"Do you love me?"

"Uh, huh."

"Will you love me always?"

"Sure."

"Will you come over and watch me play indoor?"

"Maybe."

"Aw, Hare, you don't love me. If you loved me, you'd want to come over and watch me play indoor."

24   Kreb's mother came into the dining-room from the kitchen. She carried a plate with two fried eggs and some crisp bacon on it and a plate of buckwheat cakes.

"You run along, Helen," she said. "I want to talk to Harold."

26   She put the eggs and bacon down in front of him and brought in a jug of maple syrup for the buckwheat cakes. Then she sat down across the table from Krebs.

27   "I wish you'd put down the paper a minute, Harold," she said.

Krebs took down the paper and folded it.

"Have you decided what you are going to do yet, Harold?" his mother said, taking off her glasses.

"No," said Krebs.

"Don't you think it's about time?" His mother did not say this in a mean way. She seemed worried.

"I hadn't thought about it," Krebs said.

"God has some work for every one to do," his mother said. "There can be no idle hands in His Kingdom."

"I'm not in His Kingdom," Krebs said.

"We are all of us in His Kingdom."

28   Krebs felt embarrassed and resentful as always.

"I've worried about you so much, Harold," his mother went on. "I know the temptation you must have been exposed to. I know how weak men are. I know what your own dear grandfather, my own father, told us about the Civil War and I have prayed for you. I pray for you all day long, Harold."

29   Krebs looked at the bacon fat hardening on his plate.

"Your father is worried, too," his mother went on. "He thinks you have lost your ambition, that you haven't got a definite aim in life. Charley Simmons, who is just your age, has a good job and is going to be married. The boys are all settling down; they're all determined to get somewhere; you can see that boys like Charley Simmons are on their way to being really a credit to the community.''

30   Krebs said nothing.

''Don't look that way, Harold,'' his mother said. ''You know we love you and I want to tell you for your own good how matters stand. Your father does not want to hamper your freedom. He thinks you should be allowed to drive the car. If you want to take some of the nice girls out riding with you, we are only too pleased. We want you to enjoy yourself. But you are going to have to settle down to work, Harold. Your father doesn't care what you start in at. All work is honorable as he says. But you've got to make a start at something. He asked me to speak to you this morning and then you can stop in and see him at his office.''

''Is that all?'' Krebs said.

''Yes. Don't you love your mother, dear boy?''

''No,'' Krebs said.

31   His mother looked at him across the table. Her eyes were shiny. She started crying.

''I don't love anybody,'' Krebs said.

32   It wasn't any good. He couldn't tell her, he couldn't make her see it. It was silly to have said it. He had only hurt her. He went over and took hold of her arm. She was crying with her head in her hands.

''I didn't mean it,'' he said. ''I was just angry at something. I didn't mean I didn't love you.''

33   His mother went on crying. Krebs put his arm on her shoulder.

''Can't you believe me, mother?''

His mother shook her head.

''Please, please, mother. Please believe me.''

''All right,'' his mother said chokily. She looked up at him. ''I believe you, Harold.''

34   Krebs kissed her hair. She put her face up to him.

''I'm your mother,'' she said. ''I held you next to my heart when you were a tiny baby.''

35   Krebs felt sick and vaguely nauseated.

''I know, Mummy,'' he said. ''I'll try and be a good boy for you.''

''Would you kneel and pray with me, Harold?'' his mother asked.

36   They knelt down beside the dining-room table and Kreb's mother prayed.

''Now, you pray, Harold,'' she said.

''I can't,'' Krebs said.

''Try, Harold.''

''I can't.''

''Do you want me to pray for you?''

''Yes.''

37   So his mother prayed for him and then they stood up and Krebs kissed his mother and went out of the house. He had tried so to keep his life from being complicated. Still, none of it had touched him. He had felt sorry for his mother and she had made him lie. He would go to Kansas City and get a job and she would feel all right about it. There would be one more scene maybe before he got away. He would not go down to his father's office. He would miss that one. He wanted his life to go smoothly. It had just gotten going that way. Well, that was all over now, anyway. He would go over to the schoolyard and watch Helen play indoor baseball.

                                                    2,722 words

Vocabulary

hysteria (3)
apocryphal (5)

Questions

1. Based on the experience of soldier Krebs, what is alienation? Define *alienation* in one simple sentence.
2. What are some of the specific signs of Krebs' alienation? Refer to appropriate paragraphs.
3. In paragraph 32, the author says: "It wasn't any good. He couldn't tell her, he couldn't make her see it." What couldn't Krebs make his mother see?
4. Was Krebs involved in some really decisive battles during the war, or did he just watch from the sidelines? How do you know?
5. Why aren't Krebs' acquaintances thrilled by his stories?
6. In paragraph 4, we are told that after Krebs fabricated a few lies about his war experience, "A distaste for everything that had happened to him in the war set in because of the lies he had told." How do you explain this reaction?
7. Who are some alienated people today? What are the causes?

The Sound of Silence
Paul Simon

1   Hello darkness my old friend,
    I've come to talk with you again,
    Because a vison softly creeping,
    Left its seed while I was sleeping
    And the vision that was planted in my brain
    Still remains within the sound of silence.

2   In restless dreams I walked alone,
    Narrow streets of cobble stone
    'Neath the halo of a street lamp,
    I turned my collar to the cold and damp
    When my eyes were stabbed by the flash of a neon light
    That split the night, and touched the sound of silence.

3   And in the naked light I saw
    Ten thousand people maybe more,
    People talking without speaking,
    People hearing without listening,
    People writing songs that voices never share
    And no one dares disturb the sound of silence.

4   "Fools!" said I, "You do not know
    Silence like a cancer grows.
    Hear my words that I might teach you
    Take my arms that I might reach you."
    But my words like silent raindrops fell
    And echoed, in the wells of silence.

5   And the people bowed and prayed
     To the neon God they made,
     And the sign flashed out its warning
     In the words that it was forming.
     And the sign said:
          "The words of the prophets are written
          on the subway walls and tenement halls"
     And whispered in the sound of silence.

Questions

1. What is the meaning of the poem title? How can silence have sound?
2. Who is the speaker and to whom is he speaking?
3. What is the atmosphere created in stanza 2?
4. What is your explanation of stanza 3?
5. What exactly is the poet-prophet's warning?
6. How much success does the poet-prophet have in his attempt to cure society? Why?
7. What is the meaning of the sign in stanza 5?

B. How to Write a Definition

Definition is the method of development used whenever you introduce a word that your reader might not understand or might misinterpret. What if someone accused you of being a *lamia?* Would you be angry or flattered? Or would you simply shrug your shoulders because you do not know what the word means. A *lamia* is a devouring monster. The term *lamia* is often used to label women as devious and witchlike. From Green mythology, the *lamia* was represented as a snake with the head and breasts of a woman, and was reputed to prey on humans and suck the blood of children. Used as a label, the word is hardly flattering.

The meanings of unfamiliar words are usually found merely by referring to any good dictionary. But that is only half the problem with the definition of words. A more complex problem involves familiar words that are interpreted differently from different points of view, often with rancor and prejudice. Typical examples are: *justice, freedom, liberal, conservative, truth, beauty, love, honor,* and so on. Such words are open to multiple interpretations, because they are tied to abstract concepts that can be expressed only through the use of other words. When such abstract words play a key role in an essay, the sense in which you intend to use them must be defined. Words such as *table, trumpet, pencil, necklace, smoke,* and *tree,* on the other hand, are associated with objects or images that we can define with our senses. They conjure up an image of something that we can see, hear, taste, feel, smell, or touch and consequently are simple to explain.

The writer who selects an abstract subject frequently is forced to begin his essay with a definition. For instance, if you were asked to write an essay comparing/contrasting love with hate, it would be entirely logical to begin by defining what you mean by love and hate. That accomplished, you can then get on with the comparison and contrast. Definitions thus have a way of cropping up in essays prompted by entirely different controlling ideas.

Writing Assignment

Based on your reading of "Soldier's Home" and "Sound of Silence," write an essay defining the word *alienation*. First look up *alienation* in a good dictionary, such as *Webster's Collegiate Dictionary* or *The American Heritage Dictionary of the English Language*. Choose the definition from those in the dictionary that most closely fits your idea of alienation. Then begin your essay by writing, "Alienation is _____ _____," completing the sentence with your chosen definition. Example: "Alienation is the feeling of being an outsider, isolated from one's society." This dictionary definition, also called a "lexical definition," will serve as the controlling idea from which you will develop your essay on alienation.

Specific Instructions

1. EXTEND YOUR DEFINITION THROUGH EXAMPLES, STATED FUNCTIONS, AND THE USE OF CONTRAST. Some essays set out to supply an extended definition of a word or concept, and to do nothing else. The assignment of this unit, for instance, calls for an extended definition of alienation. Here, the dictionary definition is not enough: you must supplement it by (1) supplying examples, (2) stating functions, and (3) suggesting contrasts.

Say you were writing an extended definition of love. Having parroted one of the lexical definitions such as "affection based on admiration or benevolence," you groan over its inadequacy, pitying the poor lexicographer who thinks that love is such bare-bones stuff. What can you do to invest the concept with deserving passion? You could give an *example* of how you felt when you were in love.

> Love is the pitter-patter of the heart, butterflies in the tummy, the invisible symphonies that swallows dance to on silken twilit evenings; but most of all, it is a sudden, urgent lunacy. As an example, I offer the night I met Julie. I had saved for months to go to dinner at Chez Francois. I had the meal all planned. Appetizer: oysters sauteed in olive oil. Main course: lobster steamed in wine with herb sauce. Vegetable: eggplant stuffed with mushrooms. Wine: a white Maçon, which I was just about to select when I met Julie—the cocktail waitress. I took one look in her eyes and my appetite went down the tube. I know that's slang and that I should say something more elegant, but I actually felt my appetite dropping from my belly down to my toes—as if it fell down a tube—and, with a little imagination, I thought I even saw it roll out on the carpet and scurry away like a routed mouse. The rest of the night I just kept ordering one drink after another so Julie would come around and I could talk to her. I ate part of a lobster feeler and then abandoned the carcass to the vultures; the eggplant stayed on the plate as if some lobotomized hen had laid it there by mistake. I never touched a mushroom. All I did was drink, chat with Julie, make a desperate and inaudible moan to myself, and get roaringly drunk. $54.89 later I ended up eating a McDonald's hamburger. That's love, brother, that's love.

Stating a function means telling what something does or how it works, thereby adding another dimension to your definition. For example, the sewing machine may be defined as a contraption that allows a tailor or seamstress to stitch cloth together automatically without inverting the needle. This definition can then be extended by stating specific functions, as follows:

> There are over 2,000 varieties of modern sewing machines designed for stitching processes in the great sewing industries making up clothing, boots and shoes, corsets, hats, hosiery, etc. There are machines specially designed for sewing regular or fancy shank buttons on shoes; for sewing sweat leathers into stiff felt, soft felt or straw hats; for trimming scalloping and over-edging lace curtains; for sewing silk initials, monograms or floral designs upon material at one operation. There is a seven needle machine for making seven parallel rows of fine double chain stitching simultaneously. This machine is fitted with seven needles and seven loopers, and its capacity is 20,000 stitches per minute.
>
> *Encyclopaedia Britannica*

Certain terms can be effectively defined through contrasts—that is, by stating *what they are not*. For example, one way to define *snob* is first to state that it stands for "a class-conscious person who pretends to be superior to others." The definition can then be extended by stating what a snob is *not:*

> A snob does *not* have the capacity to judge others by their genuine worth; rather, he indiscriminately labels anyone but the rich and educated as his inferiors. He is *not* a judge of what is truly noble, but only of what has obvious social rank and prestige.

In summary, your definition should be clear and complete and should not allow for any unanswered questions in the mind of your reader.

2. DEFINE; DON'T DESCRIBE. "Marriage is a boring institution" is not a definition, but a description. "Marriage is the ceremony by which two people are united in order to found a home or family" is a definition. "Communism is a dangerous political enemy" reveals the writer's attitude toward communism but does not really tell us what communism is. A better attempt is "Communism is a political system that advocates the elimination of private property by substituting common ownership."

3. MAKE YOUR DEFINITION PENETRATING, NOT CIRCULAR. For example, to define the grammatical term *dangling participle* by saying that "it is a participle that dangles" merely repeats the term without defining it. A better definition of dangling participle is "a participle that has no relationship to any other element in a sentence."

4. MAKE YOUR DEFINITION CONCISE AND UNDERSTANDABLE. The following definition is bloated with words but starving for clarity. "Enlightenment is a philosophical movement of the eighteenth century, concerned with and exclusively committed to the idea—unknown in medieval times with its dogmatic attitudes—that every-thing in the world must be critically examined and then empirically proved, so

that previously accepted doctrines and institutions were viewed from the point of view of rationalism combined with individualism." Here is an improved version: "Enlightenment is a philosophical movement of the eighteenth century that examined traditional doctrines and institutions by applying reason and the scientific method."

This extended definition of alienation is adapted by the editors from an article by Steven Kelman. Written while the author was a sophomore at Harvard University, the article originally appeared in the *New York Times Magazine,* October 22, 1967.

Professional Model

These Are Three of the Alienated
Steven Kelman

1   "If I had been brought up in Nazi Germany—supposing I wasn't Jewish—I think I would have had an absolute set of values, that is to say, Nazism, to believe in. In modern American society, particularly in the upper middle class, a very liberal group, where I'm given no religious background, where my parents always said to me, 'If you want to go to Sunday School, you *can,*' or 'If you want to take music lessons, you *can,*' but 'It's up to *you,*' where they never did force any arbitrary system of values on me—what I find is that with so much freedom, I'm left with *no* value system, and in certain ways I wish I had had a value system forced on me, so that I could have something to believe in."

2   The speaker is a sophomore at Harvard University, describing his sense of alienation and its causes. His words may surprise most adults, who tend to view the alienated youth as someone who has no respect for the values of society and who therefore seeks to destroy those values and even society itself—a sort of intellectual descendant of the Luddites. This is only one of the stereotypes that abound in the conventional literature about alienation. All the stereotypes, however, miss one central point: There is a very wide range of attitudes, activities, opinions, and experiences among those young people who call themselves "alienated." The alienated are both committed and uncommitted, present-oriented and future-oriented, political and apolitical, even happy and unhappy.

3   That such varied people are all *self-proclaimed* "alienated youths" could be an indication that alienation is becoming a sort of modern party game, without any real meaning. But I don't feel this is the case. The alienated kids I have spoken with were going through too much real anguish to make the "game" worth it. Adults may confine their alienation to cocktail commiseration; for young people it's generally a total thing.

4   Actually, it should not really be surprising that there are so many different types of alienation, because alienation in itself is only a negative reaction. It is not a set of beliefs—like Socialism, Republicanism or vegetarianism—but a rejection of or even simply an inability to accept the conventional attitudes, mores or way of life of society, a rejection that is essentially emotional and only secondarily, if at all, intellectual. There is every reason to expect, contrary to the typical adult monistic view of alienation, that from such a start the alienated can go into many worlds.

5   And they do.

6   Gene lives in Roxbury, Boston's black ghetto. He is 17, a high school dropout, has served a year in prison for car theft and armed robbery committed when he was 15. He is about to complete his parole period. Gene will refuse to go to Vietnam if drafted. "I ain't going to fight nobody's war that don't belong to me. That ain't none of *my* fight. I'd go to jail first."

7   But Gene is not, as one might think, a Black Power activist or even a Muslim. In fact he is not particularly bitter about American society, or about white America's treatment of Negroes. "I'm not saying we're being treated *wrong,* but it ain't *right* either. You know, part's right and part's wrong." Gene's equivocation is not the hesitant moderation of an Uncle Tom. The simple fact is that it is not so much injustice he feels as separation from the society at large, the world outside. Thus, when I asked him what he thought about America, he answered simply and sincerely, "I don't know too much about the place. I just live here."

8   What he meant is that, while subject to the institutions of society, he is outside when the time comes to draw up the rules of the game, and is even to an extent ignorant of what those rules are. He is, in his own words, "not where the action is." Like Meursault in Camus' *The Stranger,* a character of whom Gene strongly reminded me, the trial goes on without his participation. But this doesn't mean that he hates or flouts the rules or conventions. Consider his attitudes toward school: "School's all right, I ain't got nothing against school; I just don't like to go. I just can't sit up there in no classroom and listen to the teachers blah all afternoon."

9   Conventions and rules are foreign, and sometimes incomprehensible. Gene was puzzled, for example, that a person could be acquitted of a crime and yet his arrest might still be used against him if he were arrested a second time. "I don't even understand nothing like that," he said. "That's why I don't know too much about the place; I just *live* here." Gene's is an alienation in the most nitty-gritty sense of separation from the very day-to-day mechanisms of "normal" society.

10   Gene nonchalantly and matter-of-factly described how he and his friends stole an automobile and robbed a service station ("It wasn't so much money, but what could you do?"), a description devoid even of pride of accomplishment. It was as if he were telling me about going to the grocery to buy a loaf of bread. He started his story with, "You see, it was really nothing." He ended it with a description of his capture: "I forgot. You know, I meant to tie the guy at the gas station up, and all this sort of jive. But I forgot." As I was talking to him, trying to get across how I would have had great feelings of compunction and fear before even being able to attempt a robbery, I realized that my scruples sounded as strange to him as his nonchalance did to me. Then I saw that we were part of worlds more separate than those that separated me from the farthest-out, freakiest hippie. He was alienated, and I was not—because my world set the official rules by which his must live.

11   Nobody should fool himself by trying to explain Gene on any grounds other than those of alienation. His crime was not, for instance, the imperative of a "delinquent subculture" that demands lawbreaking as a condition for acceptance. He never admitted, although I asked him about it, any exalted feelings of power or defiance while committing a crime. His parents certainly disapproved of his getting into trouble. I had no feeling I was sitting next to a "criminal"—and, indeed, I guess I wasn't. For society's law, like society in general, is something *separate* from Gene. He recognizes it, but he is not in formal rebellion against it: "They caught me, and I served time," he noted calmly. It was like a Monopoly game—"Go direct to jail. Do not pass 'Go.' Do not collect $200." Nothing more serious than that.

12   Gene does not identify with any "black community" or even with the civil-rights movement, for which he has nothing but contempt: "They don't gain nothing by doing that but making a fool out of themselves. What are they trying to prove? That's what white people want to see anyway—see niggers making a fool of themselves. You gotta mind your own business." Would he participate in a civil-rights demonstration? "No," Gene answered, drawing it out contemptuously. "I wouldn't even bother to join." Stokely Carmichael? "Who's that? I forgot who that is." After a brief reminder: "Oh, that Black Power junk. White power, Black Power. I don't believe in that."

13   Although certain theorists have explained the civil-rights movement as the Negro's quest for the middle-class glamor he sees on television, Gene feels no such pull from the society outside. "That's a lot of bull," Gene said slowly and with disdain for the world pictured on TV. "I don't even believe in nothing like that. That's them old dumb niggers who say, 'Look at that. I'm going to get me some of that.'"

14   Not everyone in Gene's surroundings is as detached as he. One of his friends wants to go to college, maybe; he thinks that the idea of "stopping Communism" in Vietnam is "a good motive" and even, in hawkish terms, calls for escalation. But Gene has always been different. He remembers his reaction as a child to his mother's explanation of the problems of being black. "She told me that I got to be extra nice, 'cause you know how these whities are. Well, I said, 'Forget it man. If one says something to me, I'm going to kill him, that's all.'" For a black person, the rules of the game were to be "extra nice" so as not to offend anybody. Gene never accepted those rules.

15   Because his alienation was, in a sense, imposed on him; because—unlike the middle-class alienated student—he never *left* "normal" American society, Gene is open, serene and completely without the hang-ups and up-tightness that afflict all the other alienated kids I spoke with. Asked if he ever thought about whether he was happy, he replied quickly, "Yeah, I think about it all the time. Of course I'm happy. I have nothing to be sad about." Would he ever leave Roxbury? "Never. Here it's just the way I like everything, wild and crazy." It was a statement that would fill most alienated students with envy.

BILL

16   Bill is the very unhappy, very alienated Harvard sophomore quoted earlier. At times he leads a kind of non-life: "I'll find myself sitting in a chair for hours on end, doing nothing—reading until I get tired of reading, listening to the radio until I even get tired of listening (which is the most passive action I know). Then I'll just sit in the seat doing absolutely nothing, in a certain way wishing there was something I felt like doing, but with nothing being very appealing to me. I'll just sit there for hours, not even caring about getting happy."

17   As an intellectual, Bill is very verbal about his condition and very precise in defining his alienation: "In my own terms, alienation is my lack of commitment to or even interest in any one position. I hold opinions in politics, philosophy and esthetics, and I suppose also ethical opinions, but I'm not really strongly committed to any position. I can intellectually understand, hold and even approve of both sides, or all sides. Because I can appreciate more than one way of looking at things, I don't really find myself in strong approval or disapproval."

18   Although this may suggest to the unalienated person merely a healthy skepticism, the question of commitment has become for Bill a central and obsessive concern. Few people would view the rah-rah, "I'm all right, Jack" student, whose horizon extends no further than the comforts available to the upper middle class, as being committed. Yet to Bill, such a student is committed, if "only" to making money. "To me, he said,

"the difference between the kid who wants to make a pile and the kid in the New Left is a very minor one. Their commitments to me are of equal merit. One is committed to getting through school; the other is committed to overthrowing the Government."

19   Bill spoke of the things in his life that have molded him. He grew up in "a typical, loving, middle-class home," living in the same house for almost 17 years. He never had many friends or a close relationship with older brothers and sisters. He recalled that he never did much work in school, partly because he was intelligent enough to get along without working, but mainly because he could only worry about immediate problems, and grades were usually too far in the future, as he put, to "motivate" him. After losing an earlier interest in physics and math, he decided in the ninth grade that he wanted to be a writer. "I'm not sure," he said, "whether it was more writing or the idea of being a writer which excited me. At any rate, this was a value, a commitment."

20   Also, shortly after this time, he developed a few very close friendships: "I could always rely to some extent on what friends thought for an arbitrary value system." But at the start of his senior year, Bill had to move from his old home, "which made me feel a little insecure," and last fall he and his friends were spun off to the several corners of the collegiate world.

21   Nor does Bill draw any solace from association with girls. He never had a girl friend until the middle of the 12th grade, and this year he has had only one date. Thus he has no emotional ties that might provide commitment to *something* in the day-to-day world, lacking as he does any commitment to beliefs or goals.

22   Bill takes drugs. He has "turned on" with pot many times, often swallowed pep pills and—once—taken LSD. He thinks only of the moment and is not concerned about the consequences of his act. Moreover, drugs fill one of his essential needs: "When you're left with no values you believe in, it's a comforting thing to know you can take a pill, and it will give you an arbitrary set of values. Anything that comes up to do, you'll want to do." In fact, this is the way Bill gets through exams. He takes pep pills, not to keep awake, but to give him the motivation to get in some cramming.

23   What about the psychedelic drugs? "It'll make you feel good, that's the first thing. It'll impose a good mood on you. You'll see how pointless things are, but it'll give you so many beautiful things to see that you'll say, 'What difference does that make? Let's have a good time anyway.'" Marijuana? "Pot doesn't really give you any set of values. Pot just serves after a while to turn off your mind if you're feeling bad, to give you a completely neutral feeling."

24   How long can the drug "thingie" last? As with his alienation, itself, Bill hopes that it's not forever. First, there's just a limit to what drugs can do. "There are times," he commented, "when I'm so demobilized that I don't even have the motivation to turn on." After a while, too, "kicks get harder to find," in the words of a popular teenage song. Three months ago, Bill said, he never would have taken LSD. Now he was talking about a psychedelic drug called STP, which he describes as "so powerful that you either flip out for life or you die." He adds, more seriously, that "if someone put some heroin under my nose today, I wouldn't hesitate to sniff some."

25   Despite adult myths about the supposed fashionableness of alienation, the truth is that for Bill alienation is hell, and he is hoping for out. Reading about it in books, intellectually understanding it, Bill said, is easy enough, but emotionally experiencing it is something else. Talking with me in *my* world, Bill could intellectually describe his emotions; but in his own world, he can't apply his mind to solving his problems. He spoke of returning to writing again, "when I get out of this," but he cannot get "out of" it by telling himself intellectually to do so. Instead, he almost mystically holds onto those few commitments he has made. At the age of 12 he swore not to commit suicide. Recently he promised an old friend not to take LSD for three months. Mainly, he hopes.

26   "Strange though it might seem," he said, "I think I'm the only person I know in this school who's basically religious. I happen to believe in God, I think. I'm not definite about it, and that's why I'm not committed to it. But that strikes me as vaguely important." Could be.

HANK

27   Bill would not call Hank alienated at all, for Hank is an activist in Students for a Democratic Society and therefore "committed." In fact, although they are both Harvard sophomores, Hank is the opposite of Bill in many ways. Bill is from a big Northern city; Hank is from a city in the Deep South. Bill grew up, so he says, with no values forced on him; Hank grew up a practicing Christian and was president of his teen-age church group. Yet Hank, too, is very conscious of his own alienation. One day when I was speaking with him he commented: "I think that the basic difference between the New and the Old Left is in their degree of alienation."

28   For Hank, the emotional act of alienation was based on his rejection of Christianity. Although, in explaining the genesis of his alienation, he went at length into political reasons for it (the conventional ones: Southern racism, the war in Vietnam, poverty of whites and blacks), the first thing he talked about was his disillusionment with Christianity.

29   "Around 10th grade in high school," he said, "I started wondering about Christianity, wondering if all this they were feeding me for all these years wasn't a bunch of bull. I seriously questioned for a few years, but I was president of my church group through my junior year in high school, and I went through all the motions. I was actually the epitome of hypocrisy. But I finally came to the decision that I couldn't find any meaning in Christianity. I read a good deal of Camus[1] and Kierkegaard,[2] and I got hung up on some type of existential philosophy, seeing that no broad dogma could be adhered to by everyone and that each person has to find his own truth. This is part of my alienation now. I'm sort of withdrawing philosophically and religiously from the established religion, and I'm trying to grapple with myself and find some philosophy to suit my own needs."

30   In a sense, Hank was lucky to have such a clear-cut, primitive set of dogmas to rebel against—racism, hypocrisy, what he calls the "contradictions" of the particular society around him. He spoke of the contradictions between Southern hospitality ("It's not mythical what they say about that. People really are very nice—if you're white") and Southern attitudes ("These nice people then turn around and do atrocious things—like beating up Negroes or starting to shout for bombing Hanoi three years ago"). There are also the contradictions which Hank feels in American society in general, and which any radical would sense, such as between the principle of free speech and its stifling, according to Hank, as soon as it becomes "effective," that is to say, a clear and present danger. And there are the contradictions posed by his liberal parents who constantly told him, "We only want what's best for you," but "You'd better do what we want you to do," or "We want you to say what you believe in," but "You've got to be realistic." Fortunately for Hank, many of *his* contradictions can be resolved by embracing an activist political philosophy. Perhaps because he's had enough to feel alienated from in the society around him, he hasn't had the time or inclination to become, like Bill, alienated from life in general.

31   Hank's mixture of alienation and commitment is easy enough to maintain at school,

---

[1]Albert Camus, French novelist and essayist (1913–1960).
[2]Sören Aabye Kierkegaard, Danish philosopher and theologian (1813–1855).

away from the "real world," especially when one is a member of a sizable group like S.D.S. (which at Harvard numbers almost 200). His problem comes when he goes home; up to now, he has solved it by "cooling it" on some of his alienation while back, figuratively, at the Manse. Up North, he speaks boldly of the need to work outside the "Establishment," while at home he works for liberal Democratic candidates. This doesn't mean that Hank becomes a sellout at home. Last year he was the only voice in an entire state Key Club convention to come out against acceptance by acclamation of a resolution calling for escalation of the war. The resolution was adopted 177–1.

32   Hank also tries to mix radicalism and more conventional social action. This summer at home he tutored Negro high school students. Meliorism? "No, because I was tutoring them in a radical critique of American society."

33   How does someone from the South become alienated, in the face of the pressures there for conformity (Hank remembers, chanting as a child, "2, 4, 6, 8—we don't want to integrate!")? Hank explained it this way: "My parents were sort of an initial cause of my alienation, but in an unconventional way. Their being liberals sort of caused me to question at first. They got the ball rolling, but from there it just took off."

34   These alienated young people suffer with their alienation, but it may be that they will be the better for it. I have the feeling that when they finally figure out "where they're at," they'll be far ahead of many adults who never went through the painful process.

One alienated student made this point in strong terms. He had been telling me of a student he called Mr. Joe Straight ("the guy who never thinks about these problems, who's oblivious of his own existence"), and then he brought up the story of another student's father:

"He's made a lot of money, and at the age of 60 he's finally found out that, as far as he's concerned, his life is nothing. Because he sees that in five years or ten years he's going to die, and he sees that he's got all his 'goals,' and he's still nowhere. Life itself was just a vehicle for him to attain these exterior goals. So now what is he going to do? How does he handle life? Because he has no goals to preoccupy his mind, what's preoccupying his mind now is *life,* and he can't handle that.

35   "This cat at 60 is where I am at 20. When I'm 60, I don't want to be where he's at. Being desperate at 20, you still feel you can know yourself, but at 60—where do you go from there?"

3,698 words

Vocabulary

arbitrary (1)	scruples (10)	epitome (29)
Luddites (2)	imperative (11)	existential philosophy (29)
stereotypes (2)	exalted (11)	dogmas (30)
commiseration (3)	esthetics (17)	Manse (31)
monistic (4)	skepticism (18)	acclamation (31)
equivocation (7)	demobilized (24)	meliorism (32)
devoid (10)	genesis (28)	critique (32)
compunction (10)	disillusionment (28)	conformity (33)

Questions

1. How does the author attempt to engage the reader's interest in the opening paragraph?
2. A common strategy in defining is to state early what a thing is not. Where in this article does the author state what alienation is not?

3. In paragraph 2, the author discusses alienation stereotypes. Why? What does this discussion contribute to his definition of alienation?
4. Three examples are used to illustrate the meaning of alienation. What does the example of Gene illustrate? Of Bill? Of Hank?
5. What is the controlling idea behind this definition of alienation?
6. Examine paragraph 27. How is this paragraph developed? What does this development contribute to the essay?

Student Model

What Is Alienation?
Thomas Chessum

Alienation is by no means a new concept; man has encountered its darkness since he first became aware of his own existence. The very heart of the darkness seems to be inherent in man's structure, fixed in the depths of the human soul. All mankind seems condemned to some form of alienation simply by the severely limited facilities available for expressing and understanding self and for reaching out toward fellow selves. Alienation, this cloud which surrounds and isolates man, can generally be defined as the feeling of being alone. The alienated experience—the feeling of being outside of and isolated from society with no purpose in life—is a feeling which applies not only to individuals but also to entire groups.

Alienation entails a sense of removal from established social values with a subsequent loss of consistent purpose or meaning. Yet the syndrome includes more than this simple isolation and purposelessness. A secondary characteristic is a feeling of powerlessness. Powerlessness frustrates the individual and produces submission to the feeling of being victimized by destiny, chance, or institutional collaboration. Coupled with the dimension of self-estrangement, or the lack of self-understanding, powerlessness results in "normlessness," the inability to accept shared social prescriptions.

In its original definition *alienation* denoted the insane person, a definition which is still valid, for the insane suffer the severest form of alienation. In its modern sense the term most commonly denotes the situation of the estranged individual. He is estranged from society because while being subject to the rules and regulations of social institutions, he has not shared in their formulation. He, therefore, does not accept and is even ignorant of the "rules of the game," and like so many of the 60s youth, he blatantly rejects the conventional establishment.

Beyond the alienation of an individual is that of the masses, or in popular terms Riesman's "lonely crowd." Large masses of people live in close physical contact with each other without participating in a sense of commitment or community. This alienation has resulted from increasing rates of social change, automation, lack of creativity in work, affluence, leisure, and a decline in utopian ideals. In modern man's world his whole mechanistic and technolgoical creation stands above him. He does not feel himself the architect or nucleus of the creation, but its servant. The more powerful and monumental the technological structure, the more powerless and isolated man feels. In a sense, modern man has been conquered by a mechanical dictator of his own making, and must bow down to this technological creature which he can neither control nor do without. Man both individually and societally is, therefore, isolated form purpose, meaning, power, creativity, and self, by the technology he depends on. Alienation, then, is a term which is inseparably connected with twentieth century man. It connotes the isolation, estrangement, and lack of purpose that twentieth century man is so apt to suffer.

In this essay, Gordon Allport, a well-known psychologist, gets at the root of prejudice by giving it a precise definition.

The Nature of Prejudice
Gordon Allport

1   Before I attempt to define prejudice, let us have in mind four instances that I think we all would agree involve prejudice.

2   The first is the case of the Cambridge University student, who said, "I despise all Americans. But," he added, a bit puzzled, "I've never met one that I didn't like."

3   The second is the case of another Englishman, who said to an American, "I think you're awfully unfair in your treatment of Negroes. How *do* Americans feel about Negroes?" The American replied, "Well, I suppose some Americans feel about Negroes just the way you feel about the Irish." The Englishman said, "Oh, come now! The Negroes are human beings!"

4   Then there's the incident that occasionally takes place in various parts of the world (in the West Indies, for example, I'm told). When an American walks down the street the natives conspicuously hold their noses till the American goes by. The case of odor is always interesting. Odor gets mixed up with prejudice because odor has great associative power. We know that some Chinese deplore the odor of Americans. Some white people think Negroes have a distinctive smell and vice versa. An intrepid psychologist recently did an experiment; it went as follows. He brought to a gymnasium an equal number of white and colored students and had them take shower baths. When they were nice and clean he had them exercise vigorously for fifteen minutes. Then he put them in different rooms, and he put a clean white sheet over each one. Then he brought his judges in, and each went to the sheeted figures and sniffed. They were to say, "white" or "black," guessing at the identity of the subject. The experiment seemed to prove that when we are sweaty we all smell bad in the same way. It's good to have experimental demonstration of the fact.

5   The fourth example I'd like to bring before you is a piece of writing that I quote. Please ask yourselves who, in your judgment, wrote it. It's a passage about the Jews.

> The synagogue is worse than a brothel. It's a den of scoundrels. It's a criminal assembly of Jews, a place of meeting for the assassins of Christ, a den of thieves, a house of ill fame, a dwelling of iniquity. Whatever name more horrible to be found, it could never be worse than the synagogue deserves.
>
> I would say the same things about their souls. Debauchery and drunkenness have brought them to the level of lusty goat and pig. They know only one thing; to satisfy their stomachs and get drunk, kill, and beat each other up. Why should we salute them? We should have not even the slightest converse with them. They are lustful, rapacious, greedy, perfidious robbers.

6   Now who wrote that? Perhaps you say Hitler, or Goebbels, or one of our local anti-Semites? No, it was written by Saint John Chrysostom, in the fourth century A.D. Saint John Chrysostom, as you know, gave us the first liturgy in the Christian church still used in the Orthodox churches today. From it all services of the Holy Communion derive. Episcopalians will recognize him also as the author of that exalted prayer that closes

the offices of both matin and evensong in the *Book of Common Prayer.** I include this incident to show how complex the problem is. Religious people are by no means necessarily free from prejudice. In this regard be patient even with our saints.

7   What do these four instances have in common? You notice that all of them indicate that somebody is ''down'' on somebody else—a feeling of rejection, or hostility. But also, in all these four instances, there is indication that the person is not ''up'' on his subject—not really informed about Americans, Irish, Jews, or bodily odors.

8   So I would offer, first a slang definition of prejudice: *Prejudice is being down on somebody you're not up on.* If you dislike slang, let me offer the same thought in the style of St. Thomas Aquinas. Thomists have defined prejudice as *thinking ill of others without sufficient warrant.*

9   You notice that both definitions, as well as the examples I gave, specify two ingredients of prejudice. First there is some sort of faulty generalization in thinking about a group. I'll call this the process of *categorization.* Then there is the negative, rejective, or hostile ingredient, a *feeling* tone. ''Being down on something'' is the hostile ingredient; ''that you're not up on'' is the categorization ingredient; ''Thinking ill of others'' is the hostile ingredient; ''without sufficient warrant'' is the faulty categorization.

10   Parenthetically I should say that of course there is such a thing as *positive* prejudice. We can be just as prejudiced *in favor of* as we are *against.* We can be biased in favor of our children, our neighborhood or our college. Spinoza makes the distinction neatly. He says that *love prejudice* is ''thinking well of others, through love, more than is right.'' *Hate prejudice,* he says, is ''thinking ill of others, through hate, more than is right.''

840 words

Vocabulary

associative (4)	rapacious (5)	liturgy (6)
deplore (4)	perfidious (5)	matin (6)
iniquity (4)	anti-Semites (6)	

Questions

1. How does the author begin his essay? What is his purpose?
2. Why does the author think that odor often gets mixed up in prejudice?
3. The author refers to an experimental demonstration that proves that odor is not associated with race. What other firmly held beliefs have been negated by experimental demonstrations?
4. Why does the author end paragraph 6 by saying, ''In this regard be patient even with our saints''?
5. What is the author's slang definition of *prejudice?* What is his more literary definition?
6. What is a present-day example of the process of categorization?
7. What is ''positive prejudice''? What examples does the author supply?
8. Who is Spinoza? Look him up in your dictionary.
9. In your opinion, what are the pitfalls resulting from both negative and positive prejudice?
10. What is your own definition of *prejudice?* What are some of your prejudices? How do you deal with them? What prejudices in others bother you most?

---

*The book of services and prayers used in the Church of England.

Excerpted from *Modern Democracy* by Carl Becker, this selection gives a definition of the term *democracy*.

Democracy
Carl Becker

1   Democracy, like liberty or science or progress, is a word with which we are all so familiar that we rarely take the trouble to ask what we mean by it. It is a term, as the devotees of semantics say, which has no ''referent''—there is no precise or palpable thing or object which we all think of when the word is pronounced. On the contrary, it is a word which connotes different things to different people, a kind of conceptual Gladstone bag which, with a little manipulation, can be made to accommodate almost any collection of social facts we may wish to carry about in it. In it we can as easily pack a dictatorship as any other form of government. We have only to stretch the concept to include any form of government supported by a majority of the people, for whatever reasons and by whatever means of expressing assent, and before we know it the empire of Napoleon, the Soviet regime of Stalin, and the Fascist systems of Mussolini and Hitler are all safely in the bag. But if this is what we mean by democracy, then virtually all forms of government are democratic, since virtually all governments, except in times of revolution, rest upon the explicit or implicit consent of the people. In order to discuss democracy intelligently it will be necessary, therefore, to define it, to attach to the word a sufficiently precise meaning to avoid the confusion which is not infrequently the chief result of such discussions.

2   All human institutions, we are told, have their ideal forms laid away in heaven, and we do not need to be told that the actual institutions conform but indifferently to these ideal counterparts. It would be possible then to define democracy either in terms of the ideal or in terms of the real form—to define it as government of the people, by the people, for the people; or to define it as government of the people, by the politicians, for whatever pressure groups can get their interests taken care of. But as a historian I am naturally disposed to be satisfied with the meaning which, in the history of politics, men have commonly attributed to the word—a meaning, needless to say, which derives partly from the experience and partly from the aspirations of mankind. So regarded, the term democracy refers primarily to a form of government, and it has always meant government by the many as opposed to government by the one—government by the people as opposed to government by a tyrant, a dictator, or an absolute monarch. This is the most general meaning of the word as men have commonly understood it.

3   In this antithesis there are, however, certain implications, always tacitly understood, which give a more precise meaning to the term. Peisistratus, for example, was supported by a majority of the people, but his government was never regarded as a democracy for all that. Caesar's power derived from a popular mandate, conveyed through established republican forms, but that did not make his government any the less a dictatorship. Napoleon called his government a democratic empire, but no one, least of all Napoleon himself, doubted that he had destroyed the last vestiges of the democratic republic. Since the Greeks first used the term, the essential test of democratic government has always been this: the source of political authority must be and remain in the people and not in the ruler. A democratic government has always meant one in which the citizens,

or a sufficient number of them to represent more or less effectively the common will, freely act from time to time, and according to established forms, to appoint or recall the magistrates and to enact or revoke the laws by which the community is governed. This I take to be the meaning which history has impressed upon the term democracy as a form of government.

650 words

Vocabulary

devotees (1)	Gladstone bag (1)	aspirations (2)
semantics (1)	assent (1)	antithesis (3)
referent (1)	explicit (1)	tacitly (3)
palpable (1)	implicit (1)	vestiges (3)
connotes (1)		

Questions

1. What is a "referent"? What does the author mean when he says that democracy has no "referent"?
2. The author says it is not enough to define democracy simply as any form of government supported by a majority of the people. Why?
3. The author says that it is possible to define democracy in terms of either its ideal or its real form. How do these definitions of democracy differ?
4. What purpose is served by the author's dual definition of democracy as an ideal and as a reality?
5. What is the most general meaning of democracy as men have commonly understood it?
6. How did the dictator Caesar derive his powers?
7. What did Napoleon call his government?
8. What is the essential test of a democracy?
9. What has the term *democratic government* always meant?
10. In attempting to define democracy, what examples does the author use? How do these examples contribute to his definition?

Additional Writing Assignment

Beginning with a lexical definition and extending this definition into a full essay, define one of the following terms. Be sure that your essay answers the question, "What is it?"

1. racial prejudice
2. good prose
3. adolescence
4. fanatacism
5. marital fidelity
6. drug addiction
7. wit
8. autopsy
9. mental depression
10. patriotism

8

Comparison / Contrast

My two closest friends are as different as a Cape Cod cottage and a Byzantine mosque.

A. Reading for Ideas

"Señor Payroll" describes a duel between management and labor, with labor winning out in the end. The story has its serious as well as humorous side, and behind its curious plot, the sensitive reader will detect the two different worlds of transient labor and established management. As you read, try to identify and compare the characteristics of management and labor. Try also to visualize individuals with contrasting backgrounds and lifestyles, such as the educated and the ignorant, the rich and the poor. Think of specific acquaintances who have contrasting lifestyles.

Señor Payroll
William E. Barrett

1   Larry and I were Junior Engineers in the gas plant, which means that we were clerks. Anything that could be classified as paper work came to the flat double desk across which we faced each other. The Main Office downtown sent us a bewildering array of orders and rules that were to be put into effect.

2   Junior Engineers were beneath the notice of everyone except the Mexican laborers at the plant. To them we were the visible form of a distant, unknowable paymaster. We were Señor Payroll.

3   Those Mexicans were great workmen; the aristocrats among them were the stokers, big men who worked Herculean eight-hour shifts in the fierce heat of the retorts. They scooped coal with huge shovels and hurled it with uncanny aim at tiny doors. The coal streamed out from the shovels like black water from a high-pressure nozzle, and never missed the narrow opening. The stokers worked stripped to the waist, and there was pride and dignity in them. Few men could do such work, and they were the few.

4   The Company paid its men only twice a month, on the fifth and on the twentieth. To a Mexican, this was absurd. What man with money will make it last fifteen days? If he

hoarded money beyond the spending of three days, he was a miser—and when, Señor, did the blood of Spain flow in the veins of misers? Hence, it was the custom for our stokers to appear every third or fourth day to draw the money due to them.

5   There was a certain elasticity in the Company rules, and Larry and I sent the necessary forms to the Main Office and received an "advance" against a man's pay check. Then, one day, Downtown favored us with a memorandum:

6   "There have been too many abuses of the advance-against-wages privilege. Hereafter, no advance against wages will be made to any employee except in a case of genuine emergency."

7   We had no sooner posted the notice when in came stoker Juan Garcia. He asked for an advance. I pointed to the notice. He spelled it through slowly, then said, "What does this mean, this 'genuine emergency'?"

8   I explained to him patiently that the Company was kind and sympathetic, but that it was a great nuisance to have to pay wages every few days. If someone was ill or if money was needed for some other good reason, then the Company would make an exception to the rule.

9   Juan Garcia turned his hat over and over slowly in his big hands. "I do not get my money?"

10   "Next payday, Juan. On the twentieth."

11   He went out silently and I felt a little ashamed of myself. I looked across the desk at Larry. He avoided my eyes.

12   In the next hour two other stokers came in, looked at the notice, had it explained and walked solemnly out; then no more came. What we did not know was that Juan Garcia, Pete Mendoza, and Francisco Gonzalez had spread the word, and that every Mexican in the plant was explaining the order to every other Mexican. "To get money now, the wife must be sick. There must be medicine for the baby."

13   The next morning Juan Garcia's wife was practically dying, Pete Mendoza's mother would hardly last the day, there was a veritable epidemic among children, and, just for variety, there was one sick father. We always suspected that the old man was really sick; no Mexican would otherwise have thought of him. At any rate, nobody paid Larry and me to examine private lives; we made out our forms with an added line describing the "genuine emergency." Our people got paid.

14   That went on for a week. Then came a new order, curt and to the point: "Hereafter, employees will be paid ONLY on the fifth and the twentieth of the month. No exceptions will be made except in the cases of employees leaving the service of the Company."

15   The notice went up on the board, and we explained its significance gravely. "No, Juan Garcia, we cannot advance your wages. It is too bad about your wife and your cousins and your aunts, but there is a new rule."

16   Juan Garcia went out and thought it over. He thought out loud with Mendoza and Gonzalez and Ayala, then, in the morning, he was back. "I am quitting this company for a different job. You pay me now?"

17   We argued that it was a good company and that it loved its employees like children, but in the end we paid off, because Juan Garcia quit. And so did Gonzalez, Mendoza, Obregon, Ayala and Ortez, the best stokers, men who could not be replaced.

18   Larry and I looked at each other; we knew what was coming in about three days. One of our duties was to sit on the hiring line early each morning, engaging transient workers for the handy gangs. Any man was accepted who could walk up and ask for a job without falling down. Never before had we been called upon to hire such skilled virtuosos as stokers for handy-gang work, but we were called upon to hire them now.

19   The day foreman was wringing his hands and asking the Almightly if he was personally supposed to shovel this condemned coal, while there in a stolid, patient line

were skilled men—Garcia, Mendoza, and others—waiting to be hired. We hired them, of course. There was nothing else to do.

20   Every day we had a line of resigning stokers, and another line of stokers seeking work. Our paper work became very complicated. At the Main Office they were jumping up and down. The procession of forms showing Juan Garcia's resigning and being hired over and over again was too much for them. Sometimes Downtown had Garcia on the payroll twice at the same time when someone down there was slow in entering a resignation. Our phone rang early and often.

21   Tolerantly and patiently we explained: "There's nothing we can do if a man wants to quit, and if there are stokers available when the plant needs stokers, we hire them."

22   Out of chaos, Downtown issued another order. I read it and whistled. Larry looked at it and said, "It is going to be very quiet around here."

23   The order read: "Hereafter, no employee who resigns may be rehired within a period of 30 days."

24   Juan Garcia was due for another resignation, and when he came in we showed him the order and explained that standing in line the next day would do him no good if he resigned today. "Thirty days is a long time, Juan."

25   It was a grave matter and he took time to reflect on it. So did Gonzalez, Mendoza, Ayala and Ortez. Ultimately, however, they were all back—and all resigned.

26   We did our best to dissuade them and we were sad about the parting. This time it was for keeps and they shook hands with us solemnly. It was very nice knowing us. Larry and I looked at each other when they were gone and we both knew that neither of us had been pulling for Downtown to win this duel. It was a blue day.

27   In the morning, however, they were all back in line. With the utmost gravity, Juan Garcia informed me that he was a stoker looking for a job.

28   "No dice, Juan," I said. "Come back in thirty days. I warned you."

29   His eyes looked straight into mine without a flicker. "There is some mistake, Señor," he said. "I am Manuel Hernandez. I work as the stoker in Pueblo, in Santa Fe, in many places."

30   I stared back at him, remembering the sick wife and the babies without medicine, the mother-in-law in the hospital, the many resignations and the rehirings. I knew that there was a gas plant in Pueblo, and that there wasn't any in Santa Fe; but who was I to argue with a man about his own name? A stoker is a stoker.

31   So I hired him. I hired Gonzalez, too, who swore that his name was Carrera and Ayala, who had shamelessly become Smith.

32   Three days later the resigning started.

33   Within a week our payroll read like a history of Latin America. Everyone was on it: Lopez and Obregon, Villa, Diaz, Batista, Gomez, and even San Martín and Bolívar. Finally Larry and I, growing weary of staring at familiar faces and writing unfamiliar names, went to the Superintendent and told him the whole story. He tried not to grin, and said, "Damned nonsense!"

34   The next day the orders were taken down. We called our most prominent stokers into the office and pointed to the board. No rules any more.

35   The next time we hire you hombres," Larry said grimly, "come in under the names you like best, because that's the way you are going to stay on the books."

36   They looked at us and they looked at the board; then for the first time in the long duel, their teeth flashed white. "Si, Señores," they said.

37   And so it was.

1,506 words

Vocabulary

array (1)   transient (18)
Herculean (3)   virtuosos (18)
veritable (13)   dissuade (26)

Questions

1. What are the main characteristics of management and labor? List two or three characteristics for each side.
2. The ending of the story can be considered ironic. Why?
3. The gas company functioned as a benevolent dictator. Where in the story is this revealed?
4. What is the real reason the Mexican laborers win in the end? Is this realistic?
5. How is the bureaucratic nature of management revealed? How do the laborers treat it?
6. What role do the junior engineers play in the story?
7. How do you feel about the morality of the laborers? About the morality of management?

The Campus on the Hill

W. D. Snodgrass

1   Up the reputable walks of old established trees
    They stalk, children of the *nouveaux riches;* chimes
    Of the tall Clock Tower drench their heads in blessing:
    "I don't wanna play at your house;
5   I don't like you any more."
    My house stands opposite, on the other hill,
    Among meadows, with the orchard fences down and falling;
    Deer come almost to the door.
    You cannot see it, even in this clearest morning.
10 White birds hang in the air between
    Over the garbage landfill and those homes thereto adjacent,
    Hovering slowly, turning, settling down
    Like the flakes sifting imperceptibly onto the little town
    In a waterball of glass.
15 And yet, this morning, beyond this quiet scene,
    The floating birds, the backyards of the poor,
    Beyond the shopping plaza, the dead canal, the hillside lying tilted in the air,
    Tomorrow has broken out today:
20 Riot in Algeria, in Cyprus, in Alabama;
    Aged in wrong, the empires are declining,
    And China gathers, soundlessly, like evidence.
    What shall I say to the young on such a morning?—
    Mind is the one salvation?—also grammar?—

<pre>
25   No; my little ones lean not toward revolt. They
     Are the Whites, the vaguely furiously driven, who resist
     Their souls with such passivity
     As would make Quakers swear. All day, dear Lord, all day
     They wear their godhead lightly.
30   They look out from their hill and say,
     To themselves, "We have nowhere to go but down;
     The great destination is to stay."
     Surely the nations will be reasonable;
     They look at the world—don't they?—the world's way?
35   The clock just now has nothing more to say.
</pre>

Questions

1. What can you conclude about the school that is the locale of the poem?
2. The students are characterized, in part, by the quotation in lines 4 and 5. What does this quotation tell you about the students?
3. With what group of people are the students being implicitly contrasted?
4. What is the meaning of the line, "Tomorrow has broken out today."
5. What is the meaning of the second quotation attributed to the students, "We have nowhere to go but down;/ The great destination is to stay"? How are the students politically characterized by this quotation?
6. What resolution, if any, does the final line of the poem suggest? How do you think the class conflict will be resolved?

B. How to Write a Comparison/Contrast

A comparison reveals the similarities and differences between two items—a contrast assumes only differences between them. Most of our private and public decisions are based on comparison and contrast: We buy a Vega rather than a Capri because of differences we perceive between the two. An executive hires one secretary rather than another because he perceives a difference in their skills. A student selects one history class over another because he has heard that this teacher is more interesting than that one. A person chooses one religion over another because it offers greater peace of mind. Although often carried out in a slipshod manner with little or no logic, comparison is a necessary and familiar process.

Writing Assignment

Compare and contrast two of your acquaintances who come from different social backgrounds. Base your essay on the contrast between the lifestyles they represent, taking into account the differences in their attitude toward money, their treatment of people, their purpose in life, their dependence on others, and any other important basis for comparison. Place the controlling idea at the end of the introductory paragraph, making sure that it expresses the general areas of contrast you will treat in your essay—for example, "Mark and John differ in their cultural values, their treatment of people, and their goals in life."

Specific Instructions

1. CHOOSE SUITABLE BASES FOR YOUR COMPARISON.   Your assignment is to compare two acquaintances with different lifestyles. To be effective, your comparison must be systematic rather than random. The first step is therefore to establish the bases for your comparison—in this case, the three or four points on which you will examine your two acquaintances for differences and similarities between them. For example, John, the banker's son, wears flowered shirts, gold chains, and velvet trousers, while Mark, whose father is dead, wears plain T-shirts over blue Levis. The basis of this contrast is *fashion.* You have also observed that John treats everyone with impatience, whereas Mark treats people with a polite boredom. The basis of this contrast is their *treatment of people.* John's ambition is to travel all over the world with beautiful women, while Mark's dream is to buy a horse ranch in Oregon. The basis of this contrast is their respective *goals in life.* On the other hand, John loves the music of Vivaldi and so does Mark. Both are fans of Agatha Christie and devotees of Star Trek. Similarities therefore exist between them based on a mutual fondness for the same composer, mystery writer, and defunct television series.

2. LIMIT YOUR ESSAY TO MAJOR BASES FOR COMPARISON.   No doubt there are countless bases for comparing your acquaintances—looks, talent, charm, intelligence, creativity, ability to make friends, athletic prowess, and so on. However, rambling over the infinity of differences and similarities you see between John and Mark will not necessarily give your essay structure, emphasis, or clarity. To write a structured, emphatic, and clear comparison of your two acquaintances, select the major points of difference and similarity between them and restrict your essay to a contrast based on these. Once chosen and enunciated in your controlling idea, these bases will give your essay unity and structure. You should not violate this unity and structure by slipping into areas not mentioned in the controlling idea. The following paragraph begins by announcing a comparison of two girls on the bases of looks, personality, and physical strength, and lives up to its promise:

Controlling idea: Kora and Shery, though best friends, were as different as winter and summer in their looks, personality and physical strength. Kora was tall and dark, with snappy black eyes and long silken braids that fell to her hips, whereas Shery looked almost frail, with soft blue eyes and a halo of golden curls framing her delicate face. Kora wasn't afraid of anyone or anything—not even Mr. Threllkeld, the burly principal. Without the slightest abashment she could confront even the town mayor and demand that he schedule the spring prom in the civic auditorium. Strangers didn't exist for Kora. She greeted them as she would an old acquaintance, without fear or reticence. On the other hand, Shery was painfully shy. To speak up in class was a nightmare for her, as could be seen from her high blush and whispered answers. She hated meeting new people and would always wait for Kora to take over the conversation. If someone she hardly knew attempted a conversation with her, she would begin to stammer, look confused, and eventually excuse herself and hurriedly leave. Then, too, Kora was physically stronger than Shery. The boys often asked her to practice basketball or baseball with them because she could hit a basket

Looks:

Personality:

Physical strength:

and swing a bat as well as any other tenth-grader. Unlike Kora, Shery feared any physical adventure. When Kora playfully threw her a basketball, Shery would cover her face with her hands and dodge it. When coaxed to go swimming, skating or climbing, Shery would say "I'm too chicken." Kora and Shery attracted each other as opposites, not as kindred spirits.

3. DECIDE ON THE ORGANIZATION OF YOUR COMPARISON.   Basically, there are two ways to organize a comparison assignment—vertically or horizontally. For example, you intend to compare John, who is rich, with Mark, who is poor, on the basis of their attitude toward money. Organized *vertically,* the elements of your outline would look like this:

I. John has the rich boy's contempt for money.
   a. He expects it to be there when he needs it.
   b. He never hesitates over a purchase.
   c. He buys what he wants.
II. Mark has the poor boy's reverence for money.
   a. He knows it is hard to come by.
   b. He hesitates and lingers over a purchase.
   c. He buys what he can afford.

Vertical organization requires that you first write about John on points a, b, and c, and then contrast Mark with John on these same points, as in this example:

Having always lived a life of luxury and comfort, John has a rich boy's contempt for money. He expects it to be there when he needs it; he sees it as having only a utility value, enabling him to do what he likes. He never lingers or hesitates over a purchase. For him, the object of shopping is not to agonize over the amount to be spent, but simply to find the best, most suitable, and most expeditious object that will satisfy all his wants. He has a high regard for quality, and a low regard for expense. He buys what suits him best, whether it is the most or least expensive item in the store.

Mark, on the other hand, has the poor boy's reverence and respect for money. It was not always there when he needed it; what little money he has acquired has cost him in labor, sweat, and drudgery. He spends an interminable amount of time on shopping trips, endlessly comparing prices, quality, value, and listening patiently to sales spiels and technical explanations. For him, the aim of shopping is to acquire the most for the least. He regards expense on par with quality and usually ends up buying not his first choice nor even his second, but sometimes his third, or fourth, or even fifth, the acquisition always being dictated by his budget and seldom by quality.

Here is an outline of this same contrast organized *horizontally:*

John has contempt for money; Mark has reverence for money.
John buys without hesitation; Mark hesitates and compares prices.
John buys what he wants; Mark buys what he can afford.

Here is the horizontally organized written contrast:

Having lived a life of luxury and comfort, John has the rich boy's contempt for money. Mark, on the other hand, has the poor boy's reverence for it. John expects money to be there when he needs it and sees it as having a utility value, enabling him to do as he pleases. Mark, however, knows that money is not always there when he needs it, and that what little money he has acquired has cost him in labor, sweat, and drudgery. A pronounced difference shows up in their behavior on shopping trips. John never lingers or hesitates over a purchase; he shops for what he wants, buying always the most suitable, the most expeditious object which will satisfy all his wants. It is just the opposite with Mark. For him, shopping means acquiring the most for the least. He must choose his purchases not by quality alone, but also by expense. Frequently he ends up buying not his first choice, nor even his second or third, but his fourth or fifth choice, in every case the acquisition being dictated by budget rather than by quality. John buys the best if it suits him; Mark, to the contrary, buys what he can afford.

4. USE INDICATORS TO SHOW COMPARISON/CONTRAST. A good comparison should be sprinkled with *indicators* that signal similarities and differences. For example:

Similarity	*Contrast*
likewise	but
the same as	yet
too/also	however
similarly	nevertheless
in like manner	on the contrary
	contrary to
	unlike
	the opposite of

The most common student error in comparison/contrast essays is to leave out the indicators and not complete the comparison. Consider the following:

Benjamin Franklin was a more positive American than was Jonathan Edwards. For example, he had a much more developed sense of humor, as revealed in the numerous funny anecdotes in his autobiography. He could laugh at his own mistakes and at the stupidity of the world in general. Furthermore, he was much more successful in his work, becoming famous all over the world as an inventor, writer, and statesman. Then too, Franklin was more optimistic about America. His writing reflects confidence and security in America's future; they indicate an innate pride in America's potential as well as its accomplishments.

As you can see, the above conparison is hopelessly lopsided. Claiming to draw a contrast between Benjamin Franklin and Jonathan Edwards, the writer tells us only about Franklin, leaving us to guess about Edwards. Perhaps the student simply forgot that he was comparing two figures and that he was therefore obliged to give each equal treatment. However, one way a student may forestall this sort of lapse is to mechanically and consciously sprinkle the text with indicators that force him to complete the comparison with equal treatment to all parties:

> Benjamin Franklin was a more positive American than was Jonathan Edwards. First, Franklin had a developed sense of humor. He could laugh, as revealed in the numerous funny anecdotes of his autobiography. *In contrast,* the diaries of Jonathan Edwards are filled with passages in which he weeps and moans over his own sinful condition and the general wickedness of the world. Second, Benjamin Franklin was successful in everything he attempted, achieving worldwide fame as an inventor, writer, and statesman. *On the other hand,* Jonathan Edwards was doubted by most thinkers and despised by his own congregation; he ended his ministry as an outcast in the wilderness, helping the Indians. Third, Franklin was a much more optimistic man than was Jonathan Edwards. His writings show great confidence and security in America's future; they indicate an innate pride in America's potential as well as its accomplishments. *Unlike* Franklin, Edwards was burdened by a deepseated pessimism. His sermons emphasize man's utter depravity and vileness. In his view, all men except the few elect were despicable worms and the world was damned to everlasting hell.

The second version provides a clearer contrast than the first version because the contrast indicators remind the writer to treat both sides equally.

This article by Gilbert Highet, a Scottish-born, naturalized U.S. citizen, describes a meeting between two sharply contrasting personalities of history—Alexander the Great and Diogenes. This selection originally appeared in *Horizon,* the first in a series entitled Great Confrontations.

Professional Model

Diogenes and Alexander
The Dog Has His Day
Gilbert Highet

1   Lying on the bare earth, shoeless, bearded, half-naked, he looked like a beggar or a lunatic. He was one, but not the other. He had opened his eyes with the sun at dawn, scratched, done his business like a dog at the roadside, washed at the public fountain, begged a piece of breakfast bread and a few olives, eaten them squatting on the ground, and washed them down with a few handfuls of water scooped from the spring. (Long ago he had owned a rough wooden cup, but he threw it away when he saw a boy drinking out of his hollowed hands.) Having no work to go to and no family to provide for, he was free. As the market place filled up with shoppers and merchants and gossipers and sharpers and slaves and foreigners, he had strolled through it for an hour or two.

Everybody knew him, or knew of him. They would throw sharp questions at him and get sharper answers. Sometimes they threw jeers, and got jibes; sometimes bits of food, and got scant thanks; sometimes a mischievous pebble, and got a shower of stones and abuse. They were not quite sure whether he was mad or not. He knew they were mad, all mad, each in a different way; they amused him. Now he was back at his home.

2 It was not a house, not even a squatter's hut. He thought everybody lived far too elaborately, expensively, anxiously. What good is a house? No one needs privacy: natural acts are not shameful; we all do the same things, and need not hide them. No one needs beds and chairs and such furniture: the animals live healthy lives and sleep on the ground. All we require, since nature did not dress us properly, is one garment to keep us warm, and some shelter from rain and wind. So he had one blanket—to dress him in the daytime and cover him at night—and he slept in a cask. His name was Diogenes. He was the founder of the creed called Cynicism (the word means "doggishness"); he spent much of his life in the rich, lazy, corrupt Greek city of Corinth, mocking and satirizing its people, and occasionally converting one of them.

3 His home was not a barrel made of wood: too expensive. It was a storage jar made of earthenware, something like a modern fuel tank—no doubt discarded because a break had made it useless. He was not the first to inhabit such a thing: the refugees driven into Athens by the Spartan invasion had been forced to sleep in casks. But he was the first who ever did so by choice, out of principle.

4 Diogenes was not a degenerate or a maniac. He was a philosopher who wrote plays and poems and essays expounding his doctrine; he talked to those who cared to listen; he had pupils who admired him. But he taught chiefly by example. All should live naturally, he said, for what is natural is normal and cannot possibly be evil or shameful. Live without conventions, which are artificial and false; escape complexities and superfluities and extravagances: only so can you live a free life. The rich man believes he possesses his big house with its many rooms and its elaborate furniture, his pictures and expensive clothes, his horses and his servants and his bank accounts. He does not. He depends on them, he worries about them, he spends most of his life's energy looking after them; the thought of losing them makes him sick with anxiety. They possess him. He is their slave. In order to procure a quantity of false, perishable goods he has sold the only true, lasting good, his own independence.

5 There have been many men who grew tired of human society with its complications, and went away to live simply—on a small farm, in a quiet village, in a hermit's cave, or in the darkness of anonymity. Not so Diogenes. He was not a recluse, or a stylite, or a beatnik. He was a missionary. His life's aim was clear to him: it was "to restamp the currency." (He and his father had once been convicted for counterfeiting, long before he turned to philosophy, and this phrase was Diogenes' bold, unembarrassed joke on the subject.) To restamp the currency: to take the clean metal of human life, to erase the old false conventional markings, and to imprint it with its true values.

6 The other great philosophers of the fourth century before Christ taught mainly their own private pupils. In the shady groves and cool sanctuaries of the Academy, Plato discoursed to a chosen few on the unreality of this contingent existence. Aristotle, among the books and instruments and specimens and archives and research-workers of his Lyceum, pursued investigations and gave lectures that were rightly named *esoteric,* "for those within the walls." But for Diogenes, laboratory and specimens and lecture halls and pupils were all to be found in a crowd of ordinary people. Therefore he chose to live in Athens or in the rich city of Corinth, where travelers from all over the Mediterranean world constantly came and went. And, by design, he publicly behaved in such ways as to show people what real life was. He would constantly take up their spiritual coin, ring it on a stone, and laugh at its false superscription.

7   He thought most people were only half-alive, most men only half-men. At bright noonday he walked through the market place carrying a lighted lamp and inspecting the face of everyone he met. They asked him why. Diogenes answered, "I am trying to find a *man*."

8   To a gentleman whose servant was putting on his shoes for him, Diogenes said, "You won't be really happy until he wipes your nose for you: that will come after you lose the use of your hands."

9   Once there was a war scare so serious that it stirred even the lazy, profit-happy Corinthians. They began to drill, clean their weapons, and rebuild their neglected fortifications. Diogenes took his old cask and began to roll it up and down, back and forward. "When you are all so busy," he said, "I felt I ought to do *something!*"

10   And so he lived—like a dog, some said, because he cared nothing for privacy and other human conventions, and because he showed his teeth and barked at those whom he disliked. Now he was lying in the sunlight, as contented as a dog on the warm ground, happier (he himself used to boast) than the Shah of Persia. Although he knew he was going to have an important visitor, he would not move.

11   The little square began to fill with people. Page boys elegantly dressed, spearmen speaking a rough foreign dialect, discreet secretaries, hard-browed officers, suave diplomats, they all gradually formed a circle centered on Diogenes. He looked them over, as a sober man looks at a crowd of tottering drunks, and shook his head. He knew who they were. They were the attendants of the conqueror of Greece, the servants of Alexander, the Macedonian king, who was visiting his newly subdued realm.

12   Only twenty, Alexander was far older and wiser than his years. Like all Macedonians he loved drinking, but he could usually handle it; and toward women he was nobly restrained and chivalrous. Like all Macedonians he loved fighting; he was a magnificent commander, but he was not merely a military automaton. He could think. At thirteen he had become a pupil of the greatest mind in Greece, Aristotle. No exact record of his schooling survives. It is clear, though, that Aristotle took the passionate, half-barbarous boy and gave him the best of Greek culture. He taught Alexander poetry; the young prince slept with the *Iliad* under his pillow and longed to emulate Achilles, who brought the mighty power of Asia to ruin. He taught him philosophy, in particular the shapes and uses of political power: a few years later Alexander was to create a supranational empire that was not merely a power system but a vehicle for the exchange of Greek and Middle Eastern cultures.

13   Aristotle taught him the principles of scientific research: during his invasion of the Persian domains Alexander took with him a large corps of scientists, and shipped hundreds of zoological specimens back to Greece for study. Indeed, it was from Aristotle that Alexander learned to seek out everything strange which might be instructive. Jugglers and stunt artists and virtuosos of the absurd he dismissed with a shrug; but on reaching India he was to spend hours discussing the problems of life and death with naked Hindu mystics, and later to see one demonstrate Yoga self-command by burning himself impassively to death.

14   Now, Alexander was in Corinth to take command of the League of Greek States which, after conquering them, his father Philip had created as a disguise for the New Macedonian Order. He was welcomed and honored and flattered. He was the man of the hour, of the century: he was unanimously appointed commander-in-chief of a new expedition against old, rich, corrupt Asia. Nearly everyone crowded to Corinth in order to congratulate him, to seek employment with him, even simply to see him: soldiers and statesmen, artists and merchants, poets and philosophers. He received their compliments graciously. Only Diogenes, although he lived in Corinth, did not visit the new monarch. With that generosity which Aristotle had taught him was a quality of the truly

magnanimous man, Alexander determined to call upon Diogenes. Surely Dio-genes, the God-born, would acknowledge the conqueror's power by some gift of hoarded wisdom.

15   With his handsome face, his fiery glance, his strong supple body, his purple and gold cloak, and his air of destiny, he moved through the parting crowd, toward the Dog's kennel. When a king approaches, all rise in respect. Diogenes did not rise, he merely sat up on one elbow. When a monarch enters a precinct, all greet him with a bow or an acclamation. Diogenes said nothing.

16   There was a silence. Some years later Alexander speared his best friend to the wall, for objecting to the exaggerated honors paid to His Majesty; but now he was still young and civil. He spoke first, with a kindly greeting. Looking at the poor broken cask, the single ragged garment, and the rough figure lying on the ground, he said, "Is there anything I can do for you, Diogenes?"

17   "Yes," said the Dog. "Stand to one side. You're blocking the sunlight."

18   There was silence, not the ominous silence preceding a burst of fury, but a hush of amazement. Slowly, Alexander turned away. A titter broke out from the elegant Greeks, who were already beginning to make jokes about the Cur that looked at the King. The Macedonian officers, after deciding that Diogenes was not worth the trouble of kicking, were starting to guffaw and nudge one another. Alexander was still silent. To those nearest him he said quietly, "If I were not Alexander, I should be Diogenes." They took it as a paradox, designed to close the awkward little scene with a polite curtain line. But Alexander meant it. He understood Cynicism as the others could not. Later he took one of Diogenes' pupils with him to India as a philosophical interpreter (it was he who spoke to the naked *saddhus*). He was what Diogenes called himself, a *cosmopolitēs,* "citizens of the world." Like Diogenes, he admired the heroic figure of Hercules, the mighty conqueror who labors to help mankind while all others toil and sweat only for themselves. He knew that of all men then alive in the world only Alexander the conqueror and Diogenes the beggar were truly free.

2,078 words

Vocabulary

squatter (2)	superfluities (4)	fortifications (9)
Cynicism (2)	recluse (5)	barbarous (12)
satirizing (2)	stylite (5)	supranational (12)
degenerate (4)	Lyceum (6)	mystics (13)
maniac (4)	superscription (6)	ominous (18)

Questions

1. What bases govern Highet's comparison of Diogenes and Alexander?
2. How does Highet present his comparison—vertically or horizontally?
3. In what paragraph does Highet first shift from one character to another? How is the shift accomplished?
4. What other contrast is drawn besides the contrast between Diogenes and Alexander? Point to specific passages.
5. What is the analogy used in paragraph 10?
6. What are some characteristics that Diogenes and Alexander share?
7. What are the most outstanding contrasts between the old philosopher and the young emperor?

In this essay, a student contrasts her two best friends on three points: looks, personality, and attitude toward life. The contrast is vertically organized. Its clarity is its chief strength. An occasional weakness is the writer's fondness for extravagant images and diction.

Student Model

Two Friends: A Study in Contrasts
Catherine Wells

My two closest friends are as different as a Cape Cod cottage and a Byzantine mosque. Pari Ahmadi is a flamboyant dancer from Bandar, Iran, whereas Margie Warner is an unobtrusive college sophomore from Salt Lake City, Utah. The fact that both of these girls are my friends proves that my tastes are polarized. On one hand, I am drawn to the strangely exotic, but on the other hand, I need serene stability. Pari and Margie fill both of these needs. Where they differ most is in looks, personality, and attitude toward life. Let me explain.

Pari is stunning, almost embarrassingly so because everywhere we go, men turn around and give her that wow-did-you-see-that?-look. Her silky black hair hangs clear down to her waist and matches her round black snappy eyes. Everything about Pari is dark and sultry. Her skin is a deep bronze with two peach spots that blend into her cheeks, giving them a look of painted velvet. Pari wears heavy makeup, but somehow on her this bit of theatricality looks right. It gives her added boldness, extra electricity. When I look at Pari's profile, I always imagine that Cleopatra looked just like her, straight-nosed and imperious. Pari wears tight-fitting dresses and pants; nothing else would look right on her voluptuous shape. She would look silly and contrived in a fluffy little flowered piqué or a sternly tailored jumpsuit. I can imagine Pari looking only one way— enticingly erotic.

Margie's looks are the exact opposite of Pari's. Whereas Pari's appearance clamors for attention, Margie's automatically fades into the background. Her looks are refined but unassuming. Nothing about her stands out. She is simply a typical medium-haired, medium-skinned, medium-sized American girl. Only her eyes hint at remarkable inner qualities. They are a deep grey and when you look into them, they seem to contain secrets worth probing. Margie has a tranquility about her that is enviable. She is not beautiful; she is not sensual; but she is serene.

If Pari and Margie differ in looks, they differ even more in personality. One might say that Pari is a stormy sky flashing with lightning whereas Margie is a soft summer breeze. Whenever I meet Pari, she takes me by storm and hurls laughter, banter, and information at me. She is violent in her tastes, either loving ecstatically or hating bitterly. For instance, in her view all classical music is a deadly bore, whereas all jazz is magically entertaining. Every acquaintance we share is either canonized or damned; there are no medians or middle levels. When we go to a movie together, it is not unusual for Pari to take turns hitting me with suspense, clinging to me in despair, or weeping audibly if the ending is sad. Her own love affairs reflect her undulant personality. Time and again I have heard her hurling angry epithets at her latest lover only to end curled up on a couch next to him, purring like a Siamese cat. Pari's personality is as exotic as her looks.

Margie is best described as quietly content. She may never soar as high with ecstasy as does Pari, but neither will she sink as low with despair. She reminds me of one of those Rembrandt portraits where the face reflects infinite harmony and balance. When

I want excitement and titillation, I look for Pari, but when I want a quiet, sensible discussion, I go to Margie. Her influence on me is calming without being prissy. Her wry sense of humor, in fact, often sends me into gales of laughter because she is able to see the incongruity and hypocrisy in so much of the nonsense in our society today. "Come on, Cathy," she will gently scold when I get hostile toward my mother's nagging, "you know your mother wants only your best. Give her a break." So, she sets my life in proper perspective.

Where Pari and Margie differ most is in their philosophies of life. Pari worries me deeply because beyond her electric involvement in life is a gnawing feeling of futility. Twice already in her twenty-two years she has tried to commit suicide. These were not dramatic acts just to get attention, but acts of complete hopelessness. Despite her exotic beauty that holds many men hypnotized, Pari feels unloved, unwanted, and undesirable. When she is depressed, she hides by herself and reads Sylvia Plath or Anne Sexton. Nothing I or any of her friends say will cheer her up. The fact is that Pari has a sad, sick strain in her attitude toward life and unless she can overcome it, she will not survive to a satisfied old age. It hurts me to see Pari when she's down because her vulnerability reminds me of a magnificent bird whose wings have been clipped so that she can no longer fly or preen herself.

Margie's philosophy of life is much more stable than Pari's because it is based on a firm religious belief. Her Mormon background has led her to see life as purposeful and ultimately fulfilling when one does his duty. Margie accepts good times as well as bad times with equanimity. Often I envy her ability to face aggravations and sorrows without breaking down. Not that she is coldly stoical—no, she has plenty of emotions. But her emotions are controlled by her belief that a greater power than she is in charge of the universe. This supplies her with limitless confidence.

Pari and Margie are both my dearest friends. I love Pari because she is fascinating and alive, but I love Margie because she is strong and reliable.

For the sake of contrasting the unfair and unequal treatment of women throughout history, English novelist and critic Virginia Woolf (1882–1941) invents a fictitious but equally gifted sister of Shakespeare's and traces her life as she would probably have lived it in Elizabethan times.

Alternate Reading

Rewriting History
Virginia Woolf

1   It would be ambitious beyond my daring, I thought, looking about the shelves for books that were not there, to suggest to the students of those famous colleges* that they should re-write history, though I own that it often seems a little queer as it is, unreal, lop-sided; but why should they not add a supplement to history? calling it, of course, by some inconspicuous name so that women might figure there without impropriety? For one often catches a glimpse of them in the lives of the great, whisking away into the background, concealing, I sometimes think, a wink, a laugh, perhaps a tear. And, after all, we have lives enough of Jane Austen; it scarcely seems necessary to consider

---

*Newnham and Girton—women's colleges of Cambridge University.

again the influence of the tragedies of Joanna Baillie upon the poetry of Edgar Allen Poe; as for myself, I should not mind if the homes and haunts of Mary Russell Mitford were closed to the public for a century at least. But what I find deplorable, I continued, looking about the bookshelves again, is that nothing is known about women before the eighteenth century. I have no model in my mind to turn about this way and that.

2   Here am I asking why women did not write poetry in the Elizabethan age, and I am not sure how they were educated; whether they were taught to write; whether they had sitting-rooms to themselves; how many women had children before they were twenty-one; what, in short, they did from eight in the morning till eight at night. They had no money evidently; according to Professor Trevelyan they were married whether they liked it or not before they were out of the nursery, at fifteen or sixteen very likely. It would have been extremely odd, even upon this showing, had one of them suddenly written the plays of Shakespeare, I concluded, and I thought of that old gentleman, who is dead now, but was a bishop, I think, who declared that it was impossible for any woman, past, present, or to come, to have the genius of Shakespeare. He wrote to the papers about it. He also told a lady who applied to him for information that cats do not as a matter of fact go to heaven, though they have, he added, souls of a sort. How much thinking those old gentlemen used to save one! How the borders of ignorance shrank back at their approach! Cats do not go to heaven. Women cannot write the plays of Shakespeare.

3   Be that as it may, I could not help thinking, as I looked at the works of Shakespeare on the shelf, that the bishop was right at least in this; it would have been impossible, completely and entirely, for any woman to have written the plays of Shakespeare.

4   Let me imagine, since facts are so hard to come by, what would have happened had Shakespeare had a wonderfully gifted sister, called Judith, let us say. Shakespeare himself went, very probably—his mother was an heiress—to the grammar school, where he may have learnt Latin—Ovid, Virgil and Horace—and the elements of grammar and logic. He was, it is well known, a wild boy who poached rabbits, perhaps shot a deer, and had, rather sooner than he should have done, to marry a woman in the neighbourhood, who bore him a child rather quicker than was right. That escapade sent him to seek his fortune in London. He had, it seemed, a taste for the theatre; he began by holding horses at the stage door. Very soon he got work in the theatre, became a successful actor, and lived at the hub of the universe, meeting everyboy, knowing everybody, practising his art on the boards, exercising his wits in the streets, and even getting access to the palace of the queen.

5   Meanwhile his extraordinarily gifted sister, let us suppose, remained at home. She was as adventurous, as imaginative, as agog to see the world as he was. But she was not sent to school She had no chance of learning grammar and logic, let alone of reading Horace and Virgil. She picked up a book now and then, one of her brother's perhaps, and read a few pages. But then her parents came in and told her to mend the stockings or mind the stew and not moon about with books and papers. They would have spoken sharply but kindly, for they were substantial people who knew the conditions of life for a woman and loved their daughter—indeed, more likely than not she was the apple of her father's eye. Perhaps she scribbled some pages up in an apple loft on the sly, but was careful to hide them or set fire to them.

6   Soon, however, before she was out of her teens, she was to be betrothed to the son of a neighbouring wool-stapler. She cried out that marriage was hateful to her, and for that she was severely beaten by her father. Then he ceased to scold her. He begged her instead not to hurt him, not to shame him in this matter of her marriage. He would give her a chain of beads or a fine petticoat, he said; and there were tears in his eyes. How could she disobey him? How could she break his heart? The force of her own gift alone drove her to it. She made up a small parcel of her belongings, let herself down

by a rope one summer's night and took the road to London. She was not seventeen.

7   The birds that sang in the hedge were not more musical than she was. She had the quickest fancy, a gift like her brother's, for the tune of words. Like him, she had a taste for the theatre. She stood at the stage door; she wanted to act, she said. Men laughed in her face. The manager—a fat, loose-lipped man—guffawed. He bellowed something about poodles dancing and women acting—no woman, he said, could possibly be an actress. He hinted—you can imagine what. She could get no training in her craft. Could she even seek her dinner in a tavern or roam the street's at midnight? Yet her genius was for fiction and lusted to feed abundantly upon the lives of men and women and the study of their ways.

8   At last—for she was very young, oddly like Shakespeare the poet in her face, with the same grey eyes and rounded brows—at last Nick Greene the actor-manager took pity on her; she found herself with child by that gentlemen and so—who shall measure the heat and violence of the poet's heart when caught and tangled in a woman's body?—killed herself one winter's night and lies buried at some cross-roads where the omnibuses now stop outside the Elephant and Castle.

9   That, more or less, is how the story would run, I think, if a woman in Shakespeare's day had had Shakespeare's genius. But for my part, I agree with the deceased bishop, if such he was—it is unthinkable that any woman in Shakespeare's day should have had Shakespeare's genius. For genius like Shakespeare's is not born among labouring, uneducated, servile people. It was not born in England among the Saxons and the Britons. It is not born today among the working classes. How, then, could it have been born among women whose work began, according to Professor Trevelyan, almost before they were out of the nursery, who were forced to it by their parents and held to it by all the power of law and custom? Yet genius of a sort must have existed among women as it must have existed among the working classes. Now and again an Emily Brontë or a Robert Burns blazes out and proves its presence. But certainly it never got itself on paper. When, however, one reads of a witch being ducked, or a woman possessed by devils, of a wise woman selling herbs, or even of a very remarkable man who had a mother, then I think we are on the track of a lost novelist, a suppressed poet, of some mute and inglorious Jane Austen, some Emily Brontë who dashed her brains out on the moor or mopped and mowed about the highways crazed with the torture that her gift had put her to. Indeed, I would venture to guess that Anon, who wrote so many poems without signing them, was often a woman. . . .

1,380 words

Vocabulary

impropriety (1)   guffawed (7)
agog (5)   servile (9)

Questions

1. What does the author find deplorable about the place of women in recorded history?
2. According to Professor Trevelyan, at what age were Elizabethan women often married?
3. Having stated the opinion of the bishop—that it was impossible for any woman to have written like Shakespeare—why does the author then go on to give the same bishop's opinion on whether cats go to heaven?
4. What kind of paragraph is paragraph 3?
5. What was Shakespeare like as a boy?

6. How did Shakespeare's imaginary sister compare to her brother in temperament?
7. How did her education contrast with Shakespeare's?
8. To whom was Shakespeare's sister betrothed? How did she react to her betrothal?
9. In contrast to Shakespeare's reception at the theater in London, how was his sister received when she arrived and announced her ambition to become an actress?
10. Why did she commit suicide?
11. Since this is all an invention, why does the author mention the specific location of Judith Shakespeare's grave?
12. The author says that "Nick Greene the actor-manager took pity on her." In the light of what happened afterward, what tone do you think the author is using here?
13. What bases of contrast does the author use in comparing Shakespeare with his imaginary sister?

In his comparison of the behavior of rats in a labortatory experiment with that of humans in society, semanticist S. I. Hayakawa finds some interesting parallels.

Alternate Reading

Insoluble Problems

S. I. Hayakawa

1   Professor N.R.F. Maier of the University of Michigan performed a series of interesting experiments in which "neurosis" is induced in rats. The rats are first trained to jump off the edge of a platform at one of two doors. If the rat jumps to the right, the door holds fast, and it bumps its nose and falls into a net; if it jumps to the left, the door opens, and the rat finds a dish of food. When the rats are well trained to this reaction, the situation is changed. The food is put behind the other door, so that in order to get their reward they now have to jump to the right instead of to the left. (Other changes, such as marking the two doors in different ways, may also be introduced by the experimenter). If the rat fails to figure out the new system, so that each time it jumps it never knows whether it is going to get food or bump its nose, it finally gives up and refuses to jump at all. At this stage, Dr. Maier says, "Many rats prefer to starve rather than make a choice."

2   Next, the rats are forced to make a choice, being driven to it by blasts of air or an electric shock. "Animals which are induced to respond in the insoluble problem situation," says Dr. Maier, "settle down to a specific reaction (such as jumping *solely* at the left-hand door) which they continue to execute regardless of consequences. . . . The response chosen under these conditions becomes fixated. . . . Once the fixation appears, the animal is incapable of learning an adaptive response in this situation." When a reaction to the left-hand door is thus fixated, *the right-hand door may be left open so that the food is plainly visible.* Yet the rat, when pushed, *continues to jump to the left,* becoming more panicky each time. When the experimenter persists in forcing the rat to make choices, it may go into convulsions, racing around wildly,

138

injuring its claws, bumping into chairs and tables, then going into a state of violent trembling, until it falls into a coma. In this passive state, it refuses to eat, refuses to take any interest in anything; it can be rolled up into a ball or suspended in the air by its legs—the rat has ceased to care what happens to it. It has had a "nervous breakdown."*

3   It is the "insolubility" of the rat's problem that leads to its nervous breakdown, and, as Dr. Maier shows in his studies of disturbed children and adults, rats and human beings seem to go through pretty much the same stages. First, they are trained to make habitually a given choice when confronted by a given problem; secondly, they get a terrible shock when they find that the conditions have changed and that the choice doesn't produce the expected results; third, whether through shock, anxiety, or frustration, they may fixate on the original choice and continue to make that choice regardless of consequences; fourth, they sullenly refuse to act at all; fifth, when by external compulsion they are forced to make a choice, they again make the one they were originally trained to make—and again get a bump on the nose; finally *even with the goal visible in front of them,* to be attained simply by making a different choice, they go crazy out of frustration. They tear around wildly; they sulk in corners and refuse to eat; bitter, cynical, disillusioned, they cease to care what happens to them.

4   Is this an exaggerated picture? It hardly seems so. The pattern recurs throughout human life, from the small tragedies of the home to the world-shaking tragedies among nations. In order to cure her husband's faults, a wife may nag him. His faults get worse, so she nags him some more. Naturally his faults get worse still—and she nags him even more. Governed, like the rat, by a fixated reaction to the problem of her husband's faults, she can meet it only in one way. The longer she continues, the worse it gets, until they are both nervous wrecks.

5   Again, white people in a northern city, deploring the illiteracy and high crime rate among Negroes, segregate them, persecute them (it is well known that the police are almost always tougher on Negro suspects than on whites), and deny them opportunities for employment and advancement. The denial of opportunity perpetuates the illiteracy and the high crime rate, which in turn perpetuate the segregation, persecution, and denial of opportunity. The search for a way to break up this vicious circle taxes the best minds among those interested in orderly social change: city councilmen, educators, urban planners, Negro organizations, as well as state governments and federal authorities.

6   To cite another example, students trying to express themselves in writing may write poorly. In order to improve their writing, says the English teacher, I must teach them the fundamentals of grammar, spelling, and punctuation. By thus placing excessive emphasis on grammar and mechanics while ignoring the students' ideas, the teacher quickly destroys student interest in writing. That interest destroyed, the students write even more poorly. Thereupon the teacher redoubles his dose of grammer and mechanics. The students become increasingly bored and rebellious. Such students fill the ranks of "remedial English" classes in high school and college.

7   Again, a nation, believing that the only way to secure peace and dignity is through armed strength, may embark on a huge armaments program. The program arouses the fears of neighboring nations, so that they too increase their armaments to match those of the first nation. Anxiety and tension increase. It is clear, the first nation declares, that we shall continue to feel anxious about our national security so long as we are not adequately prepared for all emergencies; we must therefore *double* our armaments.

------

*Norman R. F. Maier, *Frustration: The Study of Behavior Without a Goal* (1949). See especially Chapter 2, "Experimental Evidence of Abnormal Behavior Reactions," and Chapter 6, "Comparison of Motivational and Frustration-Induced Behavior Problems in Children."

This naturally makes the neighboring nations even more anxious, so that they too double their armaments. Anxiety and tension increase even more. It is clear, the first nation declares, that our mistake has been to underestimate our defense needs. This time we must be *sure* to be sufficiently armed to preserve peace. We must *triple* our armaments. . . .

8   Of course these instances are oversimplified, but it is often because of vicious circles of this kind that we are unable to get at or do anything about the conditions that lead to disaster. The pattern is frequently recognizable; the goal may be in sight, attainable by a mere change in methods. Nevertheless, governed by fixated reactions, the rat "cannot" get food, the wife "cannot" cure her husband's faults, Negroes will have to wait two or three generations "until the time is ripe" for social change, and we "cannot afford" to stop devising and manufacturing weapons so deadly that they cannot be used without destroying civilization itself.

9   There is, however, an important difference between the insolubility of the rat's problems and the insolubility of human problems. Dr. Maier's rats were driven to their nervous breakdowns by problems more complicated than would naturally occur in a rat's environment. But human breakdowns are ordinarily caused by problems that human beings themselves have created: problems of religious and ethical belief; problems of money and credit and mortgages and trust funds and stock-market fluctuations; problems of man-made custom and etiquette and social organization and law.

10   Rats can hardly be blamed for not being able to solve problems set for them by Dr. Maier; there are limits to a rat's powers of abstraction. But there are no known limits to the human capacity to abstract and organize and make use of abstractions. Hence, if human beings find problems insoluble because of fixated reactions—if they are frustrated because they can respond in only one way, regardless of context or circumstances, to certain symbolically defined situations—they are functioning at less than full human capacity. They can be said, in Korzybski's suggestive phrase, to be "copying animals" in their reactions. Wendell Johnson summarized this idea aptly when he said, "To a mouse, cheese is cheese; that's why mousetraps work." . . .

1,345 words

Vocabulary

induced (1)	adaptive (2)
fixated (2)	perpetuate (5)

Questions

1. How does Professor Maier's experiment induce "neurosis" in rats?
2. How do the rats react when they have become neurotic?
3. Having made the rats neurotic, what does the experiment then force them to do?
4. How do the rats react to being forced?
5. What causes the rats to have a "nervous breakdown"?
6. What basis does the article use in comparing/contrasting rats and humans?
7. How does the wife who nags her husband react when his faults become worse?
8. What common failure is evident in the behavior of both humans and rats when faced with a visible and reachable goal?
9. How do the experiment findings apply to relations between blacks and whites? whites?
10. What important difference characterizes the insolubility of the rat's problems versus the insolubility of human problems?
11. How does Korzybski characterize people who develop fixed reactions?

C. Additional Writing Assignments

1. Compare the advantages of being old with the advantages of being young.
2. Develop an essay based on the following controlling idea: "Ignorance is different from stupidity."
3. Write an essay contrasting envy with jealousy.
4. After establishing the bases of your comparison, write an essay comparing a compact car with a large car, indicating the advantages of one over the other.
5. Think of an acquaintance who is totally different from you. Write an essay developing this contrast based on selected points of difference.
6. Write an essay comparing a teacher you find boring and one you think is interesting and stimulating.
7. From your travels in the United States and abroad, pick two cities or towns that are totally different from one another. Develop an essay describing these differences.
8. From your general knowledge of U.S. history, compare the eighteenth and twentieth centuries on three bases—for example, hygiene, education, women's rights—supplying examples that stress their differences.
9. Write an essay delineating the differences between a romantic and a realistic movie. Supply examples of each.
10. What do good statesmen and good ship captains have in common? Write an essay comparing the two.

9
Process

*First of all, keep your dream journal in a notebook
small enough to carry with you all the time.*

A. Reading for Ideas

As you read through the story "How Mr. Hogan Robbed a Bank," you might admire the meticulousness of Mr. Hogan's method even if you are repelled by his ethics. Ask yourself whether the means ever justifies an end. In other words, if the method is right, is the purpose also right? Also, think of some task you would like to accomplish, and see if you can put together similar meticulous, easy-to-follow directions for this task.

How Mr. Hogan Robbed a Bank
John Steinbeck

1   On Saturday before Labor Day, 1955, at 9:04½ A.M., Mr. Hogan robbed a bank. He was forty-two years old, married, and the father of a boy and a girl, named John and Joan, twelve and thirteen respectively. Mrs. Hogan's name was Joan and Mr. Hogan's name was John, but since they called themselves Papa and Mama that left their names free for the children, who were considered very smart for their ages, each having jumped a grade in school. The Hogans lived at 215 East Maple Street, in a brown-shingle house with white trim—there are two. 215 is the one across from the street light and it is the one with the big tree in the yard, either oak or elm—the biggest tree in the whole street, maybe in the whole town.

2   John and Joan were in bed at the time of the robbery, for it was Saturday. At 9:10 A.M., Mrs. Hogan was making the cup of tea she always had. Mr. Hogan went to work early. Mrs. Hogan drank her tea slowly, scalding hot, and read her fortune in the tea leaves. There was a cloud and a five-pointed star with two short points in the bottom of the cup, but that was at 9:12 and the robbery was all over by then.

3   The way Mr. Hogan went about robbing the bank was very interesting. He gave it a great deal of thought and had for a long time, but he did not discuss it with anyone. He just read his newspaper and kept his own counsel. But he worked it out to his own satisfaction that people went to too much trouble robbing banks and that got them in a

mess. The simpler the better, he always thought. People went in for too much hullabaloo and hanky-panky. If you didn't do that, if you left hanky-panky out, robbing a bank would be a relatively sound venture—barring accidents, of course, of an improbable kind, but then they could happen to a man crossing the street or anything. Since Mr. Hogan's method worked fine, it proved that his thinking was sound. He often considered writing a little booklet on his technique when the how-to rage was running so high. He figured out the first sentence, which went: "To successfully rob a bank, forget all about hanky-panky."

4   Mr. Hogan was not just a clerk at Fettucci's grocery store. He was more like the manager. Mr. Hogan was in charge, even hired and fired the boy who delivered groceries after school. He even put in orders with the salesmen, sometimes when Mr. Fettucci was right in the store too, maybe talking to a customer. "You do it, John," he would say and he would nod at the customer, "John knows the ropes. Been with me —how long you been with me, John?"

5   "Sixteen years."

6   "Sixteen years. Knows the business as good as me. John, why he even banks the money."

7   And so he did. Whenever he had a moment, Mr. Hogan went into the storeroom on the alley, took off his apron, put on his necktie and coat, and went back through the store to the cash register. The checks and bills would be ready for him inside the bankbook with a rubber band around it. Then he went next door and stood at the teller's window and handed the checks and bankbook through to Mr. Cup and passed the time of day with him too. Then, when the bankbook was handed back, he checked the entry, put the rubber band around it, and walked next door to Fettucci's grocery and put the bankbook in the cash register, continued on to the storeroom, removed his coat and tie, put on his apron, and went back into the store ready for business. If there was no line at the teller's window, the whole thing didn't take more than five minutes, even passing the time of day.

8   Mr. Hogan was a man who noticed things, and when it came to robbing the bank, this trait stood him in good stead. He had noticed, for instance, where the big bills were kept right in the drawer under the counter and he had noticed also what days there were likely to be more than other days. Thursday was payday at the American Can Company's local plant, for instance, so there would be more then. Some Fridays people drew more money to tide them over the weekend. But it was even Steven, maybe not a thousand dollars difference, between Thursdays and Fridays and Saturday mornings. Saturdays were not terribly good because people didn't come to get money that early in the morning, and the bank closed at noon. But he thought it over and came to the conclusion that the Saturday before a long weekend in the summer would be the best of all. People going on trips, vacations, people with relatives visting, and the bank closed Monday. He thought it out and looked, and sure enough the Saturday morning before Labor Day the cash drawer had twice as much money in it—he saw it when Mr. Cup pulled out the drawer.

9   Mr. Hogan thought about it during all that year, not all the time, of course, but when he had some moments. It was a busy year too. That was the year John and Joan had the mumps and Mrs. Hogan got her teeth pulled and was fitted for a denture. That was the year when Mr. Hogan was Master of the Lodge, with all the time that takes. Larry Shield died that year—he was Mrs. Hogan's brother and was buried from the Hogan house at 215 East Maple. Larry was a bachelor and had a room in the Pine Tree House and he played pool nearly every night. He worked at the Silver Diner but that closed at nine and so Larry would go to Louie's and play pool for an hour. Therefore, it was a surprise when he left enough so that after funeral expenses there were twelve hundred dollars

left. And even more surprising that he left a will in Mrs. Hogan's favor, but his double-barreled twelve-gauge shotgun he left to John Hogan, Jr. Mr. Hogan was pleased, although he never hunted. He put the shotgun away in the back of the closet in the bathroom, where he kept his things, to keep it for young John. He didn't want children handling guns and he never bought any shells. It was some of that twelve hundred that got Mrs. Hogan her dentures. Also, she bought a bicycle for John and a doll buggy and walking-talking doll for Joan—a doll with three changes of dresses and a little suitcase, complete with play make-up. Mr. Hogan thought it might spoil the children, but it didn't seem to. They made just as good marks in school and John even got a job delivering papers. It was a very busy year. Both John and Joan wanted to enter the W. R. Hearst National "I Love America" Contest and Mr. Hogan thought it was almost too much, but they promised to do the work during their summer vacation, so he finally agreed.

II

10   During that year, no one noticed any difference in Mr. Hogan. It was true, he was thinking about robbing the bank, but he only thought about it in the evening when there was neither a Lodge meeting nor a movie they wanted to go to, so it did not become an obsession and people noticed no change in him.

11   He had studied everything so carefully that the approach of Labor Day did not catch him unprepared or nervous. It was hot that summer and the hot spells were longer than usual. Saturday was the end of two weeks heat without a break and people were irritated with it and anxious to get out of town, although the country was just as hot. They didn't think of that. The children were excited because the "I Love America" Essay Contest was due to be concluded and the winners announced, and the first prize was an all-expense-paid two days trip to Washington, D.C., with every fixing—hotel room, three meals a day, and side trips in a limousine—not only for the winner, but for an accompanying chaperone; visit to the White House—shake hands with the President—everything. Mr. Hogan thought they were getting their hopes too high and he said so.

12   "You've got to be prepared to lose," he told his children. "There're probably thousands and thousands entered. You get your hopes up and it might spoil the whole autumn. Now I don't want any long faces in this house after the contest is over."

13   "I was against it from the start," he told Mrs. Hogan. That was the morning she saw the Washington Monument in her teacup, but she didn't tell anybody about that except Ruth Tyler, Bob Tyler's wife. Ruthie brought over her cards and read them in the Hogan kitchen, but she didn't find a journey. She did tell Mrs. Hogan that the cards were often wrong. The cards had said Mrs. Winkle was going on a trip to Europe and the next week Mrs. Winkle got a fishbone in her throat and choked to death. Ruthie, just thinking out loud, wondered if there was any connection between the fishbone and the ocean voyage to Europe. "You've got to interpret them right." Ruthie did say she saw money coming to the Hogans.

14   "Oh, I got that already from poor Larry," Mrs. Hogan explained.

15   "I must have got the past and future cards mixed," said Ruthie. "You've got to interpret them right."

16   Saturday dawned a blaster. The early morning weather report on the radio said "Continued hot and humid, light scattered rain Sunday night and Monday." Mrs. Hogan said, "Wouldn't you know? Labor Day." And Mr. Hogan said, "I'm sure glad we didn't plan anything." He finished his egg and mopped the plate with his toast. Mrs. Hogan said, "Did I put coffee on the list?" He took the paper from his handkerchief pocket and consulted it. "Yes, coffee, it's here."

17   "I had a crazy idea I forgot to write it down," said Mrs. Hogan. "Ruth and I are going to Altar Guild this afternoon. It's at Mrs. Alfred Drake's. You know, they just came to town. I can't wait to see their furniture."

18 "They trade with us," said Mr. Hogan. "Opened an account last week. Are the milk bottles ready?"

19 "On the porch."

20 Mr. Hogan looked at his watch just before he picked up the bottles and it was five minutes to eight. He was about to go down the stairs, when he turned and looked back through the opened door at Mrs. Hogan. She said, "Want something, Papa?"

21 "No," he said. "No," and he walked down the steps.

22 He went down to the corner and turned right on Spooner, and Spooner runs into Main Street in two blocks, and right across from where it runs in, there is Fettucci's and the bank around the corner and the alley beside the bank. Mr. Hogan picked up a hand-bill in front of Fettucci's and unlocked the door. He went through to the storeroom, opened the door to the alley, and looked out. A cat tried to force its way in, but Mr. Hogan blocked it with his foot and leg and closed the door. He took off his coat and put on his long apron, tied the strings in a bowknot behind his back. Then he got the broom from behind the counter and swept out behind the counters and scooped the sweepings into a dustpan; and, going through the storeroom, he opened the door to the alley. The cat had gone away. He emptied the dustpan into the garbage can and tapped it smartly to dislodge a piece of lettuce leaf. Then he went back to the store and worked for a while on the order sheet. Mrs. Clooney came in for a half a pound of bacon. She said it was hot and Mr. Hogan agreed. "Summers are getting hotter," he said.

23 "I think so myself," said Mrs. Clooney. "How's Mrs. standing up?"

24 "Just fine," said Mr. Hogan. "She's going to Altar Guild."

25 "So am I. I just can't wait to see their furniture," said Mrs. Clooney, and she want out.

III

26 Mr. Hogan put a five-pound hunk of bacon on the slicer and stripped off the pieces and laid them on wax paper and then he put the wax paper-covered squares in the cooler cabinet. At ten minutes to nine, Mr. Hogan went to a shelf. He pushed a spaghetti box aside and took down a cereal box, which he emptied in the little closet toilet. Then, with a banana knife, he cut out the Mickey Mouse mask that was on the back. The rest of the box he took to the toilet and tore up the cardboard and flushed it down. He went into the store then and yanked a piece of string loose and tied the ends through the side holes of the mask and then he looked at his watch—a large silver Hamilton with black hands. It was two minutes to nine.

27 Perhaps the next four minutes were his only time of nervousness at all. At one minute to nine, he took the broom and went out to sweep the sidewalk and he swept it very rapidly—was sweeping it, in fact, when Mr. Warner unlocked the bank door. He said good morning to Mr. Warner and a few seconds later the bank staff of four emerged from the coffee shop. Mr Hogan saw them across the street and he waved at them and they waved back. He finished the sidewalk and went back in the store. He laid his watch on the little step of the cash register. He sighed very deeply, more like a deep breath than a sigh. He knew that Mr. Warner would have the safe open now and he would be carrying the cash trays to the teller's window. Mr. Hogan looked at the watch on the cash register step. Mr. Kenworthy paused in the store entrance, then shook his head vaguely and walked on and Mr. Hogan let out his breath gradually. His left hand went behind his back and pulled the bowknot on his apron, and then the black hand on his watch crept up on the four-minute mark and covered it.

28 Mr. Hogan opened the charge account drawer and took out the store pistol, a silver-colored Iver Johnson .38. He moved quickly to the storeroom, slipped off his apron, put on his coat, and stuck the revolver in his side pocket. The Mickey Mouse mask he shoved up under his coat where it didn't show. He opened the alley door and looked up and down and stepped quickly out, leaving the door slightly ajar. It is sixty feet to where

the alley enters Main Street, and there he paused and looked up and down and then he turned his head toward the center of the street as he passed the bank window. At the bank's swinging door, he took out the mask from under his coat and put it on. Mr. Warner was just entering his office and his back was to the door. The top of Will Cup's head was visible through the teller's grill.

29 Mr. Hogan moved quickly and quietly around the end of the counter and into the teller's cage. He had the revolver in his right hand now. When Will Cup turned his head and saw the revolver, he froze. Mr. Hogan slipped his toe under the trigger of the floor alarm and he motioned Will Cup to the floor with the revolver and Will went down quick. Then Mr. Hogan opened the cash drawer and with two quick movements he piled the large bills from the tray together. He made a whipping motion to Will on the floor, to indicate that he should turn over and face the wall, and Will did. Then Mr. Hogan stepped back around the counter. At the door of the bank, he took off the mask, and as he passed the window he turned his head toward the middle of the street. He moved into the alley, walked quickly to the storeroom, and entered. The cat got in. It watched him from a pile of canned goods cartons. Mr. Hogan went to the toilet closet and tore up the mask and flushed it. He took off his coat and put on his apron. He looked out into the store and then moved to the cash register. The revolver went back into the charge account drawer. He punched No Sale and, lifting the top drawer, distributed the stolen money underneath the top tray and then pulled the tray forward and closed the register, and only then did he look at his watch and it was 9:07½.

30 He was trying to get the cat out of the storeroom when the commotion boiled out of the bank. He took his broom and went out on the sidewalk. He heard all about it and offered his opinion when it was asked for. He said he didn't think the fellow could get away—where could he get to? Still, with the holiday coming up—

31 It was an exciting day. Mr. Fettucci was as proud as though it were his bank. The sirens sounded around town for hours. Hundreds of holiday travelers had to stop at the roadblocks set up all around the edge of town and several sneaky-looking men had their cars searched.

32 Mrs. Hogan heard about it over the phone and she dressed earlier than she would have ordinarily and came to the store on her way to Altar Guild. She hoped Mr. Hogan would have seen or heard something new, but he hadn't. "I don't see how the fellow can get away," he said.

33 Mrs. Hogan was so excited, she forgot her own news. She only remembered when she got to Mrs. Drake's house, but she asked permission and phoned the store the first moment she could. "I forgot to tell you. John's won honorable mention."

34 "What?"
"In the 'I Love America' Contest."
"What did he win?"
"Honorable mention."
"Fine. Fine—Anything come with it?"

35 "Why, he'll get his picture and his name all over the country. Radio too. Maybe even television. They've already asked for a photograph of him."

36 "Fine," said Mr. Hogan. "I hope it don't spoil him." He put up the receiver and said to Mr. Fettucci, "I guess we've got a celebrity in the family."

37 Fettucci stayed open until nine on Saturdays. Mr. Hogan ate a few snacks from cold cuts, but not much, because Mrs. Hogan always kept his supper warming.

38 It was 9:05, or :06, or :07, when he got back to the brown-shingle house at 215 East Maple. He went in through the front door and out to the kitchen where the family was waiting for him.

39 "Got to wash up," he said, and went up to the bathroom. He turned the key in the

bathroom door and then he flushed the toilet and turned on the water in the basin and tub while he counted the money. Eight thousand three hundred and twenty dollars. From the top shelf of the storage closet in the bathroom, he took down the big leather case that held his Knight Templar's uniform. The plumed hat lay there on its form. The white ostrich feather was a little yellow and needed changing. Mr. Hogan lifted out the hat and pried the form up from the bottom of the case. He put the money in the form and then he thought again and removed two bills and shoved them in his side pocket. Then he put the form back over the money and laid the hat on top and closed the case and shoved it back on the top shelf. Finally he washed his hands and turned off the water in the tub and the basin.

40   In the kitchen, Mrs. Hogan and the children faced him, beaming, "Guess what some young man's going on?"

41   "What?" asked Mr. Hogan.

"Radio," said John. "Monday night. Eight o'clock."

"I guess we got a celebrity in the family," said Mr. Hogan.

42   Mrs. Hogan said, "I just hope some young lady hasn't got her nose out of joint."

43   Mr. Hogan pulled up to the table and stretched his legs. "Mama, I guess I got a fine family," he said. He reached in his pocket and took out two five-dollar bills. He handed one to John. "That's for winning," he said. He poked the other bill at Joan. "And that's for being a good sport. One celebrity and one good sport. What a fine family!" He rubbed his hands together and lifted the lid of the covered dish. "Kidneys," he said. "Fine."

44   And that's how Mr. Hogan did it.

3,442 words

Questions

1. What steps are taken by Mr. Hogan to rob the bank? State them in the order in which they occur.
2. What point does this story make?
3. What are some examples of the typical middle-class life of the Hogans?
4. What detail in paragraph 9 clearly indicates Mr. Hogan's double standard?
5. What is your response to the sentence in paragraph 3, ". . . if you left hanky-panky out, robbing a bank would be a relatively sound venture. . . "?

Tract
William Carlos Williams

1   I will teach you my townspeople
how to perform a funeral—
for you have it over a troop
of artists—
unless one should scour the world—
you have the ground sense necessary.

2   See! the hearse leads.
I begin with a design for a hearse.
For Christ's sake not black—
nor white either—and not polished!

Let it be weathered—like a farm wagon—
with gilt wheels (this could be
applied fresh at small expense)
or no wheels at all:
a rough dray to drag over the ground.

3   Knock the glass out!
My God—glass, my townspeople!
For what purpose? Is it for the dead
to look out or for us to see
how well he is housed or to see
the flowers or the lack of them—
or what?
To keep the rain and snow from him?
He will have a heavier rain soon:
pebbles and dirt and what not.
Let there be no glass—
and no upholstery phew!
and no little brass rollers
and small easy wheels on the bottom—
my townspeople what are you thinking of?
A rough plain hearse then
with gilt wheels and no top at all.
On this the coffin lies
by its own weight.
                    No wreaths please—
especially no hot house flowers.
Some common memento is better,
something he prized and is known by:
his old clothes—a few books perhaps—
God knows what! You realize
how we are about these things
my townspeople—
something will be found—anything
even flowers if he had come to that.
So much for the hearse.

4   For heaven's sake though see to the driver!
Take off the silk hat! In fact
that's no place at all for him—
up there unceremoniously
dragging our friend out to his own dignity!
Bring him down—bring him down!
Low and inconspicuous! I'd not have him ride
on the wagon at all—damn him—
the undertaker's understrapper!
Let him hold the reins
and walk at the side
and inconspicuously too!

5   Then briefly as to yourselves:
Walk behind—as they do in France,
seventh class, or if you ride
Hell take curtains! Go with some show
of inconvenience; sit openly—
to the weather as to grief.
Or do you think you can shut grief in?
What—from us? We who have perhaps
nothing to lose? Share with us
share with us—it will be money
in your pockets.
                    Go now
I think you are ready.

Vocabulary

memento (3)
unceremoniously (4)
understrapper (4)

Questions

1. In giving advice on how to perform a funeral, what major steps does the speaker advocate? List them in the order in which they are mentioned.
2. What is the poet's general purpose in advocating this kind of funeral?
3. In stanza 2, why does the speaker suggest the gilt wheels, applied fresh?
4. Why doesn't the speaker want the coffin to ride along smoothly (stanza 3)?
5. Instead of wreaths or hothouse flowers, what does the speaker suggest as a decoration for the coffin? Why?
6. What objections does the speaker have to the undertaker's driving the carriage in a silk top hat?
7. What is the most important thought contained in the final stanza?

B. How to Write a Process Paper

Describing a process, often called *process analysis,* is a common and indispensable assignment. A process paper involves step-by-step directions, such as giving someone directions to your home or writing instructions for your roommate on how to care for your plants while you're on vacation.

Writing Assignment

Choose a process with which you are thoroughly familiar, and give a specific and detailed set of instructions for doing it. Here are some sample process topics: "How to detect counterfeit money," "How to train a dog in obedience," "How to make French crêpes," "How to tie macramé wall hangings," "How to get ready for a camping trip," "How to balance a budget," "How to produce an antiflu serum."

Specific Instructions

1. BEGIN WITH A CLEAR STATEMENT OF PURPOSE.   A process paper should begin by announcing the directions it intends to give: "My paper will explain the steps in assembling a dictionary." Or "The purpose of this paper is to show the easiest way to gather a good collection of rock music." Or "What follows is a summary of the basic steps involved in the scientific method of investigation." This initial announcement alerts the reader to the purpose of your process paper, giving him or her a context for the individual steps that follow.

2. ASSEMBLE ALL THE INFORMATION NECESSARY TO THE COMPLETE PROCESS.   It is easier to give directions or explain the separate steps of a project when you have accurate and complete information on the process. If the process is unfamiliar and the information not at hand, you will need to do some research. Gather *all* the information you can. It is better to assemble more information than you will actually use than to overlook a detail that might have helped explain a step in the process. Collect the facts, and refer to them as you write the process.

3. DECIDE ON THE ORDER OF YOUR STEPS.   Once the facts are collected, their order of presentation will usually become apparent from the process. For example, if you are analyzing the steps in planting camelias, common sense tells you that the first step is preparation of the soil. Similarly, if you are writing a paper on how an American president is elected to office, you would begin not with his inauguration, but with the election of local delegates in the primaries.

A reasonable way to begin a process paper is to outline all the steps in the order they will logically occur and to include those details necessary for a clear presentation of each step. An example of such an outline follows:

Controlling idea: My purpose is to list the basic steps in writing a book review.

   I. Read the book carefully.
      A. Look for major ideas.
      B. Mark essential pages.
  II. Think about the book.
      A. Figure out the purpose of the book.
      B. Judge the book according to how well it has fulfilled its purpose.
      C. Make mental notes of both strengths and weaknesses.
 III. Write a fair review.
      A. State the purpose of the book.
      B. Give a brief summary of the book.
      C. Explain major passages, using quotations to give a flavor of the author's style.
      D. Pass judgment on the book.

Although the sequence of a process may be extremely simple, consisting of only one or two steps, each step may be complicated by many details. For example, the process of writing good advertising copy contains two steps complicated by detail:

Controlling idea: The purpose of this paper is to show how to write good advertising copy.

  I. Begin with a strong headline.
    A. Flag down all possible customers.
    B. Include key words associated with the product.
    C. Appeal to the reader's self-interest.
    D. Make the product sound new.
 II. Write the body as if you were answering someone's questions.
    A. Go straight to the point.
    B. Be factual and specific.
    C. Include testimonials.
    D. Give the reader some helpful advice.
    E. Write in colloquial language.

The outline makes the process easier to write by highlighting each step along with its cluster of details. Without the aid of the outline, the writer could easily become muddled and confused.

4. EACH INDIVIDUAL STEP MUST BE CLEAR AND COMPLETE.   Each step in the process must be clearly enumerated and explained; one poorly explained step can confuse an entire process. For example, suppose the third step in producing an antivenom for snake bites is to collect the serum by bleeding a horse that has been injected with the venom. A clear explanation of this step, with all the necessary details beautifully aligned, is of little use if step 1—collecting the venom by milking a snake —is never explained. A clear step-by-step presentation of material is crucial in a process paper.

In this article, Alex Haley, the co-author of *The Autobiography of Malcolm X,* tells of the step-by-step process he used in tracking down the origins of his African ancestry.

Professional Model

My Search for Roots: A Black American's Story
Alex Haley

1   My earliest memory is of Grandma, Cousin Georgia, Aunt Plus, Aunt Liz and Aunt Till talking on our front porch in Henning, Tenn. At dusk, these wrinkled, graying old ladies would sit in rocking chairs and talk, about slaves and massas and plantations —pieces and patches of family history, passed down across the generations by word of mouth. "Old-timey stuff," Mamma would exclaim. She wanted no part of it.

2   The furthest-back person Grandma and the others ever mentioned was "the African." They would tell how he was brought here on a ship to a place called "Naplis" and sold as a slave in Virginia. There he mated with another slave, and had a little girl named Kizzy.

3   When Kizzy became four or five, the old ladies said, her father would point out to her various objects and name them in his native tongue. For example, he would point to a guitar and make a single-syllable sound, *ko*. Pointing to a river that ran near the plantation, he'd say "Kamby Bolongo." And when other slaves addressed him as Toby—the name given him by his massa—the African would strenuously reject it, insisting that his name was "Kin-tay."

4   Kin-tay often told Kizzy stories about himself. He said that he had been near his village in Africa, chopping wood to make a drum, when he had been set upon by four men, overwhelmed, and kidnapped into slavery. When Kizzy grew up and became a mother, she told her son these stories, and he in turn would tell *his* children. His granddaughter became my grandmother, and she pumped that saga into me as if it were plasma, until I knew by rote the story of the African, and the subsequent generational wending of our family through cotton and tobacco plantations into the Civil War and then freedom.

5   At 17, during World War II, I enlisted in the Coast Guard, and found myself a messboy on a ship in the Southwest Pacific. To fight boredom, I began to teach myself to become a writer. I stayed on in the service after the war, writing every single night, seven nights a week, for eight years before I sold a story to a magazine. My first story in the Digest was published in June 1954: "The Harlem Nobody Knows." At age 37, I retired from military service, determined to be a full-time writer. Working with the famous Black Muslim spokesman, I did the actual writing for the book *The Autobiography of Malcolm X.*

6   I remembered still the vivid highlights of my family's story. Could this account possibly be documented for a book? During 1962, between other assignments, I began following the story's trail. In plantation records, wills, census records, I documented bits here, shreds there. By now, Grandma was dead; repeatedly I visited other sources, most notably our encyclopedic matriarch, "Cousin Georgia" Anderson in Kansas City, Kan. I went as often as I could to the National Archives in Washington, and the Library of Congress, and the Daughters of the American Revolution Library.

7   By 1967, I felt I had the seven generations of the U.S. side documented. But the unknown quotient in the riddle of the past continued to be those strange, sharp, angular sounds spoken by the African himself. Since I lived in New York City, I began going to the United Nations lobby, stopping Africans and asking if they recognized the sounds. Every one of them listened to me, then quickly took off. I can well understand: me with a Tennessee accent, trying to imitate African sounds!

8   Finally, I sought out a linguistics expert who specialized in African languages. To him I repeated the phrases. The sound "Kin-tay," he said, was a Mandinka tribe surname. And "Kamby Bolongo" was probably the Gambia River in Mandinka dialect. Three days later, I was in Africa.

9   In Banjul, the Capital of Gambia, I met with a group of Gambians. They told me how for centuries the history of Africa has been preserved. In the older villages of the back country there are old men, called *griots,* who are in effect living archives. Such men know and, on special occasions, tell the cumulative histories of clans, or families, or villages, as those histories have long been told. Since my forefather had said his name was Kin-tay (properly spelled Kinte), and since the Kinte clan was known in Gambia, they would see what they could do to help me.

10   I was back in New York when a registered letter came from Gambia. Word had been passed in the back country, and a *griot* of the Kinte clan had, indeed, been found. His name, the letter said, was Kebba Kanga Fofana. I returned to Gambia and organized a safari to locate him.

11   There is an expression called "the peak experience," a moment which, emotionally, can never again be equaled in your life. I had mine, that first day in the village of Juffure, in the back country in black West Africa.

12   When our 14-man safari arrived within sight of the village, the people came flocking

out of their circular mud huts. From a distance I could see a small, old man with a pillbox hat, an off-white robe and an aura of "somebodiness" about him. The people quickly gathered around me in a kind of horseshoe pattern. The old man looked piercingly into my eyes, and he spoke in Mandinka. Translation came from the interpreters I had brought with me.

13   "Yes, we have been told by the forefathers that there are many of us from this place who are in exile in that place called America."

14   Then the old man, who was 73 rains of age—the Gambian way of saying 73 years old, based upon the one rainy season per year—began to tell me the lengthy ancestral history of the Kinte clan. It was clearly a formal occasion for the villagers. They had grown mouse-quiet, and stood rigidly.

15   Out of the *griot's* head came spilling lineage details incredible to hear. He recited who married whom, two or even three centuries back. I was struck not only by the profusion of details, but also by the Biblical pattern of the way he was speaking. It was something like, "—and so-and-so took as a wife so-and-so, and begat so-and-so. . . ."

16   The *griot* had talked for some hours, and had got to about 1750 in our calendar. Now he said, through an interpreter, "About the time the king's soldiers came, the eldest of Omoro's four sons, Kunta, went away from this village to chop wood—and he was never seen again. . . ."

17   Goose pimples came out on me the size of marbles. He just had no way in the world of knowing that what he told me meshed with what I'd heard from the old ladies on the front porch in Henning, Tenn. I got out my notebook, which had in it what Grandma had said about the African. One of the interpreters showed it to the others, and they went to the *griot,* and they all got agitated. Then the *griot* went to the people, and *they* all got agitated.

18   I don't remember anyone giving an order, but those 70-odd people formed a ring around me, moving counterclockwise, chanting, their bodies close together. I can't begin to describe how I felt. A woman broke from the circle, a scowl on her jet-black face, and came charging toward me. She took her baby and almost roughly thrust it out at me. The gesture meant "Take it!" and I did, clasping the baby to me. Whereupon the woman all but snatched the baby away. Another woman did the same with her baby, then another, and another.

19   A year later, a famous professor at Harvard would tell me: "You were participating in one of the oldest ceremonies of humankind, called 'the laying on of hands.' In their way, these tribespeople were saying to you, 'Through this flesh, which is us, we are you and you are us.'"

20   Later, as we drove out over the back-country road, I heard the staccato sound of drums. When we approached the next village, people were packed alongside the dusty road, waving, and the din from them welled louder as we came closer. As I stood up in the Land Rover, I finally realized what it was they were all shouting: "Meester Kinte! Meester Kinte!" In their eyes I was the symbol of all black people in the United States whose forefathers had been torn out of Africa while theirs remained.

21   Hands before my face, I began crying—crying as I have never cried in my life. Right at that time, crying was all I could do.

22   I went then to London. I searched and searched, and finally in the British Parliamentary records I found that the "king's soldiers" mentioned by the *griot* referred to a group called "Colonel O'Hare's forces," which had been sent up the Gambia River in 1767 to guard the then British-operated James Fort, a slave fort.

23   I next went to Lloyds of London, where doors were opened for me to research among all kinds of old maritime records. I pored through the records of slave ships that had sailed from Africa. Volumes upon volumes of these records exist. One afternoon about 2:30, during the seventh week of searching, I was going through my 1023rd set of ship

records. I picked up a sheet that had on it the reported movements of 30 slave ships, my eyes stopped at No. 18, and my glance swept across the column entries. This vessel had sailed directly from the Gambia River to America in 1767; her name was the *Lord Ligonier;* and she had arrived in Annapolis (Naplis) the morning of September 29, 1767.

24   Exactly 200 years later, on September 29, 1967, there was nowhere in the world for me to be except standing on a pier at Annapolis, staring sea-ward across those waters over which my great-great-great-great-grandfather had been brought. And there in Annapolis I inspected the microfilmed records of the *Maryland Gazette.* In the issue of October 1, 1767, on page 3, I found an advertisement informing readers that the *Lord Ligonier* had just arrived from the River Gambia, with "a cargo of choice, healthy SLAVES" to be sold at auction the following Wednesday.

25   In the years since, I have done extensive research in 50 or so libraries, archives and repositories on three continents. I spent a year combing through countless documents to learn about the culture of Gambia's villages in the 18th and 19th centuries. Desiring to sail over the same waters navigated by the *Lord Ligonier,* I flew to Africa and boarded the freighter *African Star.* I forced myself to spend the ten nights of the crossing in the cold, dark cargo hold, stripped to my underwear, lying on my back on a rough, bare plank. But this was sheer luxury compared to the inhuman ordeal suffered by those millions who, chained and shackled, lay in terror and in their own filth in the stinking darkness through voyages averaging 60 to 70 days.

1,851 words

Vocabulary

saga (4)	matriarch (6)	aura (12)	welled (20)
plasma (4)	quotient (7)	meshed (17)	maritime (23)
wending (4)	linguistics (8)	staccato (20)	microfilmed (24)
encyclopedic (6)	archives (9)	din (20)	repositories (25)

Questions

1. What main steps did Haley take in tracing his family roots? List each step.
2. On what important information does the success of the entire process rest?
3. What characteristic of the author stands out above all else?
4. Why do you suppose the author wanted to duplicate the voyage of the African?

This process essay is a step-by-step explanation of how to keep a dream journal.

Student Model

How to Keep a Dream Journal
Deborah Lott

In keeping a dream journal you not only record the mental events of sleep, but also indirectly take account of your life. Those who have kept journals for some time are amazed at how much their journals tell about past events, which at the time seemed unrelated to their dreams. Keeping a dream journal is not just an after-the-fact passive logging of dreams, but a process that will affect your dreams, and may also increase your creativity.

First of all, keep your dream journal in a notebook small enough to carry with you all the time. Thus, if you remember some aspect of a dream, you can immediately record it. At night, put the journal beside your bed along with several pens. If you awaken during the night, write down what you were dreaming, or at least the image that was in your mind when you awakened.

In the morning, wake either naturally or to music; the jolt of an alarm will blast a dream right out of memory. Allow yourself at least fifteen minutes to work on your journal before getting out of bed. If you are one of those people who "never remember dreams," set a music alarm for every two hours, beginning two hours after you go to bed. If the anxiety of this setup does not create insomnia, you should begin to remember at least fragments.

Upon awakening in the morning, don't move. Shut your eyes and attempt to recall an image. This image will trigger other images if not whole dreams. Don't try too hard—fighting too strenuously to hold on to an image may have the opposite of the desired effect and block all memory.

Write the dream on every other line of a page, recalling as much as you can as quickly as you can. Write whatever comes to mind even if there are gaps in the sequence of images, even if a scene from one dream floats into the middle of another. Indicate gaps, discrepancies, or uncertainties with a slash or question mark. If a digression occurs to you, don't deny it, asterisk the point in the narrative at which it occurs, skip two lines and write it in parentheses. The longer you keep a journal, the more spontaneously associations and digressions will occur. These may be the real meat of the journal and are not to be spurned.

Describe the dream in detail without lingering over cloudy portions. It is crucial to include as much detail as possible because no matter how vivid the dream seems at the moment, it will quickly fade. It is a common delusion to think that "shorthand" will suffice, but words laden with significance when you write them can seem absolutely flat two hours later. Recalling their importance can be as difficult as conveying the significance of an image in your own dream to someone else.

Capture the texture of the dream. What colors and shapes predominate? Are there distortions in spatial relations or in perspective? Does time pass at a normal rate or is it warped? Write descriptions as if you were delineating a foreign terrain to an alien visitor. Use drawings. Re-create the atmosphere of the dream, *what it really felt like*. As you do this, you will remember more of the dream. The process of writing the journal will be much like the process of dreaming itself—associations engender other associations; images metamorphose into other images.

Say it all. Defy the internal censors. Do not attempt to make logical stories out of your dreams or to rationalize your behavior. If something is irrational, express it that way; tax the language to express the dream. Putting a dream into words makes it seem more real; thus, you may find some resistance to expressing negative or frightening dreams. Language tends to formalize dreams, so that once written, you will always remember the dream in those words. You may wish to express some passage in two different ways when neither feels completely "right"; retain them both. Once the dream is on paper, you will be interpreting the language as much as the original experience.

Reread the narrative, filling in details, making additional notes, such as "resistance in writing this," "cloudier than the rest of the dream," "very disturbing," etc. on the blank line below.

You may then wish to engage in some tentative analysis or commentary about the dream. This process will affect your dreams. One writer was first infatuated with Freud, then Jung, and finally Reich. He reported: "When I wrote Jungian analyses, my dreams were full of huge, black Oak trees, cloaked female figures, and caves. When I wrote Freudian analyses, my dreams changed until I had phalluses coming out of my ears!

With Reich I had the most visceral dreams and woke up every morning with a backache."

If you impose an analytical methodology, juxtapose the interpretation to the dream as a sort of story or myth in itself, not as a final explanation. Your journal will be more fruitful if you retain some perspective about deriving symbolic equivalences: "House equals psyche." "Big, black bear equals Daddy," etc.

The most exciting part of keeping a journal is seeing the way that dreams comment on one another, how one dream provides insight into another and into the events of your life. What once might have seemed totally unconnected dreams, if you had even remembered them, reveal fascinating connections when read together in a journal. Consider these entries:

> January 4, 1976.
> Floods, everywhere in the city. Especially I remember the Tujunga area that was burned in the last forest fire. It went on for several days. Water was on the floor.

> January 12, 1976.
> I had a flash of a dream in which I remembered a previous residence of Billy's and mine, the bedroom of which had many plants and an interesting architectural feature which I liked, a low box filled with soil* in which grew many plants.

> January 18, 1976
> I was in a bookstore like the Bodhi Tree. I looked at astrology books although they didn't have anything I really wanted. Then I was looking at some books on a bottom shelf near the floor. They had illustrated covers. One entitled *Jungle Doctor* showed a doctor operating on someone. I felt a sudden tugging on my heart. "I too wish to spend my life's work saving souls," I thought.

In her dreams, fire appears in association with fertility, power, and destruction. Water imagery is also prominent, being associated with fertility, and again as with fire, with destruction. Might some connection be drawn between the planter on the floor in which plants are grown in "soul" and the book about "saving souls" on the bottom shelf near the floor, in the bookstore? The jungle appears again, in proximity to fertility and to disaster:

> January 27, 1976
> I was visiting a "jungle farm." It was a residence of the strangest beasts, like Dr. Doolittle's companions. Then, the rains came—heavy, thick brown rain, turning the grounds to mud. I am reminded of the flood they had at Africa USA in '65 or '66 with the heroic tales of large beasts helping small ones to safety. Again the rains and floods!

Seen together, these dreams reveal a personal grammar of images: fire, flood, disaster, salvation—appearing in an infinite variety of representations in dream.

Once you have a body of dreams, read them all over often before going to sleep. Consider the language. What about puns? Freudian slips? Idiosyncracies of phrasing? Using a word not in your everyday vocabulary? Rewrite the endings to dreams. Rework dream plots. Program yourself to resolve a conflict left unresolved in your dreams to date. Consider the dream journal as providing a wealth of personal imagery upon which to draw for all your writing.

---

*Instead of the word *soil* she had written the word *soul*.

Euell Gibbons was a naturalist who gained a reputation from his talks and writings about wilderness survival, and the benefits of wild nuts, herbs, vegetables, and berries. The selection that follows is an excerpt from Mr. Gibbon's book *Stalking the Wild Asparagus,* published in 1962.

Alternate Reading

How to Find a Wild Bees' Nest
Euell Gibbons

1   While fishing in a pond near my camp, I noticed that a nearby patch of blooming milkweed was swarming with honeybees, so I set out to improvise some tracking device. In camp, I found a square of masonite that had been painted bright red and an aluminum cake cover that fitted well over my large square of old black honeycomb. I made a sirup by putting one cup of sugar in a bottle with two cups of water and shaking it until it dissolved. Returning to the milkweed patch, I rubbed the top of the honeycomb with a corner of the cork from the anise bottle, filled the empty comb with sirup and placed it on the square of masonite, while I rested on a stone. Then I returned to my fishing.

2   A half-hour later I checked my bee bait and, sure enough, the bees had deserted the flowers and were swarming over the sugar-filled comb. I stood and watched them come and go for many minutes, until I was satisfied that they were all leaving in the same direction. I kept them in sight as long as my eyes could pick up the flash of sun on their wings, and, by sighting over my honeycomb in the direction they were going, I picked out some landmarks to establish my beeline.

3   Now I knew in which direction the parent colony lay, but I also wanted to know how far away it was. Taking a pinch of powdered carpenter's chalk, I mixed it with a drop of water with the tip of a camel's hair brush. Then, when a bee had his head buried in a honey cell, I dabbed his rear end with the blue chalk. He didn't like it much, but, after doing an angry dance across the honeycomb, he took on a load of sirup and flew away. I noted the exact time that he left and anxiously awaited his return. In just over six minutes, there was my blue-bottomed bee, upending himself on the honeycomb and drinking up more sirup. According to my mentor, this meant that the tree was less than a mile distant, and the trail led first across an open field.

4   Now it was time to make the first crucial move in the actual tracking process. Waiting until a dozen or more bees were on the honeycomb at the same time, I suddenly clapped on the aluminum cake cover, picked up the board with my trapped bees and carried it across the field to a fence post which I had picked out as being directly on the beeline. Balancing the red masonite on the top of the post, I waited a few minutes for the bees to settle down, then lifted the cover. They flew out, circling and figure-eighting in all directions, so I really couldn't see in which direction they flew when they finally left.

5   A long ten minutes went by. I refilled the honeycomb, renewed the anise with a light touch and waited while the anxious interval passed. Then a bee darted down and buzzed suspiciously around the bait. Another one joined him. Then temptation overcame one and he dropped down on the comb. In twenty minutes the bees were coming and going regularly. I even saw my blue-spotted bee come in for a load, which satisfied me that I was still running the same beeline.

6   I made three more moves along the line. On the last move, the bees almost deserted me. When they finally settled down to carrying away sirup, they moved off in the opposite

157

direction toward which they had formerly been going. This was it! Now I knew that the tree was between this spot and my former setup. Sighting back along the line I spotted a likely looking beech tree. Walking to it, I circled it again and again, looking first high, then low, without seeing a thing. Finally, when I was about ready to give up, I caught a flash of the setting sun on wings as a bee came in for a landing on the side of a large limb. I had found my bee tree.

580 words

Vocabulary

masonite (1) mentor (3)
anise (1)

Questions

1. How early in the essay does the reader find out what process Euell Gibbons is describing?
2. What is the first step in the process of tracking the bees' nest?
3. How does the author improvise a syrup to use as bait for the bees?
4. Where were the bees when the author first noticed them?
5. How does the author establish the beeline?
6. Why does the author put blue chalk on one of the bees?
7. What is the first crucial move in the actual tracking process?
8. How long did it take before the bees were coming and going regularly between the piece of masonite and the hive?
9. How does the author reassure himself that he is running the same beeline with the same group of bees?
10. On the last move along the beeline, what does the author find out?

In this selection, Mayleas gives the prospective job-hunter a series of systematic steps to follow. The article first appeared in *Empire Magazine* and later, in condensed form, in *The Reader's Digest*.

Alternate Reading

How to Land the Job You Want

Davidyne Mayleas

1   Louis Albert, 39, lost his job as an electrical engineer when his firm made extensive cutbacks. He spent two months answering classified ads and visiting employment agencies—with zero results. Albert might still be hunting if a friend, a specialist in the employment field, had not shown him how to be his own job counselor. Albert learned how to research unlisted openings, write a forceful résumé, perform smoothly in an interview, even transform a turndown into a job.

2   Although there seemed to be a shortage of engineering jobs, Albert realized that he still persuaded potential employers to see him. This taught him something—that his naturally outgoing personality might be as great an asset as his engineering degree.

When the production head of a small electronics company told him that they did not have an immediate opening, Albert told his interviewer, "You people make a fine product. I think you could use additional sales representation—someone like me who understands and talks electrical engineer's language, and who enjoys selling." The interviewer decided to send Albert to a senior vice president. Albert got a job in sales.

3   You too can be your own counselor if you put the same vigorous effort into *getting* a job as you would into *keeping* one. Follow these three basic rules, developed by placement experts:

4   1. FIND THE HIDDEN JOB MARKET.   Classified ads and agency listings reveal only a small percentage of available jobs. Some of the openings that occur through promotions, retirements and reorganization never reach the personnel department. There are three ways to get in touch with this hidden market:

5   *Write a strong résumé with a well-directed cover letter and mail it to the appropriate department manager in the company where you'd like to work.* Don't worry whether there's a current opening. Many managers fill vacancies by reviewing the résumés already in their files. Dennis Mollura, press-relations manager in the public-relations department of American Telephone and Telegraph, says, "In my own case, the company called me months after I sent in my résumé."

6   *Get in touch with people who work in or know the companies that interest you.* Jobs are so often filled through personal referral that Charles R. Lops, executive employment manager of the J.C. Penney Co., says, "Probably our best source for outside people comes from recommendations made by Penney associates themselves."

7   *"Drop in" on the company.* Lillian Reveille, employment manager of Equitable Life Assurance Society of the United States, reports: "A large percentage of the applicants we see are 'walk-ins'—and we do employ many of these people."

8   2. LOCATE HIDDEN OPENINGS.   This step requires energy and determination to make telephone calls, see people, do research, and to keep moving despite turndowns.

9   *Contact anyone who may know of openings,* including relatives, friends, teachers, bank officers, insurance agents—anyone you know in your own or an adjacent field. When the teachers' union and employment agencies produced no teaching openings, Eric Olson, an unemployed high-school math instructor, reviewed his talent and decided that where an analytical math mind was useful, there he'd find a job. He called his insurance agent, who set up an interview with the actuarial department of one of the companies he represented. They hired Olson.

10   It's a good idea to contact not only professional or trade associations in your field, but also your local chamber of commerce and people involved in community activities. After Laura Bailey lost her job as retirement counselor in a bank's personnel department, she found a position in customer relations in another bank. Her contact: a member of the senior-citizens club that Mrs. Bailey ran on a volunteer basis.

11   *Use local or business-school libraries.* Almost every field has its own directory of companies, which provides names, addresses, products and/or services, and lists officers and other executives. Write to the company president or to the executive to whom you'd report. The vice president of personnel at Warner-Lambert Co. says, "When a résumé of someone we could use—now or in the near future—shows up 'cold' in my in-basket, that's luck for both of us."

12   *Consult telephone directories.* Sometimes the telephone company will send you free the telephone directories of various cities. Also, good-sized public libraries often have many city directories. Fred Lewis, a cabinet maker, checked the telephone directories of nine different cities where he knew furniture was manufactured. At the end of five weeks he had a sizable telephone bill, some travel expenses—and ten interviews which resulted in three job offers.

13   3. AFTER YOU FIND THE OPENING, GET THE JOB.   The applicants who actually get hired are those who polish these six job-getting skills to perfection:

14   *Compose a better résumé.* A résumé is a self-advertisement, designed to get you an interview. Start by putting yourself in an employer's place. Take stock of your job history and personal achievements. Make an inventory of your skills and accomplishments that might be useful from the employer's standpoint. Choose the most important and describe them in words that stress accomplishments. Avoid such phrases as ''my duties included . . .'' Use action words like planned, sold, trained, managed.

15   Ask a knowledgeable business friend to review your résumé. Does it stress accomplishment rather than duties? Does it tell an employer what you can do for him? Can it be shortened? (One or two pages should suffice.) Generally, it's not wise to mention salary requirements.

16   *Write a convincing cover letter.* While the résumé may be a copy, the cover letter must be personal. Sy Mann, director of research for Aceto Chemical Co., says: ''When I see a mimeographed letter that states, 'Dear Sir, I'm sincerely interested in working for your company,' I wonder, 'How many other companies got this valentine?' '' Use the name and title of the person who can give you the interview, and be absolutely certain of accuracy here. Using a wrong title or misspelling a prospective employer's name may route your correspondence directly to an automatic turndown.

17   *Prepare specifically for each interview.* Research the company thoroughly; know its history and competition. Try to grasp the problems of the job you're applying for. For example, a line in an industry journal that a food company was ''developing a new geriatric food'' convinced one man that he should emphasize his marketing experience with vitamins rather than with frozen foods.

18   You'll increase your edge by anticipating questions the interviewer might raise. Why do you want to work for us? What can you offer us that someone else cannot? Why did you leave your last position? What are your salary requirements?

19   An employer holds an interview to get a clearer picture of your work history and accomplishments, and to look for characteristics he considers valuable. These vary with jobs. Does the position require emphasis on attention to detail or on creativity? Perserverance or aggressiveness? Prior to the interview decide what traits are most in demand. And always send a thank-you note immediately after the interview.

20   *Follow up.* They said you would hear in a week; now it's two. Call them. Don't wait and hope. Hope and act.

21   *Supply additional information.* That's the way Karen Halloway got her job as fashion director with a department store. ''After my interview I sensed that the merchandise manager felt I was short on retail experience. So I wrote to him describing the 25 fashion shows I'd staged yearly for the pattern company I'd worked for.''

22   *Don't take no for an answer.* Hank Newell called to find out why he had been turned down. The credit manager felt he had insufficient collection experience. Hank thanked him for his time and frankness. The next day, Hank called back saying, ''My collection experience is limited, but I don't think I fully emphasized my training in credit checking.'' They explored this area and found Hank still not qualified. But the credit manager was so impressed with how well Hank took criticism that when Hank asked him if he could suggest other employers, he did, even going so far as to call one. Probing for leads when an interview or follow-up turns negative is a prime technique for getting personal referrals.

23   The challenge of finding a job, approached in an active, organized, realistic way, can be a valuable personal adventure. You can meet new people, develop new ideas about yourself and your career goals, and improve your skills in dealing with individuals. These in turn can contribute to your long-term job security.

1,410 words

adjacent (9)
actuarial (9)

Questions

1. What is the purpose of the example given in paragraph 1?
2. What are the three basic rules of job-hunting?
3. What is the hidden job market?
4. What are the three basic ways of getting in touch with the hidden job market?
5. What three steps can you take to locate hidden openings?
6. After you find the opening, what six steps can you take to ensure that you'll get the job?
7. Whose point of view should you take in composing a résumé?
8. What sort of phrases should you avoid in writing a résumé?
9. How can you prepare specifically for each interview?
10. Examine paragraph 17. What technique does the author use there and throughout in clarifying her suggestions?

C. Additional Writing Assignments

1. If you don't already know, find out the steps involved in getting ready for a trip to Japan. Write them down as if you were explaining them to a friend.
2. You want to bake a Thanksgiving turkey, complete with stuffings and gravy. Find out the procedure, and develop it into a process essay.
3. Write an essay explaining the several steps involved in writing a research paper. Begin with finding a subject and end with the final copy typed on white bond paper.
4. Write a 500-word essay summarizing the steps that led to President Nixon's resignation during the Watergate scandal.
5. Delineate the major steps and details involved in writing a good contrast paper.
6. Choose your favorite hobby or sport, and write a process paper on how it is best pursued.
7. Pretend that you are planning your wedding. Develop an essay in which you analyze chronologically the major events involved.
8. If you were a first-grade teacher, what events would you plan for the first day of school? Explain them in a process essay that could serve as your lesson plans.
9. Find out how to transplant a lemon tree. Write the instructions in the form of a process essay.
10. Through library research, accumulate the proper information to write an essay in which you narrate the major events that led to one of the following: the Battle of Waterloo, the bombing of Pearl Harbor, the war in Vietnam.

10

Classification

Love is divisible into four types.

A. Reading for Ideas

"The Cries of Love" reveals a most peculiar kind of love—a love expressed through hostility and mean tricks. As you read the story, ask yourself why Hattie and Alice, both desperately lonely, treat each other with such malice. From your own experience and from observing the experience of others, pick out all the different kinds of love that you have observed. Try to group them into three or four main categories.

The Cries of Love
Patricia Highsmith

1   Hattie pulled the little chain on the reading lamp, drew the covers over her shoulders and lay tense, waiting for Alice's sniffs and coughs to subside.

"Alice?" she said.

2   No response. Yes, she was sleeping already, though she said she never closed an eye before the clock struck eleven.

3   Hattie eased herself to the edge of the bed and slowly put out a white-stockinged foot. She twisted round to look at Alice, of whom nothing was visible except a thin nose projecting between the ruffle of her nightcap and the sheet pulled over her mouth. She was quite still.

4   Hattie rose gently from the bed, her breath coming short with excitement. In the semi-darkness she could see the two sets of false teeth in their glasses of water on the bed table. She giggled, nervously.

5   Like a white ghost she made her way across the room, past the Victorian settle. She stopped at the sewing table, lifted the folding top and groped among the spools and pattern papers until she found the scissors. Then, holding them tightly, she crossed the room again. She had left the wardrobe door slightly ajar earlier in the evening, and it swung open noiselessly. Hattie reached a trembling hand into the blackness, felt the two woollen coats, a few dresses. Finally she touched a fuzzy thing, and lifted the hanger down. The scissors slipped out of her hand. There was a clatter, followed by her half-suppressed laughter. She peeked round the wardrobe door at Alice, motion-

less on the bed; Alice was rather hard of hearing.

6   With her white toes turned up stiffly, Hattie climbed to the easy chair by the window where a bar of moonlight slanted, and sat down with the scissors and the angora sweater in her lap. In the moonlight her face gleamed, toothless and demoniacal. She examined the sweater in the manner of a person who toys with a piece of steak before deciding where to put his knife.

7   It was really a lovely sweater. Alice had received it the week before from her niece as a birthday present. Alice would never have indulged herself in such a luxury. She was happy as a child with the sweater and had worn it every day over her dresses.

8   The scissors cut purringly up the soft wool sleeves, between the wristbands and the shoulders. She considered. There should be one more cut. The back, of course. But only about a foot long, so it wouldn't be immediately visible.

9   A few seconds later, she had put the scissors back into the table, hung the sweater in the wardrobe, and was lying under the covers. She heaved a tremendous sigh. She thought of the gaping sleeves, of Alice's face in the morning. The sweater was quite beyond repair, and she was immensely pleased with herself.

10   They were awakened at eight-thirty by the hotel maid. It was a ritual that never failed: three bony raps on the door and a bawling voice with a hint of insolence, "Eight-thirty! You can get breakfast now!" Then Hattie, who always woke first, would poke Alice's shoulder.

11   Mechanically they sat up on their respective sides of the bed and pulled their nightgowns over their heads, revealing clean white undergarments. They said nothing. Seven years of co-existence had pared their conversation to an economical core.

12   This morning, however, Hattie's mind was on the sweater. She felt self-conscious, but she could think of nothing to say or do to relieve the tension, so she spent more time than usual with her hair. She had a braid nearly two feet long that she wound around her head, and every morning she undid it for its hundred strokes. Her hair was her only vanity. Finally, she stood shifting uneasily, pretending to be fastening the snaps on her dress.

13   Alice seemed to take an age at the washbasin, gargling with her solution of tepid water and salt. She held stubbornly to water and salt in the mornings, despite Hattie's tempting bottle of red mouthwash sitting on the shelf.

14   "What are you giggling at now?" Alice turned from the basin, her face wet and smiling a little.

15   Hattie could say nothing, looked at the teeth in the glass on the bed table and giggled again. "Here's your teeth." She reached the glass awkwardly to Alice. "I thought you were going down to breakfast without them."

"Now when did I *ever* go off without my teeth, Hattie?"

16   Alice smiled to herself. It was going to be a good day, she thought. Mrs. Crumm and her sister were back from a weekend, and they could all play gin rummy together in the afternoon. She walked to the wardrobe in her stockinged feet.

17   Hattie watched as she took down the powder-blue dress, the one that went best with the beige angora sweater. She fastened all the little buttons in front. Then she took the sweater from the hanger and put one arm into a sleeve.

18   "Oh!" she breathed painfully. Then like a hurt child her eyes almost closed and her face twisted petulantly. Tears came quickly down her cheeks. "H-Hattie—"

19   Hattie smirked, uncomfortable yet enjoying herself thoroughly. "Well, I do know!" she exclaimed. "I wonder who could have done a trick like that!" She went to the bed and sat down, doubled up with laughter.

20   "Hattie, you did this," Alice declared in an unsteady voice. She clutched the sweater to her. "Hattie, you're just wicked!"

21 Lying across the bed, Hattie was almost hysterical. "You know I didn't now, Alice . . . hah-haw! . . . Why do you think I'd—" Her voice was choked off by incontrollable laughing.

22 Hattie lay there several minutes before she was calm enough to go down to breakfast. And when she left the room, Alice was sitting in the big chair by the window, sobbing, her face buried in the angora sweater.

23 Alice did not come down until she was called for lunch. She chatted at the table with Mrs. Crumm and her sister and took no notice of Hattie. Hattie sat opposite her, silent and restless, but not at all sorry for what she had done. She could have endured days of indifference on Alice's part without feeling the slightest remorse.

24 It was a beautiful day. After lunch, they went with Mrs. Crumm, her sister, and the hotel hostess, Mrs. Holland, and sat in Gramercy Park.

25 Alice pretended to be absorbed in her book. It was a detective story by her favorite author, borrowed from the hotel's circulating library. Mrs. Crumm and her sister did most of the talking. A weekend trip provided conversation for several afternoons, and Mrs. Crumm was able to remember every item of food she had eaten for days running.

26 The monotonous tones of the voices, the warmth of the sunshine, lulled Alice into half-sleep. The page was blurred to her eyes.

27 Earlier in the day, she had planned to adopt an attitude toward Hattie. She should be cool and aloof. It was not the first time Hattie had committed an outrage. There had been the ink spilt on her lace tablecloth months ago, the day before she was going to give it to her niece . . . And her missing volume of Tennyson that was bound in morocco. She was sure Hattie had it, somewhere. She decided that that evening she should calmly pack her bag, write Hattie a note, short but well worded, and leave the hotel. She would go to another hotel in the neighborhood, let it be known through Mrs. Crumm where she was, and have the satisfaction of Hattie's coming to her and apologizing. But the fact was, she was not at all sure Hattie would come to her, and this embarrassing possibility prevented her from taking such a dangerous course. What if she had to spend the rest of her life alone? It was much easier to stay where she was, to have a pleasant game of gin rummy in the afternoons, and to take out her revenge in little ways. It was also more ladylike, she consoled herself. She did not think beyond this, of the particular times she would say or do things calculated to hurt Hattie. The opportunities would just come of themselves.

28 Mrs. Holland nudged her. "We're going to get some ice cream now. Then we're going to play some gin rummy."

29 "I was just at the most exciting part of the book." But Alice rose with the others and was almost cheerful as they walked to the drugstore.

30 Alice won at gin rummy, and felt pleased with herself. Hattie, watching her uneasily all day, was much relieved when she decreed speaking terms again.

31 Nevertheless, the thought of the ruined sweater rankled in Alice's mind, and prodded her with a sense of injustice. Indeed, she was ashamed of herself for being able to take it as lightly as she did. It was letting Hattie walk over her. She wished she could muster a really strong hatred.

32 They were in their room reading at nine o'clock. Every vestige of Hattie's shyness or pretended contrition had vanished.

33 "Wasn't it a nice day?" Hattie ventured.

"Um-hm." Alice did not raise her head.

"Well," Hattie made the inevitable remark through the inevitable yawn, "I think I'll be going off to bed."

34 And a few minutes later they were both in bed, propped up by four pillows, Hattie with the newspaper and Alice with her detective story. They were silent for a while, then Hattie adjusted her pillows and lay down.

35   ''Good night, Alice.''
    ''Good night.''

36   Soon Alice pulled out the light, and there was absolute silence in the room except for the soft ticking of the clock and the occasional purr of an automobile. The clock on the mantel whirred and began to strike ten.

37   Alice lay open-eyed. All day her tears had been restrained, and now she began to cry. But they were not the childish tears of the morning, she felt. She wiped her nose on the top of the sheet.

38   She raised herself on one elbow. The darkish braid of hair outlined Hattie's neck and shoulder against the white bedclothes. She felt very strong, strong enough to murder Hattie with her own hands. But the idea of murder passed from her mind as swiftly as it had entered. Her revenge had to be something that would last, that would hurt, something that Hattie must endure and that she herself could enjoy.

39   Then it came to her, and she was out of bed, walking boldly to the sewing table, as Hattie had done twenty-four hours before . . . and she was standing by the bed, bending over Hattie, peering at her placid, sleeping face through her tears and her shortsighted eyes. Two quick strokes of the scissors would cut through the braid, right near the head. But Alice lowered the scissors just a little to where the braid was tighter. She squeezed the scissors with both hands, made them chew on the braid, as Hattie slowly awakened with the touch of cold metal on her neck. *Whack,* and it was done.

40   ''What is it? . . . What—?'' Hattie said.
    The braid was off, lying like a dark gray snake on the bed cover.
    ''Alice!'' Hattie said, and groped at her neck, felt the stiff ends of the braid's stump. ''Alice!''

41   Alice stood a few feet away, staring at Hattie who was sitting up in bed, and suddenly Alice was overcome with mirth. She tittered, and at the same time tears started in her eyes. ''You did it to me!'' she said. ''You cut my sweater!''

42   Alice's instant of self-defense was unnecessary, because Hattie was absolutely crumpled and stunned. She started to get out of bed, as if to go to the mirror, but sat back again, moaning and weeping, feeling of the horrid thing at the end of her hair. Then she lay down again, still moaning into her pillow. Alice stayed up, and sat finally in the easy chair. She was full of energy, not sleepy at all. But toward dawn, when Hattie slept, Alice crept between the covers.

43   Hattie did not speak to her in the morning, and did not look at her. Hattie put the braid away in a drawer. Then she tied a scarf around her head to go down to breakfast, and in the dining room, Hattie took another table from the one at which Alice and she usually sat. Alice saw Hattie speaking to Mrs. Holland after breakfast.

44   A few minutes later, Mrs. Holland came over to Alice, who was reading in a corner of the lounge.

45   ''I think,'' Mrs. Holland said gently, ''that you and your friend might be happier if you had separate rooms for a while, don't you?''

46   This took Alice by surprise, though at the same time she had been expecting something worse. Her prepared statement about the spilt ink, the missing Tennyson, and the ruined angora subsided in her, and she said quite briskly, ''I do indeed, Mrs. Holland. I'm agreeable to anything Hattie wishes.''

47   Alice offered to move out, but it was Hattie who did. She moved to a smaller room three doors down on the same floor.

48   That night, Alice could not sleep. It was not that she thought about Hattie particularly, or that she felt in the least sorry for what she had done—she decidedly didn't—but that things, the room, the darkness, even the clock's ticking, were so different because she was alone. A couple of times during the night, she heard a footstep outside the door, and thought it might be Hattie coming back, but it was only people visiting the W. C. at

the end of the hall. It occurred to Alice that she could knock on Hattie's door and apologize but, she asked herself, why should she?

49   In the morning, Alice could tell from Hattie's appearance that she hadn't slept either. Again, they did not speak or look at each other all day, and during the gin rummy and tea at four, they managed to take different tables. Alice slept very badly that night also, and blamed it on the lamb stew at dinner, which she was having trouble digesting. Hattie would have the same trouble, perhaps, as Hattie's digestion was, if anything, worse.

50   Three more days and nights passed, and the ravages of Hattie's and Alice's sleepless nights became apparent on their faces. Mrs. Holland noticed, and offered Alice some sedatives, which Alice politely declined. She had her pride, she wasn't going to show anyone she was disturbed by Hattie's absence, and besides, she thought it was weak and self-indulgent to yield to sleeping pills—though perhaps Hattie would.

51   On the fifth day, at three in the afternoon, Hattie knocked on Alice's door. Her head was still swathed in a scarf, one of three that Hattie possessed, and this was one Alice had given her last Christmas.

52   "Alice, I want to say I'm sorry, if *you're* sorry," Hattie said, her lips twisting and pursing as she fought to keep back the tears.

53   This was or should have been a moment of triumph for Alice. It was, mainly, she felt, though something—she was not sure what—tarnished it a little, made it not quite pure victory. "I am sorry about your braid, if you're sorry about my sweater," Alice replied.

54   "I am," said Hattie.

"And about the ink stain on my tablecloth and . . . where is my volume of Alfred Lord Tennyson's poems?"

"I have not got it," Hattie said, still tremulous with tears.

"You haven't *got* it?"

"No," Hattie declared positively.

55   And in a flash, Alice knew what had really happened: Hattie had at some point in some place, destroyed it, so it was in a way true now that she hadn't "got" it. Alice knew, too, that she must not stick over this, that she ought to forgive and forget it, though neither emotionally nor intellectually did she come to this decision: she simply knew it, and behaved accordingly, saying, "Very well, Hattie. You may move back, if you wish."

56   Hattie then moved back, though at the card game at four-thirty they still sat at separate tables.

57   Hattie, having swallowed the biggest lump of pride she had ever swallowed in knocking on Alice's door and saying she was sorry, slept very much better back in the old arrangement, but suffered a lurking sense of unfairness. After all, a book of poems and a sweater could be replaced, but could her hair? Alice had got back at her all right, and then some. The score was not quite even.

58   After a few days, Hattie and Alice were back to normal, saying little to each other but outwardly being congenial, taking meals and playing cards at the same table. Mrs. Holland seemed pleased.

59   It crossed Alice's mind to buy Hattie some expensive hair tonic she saw in a Madison Avenue window one day while on an outing with Mrs. Holland and the group. But Alice didn't. Neither did she buy a "special treatment" for hair which she saw advertised in the back of a magazine, guaranteed to make the hair grow thicker and faster, but Alice read every word of the advertisements.

60   Meanwhile, Hattie struggled in silence with her stump of braid, brushed her hair faithfully as usual, but only when Alice was having her bath or was out of the room, so Alice would not see it. Nothing in Alice's possession now seemed important enough for Hattie's vengeance. But Christmas was coming soon. Hattie determined to wait patiently and see what Alice got then.

2,986 words

Vocabulary

petulantly (18)   vestige (32)   self-indulgent (50)
decreed (30)   subsided (46)   congenial (58)
rankled (31)

Questions

1. How would you characterize the kind of love dramatized in this story? Describe it as accurately as you can.
2. Hattie destroys Alice's angora sweater; Alice cuts off Hattie's braid. What do these two acts have in common?
3. Do you think it would be best if Alice and Hattie lived in separate rooms? Why? Why not?
4. What point do you think the author makes?
5. What is the meaning of the title?

Frankie and Johnny

Anonymous

1 Frankie and Johnny were lovers, great God how they could love!
Swore to be true to each other, true as the stars up above.
He was her man, but he done her wrong.

2 Frankie she was his woman, everybody knows.
She spent her forty dollars for Johnny a suit of clothes.
He was her man, but he done her wrong.

3 Frankie and Johnny went walking, Johnny in his brand new suit.
"O good Lawd," said Frankie, "but don't my Johnny look cute?"
He was her man, but he done her wrong.

4 Frankie went down to the corner, just for a bucket of beer.
Frankie said, "Mr. Bartender, has my loving Johnny been here?
He is my man, he wouldn't do me wrong."

5 "I don't want to tell you no story, I don't want to tell you no lie,
But your Johnny left here an hour ago with that lousy Nellie
  Blye.
He is your man, but he's doing you wrong."

6 Frankie went back to the hotel, she didn't go there for fun,
For under her red kimono she toted a forty-four gun.
He was her man, but he done her wrong.

7 Frankie went down to the hotel and looked in the window so
  high.
And there was her loving Johnny a-loving up Nellie Blye.
He was her man, but he was doing her wrong.

8   Frankie threw back her kimono, took out that old forty-four.
Root-a-toot-toot, three times she shot, right through the
    hardwood door.
He was her man, but he was doing her wrong.

9   Johnny grabbed off his Stetson, crying, "O, Frankie don't shoot!"
Frankie pulled that forty-four, went root-a-toot-toot-toot-toot.
He was her man, but he done her wrong.

10   "Roll me over gently, roll me over slow,
Roll me on my right side, for my left side hurts me so,
I was her man, but I done her wrong."

11   With the first shot Johnny staggered, with the second shot he
    fell;
When the last bullet got him, there was a new man's face in hell.
He was her man, but he done her wrong.

12   "O, bring out your rubber-tired hearses, bring out your
    rubber-tired hacks;
Gonna take Johnny to the graveyard and ain't gonna bring him
    back.
He was my man, but he done me wrong."

13   "O, put me in that dungeon, put me in that cell,
Put me where the northeast wind blows from the southeast
    corner of hell.
I shot my man, cause he done me wrong!"

Questions

1. What kind of love is depicted in this ballad? What are its characteristics?
2. What are the main ideas of the plot in this poem?
3. On whose side of the quarrel is the narrator? How can you tell?
4. Is the narrated situation a piece of impossible fiction and romance, or could it actually happen today?
5. Assuming that you dislike crimes of passion, what alternative reaction do you suggest for a woman whose lover or husband cheats on her?
6. What other kinds of devotion besides passion have you noticed among couples?

B. How to Write a Classification

Classifying means sorting people, objects, data, things, or ideas into types and groups. An essay that does this is called a *classification*. A simple example is the way we group people into the upper, middle, and lower classes. Another example is the division of work into white collar work, blue collar work, and common labor. Classification is one way of bringing order to a chaotic world. The more orderly we are, the more carefully we tend to classify the elements of the world around us. We divide cutlery into spoons, knives, and forks, and we classify ribbons according to their colors. Library books are arranged by subject, with history books on one shelf, philosophy books on another, and science books on yet another.

Writing Assignment

Write a 500-word essay classifying love into its major types. Think of all the possible types of love, and group them into three or four major categories. Begin with a clear statement of your classification, such as: "So far in life I have experienced three kinds of love: parental devotion, deep friendship, and romantic attraction." Then develop this controlling idea by discussing each type separately.

Specific Instructions

1. BASE YOUR CLASSIFICATION ON A SINGLE PRINCIPLE. If your classification is to have consistency and clarity, it must be made according to a single principle. Study the following categories of winter sports:

    a. Ice sports
    b. Snow sports
    c. African sports

Clearly, the third category of sports does not belong with the first two. The first two categories are based on the principle of surface, while the third is based on the principle of location.

    Your assignment is to classify love into types. First, you must establish a basis for the classification. Will you classify love on the basis of its intensity? On the basis of when in life it occurs? On the basis of who is doing the loving? One principle must be established and applied throughout the essay. The following are possibilities for your essay.

    I. Intensity of love
      A. Passion
      B. Infatuation
      C. Comradeship
    II. Who does the loving
      A. Divine love
      B. Human love
      C. Animal love
   III. When in life love occurs
      A. Childish love
      B. Teenage love
      C. Adult love

2. DIVIDE THE WHOLE PIE. Once you have been given a subject to classify, make sure that you discuss the entire subject. Don't leave a missing piece. For example, if you were to classify literature into short story, drama, and poetry, a significant category would be missing—the novel. The entire subject must be included in your classification.

3. MAKE EACH CATEGORY IN A CLASSIFICATION SEPARATE FROM THE OTHERS. A classification whose segments overlap acquires a fuzziness that is the mark of an inferior essay. Notice the overlapping teaching methods here:

    a. Lecture
    b. Discussion
    c. Question-answer

Question-answer and discussion overlap: there is no clear distinction between them. A discussion lesson may involve questions and answers, and a question-answer lesson may involve discussion. The classification either should be limited to lecture and discussion or it should include a third, clearly separate segment:

    a. Lecture
    b. Discussion
    c. Quizzes

4. GIVE EQUAL IMPORTANCE TO EACH SEGMENT OF THE CLASSIFICATION. Balance plays an important role in a division essay. You must curb the tendency to pamper one segment with elaborate details while paring down another to a few barren lines. Treat each segment with equal emphasis or your essay will become obviously lopsided.

John Alan Lee, a University of Toronto sociologist, based the following article on the results of his questionnaire study on types of love. The article originally appeared in *Psychology Today,* October 1974, and was adapted by the author from his book, *Colours of Love,* published in Canada by New Press.

Professional Model

The Styles of Loving
John Alan Lee

1   We will accept variety in almost anything, from roses and religions to politics and poetry. But when it comes to love, each of us believes we know the real thing, and we are reluctant to accept other notions. We disparage other people's experiences by calling them infatuations, mere sexual flings, unrealistic affairs.

2   For thousands of years writers and philosophers have debated the nature of love. Many recognized that there are different kinds of love, but few accepted them all as legitimate. Instead, each writer argues that his own concept of love is the best. C. S. Lewis[1] thought that true love must be unselfish and altruistic, as did sociologist Pitirim Sorokin. Stendhal,[2] by contrast, took the view that love is passionate and ecstatic. Others think that "real" love must be wedded to the Protestant ethic, forging a relationship that is mutually beneficial and productive. Definitions of love range from sexual lust to an excess of friendship.

---

[1]C. S. Lewis, British novelist and critic (1898–1963).
[2]Stendhal, pen name of Marie Henri Beyle, French novelist and biographer (1783–1842).

3   The ancient Greeks and Romans were more tolerant. They had a variety of words for different and, to them, equally valid types of love. But today the concept has rigidified; most of us believe that there is only one true kind of love. We measure each relationship against this ideal in terms of degree or quantity. Does Tom love me more than Tim does? Do you love me as much as I love you? Do I love you enough? Such comparisons also assume that love comes in fixed amounts—the more I give to you, the less I have for anyone else; if you don't give me everything, you don't love me enough.

4   "There is hardly any activity, any enterprise, which is started with such tremendous hopes and expectations, and yet which fails so regularly, as love," wrote Erich Fromm. I think that part of the reason for this failure rate is that too often people are speaking different languages when they speak of love. The problem is not *how much* love they feel, but *which kind*. The way to have a mutually satisfying love affair is not to find a partner who loves "in the right amount," but one who shares the same approach to loving, the same definition of love.

5   *The Structure of Love*   My research explored the literature of love and the experiences of ordinary lovers in order to distinguish these approaches. Color served me as a useful analogy in the process. There are three primary colors—red, yellow and blue—from which all other hues are composed. And empirically I found three primary types of love, none of which could be reduced to the others, and a variety of secondary types that proved to be combinations of the basic three. In love, as in color, "primary" does not mean superior; it simply refers to basic structure. Orange is no more or less a color than red, and no less worthy. In love, as in color, one can draw as many distinctions as one wishes; I have stopped, somewhat arbitrarily, with nine types.

6   EROS   Stendhal called love a "sudden sensation of recognition and hope." He was describing the most typical symptom of eros: an immediate, powerful attraction to the physical appearance of the beloved. "The first time I saw him was several weeks before we met," a typical erotic lover said in an interview, "but I can still remember exactly the way he looked, which was just the way I dreamed my ideal lover would look." Erotic lovers typically feel a chemical or gut reaction on meeting each other; heightened heartbeat is not just a figment of fiction, it seems, but the erotic lover's physiological response to meeting the dream.

7   Most of my erotic respondents went to bed with their lovers soon after meeting. This was the first test of whether the affair would continue, since erotic love demands that the partner live up to the lover's concept of bodily perfection. They may try to overlook what they consider a flaw, only to find that it undermines the intensity of their attraction. There is no use trying to persuade such a lover that personal or intellectual qualities are more lasting or more important. To do so is to argue for another approach to love.

8   My erotic respondents all spoke with delight of the lover's skin, fragrance, hair, musculature, body proportions, and so on. Of course, the specific body type that each lover considered ideal varied, but all erotics had such an ideal, which they could identify easily from a series of photographs. Erotic lovers actively and imaginatively cultivate many sexual techniques to preserve delight in the partner's body. Nothing is more deadly for a serious erotic lover than to fall in love with a prudish partner.

9   Modern usage tends to define *erotic* as *sexual;* we equate erotic art with pornography. But eros is not mere sexual attraction; it is a demanding search for the lover's ideal of beauty, a concept that is as old as Pygmalion[3]. Eros involves mental as well as sexual attraction, which is faithful to the Platonic concept. Most dictionaries define Platonic

---

[3]Pygmalion, a King of Cyprus who fell in love with a statue.

love as "devoid of sensual feeling," which is certainly not what Plato had in mind. On the contrary, it was sensual feeling for the beautiful body of another person that evoked eros as the Greeks understood it.

10   *The Dream of the Ideal*   The fascination with beauty that marks eros is the basis for personal and psychological intimacy between the lovers. The erotic lover wants to know everything about the beloved, to become part of him or her. If an erotic relationship surpasses the initial hurdles of expectation and physical ideals, this desire for intimacy can sustain the relationship for years. (And this knowledge must be first-hand. The playful lover may ask a friend what so-and-so is like in bed. No erotic lover would dream of relying on such vicarious evidence.)

11   An essential component of successful erotic love is self-assurance. It takes confidence to reveal oneself intensely to another. A lover who doubts himself, who falls into self-recriminations if his love is not reciprocated, cannot sustain eros.

12   The typical erotic lovers in my sample avoided wallowing in extremes of emotion, especially the self-pity and hysteria that characterize mania. They recalled happy and secure childhoods, and reported satisfaction with work, family, and close friends. They were ready for love when it came along, but were not anxiously searching. They consider love to be important, but they do not become obsessive about it; when separated from the beloved, they do not lose their balance, become sick with desire, or turn moody. They prefer exclusive relationships but do not demand them, and they are rarely possessive or afraid of rivals. Erotic lovers seek a deep, pervasive rapport with their partners and share development and control of the relationship.

13   But because the erotic lover depends on an ideal concept of beauty, he is often disappointed. The failure rate of eros has littered our fiction with bitter and cynical stories of love, and caused conventional wisdom to be deeply suspicious of ideal beauty as a basis for relationships. Indeed, I found that the purer the erotic qualities of a respondent's love experience, the less his chances of a mutual, lasting relationship.

14   An erotic lover may eventually settle for less, but he or she never forgets the compromise, and rarely loses hope of realizing the dream. However, I found several cases of "love at first sight" in which initial rapture survived years of married life. The success of a few keeps the dream alive for many more.

15   LUDUS   About the year One A.D. the Roman poet Ovid came up with the term *amor ludens,* playful love, love as a game. Ovid advised lovers to enjoy love as a pleasant pasttime, but not to get too involved. The ludic lover refuses, then, to become dependent on any beloved, or to allow the partner to become overly attached to him or her, or too intimate.

16   Other types of lovers dismiss ludus as not a kind of love at all; erotic types disdain its lack of commitment, moralists condemn its promiscuity and hedonism. But to make a game of love does not diminish its value. No skilled player of bridge or tennis would excuse inept playing because "it's only a game," and ludus too has its rules, strategies, and points for skill. Ludus turns love into a series of challenges and puzzles to be solved.

17   *Ludic Strategies*   For example, ludus is most easily and most typically played with several partners at once, a guarantee against someone on either side getting too involved. "Love several persons," a 17th-century manual advises, for three lovers are safer than two, and two much safer than one. A ludic lover will often invent another lover, even a spouse, to keep the partner from becoming too attached.

18   But most of my ludic respondents had other tactics. They were careful not to date a partner too often; they never hinted at including the partner in any long-range plans; they arranged encounters in a casual, even haphazard, way: "I'll give you a call"; "See

you around sometime.'' Such indefiniteness is designed to keep the partner from building up expectations or from becoming preoccupied with the affair.

19   Of course, as in many games, one must be on guard against cheats. Cheats in ludic love are cynical players who don't care how deeply involved the partner becomes, who may even exploit such intensity. Such players scandalize ludic lovers who believe in fair play. Insincerity and lies may be part of the game, so long as both partners understand this.

20   The ludic lover notices differences between bodies, but thinks it is stupid to specialize. As the ludic man said in *Finian's Rainbow,* when he is not near the girl he loves, he loves the girl he's near. But ludus is not simply a series of sexual encounters. A lover could get sex without the rituals of conversation, candles and wine. In ludus, the pleasure comes from playing the game, not merely winning the prize.

21   Actually, sexual gratification is only a minor part of the time and effort involved in ludic love. Of any group, ludic respondents showed the least interest in the mutual improvement of sex techniques. Their attitude was that it is easier to find a new sex partner than to work out sexual problems and explore new sexual pleasures with the current one; this view contrasts sharply with that of erotic and storgic lovers. Ludic people want sex for fun, not emotional rapport.

22   *Don Juans Aren't Always Doomed*   Ludus has enjoyed recurring popularity through history. Montesquieu[4] could write of 18th-century France: ''A husband who wishes to be the only one to possess his wife would be regarded as a public killjoy.'' The first Don Juan emerged in Tirso de Molina's *The Trickster of Seville* in 1630, the diametric opposite of the erotic Tristan,[5] the courtly ideal. Tirso's hero conquered only four women, but a century later Mozart's Don Giovanni won a thousand and three in España alone.

23   Of course the various fates of the legendary ludic lovers reflect society's ambivalence toward them. They usually go to hell, get old and impotent, or meet their match and surrender. Rarely is ludus tolerated, much less rewarded.

24   But I was struck by the fact that most of my ludic respondents neither suffered nor regretted their ways. Like successful erotics, they play from a base of self-confidence. They believe in their own assets so much that they convince themselves that they do not ''need'' other people, like most mortals. These ludic lovers prefer to remain in perfect control of their feelings; they do not think that love is as important as work or other activities; they are thus never possessive or jealous (except as a teasing ploy in the game). They typically recall their childhoods as ''average,'' and their current lives as ''OK, but occasionally frustrating.''

25   My ludic respondents seemed quite content with their detachment from intense feelings of love, but most failed the acid test of ludus: the ability to break off with a partner with whom they were through. Their intentions were ludic, but they had Victorian hangovers. They tended to prolong the relationship for the sake of the partner, until the inevitable break was painful. Ovid would not have approved. ''Extinguish the fire of love gradually,'' he admonished, ''not all at once . . . it is wicked to hate a girl you used to love.''

26   The legendary ludic lovers, like Don Juan and Alfie, were generally men, and only in recent years—with the pill and penicillin—have women won entry into the game. Ludus is also frequently identified with male homosexual love; the term ''gay'' may have orig-

---

[4]Baron de la Brède et de Montesquieu, French political philosopher, jurist, and writer (1689–1755).
[5]Tristan, a prince at King Arthur's court who fell in love with the Irish princess Iseult and died with her.

inated from the assumption that homosexuals adopt a noncommittal, playful approach to sex and love, which is not necessarily so.

27   There is a variant of this type of love that I call *manic ludus,* in which the lover alternates between a detached, devil-may-care attitude toward the partner, and a worried, lovesick desire for more attention. People in this conflicting state would like to be purely ludic, but they lack the vanity or self-sufficiency to remain aloof from intimacy. They both need and resent love, and they cannot control their emotions long enough to maintain a cool relationship.

28   STORGE (pronounced stor-gay) is, as Proudhon described it, "love without fever, tumult or folly, a peaceful and enchanting affection" such as one might have for a close sibling. It is the kind of love that sneaks up unnoticed; storgic lovers remember no special point when they fell in love. Since storgic lovers consider sex one of the most intimate forms of self-disclosure, sex occurs late in the relationship.

29   Storge is rarely the stuff of dramatic plays or romantic novels, except perhaps as a backdrop or point of comparison. In *Of Human Bondage,* the hero, Philip, follows a manic love affair with Mildred with a storgic marriage to Sally, whom he has known all along.

30   Storge superficially resembles ludus in its lack of great passion, but the origins of the two types are quite different. The ludic lover avoids intensity of feeling consciously aware of its risks. The storgic lover is unaware of intense feeling. It simply doesn't occur to him that a lover should be dewy-eyed and sentimental about a beloved. Such behavior is as out of place in storgic love as it would be for most of us in relating to a close friend. Storgic love "just comes naturally" with the passage of time and the enjoyment of shared activities. You grow accustomed to her face.

31   In most modern cities people do not live near each other long enough to develop the unself-conscious affection that is typical of storgic love. I found some such cases among people who grew up in rural areas. However, among my urban respondents, who usually had few lasting contacts with their childhood friends, there were some storgic types who based their love on friendship and companionship. This characteristic distinguishes storge from other types of love, in which the partners may not treat each other at all like friends.

32   When a storgic lover gets involved with another type of lover, serious misunderstandings are likely to occur. The goals of storge, for instance, are marriage, home and children, avoiding all the silly conflicts and entanglements of passion. But to the erotic or ludic lover, storge is a bore. Storge implies a life that is reasonable and predictable; why make it more complicated by engaging in emotionally exhausting types of love? Erotic lovers would never understand that question.

33   *The Strengths of Storge*   Storge is a slow-burning love, rarely hectic or urgent, though of course storgic lovers may disagree and fight. But they build up a reservoir of stability that will see them through difficulties that would kill a ludic relationship and greatly strain an erotic one. The physical absence of the beloved, for instance, is much less distressing to them than to other lovers; they can survive long separations (Ulysses and Penelope are a classic example of that ability).

34   Even if a break-up occurs, storgic lovers are likely to remain good friends. A typical storgic lover would find it inconceivable that two people who had once loved each other could become enemies, simply because they had ceased to be lovers.

35   In a ludic or erotic relationship, something is happening all the time. In eros, there is always some secret to share, a misunderstanding to mend, a separation to survive with letters and poems. In ludus, inactivity quickly leads to boredom, and a search for

new amusement. In storge, there are fewer campaigns to fight and fewer wounds to heal. There is a lack of ecstasy, but also a lack of despair.

36   Eros, ludus and storge are the three primary types of love, but few love affairs and few colors, are pure examples of one type. Most reds have a little yellow or blue in them, and most cases of eros have a little storge or ludus.

37   The color analogy led me to distinguish mixtures from blends (compounds). You can mix two colors and be aware of both components. But it may happen that two primary colors are so evenly blended that an entirely new color emerges, unclassifiable as a hue of either, with unique properties. This is the case with mania, a fourth color of love.

38   MANIA   The Greeks called it *theia mania,* the madness from the gods. Both Sappho and Plato, along with legions of sufferers, recorded its symptoms: agitation, sleeplessness, fever, loss of appetite, heartache. The manic lover is consumed by thoughts of the beloved. The slightest lack of enthusiasm from the partner brings anxiety and pain; each tiny sign of warmth brings instant relief, but no lasting satisfaction. The manic lover's need for attention and affection from the beloved is insatiable. Cases of mania abound in literature, for its components—furious jealousy, helpless obsession, and tragic endings—are the stuff of human conflict. Goethe made his own unhappy bout with mania the subject of his novel, *The Sorrows of Young Werther,* and Somerset Maugham did the same in *Of Human Bondage.* The manic lover alternates between peaks of ecstasy when he feels loved in return, and depths of despair when the beloved is absent. He knows his possessiveness and jealousy are self-defeating, but he can't help himself.

39   *From God's Curse to Popular Passion*   Rational lovers throughout the ages, from Lucretius[6] to Denis de Rougemont, have warned us to avoid mania like the plague. Fashions in love, of course, change. To the ancient Greeks, a person who fell head-over-heels, "madly" in love, had obviously been cursed by the gods. Many parents in the Middle Ages strongly disapproved of love matches, preferring their children to arrange "sensible marriages." But mania has gained popularity in the West since the 13th century; today many young people would consider it wrong to marry unless they loved "romantically."

40   So popular is mania in literature and love that I originally assumed it would be a primary type. But green, a color that occurs in nature more than any other, is not a primary, but a blend of yellow and blue. Similarly, the data from my interviews refused to reduce mania to one clear type. Instead, mania respondents derive their unique style of love from the primaries of eros and ludus.

41   These yearning, obsessed, often unhappy manic lovers are typical of frustrated eros. With eros, they share the same intensity of feeling, the same urgency to find the ideal beloved. But erotic lovers are not crushed by disappointment as manic lovers are; they keep their self-respect. Manic lovers, by contrast, are self-effacing, ambivalent, lacking in confidence. They don't have a clear idea of what they are looking for, as erotic lovers do, and they feel helpless, out of control of their emotions. "I know it was crazy, but I couldn't help myself," was a favorite explanation.

42   Oddly, manic lovers persist in falling in love with people they say they don't even like. "I hate and I love," wailed the Roman poet Catullus. "And if you ask me how, I do not know. I only feel it, and I'm torn in two." Aldous Huxley's hero in *Point Counter-Point* "wanted her against all reason, against all his ideals and principles, madly, against his wishes . . . for he didn't like Lucy, he really hated her."

---

[6]Titus Lucretius Carus, Roman poet and philosopher (96?–55 B.C.).

43   For these reasons, some psychologists consider mania to be neurotic, unhealthy. Freud was most critical of obsessive love, and Theodor Reik, in *Of Love and Lust,* explains the obsessiveness of mania as a search for the qualities in a partner that the lover feels lacking in himself. The typical manic lover in my samples seemed to feel, as the song suggests, that he was nobody until somebody loved him.

44   Paradoxically, manic lovers also behave in ways similar to ludus. They try to hold back to manipulate the lover, to play it cool. But unlike successful ludic types, manic lovers never quite succeed at detachment. Their sense of timing is off. They try to be noncommittal, only to panic and surrender in ignominious defeat.

45   *The Telephone Trauma*   Consider this typical caper. The manic realizes that he has been taking the initiative too often in calling his beloved, so he asks her to call the next time. This is a consciously ludic ploy, since no erotic or storgic lover would keep count or care. But it is part of the game in ludus to keep things in balance.

46   The hour of the expected call arrives, and the phone sits silent. The true ludic lover would not be terribly bothered; he or she would quickly make a few calls and get busy with other lovers. The manic lover falls into a frenzy of anxiety. Either he breaks down and calls the lover, or he is in such a state of emotional upset that he is incapable of ludic detachment when the lover does call: "Where were you? I was so *worried!*"

47   Manic lovers, in short, attempt to play by the rules of ludus with the passion of eros, and fail at both. They need to be loved so much that they do not let the relationship take its own course. They push things, and thereby tend to lose; mania rarely ends happily. Few lovers go to such extremes as violence or suicide, but most remain troubled by the experience for months, even years. Like malaria, it may return to seize the manic lover with bouts of nostalgia and unrest.

48   It is theoretically possible for mania to develop into lasting love, but the manic lover must find an unusual partner—who can ride out the storms of emotion, return the intensity of feeling, and ultimately convince the manic lover that he or she is lovable. A ludic partner will never tolerate the emotional extremes, and a storgic lover will be unable to reciprocate the feelings. A strong-willed erotic partner might manage it.

49   *Ludic Eros*   Mania can be reduced by resolving the underlying conditions that create and sustain the lover's lack of self-esteem and his desperate need to be in love. Then the lover may move toward a more confident eros or, perhaps, a more playful ludus. This is the part of the color chart labeled *ludic eros,* the sector between the two primaries.

50   What enables one lover to mix ludus and eros in a pleasant compromise, while another finds them compounded into mania? Having previous experience in love and many good relationships is one factor. The manic lovers in my sample were discontented with life, but ludic-erotic lovers were basically content and knew what kind of partners they wanted. Ludic-erotic people resemble ludus in their pluralism, their desire for many relationships, but they resemble eros in their preference for clearly-defined types. They do not easily accept substitutes, as ludic types do.

51   Ludic-erotic love walks an exacting tightrope between intensity and detachment. Most people think this approach is too greedy, and therefore immoral. To the ludic-erotic lover, it is just good sense.

52   *The Art of Passionate Caution*   The tightrope isn't always easy. The lover may spend an evening in the most intense intimacy with his partner, but will always back off in a ludic direction at critical moments. Just when you, the beloved, are about to react to his passion with a murmur of confirmation, he leaps from the couch to make a cup of coffee. Or just when he is about to blurt out that he loves you; he bites his lips and says something less committal: "You really turn me on."

53 The successful combination of ludus and eros is rare, but it exists. The journals of Casanova are a classic example of the bittersweet taste of this type of love. Today many attempts at "open marriages" are in fact advocating a ludic-erotic approach to love: the spouses remain primarily involved with each other, yet may have intense involvements with others so long as these remain temporary.

54 PRAGMA   is love with a shopping list, a love that seeks compatibility on practical criteria. In traditional societies, marriages were arranged on similarities of race, social class, income, and so on. In modern society the pragmatic approach to love argues that lovers should choose each other on the basis of compatible personalities, like interests and education, similar backgrounds and religious views, and the like. Computer-match services take a pragmatic view.

55 The pragmatic lover uses social activities and programs as a means to an end, and will drop them if there is no payoff in partners. By contrast, a storgic lover goes out for the activities he enjoys, and thereby meets someone who shares those interests. The storgic lover never consciously chooses a partner.

56 Pragma is not a primary type of love but a compound of storge and ludus. The pragmatic lover chooses a partner as if she had grown up with him (storge) and will use conscious manipulation to find one (ludus). Pragma is rather like manufactured storge, a faster means of achieving the time-honored version. If a relationship does not work out, the pragmatic lover will move rationally on, ludic-fashion, to search for another.

57 The pragmatic approach is not as cold as it seems. Once a sensible choice is made, more intense feelings may develop; but one must begin with a solid match that is practically based. Oriental matchmakers noted that in romantic love "the kettle is boiling when the young couple first starts out"—and cools with time, bringing disappointment. An arranged marriage, they say, is like a kettle that starts cold and slowly warms up. Pragmatic love grows over the years.

58 As pragma is the compound, so storge and ludus may combine as a mixture. The distinguishing features of a *storgic-ludic* affair are convenience and discretion. A typical example is that of a married boss and his secretary, in which the relationship is carefully managed so as to disrupt neither the boss's marriage nor the office routine. Of course, such affairs don't always stay in neat storgic-ludic boxes. In the film, *A Touch of Class,* the affair becomes too intense, threatening to interfere with the man's comfortably companionate marriage.

59 AGAPE   (pronounced ah-ga-pay) is the classical Christian view of love: altruistic, universalistic love that is always kind and patient, never jealous, never demanding reciprocity. When St. Paul wrote to the Corinthians that love is a duty to care about others, whether the love is deserved or not, and that love must be deeply compassionate and utterly altruistic, he used the Greek word, *agape.* But all the greater religions share this concept of love, a generous, unselfish, giving of oneself.

60 I found no saints in my sample. I have yet to interview an unqualified example of agape, although a few respondents had had brief agapic episodes in relationships that were otherwise tinged with selfishness. For instance, one of my subjects, seeing that his lover was torn between choosing him or another man, resolved to save her the pain of deciding; he bowed out gracefully. His action fell short of pure agape, however, because he continued to be interested in how well his beloved was doing, and was purely and selfishly delighted when she dropped the other man and returned to him.

61 Yet my initial sample of 112 people did contain eight case histories that came quite close to the sexual restraint, dutiful self-sacrifice, universality and altruism that characterize agape. These respondents mixed storge and eros; they had an almost religious attitude toward loving, but they fell short of the hypothetical ideal in loving the partner

more than anyone else. They felt intense emotion, as erotic lovers do, along with the enduring patience and abiding affection of storge.

62   Storgic-erotic respondents felt an initial attraction to their partners, distinguishable from erotic attraction by the absence of physical symptoms of excitement. And unlike eros, these people felt little or no jealousy; they seemed to find enough pleasure in the act of loving another person so that the matter of reciprocity was almost irrelevant.

63   *Testing One's Type of Love*   Why construct a typology of love in the first place? Love is a delicate butterfly, runs a certain sentiment, that can be ruined with clumsy dissection. Who cares how many species it comes in; let it fly.

64   As far as I am concerned, any analysis that helps reduce misunderstandings is worthwhile, and there is no human endeavor more ripe for misunderstandings than love. Consider. A person who has just fallen in love is often tempted to test his sensations to prove it's "really" love. Usually such tests are based on a unidimensional concept of love, and therefore they are usually 180° wrong.

65   For example, the decision to test love by postponing sex would be disastrous for an erotic love affair, the equivalent of depriving a baby of food for a week to see if it is strong enough to live. A budding erotic love thrives on sexual intimacy. But delaying sex would be absolutely natural and right for a storgic lover, and it might be a positive incentive to a manic lover.

66   The advantage of my typology, preliminary as it is, is that it teases apart some very different definitions of love, and suggests which types of love are most compatible. Generally, the farther apart two types are on the color chart, the less likely that the lovers share a common language of love. One of my ludic respondents berated his storgic lover for trying to trap him into a commitment, while she accused him of playing games just to get her body. Different types, different languages. Eros insists on rapid intimacy, storge resents being rushed. Same feelings of "love," but opposite ways to express it.

67   Obviously, two lovers who represent unlike primaries will have trouble getting along unless they both bend toward a mixture or compromise. But it all depends on what each individual wants out of a relationship. Two storgic lovers have the best chance for a lasting relationship, and two ludic lovers have the worst chance—but they will have fun while it lasts.

68   One swallow does not a summer make, and neither does one manic binge confirm you as an obsessive lover. One playful affair in a storgic marriage does not define you as ludus. While some people have enjoyed a variety of love experiences equally, most of us definitely prefer one type. We live with other kinds, as we live with many colors, but we still have our favorites.

5,264 words

Vocabulary

altruistic (2)	rapport (12)	insatiable (38)
ecstatic (2)	rapture (14)	self-effacing (41)
empirically (5)	disdain (16)	ignominious (44)
arbitrarily (5)	promiscuity (16)	nostalgia (47)
Platonic (9)	hedonism (16)	reciprocate (48)
devoid (9)	haphazard (18)	compatibility (54)
vicarious (10)	diametric (22)	pragmatic (54)
self-recriminations (11)	ambivalence (23)	hypothetical (61)
reciprocated (11)	impotent (23)	typology (63)
wallowing (12)	ploy (24)	unidimensional (64)
mania (12)	sibling (28)	

Questions

1. What is the basis of Lee's classification?
2. What part does the analogy to the color wheel play in this essay? How does it contribute to the classification?
3. What are the three main types of love identified in the essay?
4. Which types of love, according to the author, have the best chance for a lasting relationship? Which kind of love has the worst chance?
5. On what grounds does the author defend his study of love against the charge that love is ruined by dissection?
6. According to the author, which kind of love is at work in computer dating services?
7. Which kind of love was the author unable to find an unqualified example of? Why?

This essay identifies four primary categories of loved objects: children, friends, lovers, and life. The strengths of this essay are its organization and its varied syntax. Its weaknesses are its overly abstract treatment of love and its failure to cite specific examples. Literature and history abound with examples that the author could have used in his discussion of each love category.

Student Model

The Many Faces of Love
Irving C. Weill

Love—the sincere expression of concern, affection and devotion—is divisible into four primary types: the love of a parent for a child, the love of one friend for another, the love between lovers, and the love of just being alive.

The love of a parent for a child is a deep, strong bond. The joy attending the news of a birth translates into a wonderfully exhilarating feeling of love combined with pride. Visions of ways to express this love flash through the minds of father and mother. The desire of the parents to hold the child is so overwhelming that tenderness wells up and bursts into feelings of euphoria. For the new father, everything in the world is in its proper place. For the new mother, life has a purpose. Between them life has been forged, and the essence that burns in their hearts has kindled a spark in their young. Throughout history, portraits of parents holding infants, lovingly looking into the child's eyes, have symbolized this type of love.

The love of one friend for another is a marvelous and necessary kind of love. Most young people develop this feeling for a member of their own sex. The feeling is based on mutual trust and affection. Friendship is a unique arrangement of shared relationships; it is a true love in its ability to generate trust and confidence. Friends may change from time to time as goals, desires, and environments change, but the need for a companion does not change. A friend is a safety valve that allows one to let off steam by expressing whatever is bothering or troubling him. Life's joys as well as its hardships are more pleasant to bear when a friend is there to share them.

The love of lovers is a rapturous experience. Gazing into his loved one's eyes, the lover feels passion, yearning, and endearment. When lovers hold hands, they feel the thrill of electricity that sets up a communication only understood by those who also have been initiated into love. Tender caresses are signals decoded only by the lovers. A lover's eyes speak of delights yet to come; his heart pounds with expectations of closeness and intimacy. Lovers watch each other, trusting in love, knowing that their time of fulfillment will come. Their thoughts are always with each other, waiting for the next meeting when they can be together with their feelings—indulging in delicious dreams and fantasies. In all the world, the language of love is spoken in a universal rhetoric. Letters are written, hearts are laid bare, dreams are expressed—all on the altar of love.

The love of being alive, being able to breathe free, is the most fundamental love of all. Our lives tend to become humdrum, monotonous, and uninteresting because we forget to love life. We do not see the beauty around us. Our interest in business, work, and self often excludes the wondrous world in which we live. We forget to notice the trees, flowers, birds, dogs and cats, and multitudes of interesting people who are waiting to speak to us, to be friendly, and maybe to become our friends. Simple things like riding a bicycle in open spaces, walking fast, swinging a golf club, or throwing a ball with a child can reawaken a love for life. The joy of waking up each morning to see the sun again, of doing things with people who appreciate doing the unusual, is a most invigorating sensation, a sensation those in love with life shall never lose.

A visit to the country fair and a ride on the Ferris wheel provide E. B. White with a basis for a classification of people into two unusual types.

Alternate Reading

Security

E. B. White

1   It was a fine clear day for the Fair this year, and I went up early to see how the Ferris wheel was doing and to take a ride. It pays to check up on Ferris wheels these days: by noting the volume of business one can get some idea which side is ahead in the world —whether the airborne freemen outnumber the earthbound slaves. It was encouraging to discover that there were still quite a few people at the Fair who preferred a feeling of high, breezy insecurity to one of solid support. My friend Healy surprised me by declining to go aloft; he is an unusually cautious man, however—even his hat is insured.

2   I like to watch the faces of people who are trying to get up their nerve to take to the air. You see them at the ticket booths in amusement parks, in the waiting room at the airport. Within them two irreconcilables are at war—the desire for safety, the yearning for a dizzy release. My *Britannica* tells nothing about Mr. G. W. G. Ferris, but he belongs with the immortals. From the top of the wheel, seated beside a small boy, windswept and fancy free, I looked down on the Fair and for a moment was alive. Below us the old harness drivers pushed their trotters round the dirt track, old men with their legs still sticking out stiffly round the rumps of horses. And from the cluster of loud speakers atop the judges' stand came the "Indian Love Call," bathing heaven and earth in jumbo tenderness.

3   This silvery wheel, revolving slowly in the cause of freedom, was only just holding its own, I soon discovered; for farther along in the midway, in a sideshow tent, a tattoo artist was doing a land-office business, not with anchors, flags, and pretty mermaids, but with Social Security Numbers, neatly pricked on your forearm with the electric needle. He had plenty of customers, mild-mannered pale men, asking glumly for the sort of indelible

ignominy that was once reserved for prisoners and beef cattle. Drab times these, when the bravado and the exhibitionism are gone from tattooing and it becomes simply a branding operation. I hope the art that produced the bird's eye view of Sydney will not be forever lost in the routine business of putting social security numbers on people who are worried about growing old.

4   The sight would have depressed me had I not soon won a cane by knocking over three cats with three balls. There is no moment when a man so surely has the world by the tail as when he strolls down the midway swinging a prize cane.

450 words

Vocabulary

irreconcilables (2)   bravado (3)
indelible (3)   exhibitionism (3)

Questions

1. Why did the author go to the Ferris wheel at the Fair?
2. What is the author's definition of an airborne freeman? Of an earthbound slave?
3. Who declined to take a ride on the Ferris wheel with the author?
4. What "irreconcilables" does the author see in the faces of those who are trying to get up enough nerve to take to the air?
5. What artist at the Fair was doing a land-office business? Why were people lining up outside his tent?
6. Which of these two categories of people, airborne freemen or earthbound slaves, were lining up outside the artist's tent? What does this say about their character?
7. Which of these two categories of people would you rather belong to? Why?
8. What principle is this division of people based on?
9. What other names have often been given to "airborne freemen"? To "earthbound slaves"?
10. What event prevented the author from becoming depressed over the behavior of the earthbound slaves?

In this brief essay, Aaron Copland, American composer, divides the composers of musical history into four distinct types.

Alternate Reading

Different Types of Composers
Aaron Copland

1   I can see three different types of composers in musical history, each of whom conceives music in a somewhat different fashion.

2   The type that has fired public imagination most is that of the spontaneously inspired composer—the Franz Schubert type, in other words. All composers are inspired, of course, but this type is more spontaneously inspired. Music simply wells out of him. He

can't get it down on paper fast enough. You can almost tell this type of composer by his prolific output. In certain months, Schubert wrote a song a day. Hugo Wolf did the same.

3   In a sense, men of this kind begin not so much with a musical theme as with a completed composition. They invariably work best in the shorter forms. It is much easier to improvise a song than it is to improvise a symphony. It isn't easy to be inspired in that spontaneous way for long periods at a stretch. Even Schubert was more successful in handling the shorter forms of music. The spontaneously inspired man is only one type of composer, with his own limitations.

4   Beethoven symbolizes the second type—the constructive type, one might call it. This type exemplifies my theory of the creative process in music better than any other, because in this case the composer really does begin with a musical theme. In Beethoven's case there is no doubt about it, for we have the notebooks in which he put the themes down. We can see from his notebooks how he worked over his themes—how he would not let them be until they were as perfect as he could make them. Beethoven was not a spontaneously inspired composer in the Schubert sense at all. He was the type that begins with a theme; makes it a germinal idea; and upon that constructs a musical work, day after day, in painstaking fashion. Most composers since Beethoven's day belong to this second type.

5   The third type of creator I can only call, for lack of a better name, the traditionalist type. Men like Palestrina and Bach belong in this category. They both exemplify the kind of composer who is born in a particular period of musical history, when a certain musical style is about to reach its fullest development. It is a question at such a time of creating music in a well-known and accepted style and doing it in a way that is better than anyone has done it before you.

6   Beethoven and Schubert started from a different premise. They both had serious pretensions to originality: After all, Schubert practically created the song form single-handed; and the whole face of music changed after Beethoven lived. But Bach and Palestrina simply improved on what had gone before them.

7   The traditionalist type of composer begins with a pattern rather than with a theme. The creative act with Palestrina is not the thematic conception so much as the personal treatment of a well-established pattern. And even Bach, who conceived forty-eight of the most varied and inspired themes in his *Well Tempered Clavichord,* knew in advance the general formal mold that they were to fill. It goes without saying that we are not living in a traditionalist period nowadays.

8   One might add, for the sake of completeness, a fourth type of composer—the pioneer type: men like Gesualdo in the seventeenth century, Moussorgsky and Berlioz in the nineteenth, Debussy and Edgar Varese in the twentieth. It is difficult to summarize the composing methods of so variegated a group. One can safely say that their approach to composition is the opposite of the traditionalist type. They clearly oppose conventional solutions of musical problems. In many ways, their attitude is experimental—they seek to add new harmonies, new sonorities, new formal principles. The pioneer type was the characteristic one at the turn of the seventeenth century and also at the beginning of the twentieth century, but it is much less evident today.

660 words

Vocabulary

prolific (2)	pretensions (6)
improvise (3)	thematic (7)
germinal (4)	variegated (8)

1. What is the first type of composer discussed in this essay? Which composers are representative of this type?
2. Which type of composer has fired the public imagination? Why?
3. Why is the first type of composer more successful with short compositions?
4. What short musical form was Schubert more successful in handling?
5. What is the second type of composer? Who is representative of this type?
6. Which category includes most composers since Beethoven's day?
7. What is the third type of composer? What name does the author give to this type?
8. What serious pretensions did Beethoven and Schubert have in common?
9. What is the fourth and final type of composer? What name does the author give to this type?
10. How does the author characterize the approach to composition of the fourth type of composers?
11. On what principle does the author base his classification of composers? Where is it stated?
12. Could these categories also apply to rock-music composers? Give your reasons.

C. Additional Writing Assignments

1. Write an essay grouping your friends or enemies into three or four major types.
2. Divide your present life into three or four aspects, and write an essay clarifying each aspect for your reader.
3. Write an essay dividing food into major types. Establish the basis for the classification, making sure to clarify each of the types.
4. What kinds of work opportunities are you interested in? Write an essay classifying the categories of work that interest you, with examples of each category.
5. Classify all the dates you have ever had into three or four groups. Use descriptive details in naming and clarifying each group.
6. Classify people's looks according to three or four general types, and supply vivid examples of each type.
7. Divide current television shows into three to five major types, supplying examples of each.
8. Find a basis for classifying all single-dwelling houses. Name the categories and supply a description of each.
9. From your experience, how many major kinds of entertainment are there? Who indulges in each? Write an essay answering these questions.
10. Find a basis for classifying all the wars America has fought. Then write an essay supplying examples of each type of war.

11

Causal Analysis

*The most destructive force in their love affair
had been social pressure.*

A. Reading for Ideas

Read "The Girls in Their Summer Dresses." See if you can describe and explain the kind of relationship that exists between Michael and Frances. Pay attention to bits of conversation and details.

The Girls in Their Summer Dresses
Irwin Shaw

1   Fifth Avenue was shining in the sun when they left the Brevoort. The sun was warm, even though it was February, and everything looked like Sunday morning—the buses and the well-dressed people walking slowly in couples and the quiet buildings with the windows closed.

2   Michael held Frances' arm tightly as they walked toward Washington Square in the sunlight. They walked lightly, almost smiling, because they had slept late and had a good breakfast and it was Sunday. Michael unbuttoned his coat and let it flap around him in the mild wind.

3   "Look out," Frances said as they crossed Eighth Street. "You'll break your neck."

4   Michael laughed and Frances laughed with him.

"She's not so pretty," Frances said. "Anyway, not pretty enough to take a chance of breaking your neck."

Michael laughed again. "How did you know I was looking at her?"

5   Frances cocked her head to one side and smiled at her husband under the brim of her hat. "Mike, darling," she said.

"O.K.," he said. "Excuse me."

6   Frances patted his arm lightly and pulled him along a little faster toward Washington Square. "Let's not see anybody all day," she said. "Let's just hang around with each other. You and me. We're always up to our neck in people, drinking their Scotch or drinking our Scotch; we only see each other in bed. I want to go out with my husband all day long. I want him to talk only to me and listen only to me."

184

7   "What's to stop us?" Michael asked.

"The Stevensons. They want us to drop by around one o'clock and they'll drive us into the country."

"The cunning Stevensons," Mike said. "Transparent. They can whistle. They can go driving in the country by themselves."

"Is it a date?"

"It's a date."

8   Frances leaned over and kissed him on the tip of the ear.

"Darling," Michael said, "this is Fifth Avenue."

"Let me arrange a program," Frances said. "A planned Sunday in New York for a young couple with money to throw away."

"Go easy."

"First let's go to the Metropolitan Museum of Art," Frances suggested, because Michael had said during the week he wanted to go. "I haven't been there in three years and there're at least ten pictures I want to see again. Then we can take the bus down to Radio City and watch them skate. And later we'll go down to Cavanagh's and get a steak as big as a blacksmith's apron, with a bottle of wine, and after that there's a French picture at the Filmarte that everybody says—say, are you listening to me?"

9   "Sure," he said. He took his eyes off the hatless girl with the dark hair, cut dancer-style like a helmet, who was walking past him.

10 "That's the program for the day," Frances said flatly. "Or maybe you'd just rather walk up and down Fifth Avenue."

"No," Michael said. "Not at all."

"You always look at other women," Frances said. "Everywhere. Every damned place we go."

"Now, darling," Michael said, "I look at everything. God gave me eyes and I look at women and men and subway excavations and moving pictures and the little flowers of the field. I casually inspect the universe."

"You ought to see the look in your eye," Frances said, "as you casually inspect the universe on Fifth Avenue."

"I'm a happily married man." Michael pressed her elbow tenderly. "Example for the whole twentieth century—Mr. and Mrs. Mike Loomis. Hey, let's have a drink," he said, stopping.

"We just had breakfast."

"Now listen, darling," Mike said, choosing his words with care, "it's a nice day and we both felt good and there's no reason why we have to break it up. Let's have a nice Sunday."

"All right. I don't know why I started this. Let's drop it. Let's have a good time."

11 They joined hands consciously and walked without talking among the baby carriages and the old Italian men in their Sunday clothes and the young women with Scotties in Washington Square Park.

12 "At least once a year everyone should go to the Metropolitan Museum of Art," Frances said after a while, her tone a good imitation of the tone she had used at breakfast and at the beginning of their walk. "And it's nice on Sunday. There's a lot of people looking at the pictures and you get the feeling maybe Art isn't on the decline in New York City, after all—"

13 "I want to tell you something," Michael said very seriously. "I have not touched another woman. Not once. In all the five years."

"All right," Frances said.

"You believe that, don't you?"

"All right."

14   They walked between the crowded benches, under the scrubby city-park trees.

"I try not to notice it," Frances said, "but I feel rotten inside, in my stomach, when we pass a woman and you look at her and I see that look in your eye and that's the way you looked at me the first time. In Alice Maxwell's house. Standing there in the living room, next to the radio, with a green hat on and all those people."

"I remember the hat," Michael said.

"The same look," Frances said. "And it makes me feel bad. It makes me feel terrible."

"Sh-h-h, please, darling, sh-h-h."

"I think I would like a drink now," Frances said.

15   They walked over to a bar on Eighth Street, not saying anything, Michael automatically helping her over curbstones and guiding her past automobiles. They sat near a window in the bar and the sun streamed in and there was a small, cheerful fire in the fireplace. A little Japanese waiter came over and put down some pretzels and smiled happily at them.

"What do you order after breakfast?" Michael asked.

"Brandy, I suppose," Frances said.

"Courvoisier," Michael told the waiter. "Two Courvoisiers."

16   The waiter came with the glasses and they sat drinking the brandy in the sunlight. Michael finished half his and drank a little water.

"I look at women," he said. "Correct. I don't say it's wrong or right. I look at them. If I pass them on the street and I don't look at them, I'm fooling you, I'm fooling myself."

"You look at them as though you want them," Frances said, playing with her brandy glass. "Every one of them."

"In a way," Michael said, speaking softly and not to his wife, "in a way that's true. I don't do anything about it, but it's true."

"I know it. That's why I feel bad."

"Another brandy," Michael called. "Waiter, two more brandies."

17   He sighed and closed his eyes and rubbed them gently with his fingertips. "I love the way women look. One of the things I like best about New York is the battalions of women. When I first came to New York from Ohio that was the first thing I noticed, the million wonderful women, all over the city. I walked around with my heart in my throat."

"A kid," Frances said. "That's a kid's feeling."

"Guess again," Michael said. "Guess again. I'm older now, I'm a man getting near middle age, putting on a little fat and I still love to walk along Fifth Avenue at three o'clock on the east side of the street between Fiftieth and Fifty-seventh Streets. They're all out then, shopping, in their furs and their crazy hats, everything all concentrated from all over the world into seven blocks—the best furs, the best clothes, the handsomest women, out to spend money and feeling good about it."

18   The Japanese waiter put the two drinks down, smiling with great happiness.

"Everything is all right?" he asked.

"Everything is wonderful," Michael said.

"If it's just a couple of fur coats," Frances said, "and forty-five-dollar hats—"

"It's not the fur coats. Or the hats. That's just the scenery for that particular kind of woman. Understand," he said, "you don't have to listen to this."

"I want to listen."

"I like the girls in the offices. Neat, with their eyeglasses, smart, chipper, knowing what everything is about. I like the girls on Forty-fourth Street at lunchtime, the actresses, all dressed up on nothing a week. I like the salesgirls in the stores, paying attention to you first because you're a man, leaving lady customers waiting. I got all this stuff accumulated in me because I've been thinking about it for ten years and now you've asked for it and here it is."

"Go ahead," Frances said.

"When I think of New York City, I think of all the girls on parade in the city. I don't know whether it's something special with me or whether every man in the city walks around with the same feeling inside him, but I feel as though I'm at a picnic in this city. I like to sit near the women in the theatres, the famous beauties who've taken six hours to get ready and look it. And the young girls at the football games, with the red cheeks, and when the warm weather comes, the girls in their summer dresses." He finished his drink. "That's the story."

19   Frances finished her drink and swallowed two or three times extra. "You say you love me?"

"I love you."

"I'm pretty, too," Frances said. "As pretty as any of them."

"You're beautiful," Michael said.

"I'm good for you," Frances said, pleading. "I've made a good wife, a good house-keeper, a good friend. I'd do any damn thing for you."

"I know," Michael said. He put his hand out and grasped hers.

"You'd like to be free to—" Frances said.

"Sh-h-h."

"Tell the truth." She took her hand away from under his.

Michael flicked the edge of his glass with his finger. "O.K.," he said gently. "Sometimes I feel I would like to be free."

"Well," Frances said, "any time you say."

"Don't be foolish." Michael swung his chair around to her side of the table and patted her thigh.

20   She began to cry silently into her handkerchief, bent over just enough so that nobody else in the bar would notice. "Someday," she said, crying, "you're going to make a move."

21   Michael didn't say anything. He sat watching the bartender slowly peel a lemon.

"Aren't you?" Frances asked harshly. "Come on, tell me. Talk. Aren't you?"

"Maybe," Michael said. He moved his chair back again. "How the hell do I know?"

"You know," Frances persisted. "Don't you know?"

"Yes," Michael said after a while, "I know."

22   Frances stopped crying then. Two or three snuffles into the handkerchief and she put it away and her face didn't tell anything to anybody. "At least do me one favor," she said.

"Sure."

"Stop talking about how pretty this woman is or that one. Nice eyes, nice breasts, a pretty figure, good voice." She mimicked his voice. "Keep it to yourself. I'm not interested."

23   Michael waved to the waiter. "I'll keep it to myself," he said.

Frances flicked the corners of her eyes. "Another brandy," she told the waiter.

"Two," Michael said.

"Yes, Ma'am, yes, sir," said the waiter, backing away.

24   Frances regarded Michael coolly across the table. "Do you want me to call the Stevensons?" she asked. "It'll be nice in the country."

"Sure," Michael said, "Call them."

25   She got up from the table and walked across the room toward the telephone. Michael watched her walk, thinking what a pretty girl, what nice legs.

1,929 words

Questions

1. How does Frances feel about Michael? Why does she feel this way? State both the *way she feels* and the *reasons* for it in a single sentence that could serve as the controlling idea for an essay about the story.
2. What role do the "girls in their summer dresses" play in the story?
3. How does Michael feel toward Frances? Support your conclusion with evidence from the story.
4. How does Michael make Frances feel when he looks at other women? Why?
5. What would your advice be to a wife whose husband looks at other women the way Michael does? Should she ignore him? Be happy that he enjoys beauty and life? Scold him? Flirt with men in order to get even? Why? Give your reasons.
6. What is your prediction about Michael and Frances' future together? Will they eventually divorce? Will the marriage survive? Why or why not?
7. Do you believe that Michael is unusual, or do his feelings toward women represent the feelings of most men?

If I Should Learn . . .

Edna St. Vincent Millay

If I should learn, in some quite casual way,
That you were gone, not to return again—
Read from the back-page of a paper, say,
Held by a neighbor in a subway train,
How at the corner of this avenue
And such a street (so are the papers filled)
A hurrying man, who happened to be you,
At noon today had happened to be killed—
I should not cry aloud—I could not cry
Aloud, or wring my hands in such a place—
I should but watch the station lights rush by
With a more careful interest on my face;
Or raise my eyes and read with greater care
Where to store furs and how to treat the hair.

Questions

1. How does the speaker feel about the man? How do you know?
2. What is the speaker imagining throughout the poem? Why?
3. What would be the reaction of the speaker to the man's death? Why?
4. What is the meaning of lines 13 and 14? State reasons for the action described.
5. How do you think different situations would affect your reaction to news of a loved one's death? What factors would make the greatest difference?

B. How to Write an Analysis of Cause

Causal analysis is the expression used for finding connections between events. Unconsciously, you make causal analyses every day of your life. For example, you are doing causal analysis when you try to figure out why you did poorly in an exam. You also are doing causal analysis when you decide to wear warm clothing on a mountain trip so that you won't catch a cold. In the first case, you are looking at the past to find causes; in the second case, you are looking at the future to predict results.

During your college career, you often will be required to write essays that analyze cause. Your history teacher may ask you to give the causes for the Crimean War; your health teacher may ask you to name three results of a rattlesnake bite; your aviation teacher may ask you to cite the major causes for hurricanes. Such assignments are rigorous, but you can fulfill them by drawing data and facts from textbooks or lecture notes. On occasion, you will also be asked to draw causal connections of your own and these will require particularly careful thought.

Causal analysis is tricky. Few situations can be traced directly to a single, clear cause, and for this reason even experts disagree about cause. Psychologists hold opposing theories on what caused Patricia Hearst, the newspaper heiress, to join the Symbionese Liberation Army. Some maintain that she was physically forced to join; some argue that she was brainwashed; and others believe that she joined voluntarily because she was spoiled, rich, and weak to begin with. What was the real cause? Perhaps there was not one cause but a combination of causes, which is usually the case.

An effect may often be preceded by a whole chain of causes so that when you try to find the real cause, you are simply pushed further and further back from one cause to another. For instance, what is the cause of air pollution? Industrial waste. But industrial waste is caused by industry. Industry is caused by the growing needs of our exploding population. The exploding population is caused by lack of birth control, which results in part from religious beliefs. Religious beliefs come from writings in the Bible. The Bible is the word of God. Therefore, God is the cause of air pollution.

This conclusion is obviously silly. It illustrates, however, how an attempt at tracing causation can quickly lead to absurdity and serves to warn you against making haphazard, hit-or-miss, or hasty causal connections. Investigate your subject thoroughly, either from firsthand experience or by doing research. The causes for your parents' happy or miserable marriage can be identified through personal experience, but the causes of complex problems such as urban poverty or juvenile crime will require some research.

Writing Assignment

Write an essay describing a good or bad human relationship and analyzing its causes. Rummage mentally among the human relationships with which you are thoroughly familiar—relationships among your relatives or friends—picking one that strikes you as particularly good or particularly bad. Describe what you think is the most outstanding quality of the relationship. For example, you might find that two people treat each other with contempt, feed on each other's weaknesses, or are cruel to each other. On the other hand, you might find that the relationship is characterized by close communication and sharing, mutual respect, or a gracious attitude toward one another. Next, search for the major reasons why the relationship is the way it is. Finally, combine the description and cause into one sentence. Possible examples:

My Aunt Marge and Uncle George live in a coldly polite atmosphere *because* my aunt has fallen in love with another man.

Lack of money and Pete's bullheaded ways are the *reasons* my neighbors, Jan and Pete Coleman, bicker constantly.

My grandmother and grandfather have spent fifty beautiful years together *because* they have always loved God, respected each other, and worked together toward common goals.

Money and power have *caused* the love between Laura and Tyrone to corrode slowly.

Norman and Jennifer have had to overcome enormous hardships, but these have had *the effect* of strengthening their devotion.

Specific Instructions

1. USE THE PROPER WORD INDICATORS TO SHOW CAUSATION.

Wrong: Minority quotas in the job market are bad. They discriminate against the white male.

Right: Minority quotas in the job market are bad *because* they discriminate against the white male.

Whether you are listing the effects or causes of a situation, warn your reader that you intend to do a causal analysis by using such expressions as *because, therefore, since the reason is, due to, as a result, consequently,* and *thus.* Here are some examples of causal sentences:

Shakespeare is difficult to read *because* he uses antiquated English.

Because of his instability, John lost his job.

Walter is talented, practices the violin five hours a day and, *as a result,* won the Luba Lefcowitz prize for violin.

The present chaos in the world may have the following *results:* the extinction of human life, a reversion to barbarism after an atomic explosion, or the peaceful establishment of a world government.

If you are listing several causes for a certain situation, it is well to number them as in these examples:

The first cause is. . . .
The second cause is. . . .
The third cause is. . . .

190

2. BE CAUTIOUS. Don't be dogmatic in drawing causal connections. Since very few events are sufficient in themselves to bring about a result, it is prudent to qualify your assertions with "it appears that," "it seems to indicate," or "the evidence points to." These qualifiers show that you realize that the connection between events may be probable but not certain, thereby increasing your reliability to the reader. On the other hand, if your causal analysis is a result of personal experience, have the courage of your conviction. For example, don't say, "It appears that the cause for the many fights between my roommate and me is my roommate's sloppy housekeeping." Such a statement makes you sound wishy-washy. By all means, just say, "My roommate's sloppy housekeeping is the cause of the many fights between us."

3. FOCUS ON THE IMMEDIATE, NOT THE REMOTE CAUSE. Causation, we pointed out earlier, has a way of multiplying back in time, with one cause leading to another and then to another, until God becomes the cause of smog. To avoid entanglement in infinity, focus on immediate rather than on remote causation. For instance, one cause of overcrowded freeways is the population explosion, but a more immediate cause is the lack of rapid transit facilities.

4. AVOID CIRCULAR REASONING ABOUT CAUSE. The following causal statements are circular:

> The freeways are overcrowded because there are too many cars.
>
> Lung cancer is caused by the rapid and uncontrolled growth of cells in the lungs.
>
> Beauty pageants are dehumanizing because ugly women never win them.

Each statement simply restates in the second half what is already implied in the first. Overcrowded freeways obviously have too many cars on them; lung cancer is, by definition, uncontrolled cell growth in the lungs; beauty pageants are called beauty pageants because they judge women for beauty. These revisions are better:

> The freeways are overcrowded because they are inadequately engineered for need, and because rapid transit facilities are poor.
>
> Cigarette smoking is the major cause of lung cancer.
>
> Beauty pageants are dehumanizing because they emphasize a shallow and superficial evalution of woman as a sex object rather than as a whole, functioning person.

5. BEWARE OF IDEOLOGY IN ASSIGNING CAUSE. Here is an example of two causal statements that are based on ideology:

> The high divorce rate in Southern California is caused by the fact that the devil has chosen this section of the country for his own and has been especially busy working among couples here.
>
> The high divorce rate in California is caused by an astrological opposition between Neptune and the Moon, and by a weak but dangerous sextile relationship between Mars and the Sun.

In a complex universe, neither statement is refutable nor demonstrable, unless one is in ideological agreement with the writer. General essays on causation, however, ought not to exert any special ideological requirement on a reader.

This humorous narrative analyzes a misunderstanding between an anthropologist, Richard Borshay Lee, and his subjects, the !Kung Bushmen of the Kalahari Desert.

Professional Model

Eating Christmas in the Kalahari
Richard Borshay Lee

1   The !Kung Bushmen's knowledge of Christmas is thirdhand. The London Missionary Society brought the holiday to the southern Tswana tribes in the early nineteenth century. Later, native catechists spread the idea far and wide among the Bantu-speaking pastoralists, even in the remotest corners of the Kalahari Desert. The Bushmen's idea of the Christmas story, stripped to its essentials, is "praise the birth of white man's god-chief"; what keeps their interest in the holiday high is the Tswana-Herero custom of slaughtering an ox for his Bushmen neighbors as an annual goodwill gesture. Since the 1930's, part of the Bushmen's annual round of activities has included a December congregation at the cattle posts for trading, marriage brokering, and several days of trance-dance feasting at which the local Tswana headman is host.

2   As a social anthropologist working with !Kung Bushmen, I found that the Christmas ox custom suited my purposes. I had come to the Kalahari to study the hunting and gathering subsistence economy of the !Kung, and to accomplish this it was essential not to provide them with food, share my own food, or interfere in any way with their food-gathering activities. While liberal handouts of tobacco and medical supplies were appreciated, they were scarcely adequate to erase the glaring disparity in wealth between the anthropologist, who maintained a two-month inventory of canned goods, and the Bushmen, who rarely had a day's supply of food on hand. My approach, while paying off in terms of data, left me open to frequent accusations of stinginess and hardheartedness. By their lights, I was a miser.

3   The Christmas ox was to be my way of saying thank you for the cooperation of the past year; and since it was to be our last Christmas in the field, I determined to slaughter the largest, meatiest ox that money could buy, insuring that the feast and trance dance would be a success.

4   Through December I kept my eyes open at the wells as the cattle were brought down for watering. Several animals were offered, but none had quite the grossness that I had in mind. Then, ten days before the holiday, a Herero friend led an ox of astonishing size and mass up to our camp. It was solid black, stood five feet high at the shoulder, had a five-foot span of horns, and must have weighed 1,200 pounds on the hoof. Food consumption calculations are my specialty, and I quickly figured that bones and viscera aside, there was enough meat—at least four pounds—for every man, woman, and child of the 150 Bushmen in the vicinity of /ai/ai who were expected at the feast.

5   Having found the right animal at last, I paid the Herero £20 ($56) and asked him to keep the beast with his herd until Christmas day. The next morning word spread among

the people that the big solid black one was the ox chosen by /ontah (my Bushman name; it means, roughly, "whitey") for the Christmas feast. That afternoon I received the first delegation. Ben!a, an outspoken sixty-year-old mother of five, came to the point slowly.

6 "Where were you planning to eat Christmas?"

"Right here at /ai/ai," I replied.

"Alone or with others?"

"I expect to invite all the people to eat Christmas with me."

"Eat what?"

"I have purchased Yehave's black ox, and I am going to slaughter and cook it."

"That's what we were told at the well but refused to believe it until we heard it from yourself."

"Well, it's the black one," I replied expansively, although wondering what she was driving at.

7 "Oh, no!" Ben!a groaned, turning to her group. "They were right." Turning back to me she asked, "Do you expect us to eat that bag of bones?"

"Bag of bones! It's the biggest ox at /ai/ai."

"Big, yes, but old. And thin. Everybody knows there's no meat on that old ox. What did you expect us to eat off it, the horns?"

Everybody chuckled at Ben!a's one-liner as they walked away, but all I could manage was a weak grin.

8 That evening it was the turn of the young men. They came to sit at our evening fire. /gaugo, about my age, spoke to me man-to-man.

"/ontah, you have always been square with us," he lied. "What has happened to change your heart? That sack of guts and bones of Yehave's will hardly feed one camp, let alone all the Bushmen around /ai/ai." And he proceeded to enumerate the seven camps in the /ai/ai vicinity, family by family. "Perhaps you have forgotten that we are not few, but many. Or are you too blind to tell the difference between a proper cow and an old wreck? That ox is thin to the point of death."

"Look, you guys," I retorted, "that is a beautiful animal, and I'm sure you will eat it with pleasure at Christmas."

"Of course we will eat it; it's food. But it won't fill us up to the point where we will have enough strength to dance. We will eat and go home to bed with stomachs rumbling."

9 That night as we turned in, I asked my wife, Nancy: "What did you think of the black ox?"

"It looked enormous to me. Why?"

"Well, about eight different people have told me I got gypped; that the ox is nothing but bones."

"What's the angle?" Nancy asked. "Did they have a better one to sell?"

"No, they just said that it was going to be a grim Christmas because there won't be enough meat to go around. Maybe I'll get an independent judge to look at the beast in the morning."

10 Bright and early, Halingisi, a Tswana cattle owner, appeared at our camp. But before I could ask him to give me his opinion on Yehave's black ox, he gave me the eye signal that indicated a confidential chat. We left the camp and sat down.

"/ontah, I'm surprised at you: you've lived here for three years and still haven't learned anything about cattle."

"But what else can a person do but choose the biggest, strongest animal one can find?" I retorted.

"Look, just because an animal is big doesn't mean that it has plenty of meat on it.

The black one was a beauty when it was younger, but now it is thin to the point of death."

"Well I've already bought it. What can I do at this stage?"

"Bought it already? I thought you were just considering it. Well, you'll have to kill it and serve it, I suppose. But don't expect much of a dance to follow."

11 My spirits dropped rapidly. I could believe that Ben!a and /gaugo just might be putting me on about the black ox, but Halingisi seemed to be an impartial critic. I went around that day feeling as though I had bought a lemon of a used car.

12 In the afternoon it was Tomazo's turn. Tomazo is a fine hunter, a top trance performer . . . and one of my most reliable informants. He approached the subject of the Christmas cow as part of my continuing Bushman education.

13 "My friend, the way it is with us Bushmen," he began, "is that we love meat. And even more than that, we love fat. When we hunt we always search for the fat ones, the ones dripping with layers of white fat: fat that turns into a clear, thick oil in the cooking pot, fat that slides down your gullet, fills your stomach and gives you a roaring diarrhea," he rhapsodized.

14 "So, feeling as we do," he continued, "it gives us pain to be served such a scrawny thing as Yehave's black ox. It is big, yes, and no doubt its giant bones are good for soup, but fat is what we really crave and so we will eat Christmas this year with a heavy heart."

The prospect of a gloomy Christmas now had me worried, so I asked Tomazo what I could do about it.

"Look for a fat one, a young one . . . smaller, but fat. Fat enough to make us //gom ('evacuate the bowels'), then we will be happy."

15 My suspicions were aroused when Tomazo said that he happened to know of a young, fat, barren cow that the owner was willing to part with. Was Tomazo working on commission, I wondered? But I dispelled this unworthy thought when we approached the Herero owner of the cow in question and found that he had decided not to sell.

16 The scrawny wreck of a Christmas ox now became the talk of the /ai/ai water hole and was the first news told to the outlying groups as they began to come in from the bush for the feast. What finally convinced me that real trouble might be brewing was the visit from u!au, an old conservative with a reputation for fierceness. His nickname meant spear and referred to an incident thirty years ago in which he had speared a man to death. He had an intense manner; fixing me with his eyes, he said in clipped tones:

17 "I have only just heard about the black ox today, or else I would have come here earlier. /ontah, do you honestly think you can serve meat like that to people and avoid a fight?" He paused, letting the implications sink in. "I don't mean fight you, /ontah; you are a white man. I mean a fight between Bushmen. There are many fierce ones here, and with such a small quantity of meat to distribute, how can you give everybody a fair share? Someone is sure to accuse another of taking too much or hogging all the choice pieces. Then you will see what happens when some go hungry while others eat."

18 The possibility of at least a serious argument struck me as all too real. I had witnessed the tension that surrounds the distribution of meat from a kudu or gemsbok kill, and had documented many arguments that sprang up from a real or imagined slight in meat distribution. The owners of a kill may spend up to two hours arranging and rearranging the piles of meat under the gaze of a circle of recipients before handing them out. And I also knew that the Christmas feast at /ai/ai would be bringing together groups that had feuded in the past.

19 Convinced now of the gravity of the situation, I went in earnest to search for a second cow; but all my inquiries failed to turn one up.

20 The Christmas feast was evidently going to be a disaster, and the incessant com-

plaints about the meagerness of the ox had already taken the fun out of it for me. Moreover, I was getting bored with the wisecracks, and after losing my temper a few times, I resolved to serve the beast anyway. If the meat fell short, the hell with it. In the Bushmen idiom, I announced to all who would listen:

21   "I am a poor man and blind. If I have chosen one that is too old and too thin, we will eat it anyway and see if there is enough meat there to quiet the rumbling of our stomachs."

22   On hearing this speech, Ben!a offered me a rare word of comfort. "It's thin," she said philosophically, "but the bones will make a good soup."

23   At dawn Christmas morning, instinct told me to turn over the butchering and cooking to a friend and take off with Nancy to spend Christmas alone in the bush. But curiosity kept me from retreating. I wanted to see what such a scrawny ox looked like on butchering, and if there *was* going to be a fight, I wanted to catch every word of it. Anthropologists are incurable that way.

24   The great beast was driven up to our dancing ground, and a shot in the forehead dropped it in its tracks. Then, freshly cut branches were heaped around the fallen carcass to receive the meat. Ten men volunteered to help with the cutting. I asked /gaugo to make the breast bone cut. This cut, which begins the butchering process for most large game, offers easy access for removal of the viscera. But it also allows the hunter to spot-check the amount of fat on the animal. A fat game animal carries a white layer up to an inch thick on the chest, while in a thin one, the knife will quickly cut to bone. All eyes fixed on his hand as /gaugo, dwarfed by the great carcass, knelt to the breast. The first cut opened a pool of solid white in the black skin. The second and third cut widened and deepened the creamy white. Still no bone. It was pure fat; it must have been two inches thick.

25   "Hey /gau," I burst out, "that ox is loaded with fat. What's this about the ox being too thin to bother eating? Are you out of your mind?"

26   "Fat?" /gau shot back, "You call that fat? This wreck is thin, sick, dead!" And he broke out laughing. So did everyone else. They rolled on the ground paralyzed with laughter. Everybody laughed except me; I was thinking.

27   I ran back to the tent and burst in just as Nancy was getting up. "Hey, the black ox. It's fat as hell! They were kidding about it being too thin to eat. It was a joke or something. A put-on. Everyone is really delighted with it!"

"Some joke," my wife replied. "It was so funny that you were ready to pack up and leave /ai/ai."

28   If it had indeed been a joke, it had been an extraordinarily convincing one, and tinged, I thought, with more than a touch of malice as many jokes are. Nevertheless, that it was a joke lifted my spirits considerably, and I returned to the butchering site where the shape of the ox was rapidly disappearing under the axes and knives of the butchers. The atmosphere had become festive. Grinning broadly, their arms covered with blood well past the elbow, men packed chunks of meat into the big cast-iron cooking pots, fifty pounds to the load, and muttered and chuckled all the while about the thinness and worthlessness of the animal and /ontah's poor judgment.

29   We danced and ate that ox two days and two nights; we cooked and distributed fourteen potfuls of meat and no one went home hungry and no fights broke out.

30   But the "joke" stayed in my mind. I had a growing feeling that something important had happened in my relationship with the Bushmen and that the clue lay in the meaning of the joke. Several days later, when most of the people had dispersed back to the bush camps, I raised the question with Hakekgose, a Tswana man who had grown up among the !Kung, married a !Kung girl, and who probably knew their culture better than any other non-Bushman.

31   "With us whites," I began, "Christmas is supposed to be the day of friendship and brotherly love. What I can't figure out is why the Bushmen went to such lengths to criticize and belittle the ox I had bought for the feast. The animal was perfectly good and their jokes and wisecracks practically ruined the holiday for me."

32   "So it really did bother you," said Hakekgose. "Well, that's the way they always talk. When I take my rifle and go hunting with them, if I miss, they laugh at me for the rest of the day. But even if I hit and bring one down, it's no better. To them, the kill is always too small or too old or too thin; and as we sit down on the kill site to cook and eat the liver, they keep grumbling, even with their mouths full of meat. They say things like, 'Oh this is awful! What a worthless animal! Whatever made me think that this Tswana rascal could hunt!' "

33   "Is this the way outsiders are treated?" I asked.

"No, it is their custom; they talk that way to each other too. Go and ask them."

/gaugo had been one of the most enthusiastic in making me feel bad about the merit of the Christmas ox. I sought him out first.

"Why did you tell me the black ox was worthless, when you could see that it was loaded with fat and meat?"

34   "It is our way," he said smiling. "We always like to fool people about that. Say there is a Bushman who has been hunting. He must not come home and announce like a braggard, 'I have killed a big one in the bush!' He must first sit down in silence until I or someone else comes up to his fire and asks, 'What did you see today?' He replies quietly, 'Ah, I'm no good for hunting. I saw nothing at all [pause] just a little tiny one.' Then I smile to myself," /gaugo continued, "because I know he has killed something big.

35   "In the morning we make up a party of four or five people to cut up and carry the meat back to the camp. When we arrive at the kill we examine it and cry out, 'You mean to say you have dragged us all the way out here in order to make us cart home your pile of bones? Oh, if I had known it was this thin I wouldn't have come.' Another one pipes up, 'People, to think I gave up a nice day in the shade for this. At home we may be hungry but at least we have nice cool water to drink.' If the horns are big, someone says, 'Did you think that somehow you were going to boil down the horns for soup?'

36   "To all this you must respond in kind. 'I agree,' you say, 'this one is not worth the effort; let's just cook the liver for strength and leave the rest for the hyenas. It is not too late to hunt today and even a duiker or a steenbok would be better than this mess.'

37   "Then you set to work nevertheless; butcher the animal, carry the meat back to the camp and everyone eats," /gaugo concluded.

Things were beginning to make sense. Next, I went to Tomazo. He corroborated /gaugo's story of the obligatory insults over a kill and added a few details of his own.

"But," I asked, "why insult a man after he has gone to all that trouble to track and kill an animal and when he is going to share the meat with you so that your children will have something to eat?"

"Arrogance," was his cryptic answer.

"Arrogance?"

38   "Yes, when a young man kills much meat he comes to think of himself as a chief or a big man, and he thinks of the rest of us as his servants or inferiors. We can't accept this. We refuse one who boasts, for someday his pride will make him kill somebody. So we always speak of his meat as worthless. This way we cool his heart and make him gentle."

"But why didn't you tell me this before?" I asked Tomazo with some heat.

"Because you never asked me," said Tomazo, echoing the refrain that has come to haunt every field ethnographer.

39   The pieces now fell into place. I had known for a long time that in situations of social conflict with Bushmen I held all the cards. I was the only source of tobacco in a thousand square miles, and I was not incapable of cutting an individual off for noncooperation. Though my boycott never lasted longer than a few days, it was an indication of my strength. People resented my presence at the water hole, yet simultaneously dreaded my leaving. In short I was a perfect target for the charge of arrogance and for the Bushmen tactic of enforcing humility.

40   I had been taught an object lesson by the Bushmen; it had come from an unexpected corner and had hurt me in a vulnerable area. For the big black ox was to be the one totally generous, unstinting act of my year at /ai/ai, and I was quite unprepared for the reaction I received.

41   As I read it, their message was this: There are no totally generous acts. All "acts" have an element of calculation. One black ox slaughtered at Christmas does not wipe out a year of careful manipulation of gifts to serve your own ends. After all, to kill an animal and share the meat with people is really no more than Bushmen do for each other every day and with far less fanfare.

42   In the end, I had to admire how the Bushmen had played out the farce—collectively straight-faced to the end. Curiously, the episode reminded me of the *Good Soldier Schweik* and his marvelous encounters with authority. Like Schweik, the Bushmen had retained a thorough-going skepticism of good intentions. Was it this independence of spirit, I wondered, that had kept them culturally viable in the face of generations of contact with more powerful societies, both black and white? The thought that the Bushmen were alive and well in the Kalahari was strangely comforting. Perhaps, armed with that independence and with their superb knowledge of their environment, they might yet survive the future.

3,537 words

Vocabulary

catechists (1)	commission (15)	corroborated (37)
pastoralists (1)	recipients (18)	ethnographer (38)
anthropologist (2)	feuded (18)	unstinting (40)
disparity (2)	carcass (24)	skepticism (42)
grossness (4)	dispersed (30)	collectively (42)
viscera (4)	cryptic (37)	viable (42)
evacuate (14)	obligatory (37)	

Questions

1. What incident does the author analyze for cause?
2. Why are the bushmen so contemptuous of the author's ox?
3. What effect does the author suggest that the bushmen's sense of pride may have had on their culture?
4. How did the author proceed with his causal analysis of the bushmen's attitude toward his Christmas gift?
5. What is the controlling idea of this essay? State it in one sentence, including both the effect and the cause.
6. Throughout the essay, how does the author achieve a sense of reader participation in the drama?

Student readers of this book probably will be required to do a more theoretical and abstract analysis of cause than this one. The particular assignment for which this was written allowed students to conduct an analysis of cause within a narrative context. The preceding professional model is a more formal analysis of cause.

Student Model

A Reason or Three
Donald Traylor

Don pulled the big white freightliner out of the yards, pointing it down the on-ramp and into the night. A quick check in his mirrors reflected the lights of other rigs merging from on-ramps, and he knew that most of his friends who ran this route would be forming up for a little convoy as they usually did three nights a week. He stuffed the Road Ranger transmission into thirteen and over, settled into his seat, lit a smoke, and pulled the mike to his C.B. unit from its clip.

"Break-Break. This is the White Knight, mobil truckin' north-bound on I-10 for Frisco town. How 'bout it, Cotton Mouth—you got a copy on this eighteen wheeler? We're lookin', how 'bout it?"

The C.B. cracked and suddenly the cab of the tractor was filled with the voice of his friend Cotton Mouth.

"Ten-roger-four, good buddy. You got the Cotton Mouth. Yea, you definitely got the front door, good buddy, but you better maintain that ol' double nickel for awhile. Susie homemaker up on channel twenty-one just told me that Smokey is out takin' pictures tonight from a plain brown wrapper, some place around the 76 Truck plaza. Your turn, come on."

"That's a big ten-four there, Cotton Mouth. Read you five by five and wall to wall. Guess I'll comb my hair and look real legal for the man. Your turn, go ahead."

Another quick check in the mirrors showed Don that three other trucks had joined the line and that Cotton Mouth was the last truck in the line. The C.B. hissed with greetings and truck talk.

"That's a roger on the double nickle ol' buddy. Go ahead."

"Cotton Mouth, I'm going to power down my unit for awhile. I don't have the motor-mouth tonight and I got some thinkin' to do. So pass the good numbers around for me. And this is the White Knight and we're gonna back on out 'a here for awhile and we're standin' by and on the side. We're gone."

Don replaced the mike in the clip, raised the squelch, lit up another smoke, and muttered to himself, "Christ, radar on the very night I want to drive my brains out." The blue green glow of the instrument panel, mixed with the gray smoke of his cigarette, matched his mood. He shifted in his seat once more and as the sixty-five-foot-long tractor trailer cut through the night with its burden of forty-two thousand pounds of steel, Don's thoughts rolled back to yesterday.

Ellen had laid the keys to his apartment on the glass-top dining room table, turned to collect a few pieces of their time together, then quietly walked out of his life.

Don grimaced as the cold icicle of pain and loss plunged into his heart. His mind slowly sorted through the memories of this love affair gone bad and he began to reflect on why they had parted.

Age had played its part. He had grown up fast and hard, his experiences far surpassing even his age. Two tours in Vietnam with a marine recon unit had put the frosting on the cake, especially the day he lay and watched his squad cut to pieces by a V.C. ambush. But when he met her, his cold, hard exterior had melted away like sugar in a rain storm. He knew he wanted this fresh, innocent girl to hold and cherish forever. But her words rang in his brain like a ricocheting bullet: "Don, I do love you, too, but don't box me in yet. Don't stunt my growth. I want to experience life as you have. I want to enjoy my youth. We have lots of time to settle down together." What she could not realize was that Don wanted to protect her from this unforgiving world and let her see only the good and not the bad. He did not want to possess her, just to love her. He knew that freedom and adventure could be horrible and ugly. Tired from the Vietnam war, he was looking for comfort and safety in a warm, stable relationship. Her needs were different. Eager for new experiences, she was looking for an open, unstructured relationship.

Religion had been another sore point between them, occasionally flaring up into angry arguments. Don was an agnostic. He had tried several formal religions but found each stultifying and hypocritical. He believed in God all right, but he was more at peace with himself when he worshiped in his own mind than when he performed church rituals. He didn't know about Heaven for sure, but he did know about Hell. He had lived in it every day of his life until he left the service. She, on the other hand, was a practicing, full-fledged Irish Roman Catholic with a head full of fine parochial school attitudes and values. He thought he had ignored most of her hints about his lack of devotion to God, in that way avoiding big destructive battles; but in the end his refusal to go to mass and his sarcasms about nuns and priests had hardened her toward him.

The most destructive force in their love affair had been social pressure. Ellen came from a proper and socially prominent family whereas Don grew up in a big family where money was always short. He blushed as he recalled one of his first meetings with her family. It was a small dinner party at her parents' Westlake home. He did not like the sympathetic glance Ellen had passed him as the afterdinner conversation turned to how nice it was that one of her old beaux had finished law school or how well her little brother was doing at Harvard Prep. Hell, man, public high school, then the service, and now night school at Riverdale City College was as well as he could do! He, too, wanted to be a lawyer, but his education would have to be assembled in segments. He had bitten his tongue a hundred times whenever her dad complained about labor ruining the country, or hippies destroying the atmosphere of their summer mansion at Lake Tahoe, or Maddy, the maid, taking advantage of them by refusing to wash down the walls. Once in a while Don couldn't help sullenly noting that Ellen's father seemed to forget that some people made a living by driving trucks during the day so that they could go to school at night. And once, when he was especially tired and grouchy, he had told her that her old man was "a fat-bellied tycoon" who lived in a fantasy world, removed from the sweat of reality. That remark had made her cry.

There it was: age, religion, and social status. Any of these problems separately and individually might have been overcome through patience and maturity. But together they combined into an overwhelming opposition. They had intruded slowly but inevitably and had gradually split Don and Ellen apart. They had blended and jelled into a sharp wedge that had lodged between them. And now he was alone without her.

Suddenly Cotton Mouth was back on the radio, just finishing a sign-off to someone. It was some time before Don realized that Cotton Mouth was trying to get his attention: "Break-break, White Knight. What happened to you, good buddy? That front door put you to sleep up there? Your turn, go ahead. Go ahead."

Don's answer was delivered in slow, measured words: "Negative, Cotton Mouth. I was just truckin'."

In this selection, Arnold Bennett (1867–1931), English novelist, presents a common-sense analysis of why some books achieve the status of a classic.

Alternate Reading

Why a Classic Is a Classic
Arnold Bennett

1   The large majority of our fellow citizens care as much about literature as they care about archaeology or the program of the Legislature. They do not ignore it; they are not quite indifferent to it. But their interest in it is faint and perfunctory; or, if their interest happens to be violent, it is spasmodic. Ask the two hundred thousand persons whose enthusiasm made the vogue of a popular novel ten years ago what they think of that novel now, and you will gather that they have utterly forgotten it, and that they would no more dream of reading it again than of reading Bishop Stubb's *Select Charters*. Probably if they did read it again they would not enjoy it—not because the said novel is a whit worse now than it was ten years ago; not because their taste has improved—but because they have not had sufficient practice to be able to rely on their taste as a means of permanent pleasure. They simply don't know from one day to the next what will please them.

2   In the face of this one may ask: Why does the great and universal fame of classical authors continue? The answer is that the fame of classical authors is entirely independent of the majority. Do you suppose that if the fame of Shakespeare depended on the man in the street it would survive a fortnight? The fame of classical authors is originally made, and it is maintained, by a passionate few. Even when a first-class author has enjoyed immense success during his lifetime, the majority have never appreciated him so sincerely as they have appreciated second-rate men. He has always been reinforced by the ardor of the passionate few. And in the case of an author who has emerged into glory after his death the happy sequel has been due solely to the obstinate perseverance of the few. They could not leave him alone; they would not. They kept on savoring him, and talking about him, and buying him, and they generally behaved with such eager zeal, and they were so authoritative and sure of themselves, that at last the majority grew accustomed to the sound of his name and placidly agreed to the proposition that he was a genius; the majority really did not care very much either way.

3   And it is by the passionate few that the renown of genius is kept alive from one generation to another. These few are always at work. They are always rediscovering genius. Their curiosity and enthusiasm are exhaustless, so that there is little chance of genius being ignored. And, moreover, they are always working either for or against the verdicts of the majority. The majority can make a reputation, but it is too careless to maintain it. If, by accident, the passionate few agree with the majority in a particular instance, they will frequently remind the majority that such and such a reputation has been made, and the majority will idly concur: "Ah, yes. By the way, we must not forget that such and such a reputation exists." Without that persistent memory-jogging the reputation would quickly fall into oblivion which is death. The passionate few only have their way by reason of the fact that they are genuinely interested in literature, that literature matters to them. They conquer by their obstinacy alone, by their eternal repetition of the same statements. Do you suppose they could prove to the man in the street that Shakespeare was a great artist? The said man would not even understand the terms they employed. But when he is told ten thousand times, and generation after generation, that Shake-

speare was a great artist, the said man believes—not by reason, but by faith. And he too repeats that Shakespeare was a great artist, and he buys the complete works of Shakespeare and puts them on his shelves, and he goes to see the marvellous stage effects which accompany *King Lear* or *Hamlet,* and comes back religiously convinced that Shakespeare was a great artist. All because the passionate few could not keep their admiration of Shakespeare to themselves. This is not cynicism; but truth. And it is important that those who wish to form their literary taste should grasp it.

4   What causes the passionate few to make such a fuss about literature? There can be only one reply. They find a keen and lasting pleasure in literature. They enjoy literature as some men enjoy beer. The recurrence of this pleasure naturally keeps their interest in literature very much alive. They are forever making new researches, forever practising on themselves. They learn to understand themselves. They learn to know what they want. Their taste becomes surer and surer as their experience lengthens. They do not enjoy today what will seem tedious to them tomorrow. When they find a book tedious, no amount of popular clatter will persuade them that it is pleasurable; and when they find it pleasurable no chill silence of the street crowds will affect their conviction that the book is good and permanent. They have faith in themselves. What are the qualities in a book which give keen and lasting pleasure to the passionate few? This is a question so difficult that it has never yet been completely answered. You may talk lightly about truth, insight, knowledge, wisdom, humor, and beauty, but these comfortable words do not really carry you very far, for each of them has to be defined, especially the first and last. It is all very well for Keats in his airy manner to assert that beauty is truth, truth beauty, and that that is all he knows or needs to know. I, for one, need to know a lot more. And I shall never know. Nobody, not even Hazlitt[1] nor Sainte-Beuve,[2] has ever finally explained why he thought a book beautiful. I take the first fine lines that come to hand—

> The woods of Arcady are dead,
> And over is their antique joy—

and I say that those lines are beautiful, because they give me pleasure. But why? No answer! I only know that the passionate few will, broadly, agree with me in deriving this mysterious pleasure from those lines. I am only convinced that the liveliness of our pleasure in those and many other lines by the same author will ultimately cause the majority to believe, by faith, that W. B. Yeats[3] is a genius. The one reassuring aspect of the literary affair is that the passionate few are passionate about the same things. A continuance of interest does, in actual practice, lead ultimately to the same judgments. There is only the difference in width of interest. Some of the passionate few lack catholicity, or, rather, the whole of their interest is confined to one narrow channel; they have none left over. These men help specially to vitalize the reputations of the narrower geniuses: such as Crashaw.[4] But their active predilections never contradict the general verdict of the passionate few; rather they reinforce it.

5   A classic is a work which gives pleasure to the minority which is intensely and permanently interested in literature. It lives on because the minority, eager to renew the sensation of pleasure, is eternally curious and is therefore engaged in an eternal process of rediscovery. A classic does not survive for any ethical reason. It does not survive because it conforms to certain canons, or because neglect would not kill it. It survives

---

[1]William Hazlitt (1778–1830), English essayist.
[2]Charles Sainte-Beuve (1804–1869), French literary critic and writer.
[3]W. B. Yeats (1865–1939), Irish poet, playwright, and essayist.
[4]Richard Crashaw (1613?–1649), English religious poet.

because it is a source of pleasure, and because the passionate few can no more neglect it than a bee can neglect a flower. The passionate few do not read "the right things" because they are right. That is to put the cart before the horse. "The right things" are the right things solely because the passionate few *like* reading them. Hence—and I now arrive at my point—the one primary essential to literary taste is a hot interest in literature. If you have that, all the rest will come. It matters nothing that at present you fail to find pleasure in certain classics. The driving impulse of your interest will force you to acquire experience, and experience will teach you the use of the means of pleasure. You do not know the secret ways of yourself: that is all. A continuance of interest must inevitably bring you to the keenest joys. But, of course, experience may be acquired judiciously or injudiciously, just as Putney may be reached via Walham Green or via Moscow.[5]

1,425 words

Vocabulary

perfunctory (1)   catholicity (4)
spasmodic (1)   predilections (4)
concur (3)   canons (5)

Questions

1. What is the attitude of the large majority of people toward literature?
2. Why can't the large majority of people rely on their literary taste as a means of permanent pleasure?
3. What is the basis for the great fame that classical authors enjoy? Where is this stated in the essay?
4. Throughout the essay, the author frequently poses questions to himself, which he then answers. What does this self-questioning technique contribute to the essay?
5. How do the passionate few succeed in conferring fame on an author who is dead?
6. Why do the passionate few have their way in literary matters?
7. Why does the man on the street believe the proposition that Shakespeare is a great artist?
8. Why do the passionate few take such an interest in literature?
9. One man has a greater interest in literature than another. Does it follow that the literary taste of the first man is superior to that of the second? Justify your reasoning.
10. Why does a classic survive? What causes the passionate few to agree that a work is a classic?
11. What is essential to the formation of literary taste?

---

[5]The names of certain districts of London, which also designate stops for the extensive London underground railway system. Putney may be reached via Walham Green or Moscow in the same way that a person can fly from Los Angeles to New York via New Orleans or Chicago.

Popular columnist Dr. Joyce Brothers analyzes in this selection why women react with hostility to the Women's Liberation movement.

Alternate Reading

Women's Lib Backlash

Joyce Brothers

1   From the beginning, some men feared and hated the Women's Liberation movement. That was to be expected. What's surprising is the number of women who feel the same way.

2   How has it happened that a movement designed to free women for a wider life, to raise their consciousness and build their self-esteem, has seemed to so many women a gigantic put-down?

3   Today, for instance, my mail contains a letter from a devoted mother of five. "In spite of the common cartoon image of the average homemaker glued to the TV," she writes, "I work all day at my job. I take pride in keeping my house not only clean but beautiful. Our family is caught up in the celebration of every season and holiday. I cook 'real' meals rich in nutrition and flavor. I do the research necessary so that my family can know and enjoy Strufoli at Christmas, Cassata di Grano at Easter. I pass along to them their rich Italian heritage—songs I remember from my own childhood, stories I was told. I plan our vacations carefully. Yet liberated women keep asking me, *'Aren't you working yet?' What do they think I've been doing these past 18 years?"*

SOME DEMANDS SUPPORTED

4   Surveys show that most American women support the central demands of the liberation movement: equal pay for equal work, fair hiring and promotion practices, an end to the many legal discriminations against women. But many resent the movement's rejection of homemaking as an appropriate and fulfilling female role. "That get-in-there-and-fight talk is fine for a professionally qualified woman," a friend said to me recently. "It doesn't mean much to someone who has no salable skills and who's really happy at home with the kids."

5   Though officially the Women's Lib platform supports the freedom of women to do whatever they choose, prominent liberationists often speak as if those who choose to stay home are either victims or fools. Homemakers who insist they are neither are told they've been so brainwashed by society that they don't even realize how they're being exploited. Is it any wonder that the response is anger?

6   Of course the backlash is not really new. It's been there all along. In the beginning, though, it was the flamboyant reformers who caught the public eye and the TV cameras. Now that the first excitements are over—the parades and strikes and tales of bra-burning (which never really occurred anywhere)—the news media has turned its attention to a silent majority that's just now finding its voice. And they've discovered that for every woman who renounces men-and-marriage there are many more who say, as did a respondent in a consumer poll: "As a housewife and mother, I would rather be a feminine woman than a woman feminist."

7   The opposition to Women's Lib doesn't all come from aggrieved homemakers. Some people are, quite simply, put off by the flagrant behavior of the movement's leaders. Betty Friedan, an intelligent and dedicated champion of women, doesn't exactly melt the heart. Nor do you have to be a shrinking violet to shrink a little at the image of Jill Johnson leaping topless into a pool at an elegant public gathering, or of Kate Millett in karate garb. Then there are those spokeswomen who describe childbearing as humiliating slavery, and heterosexual love as a form of rape.

8   In defense of the bizarre exhibitionism of some women's libbers, it's worth pointing out that without just this sort of excess, no one would have paid much attention to demands for women's equality. "Typical" women don't make news. Whatever the justification for the movement's histrionics, though, a great many women simply cannot identify with Gloria Steinem and Germaine Greer. (And no doubt at least some resent these glamorous creatures for their almost incredible combinations of brains, beauty and success.)

9   Though there's surprising agreement on women's rights to job equality with men, other planks in the reform platform are by no means universally supported. Abortion is a hotly disputed, emotionally charged issue; so are day-care centers, since some women (as well as men) fear they will ultimately contribute to child neglect and the further decline of family life. Conservative women are repelled by the movement's association with Gay Liberation, to say nothing of its implied endorsement of bisexuality. The proposed designation of *Ms.* for all women gets a cold eye from many. ("I like Mrs.," Mayor John Lindsay's wife said recently. "It took me long enough to get it.") As for cosmetics, perfumes and bras, abhorred by militant libbers because they're part of the sex-object mentality—how a women feels in this area is likely to be determined by her natural endowments. I like the realism of the woman who, asked about giving up her bra, shrugged, "That's fine if you're a 30AAA. But what about us 36D's?"

10   The message from Women's Liberation is that male-female relationships must be radically restructured. No more man-the-master, no more woman-on-a-pedestal, no more Daddy-the-strong-protector and Mommy-the-gentle-caretaker. It's clear, though, that not all females have rallied to this cry. Maybe it *is* the result of brainwashing, but a lot of women don't *want* restructure. They enjoy having doors opened for them. And I'm not thinking only of super-frillies like the members of the anti-lib organization, Pussycats (motto: "The lamb chop is mightier than the karate chop"). Even women who've made it in a man's world, successful career types, are just as likely to expect that their coats will be held and their cigarettes lit. And some ardent feminists themselves may be inconsistent. A national poll last year found that while a majority of women under 25 didn't want to be "treated as sex objects," an even larger majority enjoyed being whistled at! And while most women of all ages opposed discrimination in hiring, nearly all were against women being drafted into the armed services—though plenty of service-connected jobs could be performed equally well by either men or women.

11   Some of what's called "backlash" against Women's Lib is more properly described as indifference. Basically, the movement speaks to white, middle-class Americans. It has little relevance for blacks of any class: their experience is too separate. "The Women's Liberation movement," says Ida Lewis, former editor of *Essence,* "is basically a family quarrel between white women and white men. And on general principles, it's not good to get involved in family disputes. The role of black women is to continue the struggle in concert with black men for the liberation and self-determination of blacks." Women's Lib also says little to a woman who, for instance, left school after the eighth grade and now lives on welfare with her family. Even the movement's natural constituency, educated urban or suburban women, often remains aloof—for the most ele-

mentary human reason: Caught up in the concrete problems of daily life (jobs, cooking, pregnancies, whatever), they are bored by abstract arguments—and vividly aware that a point-by-point marriage contract wouldn't help them solve the current crisis of a broken dishwasher or the baby-sitter who didn't show.

12   Other reasons for the backlash can be dismissed briefly. There's the professional woman who says, "I made it on my own. Why can't other women do the same?" (To movement leaders, she's an Aunt Tom.) There's the woman who really isn't interested in anything except having fun (*So what on earth are they yammering about, all those neurotic females hung up on achievement?*). There's the sour-grapes type (*It's too late for me to be liberated, so why should those others get all the advantages?*).

13   But probably the most interesting opposition to the movement is the result of what psychologists call "reaction formation." In plain language, this is an individual's attempt to protect himself against unacceptable impulses by going to the opposite extreme. So, the mother who feels resentment toward her child may become oversolicitous, the hostile person may become overfriendly—and the woman who, deep down, smoulders over her housewife role may attack the liberation movement because it speaks to her suppressed desires. Reading about those emancipated wives who leave husbands and children in order to find their real selves, she feels a disproportionate fury. Hussies, sluts, tramps, they're a disgrace to womenhood. . . . The louder she rages, the less she hears that small, uneasy-making inner voice: "I'd like to do that too!"

14   A woman who finds herself unreasonably upset by Women's Liberation would do well to attempt an honest self-appraisal. What is it in her life that makes the movement's demands so galling? Such probing can be painful but productive. If, having seriously explored her feelings, she can say she's a housewife by free choice, because home-making satisfies her deepest needs, then she has no reason to feel apologetic or threatened. By the same token, she has no reason to remind her family of sacrifices made for their sake—or to expect them to put her on a pedestal.

15   What if self-examination does not produce such reassuring results? What if a women feels, frankly, that she would have made a better chemist than cook, a happier business-woman than baby-sitter? Coming to such a conclusion hurts. It takes courage. But it can be constructive too, for only by facing up to real feelings can one deal with them effectively. A woman who realizes that she's been pushing the lid down on a kettleful of boiling discontents can be helped, by Women's Lib, to come to terms with these feelings and work out a happier compromise.

16   Women's Lib is, like most things human, a mixed bag—a combination of lofty rhetoric and petty complaints, of reason and illogic, idealism and sheer vindictiveness. But what it's really talking about is free choice: freedom to take a job and freedom to stay home, freedom for women to fulfill themselves and equal freedom for men. The consciousness-raising it advocates can lead to new self-confidence, making women aware of the choices they have made and those still open to them. Above all, it urges that people respect each other as individuals, not as symbols. In the tumult and shouting, this message sometimes gets overlooked.

1,655 words

Vocabulary

flamboyant (6)	militant (9)
renounces (6)	endowments (9)
flagrant (7)	oversolicitous (13)
histrionics (8)	vindictiveness (16)
abhorred (9)	tumult (16)

Questions

1. What is the function of paragraph 2 of this article?
2. According to surveys, what central demands of the Women's Lib movement do most American women support?
3. What do many women resent about the Women's Lib movement?
4. What do many people dislike about the leaders of the Women's Lib movement? Who are some of these leaders?
5. What justification does the author give for the bizarre exhibitionism of some Women's Libbers?
6. What are some of the hotly contested planks in the Women's Lib reform movement?
7. What is the message of the Women's Lib movement? How do women feel about this message?
8. To which class of Americans does the Women's Lib movement basically speak? What relevance does the movement have for black Americans?
9. What is reaction formation? What does it have to do with a woman's reaction to the Women's Lib movement?
10. What message of the Women's Lib movement is frequently overlooked?
11. What is the essential aim of this article? What cause or effect is it analyzing?

C. Additional Writing Assignments

1. What do you consider the major causes of juvenile crime in our country? Develop a 500-word causal analysis in which you deal with this question.
2. Think of the person in this world whom you most dislike. Describe the trait that makes you dislike him or her, and find reasons for this trait. State both the trait and the reasons for it in a controlling idea. Develop this into an essay.
3. Write an essay projecting the effects of a third world war. Begin with a controlling idea.
4. Explore the major reasons for the high dropout rate in college. Summarize these reasons in your controlling idea, and develop them in an essay.
5. Think back to the last time you and your parents (or you and a friend) had a serious quarrel, and write a causal analysis on the reasons for the quarrel.
6. What is your favorite city in the world? Write an essay giving detailed reasons for your choice.
7. Write a causal analysis on one of the following historical events:
   a. The Salem witch trials
   b. The Aaron Burr–Alexander Hamilton duel
   c. The 1930 depression
   d. The creation of labor unions

   Begin with a controlling idea.
8. In an essay, give your views on the high divorce rate in America. State each reason in a separate, well-developed paragraph.
9. Write a causal analysis stating three or four good effects of a college education. Supply appropriate examples for each effect.

12

Argumentation

The social security system should be reformed to provide
free room and board for the elderly, rather than
continuing the benefit system now employed.

A. Reading for Ideas

The short story "War," by Luigi Pirandello, is a subtle and moving argument
against war that resurrects the universal questions men have always asked: Is war
glorious? Is war worth the sacrifice of a loved one? Is there honor in dying at war?
As the story progresses, you will see that it is an eloquent and persuasive argument.
Use the story as a springboard to an argument of your own. Ask yourself what
traditions, institutions, customs, or stereotypes bother you. Why do you dislike
them? If you could do away with them, would you? Why?

War

Luigi Pirandello

1   The passengers who had left Rome by the night express had had to stop until dawn at
the small station of Fabriano in order to continue their journey by the small old-fashioned
local joining the main line with Sulmona.

2   At dawn, in a stuffy and smoky second-class carriage in which five people had already
spent the night, a bulky woman in deep mourning was hoisted in—almost like a shape-
less bundle. Behind her—puffing and moaning, followed her husband—a tiny man, thin
and weakly, his face death-white, his eyes small and bright and looking shy and uneasy.

3   Having at last taken a seat he politely thanked the passengers who had helped his
wife and who had made room for her; then he turned round to the woman trying to
pull down the collar of her coat, and politely inquired:

4   "Are you all right, dear?"

5   The wife, instead of answering, pulled up her collar again to her eyes, so as to hide
her face.

6   "Nasty world," muttered the husband with a sad smile.

7   And he felt it his duty to explain to his traveling companions that the poor woman was
to be pitied for the war was taking away from her her only son, a boy of twenty to whom

both had devoted their entire life, even breaking up their home at Sulmona to follow him to Rome, where he had to go as a student, then allowing him to volunteer for war with an assurance, however, that at least for six months he would not be sent to the front and now, all of a sudden, receiving a wire saying that he was due to leave in three days' time and asking them to go and see him off.

8   The woman under the big coat was twisting and wriggling, at times growling like a wild animal, feeling certain that all those explanations would not have aroused even a shadow of sympathy from those people who—most likely—were in the same plight as herself. One of them, who had been listening with particular attention, said:

9   "You should thank God that your son is only leaving now for the front. Mine has been sent there the first day of the war. He has already come back twice wounded and been sent back again to the front."

10   "What about me? I have two sons and three nephews at the front," said another passenger.

11   "Maybe, but in our case it is our *only* son," ventured the husband.

12   "What difference can it make? You may spoil your only son with excessive attentions, but you cannot love him more than you would all your other children if you had any. Paternal love is not like bread that can be broken into pieces and split amongst the children in equal shares. A father gives *all* his love to each one of his children without discrimination, whether it be one or ten, and if I am suffering now for my two sons, I am not suffering half for each of them but double . . ."

13   "True . . . true . . ." sighed the embarrassed husband, "but suppose (of course we all hope it will never be your case) a father has two sons at the front and he loses one of them, there is still one left to console him . . . while . . ."

14   "Yes," answered the other, getting cross, "a son left to console him but also a son left for whom he must survive, while in the case of the father of an only son if the son dies the father can die too and put an end to his distress. Which of the two positions is the worse? Don't you see how my case would be worse than yours?"

15   "Nonsense," interrupted another traveler, a fat, red-faced man with bloodshot eyes of the palest gray.

16   He was panting. From his bulging eyes seemed to spurt inner violence of an uncontrolled vitality which his weakened body could hardly contain.

17   "Nonsense," he repeated, trying to cover his mouth with his hand so as to hide the two missing front teeth. "Nonsense. Do we give life to our children for our own benefit?"

18   The other travelers stared at him in distress. The one who had had his son at the front since the first day of the war sighed: "You are right. Our children do not belong to us, they belong to the Country. . . ."

19   "Bosh," retorted the fat traveler. "Do we think of the Country when we give life to our children? Our sons are born because . . . well, because they must be born and when they come to life they take our own life with them. This is the truth. We belong to them but they never belong to us. And when they reach twenty they are exactly what we were at their age. We too had a father and mother, but there were so many other things as well . . . girls, cigarettes, illusions, new ties . . . and the Country, of course, whose call we would have answered—when we were twenty—even if father and mother had said no. Now, at our age, the love of our Country is still great, of course, but stronger than it is the love for our children. Is there any one of us here who wouldn't gladly take his son's place at the front if he could?"

20   There was a silence all round, everybody nodding as to approve.

21   "Why then," continued the fat man, "shouldn't we consider the feelings of our children when they are twenty? Isn't it natural that at their age they should consider

the love for their Country (I am speaking of decent boys, of course) even greater than the love for us? Isn't it natural that it should be so, as after all they must look upon old boys who cannot move any more and must stay at home? If Country exists, if Country is a natural necessity, like bread, of which each of us must eat in order not to die of hunger, somebody must go to defend it. And our sons go, when they are twenty, and they don't want tears, because if they die, they die inflamed and happy (I am speaking, of course, of decent boys). Now, if one dies young and happy, without having the ugly sides of life, the boredom of it, the pettiness, the bitterness of disillusion . . . what more can we ask for him? Everyone should stop crying; everyone should laugh, as I do . . . or at least thank God—as I do—because my son, before dying, sent me a message saying that he was dying satisfied at having ended his life in the best way he could have wished. That is why, as you see, I do not even wear mourning. . . .''

22   He shook his light fawn coat as to show it; his livid lip over his missing teeth was trembling, his eyes were watery and motionless, and soon after he ended with a shrill laugh which might well have been a sob.

23   ''Quite so . . . quite so . . .'' agreed the others.

24   The woman who, bundled in a corner under her coat, had been sitting and listening had—for the last three months—tried to find in the words of her husband and her friends something to console her in her deep sorrow, something that might show her how a mother should resign herself to send her son not even to death but to a probable danger of life. Yet not a word had she found amongst the many which has been said . . . and her grief had been greater in seeing that nobody—as she thought—could share her feelings.

25   But now the words of the traveler amazed and almost stunned her. She suddenly realized that it wasn't the others who were wrong and could not understand her but herself who could not rise up to the same height of those fathers and mothers willing to resign themselves, without crying, not only to the departure of their sons but even to their death.

26   She lifted her head, she bent over from her corner trying to listen with great attention to the details which the fat man was giving to his companions about the way his son had fallen as a hero, for his King and his Country, happy and without regrets. It seemed to her that she had stumbled into a world she had never dreamt of, a world so far unknown to her and she was so pleased to hear everyone joining in congratulating that brave father who could so stoically speak of his child's death.

27   Then suddenly, just as if she had heard nothing of what had been said and almost as if waking up from a dream, she turned to the old man, asking him:

28   ''Then . . . is your son really dead?''

29   Everybody stared at her. The old man, too, turned to look at her, fixing his great, bulging, horribly watery light gray eyes, deep in her face. For some little time he tried to answer, but words failed him. He looked and looked at her, almost as if only then—at that silly incongruous question—he had suddenly realized at last that his son was really dead—gone for ever—for ever. His face contracted, became horribly distorted then he snatched in haste a handkerchief from his pocket and, to the amazement of everyone, broke into harrowing, heartrending, uncontrollable sobs.

1,576 words

Vocabulary

livid (22)	incongruous (29)
stoically (26)	harrowing (29)

Questions

1. What is the controlling idea of the story? State it in one concise sentence.
2. What is the fat man's *pretended* attitude toward the loss of a son at war? How does this contrast with his *real* attitude?
3. The story contains little action. What is the conflict of the story?
4. What exactly triggers off the sudden change in the fat man's attitude?
5. Is there any hint earlier in the story that the fat man was not as sure of his argument as he claimed to be?
6. How would you counter the fat man's argument?

Dooley Is a Traitor
James Michie

1   "So then you won't fight?"
    "Yes, your Honour," I said, "that's right."
    "Now is it that you simply aren't willing,
    Or have you a fundamental moral objection to killing?"
    Says the judge, blowing his nose
    And making his words stand to attention in long rows.
    I stand to attention too, but with half a grin
    (In my time I've done a good many in).
    "No objection at all, sir," I said.
    "There's a deal of the world I'd rather see dead—
    Such as Johnny Stubbs or Fred Settle or my last landlord, Mr. Syme.
    Give me a gun and your blessing, your Honour, and I'll be killing
    them all the time.
2   But my conscience says a clear no
    To killing a crowd of gentlemen I don't know.
    Why, I'd as soon think of killing a worshipful judge,
    High-court, like yourself (against whom, God knows, I've got no grudge—
    So far), as murder a heap of foreign folk.
    If you've got no grudge, you've got no joke
    To laugh at after."
3   Now the words never come flowing
    Proper for me till I get the old pipe going.
    And just as I was poking
    Down baccy, the judge looks up sharp with "No smoking,
    Mr. Dooley. We're not fighting this war for fun.
    And we want a clearer reason why you refuse to carry a gun.
    This war is not a personal feud, it's a fight
    Against wrong ideas on behalf of the Right.
    Mr. Dooley, won't you help to destroy evil ideas?"
4   "Ah, your Honour, here's
    The tragedy," I said. "I'm not a man of the mind.
    I couldn't find it in my heart to be unkind.
    To an idea. I wouldn't know one if I saw one. I haven't one of my own.
5   So I'd best be leaving other people's alone."

"Indeed," he sneers at me, "this defence is
Curious for someone with convictions in two senses.
A criminal invokes conscience to his aid
To support an individual withdrawal from a communal crusade.
Sanctioned by God, led by the Church, against a godless, churchless nation!"

6   I asked his Honour for a translation.
"You talk of conscience," he said. "What do you know of the Christian creed?"
"Nothing, sir, except what I can read,
That's the most you can hope for from us jail-birds.
I just open the Book here and there and look at the words.
And I find when the Lord himself misliked an evil notion
He turned it into a pig and drove it squealing over a cliff into the ocean,

7   And the loony ran away
And lived to think another day.
There was a clean job done and no blood shed!
Everybody happy and forty wicked thoughts drowned dead.
A neat and Christian murder. None of your mad slaughter
Throwing away the brains with the blood and the baby with the bathwater.

8   Now I look at the war as a sportsman. It's a matter of choosing
The decentest way of losing.
Heads or tails, losers or winners,
We all lose, we're all damned sinners.
And I'd rather be with the poor cold people at the wall that's shot
Than the bloody guilty devils in the firing-line, in Hell and keeping hot."
"But what right, Dooley, what right," he cried,
"Have you to say the Lord is on your side?"
"That's a dirty crooked question," back I roared.
"I said not the Lord was on my side, but I was on the side of the Lord."
Then he was up at me and shouting.

9   But by and by he calms: "Now we're not doubting
Your sincerity, Dooley, only your arguments,
Which don't make sense."
('Hullo,' I thought, 'that's the wrong way round.
I may be skylarking a bit, but my brainpan's sound.')
Then biting his nail and sugaring his words sweet:
"Keep your head, Mr. Dooley. Religion is clearly not up your street.
But let me ask you as a plain patriotic fellow
Whether you'd stand there so smug and yellow
If the foe were attacking your own dear sister."
"I'd knock their brains out, mister,
On the floor," I said. "There," he says kindly, "I knew you were no pacifist.

10   It's your straight duty as a man to enlist.
The enemy is at the door." You could have downed
Me with a feather. "Where?" I gasp, looking round.
"Not this door," he says angered. "Don't play the clown.
But they're two thousand miles away planning to do us down.
Why, the news is full of the deeds of those murderers and rapers."
"Your Eminence," I said, "my father told me never to believe the papers
But to go by my eyes,
And at two thousand miles the poor things can't tell the truth from lies."

11   His fearful spectacles glittered like the moon: "For the last time what right

Has a man like you to refuse to fight?"
"More right," I said, "than you.
You've never murdered a man, so you don't know what it is I won't do.
I've done it in good hot blood, so haven't I the right to make bold
To declare that I shan't do it in cold?"
Then the judge rises in a great rage
And writes DOOLEY IS A TRAITOR in black upon a page
And tells me I must die.
"What, me?" says I.
"If you still won't fight."
"Well, yes, your Honour," I said, "that's right."

Questions

1. Dooley is labeled a traitor because he refuses to join the army and fight in the war. What is the controlling idea of his objection?
2. What is the judge's counterargument to Dooley's position?
3. When the judge tries to trick Dooley by bringing up the Christian creed (paragraph 6), what does Dooley answer? Why?
4. When the judge tries to trick Dooley again by asking what he would do if an enemy were suddenly to attack Dooley's sister, what is Dooley's answer?
5. How would you characterize Dooley's logic? How does his logic differ from the judge's?
6. According to Dooley, who wins in a war?
7. What supportive evidence can you present to advance either Dooley's or the judge's argument?
8. Dooley is a confessed murderer and criminal. What effect does this have on his view about war?

B. How to Write an Argument

Specific Instructions

An argument assumes more than one side to a question. In a debate, two people get up and dispute back and forth, each trying to convince the other of the basic wisdom and rightness of his position. A written argument, however, has no immediate, vocal opposition. You must understand both the pro and the con and be able to deal with each, for you—the writer—are the only expositor of the argument.

Arguments usually convince not because of their intrinsic merits but because they are persuasively presented. How often have you heard this comment about some quick-witted person: "He can make you believe that black is white"? Doubtless such a person knows how to present his case with fiendish skill. Our point is not that you should become a silver-tongued rogue, but that you should learn the art of arguing effectively.

Writing Assignment

Select a tradition, a custom, an institution, or a stereotype that you distrust or dislike, and write an argument against it. Begin with a controlling idea expressing clearly the hub of your opposition—for example, "I deplore the professionalism that infiltrates the Winter Olympic Games because it gives some countries an unfair advantage." Or "The white wedding gown is outmoded and hypocritical." Or "Tax loopholes should be stopped because they help only the rich." To be convincing, the controlling idea, once argumentatively expressed, must be supported with evidence, testimonials, reasons, and data.

1. BE HARD-HEADED IN YOUR USE OF EVIDENCE. Nothing takes the place of facts, experience, statistics, or exhibits that supply a finite, definite, and incontestable edge to your assertions. Naturally, no one is an expert on all things, and hard evidence is often difficult to come by. However, the campus library is still a storehouse of innumerable facts, uncountable numbers, and irrefutable data. Look up the information you need. Here are some assertions of mush and assertions of granite:

Mush: Hotdogs are horrible things to eat and have been proven to be very bad for you since they are very high in fat and chemicals.

Granite: According to the U.S. Department of Agriculture, since 1937 the frankfurter has gone from 19% fat and 19.6% protein to 28% fat and only 11.7% protein. (The rest is water, salt, spices and preservatives.) This deterioration is yet another of technology's ambiguous gifts.

"The Decline and Fill of the American Hotdog," Time

Mush: People can reduce and lose weight. Many celebrities, including well-known actors, athletes, and politicians, have successfully lost weight. If they can, so can everyone.

Granite: People can reduce and lose weight. Alfred Hitchcock went from 365 lbs. to a weight of 200 lbs. by eating only steak and cutting down on liquor; Jackie Gleason scaled down from 280 lbs. to 221 lbs. Maria Callas likewise went from a tumorous 215 lbs. to a trim 135 lbs. Even Lyndon Johnson, when he was Vice President, lost 31 lbs. in less than 10 weeks after being elected to the post in 1961.

Jean Meyer, Overweight: Causes, Cost, and Control

2. SUPPORT YOUR ARGUMENT WITH SPECIFIC GRAPHIC DETAILS. All factual prose writing depends on specifics. Pack a series of pinpoint specifics in a paragraph, and it will acquire a zesty sting that will do honor to your wit and style. When the paragraph is part of an argument whose intent is to convince and persuade a reader, the specifics are even more indispensable. This applies not only to the use of facts, but to the use of general detail.

Some arguments fare badly with facts, but do better with overall detail. For instance, if you were writing an essay opposing beauty contests, facts about them would probably not dissuade your reader. Love or hate for beauty contests is not usually founded on fact alone, but on a person's underlying values. You may hate beauty contests because you think they *degrade* woman into a sex object while another person may love beauty contests because he thinks they *elevate* woman into an art object. A barrage of remorseless facts about the number of beauty contests held in America will probably not change your reader's mind about them. What you must do is draw a graphic picture showing the grotesque side of beauty contests. To do this, you desperately need specific, graphic detail. Here are two examples of arguments against beauty contests. The first is mush in its use of detail:

> I am against beauty pageants because they degrade women. They show the superficial side of the contestants. They never really evaluate the inside person. The whole deal is about bosoms and legs. Then all the women watching the contestants feel inferior because they don't feel as beautiful and desirable as the girls up on the stage. To me that is degrading womanhood. When the time comes for the winner to receive the flowers and the crown, I feel depressed that our country wastes its time and money on beauty pageants.

The argument started out with a strong controlling idea, but had not amounted to two sentences before we realized that the writer has little to say. His detail is weak or nonexistent. One has the urge to yell: "Prove to me that you are right! Show me!" The following has a better beginning, and is sharper and more specific in the use of detail:

> I am against beauty pageants because they degrade women. By "degrade" I mean they force women to be less than what they really are. What the audience sees is a beautifully proportioned smiling mannequin, parading gracefully up and down a light-flooded ramp, to the tune of some lilting band music. Her smile is fixed, her beauty is lacquered. The master of ceremonies asks her some inane question, such as: "How does it feel to be a runner-up in the Miss Rootbeer of Indiana Contest?" The mannequin twirps a delighted giggle and spreads her lips into a wide smile that exhibits gleamingly white teeth. If the girl has an I.Q., the judges could never discern it because she is treated as if she were made of plastic, not flesh and blood. Each year, 150 such pageants are held in California alone, sponsored as advertising by big companies that sell every sort of commodity from oranges to toothpaste. And in each pageant between ten and fifty girls must go through this degrading demotion to mannequin status. The last pageant I attended was the Miss International Trade competition. And when the girls walked out on stage, I almost expected them to jump through circus hoops held by the M.C., some honey-voiced executive who stood to gain from the advertising of the pageant.

Detail designed to show the grotesqueness of beauty contests is hammered home by this passage. The author appears to have actually attended beauty pageants and to know some facts about them—the number in California each year, what questions the girls are asked, the names of some pageants, and who profits from them. If you thought that beauty contests elevate women, here is an argument showing how they degrade. Chances are that this passage—replete with vivid details and graphic adjectives—is more likely to persuade you than the first.

Evidence is gathered through work. Checking library sources, consulting encyclopedias, and plodding through stacks of articles, books, or pamphlets is work, no question about that. But if you want to formulate a strong argument, that's what you'll have to do.

The rewards for this sort of research are numerous, some tangible, like a better grade, some intangible, like not looking foolish. For the second reward, the best illustration we can think of comes from the current controversy about the Bermuda Triangle, an area of the Atlantic and Caribbean that is luridly billed by writers as "a graveyard of lost ships," an area where UFOs regularly capture human specimens, or giant squids burst through the surface of the sea to gobble up hapless seamen. Here is one popular version of the "disappearance" of a triangle victim, the Japanese freighter *Raifuku Maru:*

> "It's like a dagger! Come quick," the frantic voice pleaded over the wireless. "Please come, we cannot escape." Then the cries from the *Raifuku Maru* faded away into the stillness of the tranquil sea. Other ships in the Bermuda Triangle were puzzled as to why a ship would send such a message on so calm a day. Nothing has ever been heard or seen of the freighter or its crew since that April morning in 1925.
>
> Lawrence D. Kusche, *The Bermuda Triangle Mystery Solved*

The same disaster was listed in the *Dictionary of Disasters during the Age of Steam,* a work compiled from the files of Lloyd's Register of Shipping. Lloyd's is the largest and oldest maritime insurer in the world. Here is the Lloyd's account:

> The Japanese steamship *Raifuku Maku* left Boston on April 18th, 1925, for Hamburg with a cargo of wheat. Shortly after leaving port the steamship encountered very heavy weather and by the morning of the 19th was in distress. An S.O.S. call was sent out which was picked up by the White Star liner *Homeric,* 34,356 tons, Capt. Roberts, 70 miles distant. Shortly afterwards another message was received stating that all lifeboats had been smashed. A last message in broken English, "Now very danger. Come quick," came just before the Homeric sighted the derelict. The liner drove through the mountainous seas at a speed of 20 knots to the spot indicated, lat. 41 43′N., long. 61 39′W. (400 miles directly east of Boston, and 700 miles north of Bermuda), to find the *Raifuku Maru* with a list of 30 degrees and quite unmanageable. Approaching as near as she dared the liner stood by in the hope of picking up survivors, but none could survive in such a sea, and all 48 of the crew were drowned.

Assuming a love of truth, which version of the *Raifuku Maru* story would you rather have written?

3. QUOTE WITNESSES.   An argument is strengthened by the support of an *authority*—a person who is generally accepted by his peers as an expert. Usually, he or she is an authority on a particular subject, and is known to be fair and objective. For example, Jack Landau, a respected journalist known for his support of a free press, might be quoted in an argument against the gag rule forbidding publicity in certain trials so as not to prejudice a case. Or an argument insisting that fairy tales have profound psychological meanings could quote Bruno Bettelheim, an internationally respected child psychiatrist who shares that view.

How do you find authorities or experts? By reading and by checking library sources such as the *Reader's Guide to Periodical Literature,* encyclopedias, or magazines dealing with specialized areas of science, literature, or the arts. Your personal experience can also be used as witness evidence. There is no better witness in an argument on rape, for example, than someone who has been raped. Who could witness more powerfully against the difficulties of the welfare system than a mother who, with four children, has lived on welfare? Don't disregard your own experience or the experiences of others; use such evidence whenever it is relevant.

No witness: Thomas Jefferson was not the moral saint students study in grade school.

With witness: Thomas Jefferson, far from being the moral saint studied by grade school students, was a man attracted to forbidden women, as indicated by Fawn Brodie's intimate history entitled *Thomas Jefferson.*

No witness: America is deep into the porno bit, but nobody stops the porno promoters.

With witness: According to Morris Goldings, Boston's leading obscenity attorney, the pornography business continues to thrive because once busted, porno pushers rarely suffer conviction.

No witness: The quality of medical care in America varies with how much you can afford to pay, and how quickly you can demonstrate your ability to pay. Accident victims are sometimes turned away by hospitals because they have no insurance nor proof of financial ability to pay.

With witness: The quality of medical care in America varies with how much you can afford to pay and how quickly you can demonstrate your ability to pay. Last summer, for instance, while climbing El Capitan in Yosemite, I fell and broke my leg. I was carried by passing hikers to the nearest hospital which, however, refused to admit me because I had no proof of insurance. I was dressed in mountain climbing gear and sported a five-day growth of stubble on my face; my clothes had been shredded by the fall. To all appearances, I was a penniless tramp. Before the admitting nurse could dispatch me to a county hospital, one of the hikers, a well-known businessman in the area, vouched for my ability to pay. Only then was I admitted.

Witness evidence allows you to share the burden of proof in your argument.

4. BASE YOUR ARGUMENT ON A SOUND PREMISE.   Arguments evolve from premises. A premise is a basic assumption about reality. The premise of an argument is true when it states accurately conditions or events that have been verified by observation and study. Here are some examples of true premises:

Disease is caused by germs.

Money is the basic trading medium of all industrialized countries.

Venereal disease is spread primarily by sexual contact.

Other premises lie in the borderline area of belief; that is, they are believed by some people but have not been verified by study and observation. Here are some examples of unverified premises:

A study of astrology can give us advance warning of either good or bad fortune.

Unidentified flying objects are transportation vehicles peopled with citizens from other planets.

None of these premises has been proven, and an argument based on any one of them would be unsound. The following argument is faulty because its underlying premise is based on superstition:

No more than Nature desires the mating of weaker with stronger individuals, even less does she desire the blending of a higher with a lower race, since, if she did, her whole work of higher breeding, over perhaps hundreds of thousands of years, might be ruined with one blow.

Historical experience offers countless proofs of this. It shows with terrifying clarity that in every mingling of Aryan blood with that of lower peoples the result was the end of the cultured people. North America, whose population consists in by far the largest part of Germanic elements who mixed but little with the lower colored people shows a different humanity and culture from Central and South America, where the predominantly Latin immigrants often mixed with the aborigines on a large scale. By this one example, we can clearly and distinctly recognize the effect of racial mixture. The Germanic inhabitant of the American continent, who has remained racially pure and unmixed, rose to be master of the continent; he will remain the master as long as he does not fall a victim to defilement of the blood.

Adolf Hitler, *Mein Kampf*

Viewed from a modern scientific point of view, this is patent nonsense.

A wrong premise can also result from hasty generalization based on poor sampling. Notice the following argument:

In 1898, the United States declared war on Spain. In 1910, United States troops invaded Mexico. In 1917, the United States declared war on Germany. Within thirty years, the United States was involved in World War II. All these facts point to the premise my paper has set out to prove: that the United States is a warmonger.

From four instances of war during a fifty-year period it does not necessarily follow that the United States has consistently instigated war. Numerous other factors must also be considered. The conclusion and premise are improbable and shaky. Here are some other examples of hasty generalizations:

The permissive abortion laws in America have contributed to the moral decay of our society.

The popularization of male vasectomies as a method of birth control is a female plot to castrate the American male.

We have nothing to fear from marijuana; it is a healthy relaxation-producing drug.

These generalizations share a lack of incontrovertible proof. They produce no evidence of careful research and sampling.

In everyday conversation we tend to ignore exceptions and play the averages, fully realizing that no one will take us literally when, for instance, we say, "Nobody makes a living in this town," or, "My company is the most radical operation this side of the Missouri." A listener accepts the fact that we are speaking in approximate terms and discounts our exaggeration. But a written argument must be more carefully constructed, and its statements painstakingly checked for accuracy.

5. DON'T IGNORE THE OPPOSITION. A well-shaped argument anticipates an opponent's objection by identifying it clearly and then showing its unreasonableness. This alerts the reader to the writer's knowledge of opposing arguments. If you neglect this step in arguing, you lay yourself wide open to the accusation of ignorance. In the following argument against the wasteful extravagance of using paper grocery bags, notice how the writer anticipates two major arguments of the opposition:

> Can you believe that in the most well-educated, cultured nation in the world we consume and destroy a vital part of our natural resources without a second thought? Consider the average brown paper grocery bag, which is made from the pulp of trees. One of our most vital resources is transformed into a convenience that is used no place else in the world with such careless extravagance as here in the United States. And for what? To move groceries from store to car to home—to be used briefly as a trash bag and then to be pulverized by chemical action into a city sewage plant. How foolish and spoiled we are. A billion tons of lovely trees are destroyed annually, just to satisfy our compulsive need for convenience. How shallow we are to make this tradeoff from lush green beauty to tacky brown bags. One day in the future, men will have to look at pictures to be reminded that the Ozark Mountains were breathlessly beautiful in the fall as the deep green leaves turned to shimmering gold. Personal memories they will not have.
>
> Of course, the big industries try to make us think that high living standards are more important than beauty. For example, George I. Kneeland, Chairman of the Board and Executive Officer of the St. Regis Paper Company, insists that "providing the highest possible standard of living for America is an urgent national priority." But I ask, what kind of value system is it that places higher priority on a trivial convenience than on the survival of Mother Earth?
>
> Another argument is that paper is biodegradable and consequently not

as polluting as plastic. But plastic bags do not have to be the substitute. People all over the world adapt to grocery carts, fishnet bags, or cloth containers. We could get into the habit of doing this too and we would be stopping our insane path of ecological mass murder.

In this example, two opposing arguments—maintaining a high standard of living and the biodegradability of paper—are anticipated and rebutted.

"The Naked Nomads," as it is presented here, was adapted from the book of the same title and first appeared in the Boston *Globe*, February 9, 1975. It is a strong persuasive argument against the stereotype of the single male.

Professional Model

The Naked Nomads
George F. Gilder

1   The single man. An image of freedom and power. A man on horseback, riding into the sunset with his gun. The town and its women would never forget, never be the same. But the man would never change, just move on. To other women, other towns. As he rides away, the sunset gives him a romantic glow.

2   The single man. The naked nomad in the bedrooms of the land. The celebrity at the party, combed by eyes of envy and desire. The hero of the film and television drama: cool, violent, sensuous, fugitive, *free*.

3   The American dream, the Superstar. If one were only rich, young, famous, one would revel as a single man. One would be—Namath? Dylan? McCartney? George Plimpton? Jay Rockefeller? Dick Cavett? Mick Jagger? Jean Claude Killy? O.J. Simpson?

4   In fact, if one were young, rich and famous, one most likely would be—as every society hostess learns when she seeks "eligible" escorts for the successful single women at her parties—one would be a married man. Of the listed celebrities, only Namath is still single.

5   If one were actually a single man, unattached—free in the spirit of our dream, our memory of youth that improves with age, our love 'em and leave 'em Lancelot, our easy-riding ranger—one would be . . . ? Well, we know from the statistics: the single man in general, compared to others in the population, is poor and neurotic. He is disposed to criminality, drugs and violence.

6   Of course, there are many exceptions. One must expect a barrage of indignant testimony from the single men who ostensibly violate the pattern of irresponsibility and neurosis. There is no doubt that millions of single men have managed to become disciplined and valuable citizens, and millions of divorced men have survived to a happy and productive old age.

7   In addition, bachelors form a fluid group. Every man is single at least for a while. Many men are divorced or widowed. Millions are merely temporary bachelors looking for a wife. Most will eventually find one. Some will not, but will spend their lives in the quest. An indeterminate number are homosexuals. Even some of them will marry.

8   Underlying all the superficial diversity of bachelor life is a syndrome of psychological instability. In a sense, the bachelor may never grow up. Thus the older unmarried man

in many ways may resemble the young man, unless he acquires direct dependents and responsibilities. The homosexual may display a pattern of neurosis quite similar to the pattern of other committed bachelors.

9   All, under the garments of culture, may be naked nomads, lacking roots in the past and connections to the future. And the erratic and impulsive course of the single man, however attractive among the young, becomes pathological as a man grows older unmarried.

10   An appreciation of the futility of a singles pattern for people of all ages beyond the early 20s can be the beginning of wisdom about human life itself. Understanding the failure of the singles style, one can comprehend the real potentialities and limits of men and women, the real possibilities for freedom and the real needs for dependency and responsibility. One can explain the barrenness of much of our popular culture and the shallowness of much of our most highly sophisticated literature and cinema. One can gain a deeper perspective of the breakdown of many of our government's social programs.

11   The failure of the singles ideal is a major sociological fact of the last decade. Many more publicized developments are related to this failure. Yet it is still to be studied. Census figures by marital status are inadequate. Few government agencies assemble statistics on singles life. But the statistics as they emerge are devastating.

12   The key to the failure is not, as often supposed, the insistent need of women for marriage. Although they make claims to the contrary, women, in fact, can often do without marriage: single women at least can live to a stable and productive old age.

13   The key to the singles failure is the profound biological dependence of men on women—deeper than any feminist or male chauvinist understands. Men without women frequently become the "single menace" and tend to live short and destructive lives—destructive both to themselves and to the society.

14   Our major social problem thus comes from single men, the very people who have apparently best achieved the national ideal of independence and freedom. The most liberated Americans are also the most afflicted—and afflictive.

15   One striking aspect of the bachelor pattern is low income. Because of their tendency toward mental instability, physical disease and early mortality, single men earn less over their lifetime than any other major category of workers. Although discrimination is not a serious problem for white bachelors, they make no higher yearly incomes, on the average, than such official victims of bias as married blacks and single women.

16   In economic terms, the group most representative of the single male condition is never-married bachelors between the ages of 25 and 65. The incomes of the divorced and widowed benefit from their time as married men, while the figures for single men below 25 are distorted by schooling commitments. In addition, the young men are getting married so fast that it is difficult to sort out the real bachelors from those just passing through on the way to church.

17   Excluding the divorced and widowed, there are a little over 4,000,000 single men between 25 and 75. About 7 percent are inmates in correctional or mental institutions. This leaves about 3,650,000 on the loose. Of these, about 330,000 are unemployed or unregistered in the labor force, leaving 3,320,000 single men at work. They do not tend to work very hard, however. Only a little more than 60 percent were on the job full time—a little higher than single women, about 20 percent behind married men.

18   In general, the 3,320,000 single male workers hardly earned enough to feed themselves and buy Playboy magazine, let alone follow its philosophy. In 1970, their average income was approximately $6000, their median income $5800.

19   In general, men have more psychological problems than women, and single men have the most problems of all. Much of the relevant data, ironically, was presented

two years ago by Phyliss Chesler in her best-selling book *Women and Madness.* Although she shows that women constitute 52 percent of the ''psychiatrically involved,'' women constitute about 54 percent of the adult population. Proportionately, therefore, men are more heavily represented.

20   As far as the society is concerned, however, the main problem of single men is not mental or physical illness, or related afflictions like alcoholism and loneliness. It is not discrimination or poverty. It is not that thriving old specialty of single men and their intimates: venereal disease. Single men have another way of getting the rest of the society, however reluctantly and unconsciously, to take part in their problems. That way is crime.

21   Much verbiage has been shed on the issue of whether crime is chiefly a function of mental disease—psychological ''madness''—or whether it is chiefly an effect of social conditions, an expression of ''madness'' against ''an unjust society.''

22   Some 3 percent of criminals are women; only 33 percent are married men. Although single men number 13 percent of the population over age 14, they comprise 60 percent of the criminals and commit about 90 percent of major and violent crimes. If one includes divorced men among the singles, the percentage of single criminals rises toward 75 percent, but the statistics are unclear on what proportion were divorced after they were convicted of crime.

23   Of course, a large number of all crimes—and a still larger proportion of violent crimes—are committed by single men under 25. In fact, about 55 percent of all single male prisoners in 1970 were between the ages of 14 and 24. But even in the age group between 20 and 24, single men were proportionately almost two and a half times more likely than married men to be imprisoned; and in the 25 to 65 group, single men were proportionately over seven times more likely to be incarcerated than married men.

24   So violence and crime join with ''madness,'' mental illness, mild neurosis, depression, addiction, venereal disease, chronic disability, psychiatric treatment, loneliness, insomnia, institutionalization, poverty, ''discrimination,'' unemployment and nightmares as part of the specialized culture of single men in America.

25   The climax of the grim story, however, is death. It is not surprising that the single male mortality rate, also, is the highest of all.

26   Single men are not in general very good at life. Often they know little about the most important parts of it. But they are sometimes fiercely ingenious at death. If you want a troop of killers, the military has learned, it is best to stick with the singles.

27   Women and children and dominant males are obviously more important to the survival of a group. And the young men have accepted this order of life, or it could not have prevailed. They have known in their bones and hearts that ultimately they are dispensable. They are the ones to leap on the grenade or charge the enemy bunker.

28   Single male suicides do not mess around: no half-hacked wrists, or semi-signaled sleeping pills, or window ledge posturings. They *do* it, coolly, fiercely, efficiently. They do it four times as often as young married men, five times as often as married women, four times as often as single women.

29   One of them I know about—a charming, intelligent young man—was interrupted by the milkman as he tried to gas himself. The boy conversed calmly for twenty minutes, disarming all suspicion, and then proceeded to finish the job. Another acquaintance, an extraordinary boy, escaped from a mental hospital and used his expert mechanical and tactical knowledge to build a perfect gallows in a darkened cellar, where he would be discovered by his mother when she turned on the lights to do the laundry.

30   Suicide is increasingly how young men die.

31   It is not restricted to young men, however. In fact, after the perilous 20s, the older a man gets without marrying the more likely he is to kill himself. In addition, there are

many forms of suicide that are listed under other names. Single men have almost double the mortality rate of married men and three times the mortality rate of single women from all causes: from automobile accidents and other mishaps, as well as from the whole range of conventional diseases.

32   Most of the illnesses do not become evident until after age 45. Many of them, it is safe to say, represent various forms of disguised or unconscious suicide.

33   In analyzing the high death rates of single men, sociologists normally focus on the bachelor's lack of the kind of "personal maintenance" married men enjoy from their wives. Feminists talk of the failure of sexist society to teach male children how to cook and take care of themselves. But this notion completely misses the point. Single men are perfectly capable of taking care of their physical needs when they want to. Most of them can cook, sew, clean up, and perform other "maintenance" tasks. The problem is the will, not the way; they don't care enough.

34   The maintenance explanations are inadequate to explain the all-encompassing reach of single male afflictions. Is it not more likely, for example, that if the heart attacks were banished, one would merely find many of these men dying in other ways—or swelling the ranks of the mentally ill? Altogether the pattern of mortality among single men is so various and inexorable that it suggests an organic source: a failure of the will to live, a disconnection from the life force itself as it arises in society.

35   Men need women—far more than women need men—for their very survival. Men need a biological and sexual tie of the sort uniquely provided by marriage and children. The struggle for marriage and family becomes a struggle for life itself.

36   The problem is that men do not necessarily know this. They continue to pursue an obsolescent manhood of the hunting party. They become increasingly alienated from the patterns of family life, which offer the only widely available way to work out a full manhood of 70 years.

37   Perhaps the most dramatic evidence of the importance of the marriage tie to men is the impact of its rupture by divorce or widowhood. Contrary to the usual images of the helpless and abandoned wife, the statistics show far greater evidence of helpless and traumatized husbands. It is men, surprisingly enough, who seem to be the divorce losers.

38   There are millions of single men, unconnected to any promising reality, dissipating their lives by the years, moving from job to job, woman to woman, illusion to embitterment. Yet they are not hopeless.

39   Many more millions have passed through the same slough, incurred the same boozy dreams, marijuana highs, acid crashes, sex diseases, job vapors, legal scrapes, wanderings. They follow the entire syndrome and then break out of it.

40   Normally they do not escape through psychiatrists' offices, sex education courses, VISTA or Peace Corps programs, reformatories, or guidance counseling uplifts. What happens, most of the time—the only effective thing that happens, the only process that reaches the sources of motivation and character—is falling in love.

41   Love is effective because it works at a deeper, more instinctual level than the other modes of education and change.

42   Love and marriage are products of 35 million years of evolution rather than a few years of instruction at school, a few hours of threats and promises from counselors and policemen, or a few months of unpleasant experiences with the singles life.

43   A man is depressed but not transfigured by vision of 40 years of dirty sheets and unmade mornings. It is not enough to see the light over a sleeping body without a remembered face. It is not enough to trudge home alone at 3 a.m.—after insults from three different women—thinking of the hangover at work just six hours hence. It should be enough, one would suppose, if men were reasonable and could be changed by reason alone.

44   But reason has a hundred voices: pointing plausibly to the flaws of each successive lover; depicting orgiastic futures for liberated singles; describing clinically the snares and pitfalls of marriage; disparaging choices that are made to be irrevocable in a life of changing sentiments and fortunes.

45   There are intelligent men and women making the case against wedlock and children. There are urbane professors expounding their eloquent dolor of the future of the race. There are reasonable projections of depression and holocaust, of petty dictators with doomsday machines.

46   Why bring children into such a world? ask the cooly reasonable voices of Zero Population Growth.

47   But it is not just an intelligent appraisal of his circumstances that transforms the single man. It is not merely a desire for companionship or "growth." It is a deeper alchemy of change, flowing from a primal source. The change that leads to love often comes slowly. Many of the women he finds will not help. They tend to go along with him and affirm his single life. Most of the time, though, the singles circuit finally becomes insufferable, offering neither sexual fulfillment nor manhood.

48   One morning he turns to the body sleeping next to him, whose name he hardly knows, whose health he hardly trusts, and who has nothing to say to him, and he decides he has to find something better.

49   One day while joking with friends about the latest of his acquaintances to be caught and hitched, he silently wonders, for a moment, whether he wishes it were he.

50   Suddenly he has a new glimpse of himself. His body is beginning to decline, grow weaker and slower, even if he keeps it fit. His body, which once measured out his few advantages over women, is beginning to intimate its terrible plan to become as weak as an older woman's. His aggressiveness, which burst in fitful storms throughout his young life but never seemed to cleanse him—his aggression for which he could so rarely find the adequate battle, the harmonious chase—is souring now. His job, so below his measure as a man, so out of tune with his body and his inspiration, now stretches ahead without joy or relief.

51   His sex, the force that drove the flower of his youth, drives still, drives again and again the same hard bargain—for which there are fewer and fewer takers, in a sexual arena with no final achievement for the single man, in which sex itself becomes work that is never done.

52   The single man is caught on a reef and the tide is running out. He is being biologically stranded and he has a hopeless dream. Studs Terkel's book *Working* registers again and again men's desire to be remembered. Yet who in this world is much remembered for his job?

53   Stuck with what he may sense as a choice between being trapped and being stranded, he still may respond by trying one more fling, perhaps with a new girl down at the bar. The biological predicament can be warded off for a time, like Hemingway's hyena.* Death often appears in the guise of eternal youth, at the ever-infatuating fountains: alcohol, drugs, hallucinogenic sex. For a while we believe in the disguise. But the hyena returns and there is mortality in the air—diseases, accidents, concealed suicides, the whole range of the single man's aggression turned inward.

54   But where there is death, there is hope. For the man who is in touch with his mortality, but not in the grips of it, is also in touch with the sources of his love. He is in contact with the elements—the natural fires and storms that we so often use as metaphors for his passions. He is a man who can be deeply and effectively changed. He can find his

---

*A reference to Ernest Hemingway's "The Snows of Kilimanjaro," in which a fatally wounded hunter is haunted by the cry of a hyena. The cry symbolizes the hunter's approaching death.

age, his relation to the world, his maturity, his future. He can burn his signature into the covenant of a specific life.

55   The man has found a vital energy and a possibility of durable change. It has assumed the shape of a woman. It is the same form that has caught his eye and roiled his body all these years. But now there will be depths below the pleasing surfaces, meanings beyond the momentary ruttings. There will be a sense that this vessel contains the secrets of new life, that the womb and breasts bear a gestalt of immortality. There will be a knowledge that to treat this treasure as an object—a mere body the equal of his own, a mere matrix of his pleasure—is to defile life itself. It is this recognition that she offers a higher possibility; it is this consciousness that he has to struggle to be worthy of her which finally issues the spark. And then arises the fire that purges and changes him as it consumes his own death.

56   The man's love begins in a knowledge of inferiority, but it offers a promise of dignity and purpose. For he then has to create, by dint of his own effort, and without the miracle of a womb, a life that a woman could choose. Thus are released and formed the energies of civilized society. He provides, and he does it for a lifetime, for a life.

3,207 words

Vocabulary

nomad (title)	inexorable (34)	expounding (45)
sensuous (2)	organic (34)	holocaust (46)
fugitive (2)	obsolescent (36)	alchemy (47)
ostensibly (6)	alienated (36)	primal (47)
syndrome (8)	traumatized (37)	insufferable (47)
erratic (9)	illusion (38)	metaphors (54)
pathological (9)	modes (41)	covenant (54)
afflicted, afflictive (14)	transfigured (40)	roiled (55)
median (18)	plausibly (44)	ruttings (55)
ironically (19)	orgiastic (44)	gestalt (55)
ingenious (26)	urbane (45)	matrix (55)
perilous (31)		

Questions

1. What stereotype does this essay argue against?
2. What is the controlling idea of Gilder's argument? Where is it stated?
3. What is the key to the single male's failure?
4. What are the chief characteristics of the single man? Where are they all summarized?
5. What comments does the author make about death and single males?
6. Why are love and marriage more effective than schooling, counseling, or guidance in curing the evils besetting the single male?
7. What is the argument's major premise? How does the author strengthen his premise?

224

This essay is a well-organized argument for changing the Social Security System to provide for different kinds of benefits. The essay's weakness is an overly developed attack on the current system, with a correspondingly deficient explanation of the new system. The author supports his argument well, however, with various testimonials and data.

Student Model

Our Old People Deserve a Break
David L. Gasser

The old people are crowded in the waiting room; phones ring convulsively; a secretary takes down the names of the new arrivals. But few of the aged seem to mind as they wait for a chance to untangle their problems. They can't afford to mind; they are all broke. This is the scene at the local Social Security office. A haven for the derelict elderly, this office, according to current census figures, draws more customers than the Welfare and Unemployment offices combined. As the numbers swell, so does the problem. A solution, urgently needed, is this: The Social Security system should be reformed to provide free room and board for the elderly, rather than continuing the benefit system now employed.

How does the present system work? What are its problems? The answers to these questions can only be supplied by an investigation of the basic practices of the Social Security Administration. A billion dollar operation, Social Security serves the swarms of elderly people from retirement age to death. No other organization can lay claim to the great power this system wields in this country.

Social Security is basically funded by workers who earn a taxable income and by their employers. A set amount (currently 5.85 percent) is subtracted on a weekly, biweekly, or monthly basis from each paycheck received by the worker, and this money, along with a matching amount paid by the employer, is sent to the coffers of the Social Security Administration. This money is then drawn on to pay the monthly checks received by those on Social Security. As the *Los Angeles Times* stated, the moneys taken from the employee "are not annuities to be returned to him later as a pension. They are actually direct transfer payments from one generation of workers to another." In this way the program is funded.

What this means is that our current work force pays the living expenses of those who are now retired. This system has worked well in the past, but drastic revisions are necessary if the Administration is to continue its high level of service. Because of population growth and because of rising standards of living, there is currently a funding crisis of unmatched proportions in the social welfare sector of government. The big question is, Where, in the future, will the needed money come from? Proponents of increased benefits feel that the payroll tax should be increased. Opponents feel that tax increase is out of the question or our entire nation will become bankrupt.

Currently there are four proposed solutions to the Social Security tangle: (1) cut back on benefit increases, (2) postpone the retirement age, (3) increase the payroll tax, and (4) pay for the benefits out of general federal revenues. Each of these alternatives will be examined in turn.

The first proposed solution, cutting back on benefit increases which help keep the elderly abreast of inflation, is unworkable because of the effect it would have on the elderly income level. This level is already ridiculously low. For example, according to the *Los Angeles Times,* "Social Security statistics show the average individual benefit to be $2,400 a year—*well below the current poverty line of $2,720* (my italics). Moreover, half of the elderly receive even less than $2,400; a third get as little as $1,600." No wonder some old people are forced to eat dog food. These shocking statistics should lay to rest any notion of solving the funding problem by cutting back on benefits.

The second alternative, raising the retirement age, is unacceptable because of the effect it would have on the elderly's later working years. Despite poor health and failing energy, many workers would be forced to continue working for a living at a time when they should be enjoying their retirement. The elderly should not be forced to give up the comforts of later life. Nor should they be expected to compete in an already overly strained job market. The situation in this area is already bad enough.

The alternative of raising the payroll tax is also unworkable. As *U.S. News and World Report* states, the payroll tax would have to be subjected to "substantial raising" in order to provide money adequate to meet our Social Security needs. With wages and inflation already extravagantly high, the means of solving the funding problem would not be found in an increased payroll tax. This would inevitably lead to higher and higher wage demands and a continued spiral of inflation, with no end in sight. Such fiscal irresponsibility must be avoided.

The last alternative, funding Social Security from general federal revenues, is unrealistic. Social Security now already costs seventy billion dollars annually. It is illogical to expect this sum to be provided by federal revenues, already totaling 281 billion. It would require a tax increase of a full twenty-five percent. This is, of course, unreasonable.

With all these alternatives found unrealistic or unworkable, we are forced to turn to yet another alternative—my proposal, mentioned at the beginning of the essay, to provide free room and board for the elderly. This would entail a complete reworking of the Social Security system as it now stands, but such an innovation may be necessary to salvage what is left of the current program.

Free housing is not a new concept. It has been inaugurated many times in federal housing programs for the poor. The success of these programs lends credence to the belief that free housing could be implemented to help the elderly. One enormous boon of this proposal is its independence from inflation. The present benefits awarded are subject to the rise in costs nationwide, and as such must be reevaluated each year. But housing, once built, is fully paid for. It would be nontaxable, being owned by the federal government. It would be a continuing resource, and would not require reevaluation each year. Except for upkeep, the initial expense of the housing would be its total cost. Once paid for, it would not only be free and clear, but its real estate value would probably increase.

As for the board, I propose that each housing unit contain a well-run cafeteria, where tastefully prepared meals would be served three times a day. Since these meals would be prepared in large quantities, they would cost less in the aggregate than what each elderly person or couple would pay to shop and to cook individually. Furthermore, the cafeteria dining room could double as a place for convivial entertainment and hospitality, alleviating some of the loneliness so often felt by the aged.

Another point in this proposal's favor is the beneficial effect it would have on unemployment. Jobs in great numbers would be created by this system. Carpenters, bricklayers, steel workers—all would be hired to build the housing units. This employment would continue for several years, as more and more units would be built in major cities. Expansion and growth would result.

These are the arguments in favor of free housing and board for the aged. Those opposed to this proposal will no doubt cite cost as a major prohibitive factor. But hasn't this always been cited whenever a new solution raises its head? Should we be swayed by it? My answer is, No. This proposal offers a legitimate solution to a difficult problem, and as such should be given serious consideration. In an open society we can ask nothing less.

With the increasing environmental awareness brought by the ecology movement and the realization that many animal species face extinction, hunting and killing seem to have fallen into public disfavor. In this selection, however, a minister undertakes the defense of the hunter and his pastime.

Alternate Reading

In Defense of Deer Hunting and Killing
Arthur C. Tennies

1   "You hunt deer?" When I nodded, my shocked colleague went on to say, "Why my whole image of you has been shattered. How can you kill such beautiful creatures?"

2   And so would many others who view the deliberate killing of deer as brutal and senseless. Such people look upon the hunter as a barbaric hangover from the distant past of the human race. To my colleague, the incongruity between the barbarism of hunting and normal civilized conduct was made more intense because I was a minister. How could I as a minister do such a thing?

3   I thought about that as I drove through the early morning darkness toward the southeastern part of Chenango County. It was a little after 5 a.m. I had gotten up at 4, something I do only in the case of an emergency or when I am going deer hunting. It was cold, the temperature in the 20s. With the ground frozen, it would be too noisy for still hunting until the sun had had a chance to thaw the frost. So it would be wait and freeze. My first thoughts about why I would hunt deer had nothing to do with the supposed barbarism of it. I thought of the foolishness of it. Wait hour after hour in the cold, feet numb, hands numb, and small chance of getting a deer.

4   I was going to hunt on Schlafer Hill on the farm of Pershing Schlafer. My choice of a place to hunt had been determined by the party permit that three of us had, which allowed us to kill one other deer of either sex besides the three bucks that we were allowed.

5   I thought about the party system in New York, the way the state controlled the size of the deer herd. The state is divided into about 40 deer-management areas. The state biologists know how many deer each area can handle, how many deer can feed on the browse available without destroying it. If there are too many deer, they will kill the plants and bushes upon which they depend. The next step is starvation for large numbers. Since the deer's natural predators were wiped out by the first settlers, the only control over their numbers now is starvation or hunting. Thus, so many deer must be killed in a deer-managment area. A certain number will be killed by motor vehicles. The biologists can estimate how many will be killed on the highways and also the number of bucks that will be killed. The surplus is taken care of by issuing a set number of party permits.

6   I have often marveled at the state biologists, their skill and knowledge in managing the deer herd. As I have pondered the problems of people—poverty, starvation, in-

justice, and all the others—and our frantic and often futile efforts to solve these problems, I have thought, "If only we could manage the problems of people as well as we can manage a deer herd."

7   Then I realize the great difference between the two. People are not for being managed. We manage people only by robbing them of the right to choose—and the most brutal attempts to manage are ultimately frustrated by the obstinacy of human nature, its refusal to be managed. A handful of biologists may manage a deer herd and a handful of scientists may be able to put a man on the moon, but no handful of planners will ever manage the human race. And so I thought again, as the car rushed through the dark, that all of our modern management techniques would fail to come up with quick and perfect solutions to the problems of people.

8   While the darkness was still on the land, I reached the bottom of the hill. I parked the car, put on my hunting shirts, took my gun, and began the long climb up the hill. For a few minutes, I could hardly see the old road. Slowly my eyes adjusted to the dark. The trees in the woods on my right took shape and the road became clearly visible. I walked with greater confidence. As I climbed, the sun climbed toward the horizon to drive away the night. By the time I reached the top of the hill, the half-light of dawn had arrived.

9   Off to my left in the valley were lights and people, but on the hill I was alone. It had not always been that way. Once long ago the hilltop had been filled with people. Following the Revolution, white settlers came into Chenango County, and some had chosen that hilltop. I stopped and tried to picture in my mind their struggles to turn the forest into farms. I looked at the stone fence off to my right and wondered how many days it had taken to clear the stones from the fields and pile them into a fence. The fence ran into the woods. Woods again where there had been fields or pasture.

10   I looked on down the road. I could not see the old barn down farther on the left, the only structure from the past still standing. All of the others were gone. I had seen before the crumbling stone foundations where once houses had stood. A half century or more ago, if I had stood there, I could have seen a half-dozen houses. Smoke would have been rolling out of chimneys as fires were started to chase away the cold. Men and boys would have been outside and in the barns getting the chores done. Women and girls would have been busy in the kitchen getting breakfast. The hill would have been full of people and empty of deer. Now it was empty of people and full of deer.

11   On that hill and on many others, like Bucktooth Run, is a story of the hand of a man upon the land. Before the settlers came, only a few deer lived on that hill, far fewer than there are now, because the forests provided little food for the deer. The few were soon killed off. While the disappearance of the deer was the fault of the early hunters, there was more to it than that. There was no room for deer on the hill. As my Dad, who was born on Bucktooth Run, has pointed out:

12   *These farms were worked over morning and evening by the farmers and their sons and their dogs going after the cattle. The wood lots were worked over during the winter for wood. The larger tracts of woodland were worked over by the lumbermen.*

13   *Then came World War I and the years following. Large areas of land were abandoned. Where once the woods resounded to the call of "Come, boss!" and in the winter the woods echoed the ring of the ax and whine of the saw, the sylvan stillness, for months on end, was unbroken by the human voice. Where once the deer had no place to rest from the constant activity of the busy farmer and lumberman, there was now a chance for the deer to carry on its life in solitude.*

14   *In 1900 there were no deer in much of New York. The state did some stocking shortly after that, and deer came across the border from Pennsylvania. The abandoned land provided a perfect setting for the deer and there were no natural enemies to stay their march. By the late 1930s, most of the state had a deer season.*

15   So as the farmers retreated from the hill, the deer returned. Now the hill is perfect for deer . . . some fields used by farmers, like Pershing, for pasture and hay, good feed for deer for most of the year . . . brush for browse during the winter . . . woods, old and new, mixed with evergreen for cover. And most of the year, except during the hunting season, only a few people make their way to the top of the hill.

16   Let nature have her way and in another century nature's hospitality to the deer will be withdrawn as large trees again cover the hill as they did before the first white settlers came.

17   I started to walk again and felt like I had left one world, the world of technology, and entered another one, the world of nature. The rush to get things done had to give way to waiting and patience, for nature does not live at our frantic pace. The noise had to give way to quietness, for only in silence can one get close to a deer.

18   But the ground crunched beneath my feet, so I walked to a likely spot and waited. Two hours and nothing, except a few small birds. Finally the cold forced me to move. I walked and found some fresh tracks in the snow. I followed them for an hour, trying to get close enough to the deer wandering in the woods ahead of me. But I was too noisy. All I saw was the flash of brown bodies and white tails too far ahead. I waited some more. No luck. I walked to another spot where deer cross.

19   I waited another hour. It was warmer now. Finally a deer appeared, a head above a rise. It started to come nearer. Then it stopped. Something was wrong. It decided to leave. As it turned, my gun came up and I shot. It lurched sideways, kicking and thrashing, disappearing under a pine tree. I walked to the spot. No deer. I went around the tree and there it lay. In a second it was dead.

20   I looked down at the deer, a button buck, and I thought: This is the way of nature, one creature feeding on another. Thousands of years ago our forebearers survived in just this way. They killed, gutted, butchered, and ate. Now we buy in a supermarket or order in a restaurant.

21   The first task was to gut the deer, kind of a messy process. I got may knife out, turned the deer on his back, and slit him open. I spilled the guts out on the ground. I saved the liver and heart, even though the heart had been mangled by the bullet. I cut through the diaphragm and pulled the lungs out.

22   Then I was ready to pull the deer back to the car. It was 3 p.m. when I got to the car. Time yet to hunt for a buck, so I dumped the deer into the trunk. Back up the hill, but no luck. As night came on, I got back to the car. I tied the deer on the top of the trunk and started for home.

23   As I drove toward home, I had a sense of satisfaction. I had fitted myself to nature's way and had been successful. For a few short hours, I had marched to the beat of nature's drum, not that of our modern world. At least for me, the barrier that we had built between nature and us could still be breached.

24   Back in suburbia, I parked the car in the driveway and went into the house. Jan and the kids were eating supper.
      "Any luck?" Jan asked.
      "Not much."
      "Did you get a deer?" one of the kids asked.
      "Yup, a button buck."
      Then the excited rush to see the deer, and the thrill of shared success.

25   After that there was the tedious job of butchering. I hung the deer in the garage. Then I began the task of skinning it. Once skinned, I cut the deer in half, then in quarters. Jan washed the blood and hair off of each quarter. I then cut the quarters into smaller pieces, and then Jan sliced it up into roasts, steaks, and stew meat.

26   "Can you get the brains out?" Jan wanted to know.
      "I can try, but why the brains?"

"We always had brains when we butchered."

So I went to work to cut the skull open and get the brains out.

When I got back into the kitchen, Jan had a skillet on.

"Let's have some venison," she said.

"At this hour?"

"Sure."

27   So she had some brains and I had some liver. As I sat there weary, eating the liver, I thought, "This meat is on the table because I put it there." By our efforts, and ours alone, it had gone from field to table.

28   "Don't you want some brains?" Jan asked.

"No."

"But they are a delicacy."

"That may be, but I'll stick to the liver."

29   As I went to sleep that night I thought: "I suppose that no matter what I say, a lot of people will still never understand why I hunt deer. Well, they don't have to, but let only vegetarians condemn me."

2,090 words

Vocabulary

incongruity (2)

sylvan (13)

Questions

1. How, according to the author, do people regard the killing of deer? How do some people regard the hunter? Why do you think he mentions people's views of the hunter and deer killing?

2. Why do you think the author mentions that he is a minister?

3. In paragraph 3 and throughout the essay, the author emphasizes the tediousness, cold, and discomfort associated with deer hunting. Why? What purpose does this serve in his defense of deer hunting?

4. What determined the author's choice of a place to hunt?

5. What is the purpose of paragraph 5? Why does the author go into deer management in such detail?

6. Why does the author reminisce about the people who used to live on the land? What does the reminiscence have to do with his argument in favor of deer hunting?

7. Where did the deer in New York come from? How did they get there?

8. In paragraph 19, the author describes how he shot and killed a deer. What does his description contribute to his defense of deer hunting?

9. What does the author contend would happen to the deer if nature had her way?

10. The author writes: "This is the way of nature, one creature feeding on another." Do you agree with this statement? Why, or why not?

11. In paragraph 20, the author compares the way our forebears survived with the way we eat today. Why? What effect does this comparison have on his defense of hunting?

12. The author makes a point of mentioning that his wife ate the brains of the deer, while he ate its liver. What is he trying to emphasize?

Max Shulman, creator of Dobey Gillis, explains some of the major logical fallacies while telling a humorous story about the eternal love triangle.

Alternate Reading

Love Is a Fallacy

Max Shulman

1   Cool was I and logical. Keen, calculating, perspicacious, acute and astute—I was all of these. My brain was as powerful as a dynamo, as precise as a chemist's scales, as penetrating as a scalpel. And—think of it!—I was only eighteen.

2   It is not often that one so young has such a giant intellect. Take, for example, Petey Burch, my roommate at the University of Minnesota. Same age, same background, but dumb as an ox. A nice enough fellow, you understand, but nothing upstairs. Emotional type. Unstable. Impressionable. Worst of all, a faddist. Fads, I submit, are the very negation of reason. To be swept up in every new craze that comes along, to surrender yourself to idiocy just because everybody else is doing it—this, to me, is the acme of mindlessness. Not, however, to Petey.

3   One afternoon I found Petey lying on his bed with an expression of such distress on his face that I immediately diagnosed appendicitis. "Don't move," I said. "Don't take a laxative. I'll get a doctor."

   "Raccoon," he mumbled thickly.

5   "Raccoon?" I said, pausing in my flight.

   "I want a raccoon coat," he wailed.

   I perceived that his trouble was not physical, but mental. "Why do you want a raccoon coat?"

8   "I should have known it," he cried, pounding his temples. "I should have known they'd come back when the Charleston came back. Like a fool I spent all my money for textbooks, and now I can't get a raccoon coat."

   "Can you mean," I said incredulously, "that people are actually wearing raccon coats again?"

10   "All the Big Men on Campus are wearing them. Where've you been?"

   "In the library," I said, naming a place not frequented by Big Men on Campus.

   He leaped from the bed and paced the room. "I've got to have a raccoon coat," he said passionately, "I've got to!"

   "Petey, why? Look at it rationally. Raccoon coats are unsanitary. They shed. They smell bad. They weigh too much. They're unsightly. They—"

   "You don't understand," he interrupted impatiently. "It's the thing to do. Don't you want to be in the swim?"

   "No," I said truthfully.

   "Well, I do," he declared. "I'd give anything for a raccoon coat. Anything!"

   My brain, that precision instrument, slipped into high gear. "Anything?" I asked, looking at him narrowly.

   "Anything," he affirmed in ringing tones.

19   I stroked my chin thoughtfully. It so happened that I knew where to get my hands on a raccoon coat. My father had had one in his undergraduate days; it lay now in a trunk in the attic back home. It also happened that Petey had something I wanted. He didn't *have* it exactly, but at least he had first rights on it. I refer to his girl, Polly Espy.

20   I had long coveted Polly Espy. Let me emphasize that my desire for this young woman was not emotional in nature. She was, to be sure, a girl who excited the emotions, but

I was not one to let my heart rule my head. I wanted Polly for a shrewdly calculated, entirely cerebral reason.

21   I was a freshman in law school. In a few years I would be out in practice. I was well aware of the importance of the right kind of wife in furthering a lawyer's career. The successful lawyers I had observed were, almost without exception, married to beautiful, gracious, intelligent women. With one omission, Polly fitted these specifications perfectly.

22   Beautiful she was. She was not yet of pin-up proportions, but I felt sure that time would supply the lack. She already had the makings.

23   Gracious she was. By gracious I mean full of graces. She had an erectness of carriage, an ease of bearing, a poise that clearly indicated the best of breeding. At table her manners were exquisite. I had seen her at the Kozy Kampus Korner eating the specialty of the house—a sandwich that contained scraps of pot roast, gravy, chopped nuts, and a dipper of sauerkraut—without even getting her fingers moist.

24   Intelligent she was not. In fact, she veered in the opposite direction. But I believed that under my guidance she would smarten up. At any rate, it was worth a try. It is, after all, easier to make a beautiful dumb girl smart than to make an ugly smart girl beautiful.

25   "Petey," I said, "are you in love with Polly Espy?"

"I think she's a keen kid," he replied, "but I don't know if you'd call it love. Why?"

"Do you," I asked, "have any kind of formal arrangement with her? I mean are you going steady or anything like that?"

"No. We see each other quite a bit, but we both have other dates. Why?"

"Is there," I asked, "any other man for whom she has a particular fondness?"

30   "Not that I know of. Why?"

I nodded with satisfaction. "In other words, if you were out of the picture, the field would be open. Is that right?"

"I guess so. What are you getting at?"

"Nothing, nothing," I said innocently, and took my suitcase out of the closet.

"Where are you going?" asked Petey.

35   "Home for the weekend." I threw a few things into the bag.

"Listen," he said, clutching my arm eagerly, "while you're home, you couldn't get some money from your old man, could you, and lend it to me so I can buy a raccoon coat?"

"I may do better than that," I said with a mysterious wink and closed by bag and left.

"Look," I said to Petey when I got back Monday morning. I threw open the suitcase and revealed the huge, hairy, gamy object that my father had worn in his Stutz Bearcat in 1925.

"Holy Toledo!" said Petey reverently. He plunged his hands into the raccoon coat and then his face. "Holy Toledo!" he repeated fifteen or twenty times.

40   "Would you like it?" I asked.

"Oh yes!" he cried, clutching the greasy pelt to him. Then a canny look came into his eyes. "What do you want for it?"

"Your girl," I said, mincing no words.

"Polly?" he said in a horrified whisper. "You want Polly?"

"That's right."

45   He flung the coat from him. "Never," he said stoutly.

I shrugged. "Okay. If you don't want to be in the swim, I guess it's your business."

47   I sat down in a chair and pretended to read a book, but out of the corner of my eye I kept watching Petey. He was a torn man. First he looked at the coat with the expression of a waif at a bakery window. Then he turned away and set his jaw resolutely. Then

he looked back at the coat, with even more longing in his face. Then he turned away, but with not so much resolution this time. Back and forth his head swiveled, desire waxing, resolution waning. Finally he didn't turn away at all; he just stood and stared with mad lust at the coat.

48 "It isn't as though I was in love with Polly," he said thickly. "Or going steady or anything like that."

"That's right," I murmured.

50 "What's Polly to me, or me to Polly?"

"Not a thing," said I.

"It's just been a casual kick—just a few laughs, that's all."

"Try on the coat," said I.

54 He complied. The coat bunched high over his ears and dropped all the way down to his shoe tops. He looked like a mound of dead raccoons. "Fits fine," he said happily.

55 I rose from my chair. "Is it a deal?" I asked, extending my hand.

56 He swallowed. "It's a deal," he said and shook my hand.

57 I had my first date with Polly the following evening. This was in the nature of a survey; I wanted to find out just how much work I had to do to get her mind up to the standard I required. I took her first to dinner. "Gee, that was a delish dinner," she said as we left the restaurant. Then I took her to a movie. "Gee, that was a marvy movie," she said as we left the theater. And then I took her home. "Gee, I had a sensaysh time," she said as she bade me good night.

58 I went back to my room with a heavy heart. I had gravely underestimated the size of my task. This girl's lack of information was terrifying. First she had to be taught to *think.* This loomed as a project of no small dimensions, and at first I was tempted to give her back to Petey. But then I got to thinking about her abundant physical charms and about the way she entered a room and the way she handled a knife and fork, and I decided to make an effort.

59 I went about it, as in all things, systematically. I gave her a course in logic. It happened that I, as a law student, was taking a course in logic myself, so I had all the facts at my finger tips. "Polly," I said to her when I picked her up on our next date, "tonight we are going over to the Knoll and talk."

60 "Oo, terrif," she replied. One thing I will say for this girl: you would go far to find another so agreeable.

We went to the Knoll, the campus trysting place, and we sat down under an old oak, and she looked at me expectantly. "What are we going to talk about?" she asked.

"Logic."

She thought this over for a minute and decided she liked it. "Magnif," she said.

"Logic," I said, clearing my throat, "is the science of thinking. Before we can think correctly, we must first learn to recognize the common fallacies of logic. These we will take up tonight."

65 "Wow-dow!" she cried, clapping her hands delightedly.

I winced, but went bravely on. "First let us examine the fallacy called Dicto Simpliciter."

"By all means," she urged, batting her lashes eagerly.

"Dicto Simpliciter means an argument based on an unqualified generalization. For example: Exercise is good. Therefore everybody should exercise."

"I agree," said Polly earnestly. "I mean exercise is wonderful. I mean it builds the body and everything."

70 "Polly," I said gently, "the argument is a fallacy. *Exercise is good* is an unqualified generalization. For instance, if you have heart disease, exercise is bad, not good. Many people are ordered by their doctors *not* to exercise. You must *qualify* the gen-

eralization. You must say exercise is *usually* good, or exercise is good *for most* people. Otherwise you have committed a Dicto Simpliciter. Do you see?

71 "No," she confessed. "But this is marvy. Do more! Do more!"

72 "It will be better if you stop tugging at my sleeve," I told her, and when she desisted, I continued. "Next we take up a fallacy called Hasty Generalization. Listen carefully: You can't speak French. I can't speak French. Petey Burch can't speak French. I must therefore conclude that nobody at the University of Minnesota can speak French."

73 "Really?" said Polly, amazed. "*Nobody?*"

74 I hid my exasperation. "Polly, it's a fallacy. The generalization is reached too hastily. There are two few instances to support such a conclusion."

75 "Know any more fallacies?" she asked breathlessly. "This is more fun than dancing even."

76 I fought off a wave of despair. I was getting nowhere with this girl, absolutely nowhere. Still, I am nothing if not persistent. I continued. "Next comes Post Hoc. Listen to this: Let's not take Bill on our picnic. Every time we take him out with us, it rains."

Causal trap

77 "I know somebody just like that," she exclaimed. "A girl back home—Eula Becker, her name is. It never fails. Every single time we take her on a picnic—"

78 "Polly," I said sharply, "it's a fallacy. Eula Becker doesn't *cause* the rain. She has no connection with the rain. You are guilty of Post Hoc if you blame Eula Becker."

79 "I'll never do it again," she promised contritely. "Are you mad at me?"

80 I sighed deeply. "No, Polly, I'm not mad."

"Then tell me some more fallacies."

"All right. Let's try Contradictory Premises."

"Yes, let's," she chirped, blinking her eyes happily.

I frowned, but plunged ahead. "Here's an example of Contradictory Premises: If God can do anything, can He make a stone so heavy that He won't be able to lift it?"

85 "Of course," she replied promptly.

"But if He can do anything, He can lift the stone," I pointed out.

"Yeah," she said thoughtfully. "Well, then I guess He can't make the stone."

"But He can do anything," I reminded her.

She scratched her pretty, empty head. "I'm all confused," she admitted.

90 "Of course you are. Because when the premises of an argument contradict each other, there can be no argument. If there is an irresistible force, there can be no immovable object. If there is an immovable object, there can be no irresistible force. Get it?"

91 "Tell me some more of this keen stuff," she said eagerly.

92 I consulted my watch. "I think we'd better call it a night. I'll take you home now, and you go over all the things you've learned. We'll have another session tomorrow night."

93 I deposited her at the girl's dormitory, where she assured me that she had had a perfect terrif evening, and I went glumly home to my room. Petey lay snoring in his bed, the raccoon coat huddled like a great hairy beast at his feet. For a moment I considered waking him and telling him that he could have his girl back. It seemed clear that my project was doomed to failure. The girl simply had a logic-proof head.

94 But then I reconsidered. I had wasted one evening; I might as well waste another. Who knew? Maybe somewhere in the extinct crater of her mind, a few embers still smoldered. Maybe somehow I could fan them into flame. Admittedly it was not a prospect fraught with hope, but I decided to give it one more try.

95 Seated under the oak the next evening I said, "Our first fallacy tonight is called Ad Misericordiam."

96 She quivered with delight.

97 "Listen closely," I said. "A man applies for a job. When the boss asks him what his

234

qualifications are, he replies that he has a wife and six children at home, the wife is a helpless cripple, the children have nothing to eat, no clothes to wear, no shoes on their feet, there are no beds in the house, no coal in the cellar, and winter is coming.''

98   A tear rolled down each of Polly's pink cheeks. ''Oh, this is awful, awful,'' she sobbed.

99   ''Yes, it's awful,'' I agreed, ''but it's no argument. The man never answered the boss's question about his qualifications. Instead he appealed to the boss's sympathy. He committed the fallacy of Ad Misericordiam. Do you understand?''

100   ''Have you got a handkerchief?'' she blubbered.

101   I handed her a handkerchief and tried to keep from screaming while she wiped her eyes. ''Next,'' I said in a carefully controlled tone, ''we will discuss False Analogy. Here is an example: Students should be allowed to look at their textbooks during examinations. After all, surgeons have X-rays to guide them during an operation, lawyers have briefs to guide them during a trial, carpenters have blueprints to guide them when they are building a house. Why, then, shouldn't students be allowed to look at their textbooks during an examination?''

102   ''There now,'' she said enthusiastically, ''is the most marvy idea I've heard in years.''

103   ''Polly,'' I said testily, ''the argument is all wrong. Doctors, lawyers, and carpenters aren't taking a test to see how much they have learned, but students are. The situations are altogether different, and you can't make an analogy between them.''

''I still think it's a good idea,'' said Polly.

105   ''Nuts,'' I muttered. Doggedly I pressed on. ''Next we'll try Hypothesis Contrary to Fact.''

''Sounds yummy,'' was Polly's reaction.

''Listen: If Madame Curie had not happened to leave a photographic plate in a drawer with a chunk of pitchblende, the world today would not know about radium.''

''True, true,'' said Polly, nodding her head. ''Did you see the movie? Oh, it just knocked me out. That Walter Pidgeon is so dreamy. I mean he fractures me.''

109   ''If you can forget Mr. Pidgeon for a moment,'' I said coldly, ''I would like to point out that the statement is a fallacy. Maybe Madame Curie would have discovered radium at some later date. Maybe somebody else would have discovered it. Maybe any number of things would have happened. You can't start with a hypothesis that is not true and then draw any supportable conclusions from it.''

110   ''They ought to put Walter Pidgeon in more pictures,'' said Polly. ''I hardly ever see him any more.''

111   One more chance, I decided. But just one more. There is a limit to what flesh and blood can bear. ''The next fallacy is called Poisoning the Well.''

112   ''How cute!'' she gurgled.

113   ''Two men are having a debate. The first one gets up and says, 'My opponent is a notorious liar. You can't believe a word that he is going to say.' . . . Now, Polly, think. Think hard. What's wrong?''

114   I watched her closely as she knit her creamy brow in concentration. Suddenly a glimmer of intelligence—the first I had seen—came into her eyes. ''It's not fair,'' she said with indignation. ''It's not a bit fair. What chance has the second man got if the first man calls him a liar before he even begins talking?''

115   ''Right!'' I cried exultantly. ''One hundred percent right. It's not fair. The first man has *poisoned the well* before anybody could drink from it. He has hamstrung his opponent before he could even start. . . . Polly, I'm proud of you.''

116   ''Pshaw,'' she murmured, blushing with pleasure.

117   ''You see, my dear, these things aren't so hard. All you have to do is concentrate. Think—examine—evaluate. Come now, let's review everything we have learned.''

118   ''Fire away,'' she said with an airy wave of her hand.

119   Heartened by the knowledge that Polly was not altogether a cretin, I began a long, patient review of all I had told her. Over and over and over again I cited instances, pointed out flaws, kept hammering away without letup. It was like digging a tunnel. At first everything was work, sweat, and darkness. I had no idea when I would reach the light, or even *if* I would. But I persisted. I pounded and clawed and scraped, and finally I was rewarded. I saw a chink of light. And then the chink got bigger and the sun came pouring in and all was bright.

120   Five grueling nights this took, but it was worth it. I had made a logician out of Polly; I had taught her to think. My job was done. She was worthy of me at last. She was a fit wife for me, a proper hostess for my many mansions, a suitable mother for my well-heeled children.

121   It must not be thought that I was without love for this girl. Quite the contrary. Just as Pygmalion loved the perfect woman he had fashioned, so I loved mine. I determined to acquaint her with my feelings at our very next meeting. The time had come to change our relationship from academic to romantic.

122   "Polly," I said when next we sat beneath our oak, "tonight we will not discuss fallacies."

123   "Aw, gee," she said, disappointed.

124   "My dear," I said, favoring her with a smile, "we have now spent five evenings together. We have gotten along splendidly. It is clear that we are well matched."

125   "Hasty Generalization," said Polly brightly.

126   "I beg your pardon," said I.

        "Hasty Generalization," she repeated. "How can you say that we are well matched on the basis of only five dates?"

128   I chuckled with amusement. The dear child had learned her lessons well. "My dear," I said, patting her hand in a tolerant manner, "five dates is plenty. After all, you don't have to eat a whole cake to know that it's good."

        "False Analogy," said Polly promptly. "I'm not a cake. I'm a girl."

130   I chuckled with somewhat less amusement. The dear child had learned her lessons perhaps too well. I decided to change tactics. Obviously the best approach was a simple, strong, direct declaration of love. I paused for a moment while my massive brain chose the proper words. Then I began:

131   "Polly, I love you. You are the whole world to me, and the moon and the stars and the constellations of outer space. Please, my darling, say that you will go steady with me, for if you will not, life will be meaningless. I will languish. I will refuse my meals. I will wander the face of the earth, a shambling, hollow-eyed hulk."

        There, I thought, folding my arms, that ought to do it.

        "Ad Misericordiam," said Polly.

        I ground my teeth. I was not Pygmalion; I was Frankenstein, and my monster had me by the throat. Frantically I fought back the tide of panic surging through me. At all costs I had to keep cool.

135   "Well, Polly," I said, forcing a smile, "you certainly have learned your fallacies."

        "You're darn right," she said with a vigorous nod.

        "And who taught them to you, Polly?"

        "You did."

        "That's right. So you do owe me something, don't you, my dear? If I hadn't come along you never would have learned about fallacies."

140   "Hypothesis Contrary to Fact," she said instantly.

        I dashed perspiration from my brow. "Polly," I croaked, "you mustn't take all these things so literally. I mean this is just classroom stuff. You know that the things you learn

236

in school don't have anything to do with life.''

''Dicto Simpliciter,'' she said, wagging her finger at me playfully.

That did it. I leaped to my feet, bellowing like a bull. ''Will you or will you not go steady with me?''

''I will not,'' she replied.

145 ''Why not?'' I demanded.

''Because this afternoon I promised Petey Burch that I would go steady with him.''

I reeled back, overcome with the infamy of it. After he promised, after he made a deal, after he shook my hand! ''The rat!'' I shrieked, kicking up great chunks of turf. ''You can't go with him, Polly. He's a liar. He's a cheat. He's a rat.''

''Poisoning the well,'' said Polly, ''and stop shouting. I think shouting must be a fallacy too.''

149 With an immense effort of will, I modulated my voice. ''All right,'' I said. ''You're a logician. Let's look at this thing logically. How could you choose Petey Burch over me? Look at me—a brilliant student, a tremendous intellectual, a man with an assured future. Look at Petey—a knothead, a jitterbug, a guy who'll never know where his next meal is coming from. Can you give me one logical reason why you should go steady with Petey Burch?''

150 ''I certainly can,'' declared Polly. ''He's got a raccoon coat.''

3,840 words

Vocabulary

perspicacious (1)	pitchblende (105)
coveted (20)	cretin (119)
cerebral (20)	shambling (131)
trysting (60)	infamy (145)
testily (103)	modulated (149)

Questions

1. What trade does the narrator make with his roommate, Petey Burch?
2. Why does the narrator desire Polly Espy?
3. What is the Dicto Simpliciter fallacy? What example of it does the author give?
4. What is a hasty generalization? Give an example.
5. What is the Post Hoc fallacy? Give an example.
6. What are contradictory premises? Give an example.
7. What is the Ad Misericordiam fallacy? Give an example.
8. What is a false analogy? Make up your own example.
9. What is a hypothesis contrary to fact? Give your own example.
10. What is the fallacy of poisoning the well? Make up an example.
11. What attitudes toward women are evident in this story? How do you regard these attitudes?
12. How do you regard the characters in this story? Do you see them as humorous caricatures? Or do you see them as a reflection of the 1950s?

C. Additional Writing Assignments

1. Argue for or against recreational facilities in our nation's prisons.
2. It is often stated that newspapers give a distorted view of life because they report only the sensational. Argue for or against this proposition.
3. Should movies be subject to censorship? Rely on the rules of good argument in supporting your answer to this question.
4. Instructors of political science should never express their own political opinions in class. Argue for or against this statement.
5. Write a well-shaped argument in favor of allowing 18-year-olds to purchase liquor.
6. Write a carefully reasoned argument either for or against coeducational dormitories.
7. Write a 500-word argument supporting the statement that the American consumer is a victim of planned obsolescence.
8. Read through the editorial section in several issues of your local newspaper until you find an article containing a controlling idea with which you disagree. Counter with your own argument.
9. Write 250 words arguing that drivers should be forced by law to wear seat belts; then turn around and write a 250-word argument arguing that drivers should *not* be forced to wear seat belts.
10. As persuasively as you can, argue in favor of a research paper requirement for Freshman English.

Part III

Revising the Essay:

a brief handbook

13

Grammar Fundamentals

A. The Sentence

A sentence is *a group of words that expresses a complete thought.* "Because I'm happy" and "singing in the rain" do not express complete thoughts and are therefore not sentences. The following express complete thoughts and are therefore classified as sentences:

1. Because I am happy, I like to see other people happy.
2. John is singing in the rain.

The Subject and Predicate

Every sentence is divisible into two parts—a *subject* and a *predicate*. The subject is the word or word group about which something is said; the predicate is the word or word group that asserts something about the subject:

subject	predicate
The bird	fell out of the sky.
It	angered him deeply.
All the boys	left without saying a word.

The *simple subject* of a sentence is the single word—usually a noun or pronoun—about which the sentence says something:

1. The *beggar* suddenly blinked his eyes.
2. The ugly *frog* turned into a handsome young prince.

The *simple predicate* is the verb or verb phrase that makes a statement about the subject:

1. Fred *decided* to play in the tournament.
2. Before dinner we *had welcomed* all the guests.

Complete Subjects and Predicates

The *complete subject* is the simple subject and all the words associated with it. The *complete predicate* is the simple predicate and all the words associated with it. A vertical line divides the complete subject from the complete predicate in these sentences:

1. Diseases of the mind | are often caused by the pressures of city living.
2. The regular bus driver | knows his passengers by name.

The student who is unable to distinguish between the simple subject and simple predicate, and between the complete subject and complete predicate in sentences, will have trouble with the construction and punctuation of sentences.

Compound Subjects and Predicates

A compound subject is made up of two or more nouns or pronouns tied together; a compound predicate is made up of two or more verbs tied together:

1. *Terror and hate* were in their eyes.   compound subject
2. The soldier *stopped and saluted.*   compound predicate
3. *Ghosts and witches* were the main characters in the story.   compound subject
4. In the recesses of his mind, the villain *remembered and felt guilty.*   compound predicate
5. *John and Mary laughed and sang.*   compound subject/compound predicate

Exercises

Underline the simple subject once and the simple predicate twice in the following sentences. Identify the verb first. To find the subject, ask "Who or what did it?"

1. The teacher arrived ten minutes after the class was to begin.

2. Mary believes in the intelligence and honesty of dogs.

3. After seeing the movie twice, Alice was sure she was in love with Robert Redford.

4. At the end of the first act, the big star made his appearance.

5. People all over the world expect America to feed them.

6. Ted was elected to run as vice-president.

7. We danced in the hallway, in the cellar, and on the patio.

8. Grace, her voice controlled and her head held high, debated the issues with her rival.

9. My father, a businessman, took the paper and tore it to shreds.

10. At the end of the examination, Bill broke down and laughed hysterically.

In the following sentences, draw a vertical line between the complete subject and the complete predicate.

1. Jane arranged her schedule to allow for study.

2. As an usher as well as a waiter, Bruce worked to save $300.00.

3. Alaska, with all of its natural beauty, appealed to the Smiths.

4. Playing a guitar demands skill and sensitivity.

5. Angry and tired, the dean arrived and was hit with a water balloon.

6. Separate wills are recommended for couples who have been married twice.

7. The top of Mt. Whitney offers a breathtaking view of the Sierras.

8. The undefeatable Johnson was dropped from the squad.

9. Horses, covered with flies, stood scratching their backs on the fence.

10. Honor is more important than love.

B. Clauses and Phrases

The Clause

A clause is a *group of related words that form part of a sentence.* Every clause has a subject and a predicate. There are two types of clauses: *independent* and *dependent.* An independent clause expresses a complete thought by making a complete statement, asking a question, giving a command, or making an exclamation. An independent clause, therefore, could stand alone as a complete sentence, but it is combined with other independent or dependent clauses to form a full sentence, as in the following examples:

1. John was happy at home, but he left to make money.

    independent clause   independent clause

2. The children played until their parents arrived.

    independent clause   dependent clause

3. Is the soldier happy because he left home?

    independent clause   dependent clause

There is a crucial difference between an independent and a dependent clause: Standing alone, an independent clause makes sense, but a dependent clause does not. A dependent clause depends for its meaning on an independent clause that either precedes or follows it. Dependent clauses are therefore said to be *subordinate* to independent clauses.

The Phrase

A phrase is a group of two or more associated words having neither subject nor predicate. A phrase does not make a complete statement, is never a clause, and is certainly not a sentence. A phrase is only part of a clause or a sentence. The following groups of words are phrases:

1. for his fiftieth birthday
2. practicing the flute
3. under the table
4. after a long time

Exercises

Label the following passages as *I* (independent clause), *D* (dependent clause), or *P* (phrase).

1. Spring has begun   _____

2. Since their parents died   _____

3. Although Sam is an atheist   _____

4. Follow the main road for a mile   _____

5. Between the two houses   _____

6. Everyone told him to stay home   _____

7. For your country   _____

8. If Mary enrolled in the class   _____

9. You may wish to return the picture today   _____

10. Who attend religious services   _____

11. Begging her to love him   _____

12. Flowers blossom   _____

13. Have you seen the five napkins   _____

14. He seldom speaks his mind   _____

15. Because she grew up in Poland   _____

C. Sentence Types

Sentences are punctuated according to their function and their form. The examples in this section will assist you in recognizing the function a sentence serves and the forms it can take.

244

Classification according to Function

A *declarative sentence* tells something; it states a fact or a possibility:

1. The jet fighter died in the crash. (fact)
2. The stock market may go up tomorrow. (possibility)

A declarative sentence always ends with a period.

An *interrogative sentence* asks a question:

1. Is it true what they say about Dixie?
2. Have you decided which courses you will take?

An interrogative sentence always ends with a question mark.

An *imperative sentence* makes a request or gives an order:

1. Don't park your car here.
2. Turn over the cash to the cashier.

An imperative sentence ends with a period unless the command is filled with strong emotion, in which case it ends with an exclamation mark:

1. Shut your mouth, you fool!
2. It's an earthquake. Fall to the floor!

An *exclamatory sentence* expresses strong or sudden feeling:

1. Oh, the pain is terrible!
2. How cruel you are!

The exclamatory sentence ends with an exclamation mark.

Classification according to Form

A *simple sentence* consists of one independent clause that contains one subject and one predicate, and expresses one complete thought:

1. The tree fell.
2. The heavens declare the glory of God.
3. There is no peace in being greedy.

Although a simple sentence has only one subject and one predicate, either the subject or the predicate or both may be compound. Not all simple sentences are short, for both the subject and the predicate may have many modifying words:

Staggering from his wound, inflicted during the heat of battle, and exhausted from the endless trudging through jungles, the young marine found a place near a brook shaded by trees and rested awhile.

A *compound sentence* consists of two or more independent clauses connected by one of the following coordinating conjunctions: *and, or, nor, but, yet, for, as.* For example:

1. The flowers were blossoming, but patches of snow still covered the earth.

2. He studied hard for the examination, yet he failed.
3. Jim smiled and Fred frowned.

A *complex sentence* consists of one independent clause to which one or more dependent clauses have been connected:

1. The foreman ordered the men to work because five days had elapsed.   one dependent clause
2. Since life is not perfect, everyone must expect to find that difficulties will confront him as he attempts to achieve his goal.   three dependent clauses

A *compound-complex sentence* consists of two or more independent clauses and at least one dependent clause.

1. The company figured the values of all the pieces of property that lay within the city limits, and the manager then wrote each property owner a letter that explained the cost of curbing.
2. The Christmas holiday contained one big surprise; while the girls went skiing, the boys washed the dishes.

Exercises

Place the appropriate punctuation mark at the end of each of the following sentences.

1. Oh, crime and violence, how long will you continue to rob us of peace
2. This is the time for all good men to come to the aid of their country
3. Come here, right this minute
4. Have you, by chance, already met this gentleman
5. Help I am caught in a mousetrap
6. Go to the store and buy me a quart of milk
7. If I need you, will you be available
8. What an exciting evening
9. Should we never meet again, I wish you the best of luck
10. I asked him if he had been paid for his time

Classify each of the following sentences as (1) simple, (2) compound, (3) complex, (4) compound-complex. Justify your classification by identifying the various clauses.

1. At the end of the day, Alice made an appearance; however, she did not smile once.   _____
2. Because the winter was nearly over, Maxine arranged to be home with her mother, her grandmother, and her sisters.   _____
3. After he had reached the end of the road, Mr. Leffingwell began to cross the bridge.   _____
4. Big Tom was dropped from the club after one month of membership; he now is trying out for the swimming team.   _____

5. At the end of the race, Jane let out a yell, for she had finished in third place. _____

6. Maybelle operated an elevator for three years to save enough money to go to night school, to buy a new car, and to pay her mother's doctor bills. _____

7. In the top drawer you will find two pairs of old gloves, three torn sweaters, and a yellowed picture album. _____

8. We all believe that the American constitution must be preserved, because our liberties, which our ancestors paid for with their lives, must be nurtured with care. _____

9. After freezing all night, Nancy decided she should have worn a sweater. _____

10. When my family left for New Orleans, I thought they would return within two weeks; instead, they stayed there a full year. _____

11. My uncle, a famous poet, gave me a handwritten manuscript and asked me to take care of it for him. _____

12. Your letter was delightful; I am sure that it offended no one. _____

13. Because Tom gave the most forceful peptalk, he was asked to represent the senior class at the Fine Arts Festival. _____

14. The mayor, his voice trembling with rage, denounced his opponent, Jack Wilson. _____

15. He flew to New York, and she drove to Chicago because she was afraid to fly with him. _____

D. Parts of Speech

The Verb

The verb is a word that suggests *action,* a *state of being,* or a *condition:*

1. The cat *leaped* off the roof.   action
2. The antique cup *sat* on the lace cloth.   state of being
3. Her eyes *were* big and luminous.   condition

The Noun

Nouns are *names* of persons, animals, things, places, characteristics, or ideas. The following are nouns:

engineer	Westwood Village
dog	jealousy
box	communism

You should be able to distinguish among four kinds of nouns:

1. *concrete* nouns, indicating tangible things such as: men, cat, towns, teachers, coat
2. *proper* nouns, indicating capitalized names of specific persons, places, things, organizations, and events, such as: Mt. Everest, Mary, French, Mr. Jones, the Eiffel Tower
3. *abstract* nouns, indicating qualities or concepts such as: love, justice, hate, credibility, intimacy
4. *collective* nouns, indicating groups that are singular in form, but singular or plural in meaning, such as: jury, group, family, council, committee

The ability to recognize these four kinds of nouns will help you to avoid common errors in capitalization, agreement of subject and predicate, and agreement of pronouns with their *antecedents*—the words the pronouns stand for.

The Pronoun

Pronouns are words used *in place of nouns*. For example, you may use the pronoun *she* instead of the noun *mother*. You may speak of "the *children's* toys" or *"their* toys." There are eight kinds of pronouns, listed below. While it is not important that you be able to name each kind, you should be able to recognize each as a pronoun:

1. personal   *You* and *they* will help *us.*
2. interrogative   *Who* is it? *What* do you want? *Which* is best?
3. relative   The man *who* killed her is the one *that* I saw.
4. demonstrative   *This* is older than *that.*
5. indefinite   *Each* of us must accomplish *something.*
6. reciprocal   Let us help *each other* and trust *one another.*
7. reflexive   John did it *himself.* I blame *myself.*
8. intensive   *I myself* heard him. *We* need money *ourselves.*

The Adjective

Adjectives are words that *modify* (describe or qualify) nouns and pronouns:

1. The *shiny, black* cat   The noun *cat* is modified.
2. *Morose* and *depressed,* he sat in the corner.   The pronoun *he* is modified.
3. The beggar wanted *five* nickels.   The word *nickels* is modified.

Adjectives usually precede, but sometimes follow, the nouns they modify (a *tall, handsome* man). *Appositive adjectives* immediately follow a noun and are set off by commas from the nouns they follow:

1. The attorney, *pale* with anger, jumped forward.
2. The little boy, *dusty* and *tired,* fell asleep.

Sometimes the adjective follows the predicate, in which case it is called a *predicate adjective:*

1. The sunset looks *splendid*.
2. The newlyweds seem *happy*.
3. Women are *strong*.

Occasionally, the adjective modifies the object of the sentence, in which case it is called an *objective complement*:

1. The cream sauce made her *sick*.
2. The sun turned him *crimson red*.

The Article

The article is a kind of adjective that *limits* a noun:

1. *the* people
2. *a* balloon, *an* orange

The Adverb

Adverbs modify verbs, adjectives, and other adverbs. They are next to verbs and nouns in importance. Good writers tend to use more adverbs than adjectives. Note the use of adverbs in the following sentences:

1. Cecil will work *slowly* and *deliberately*.   adverb modifying a verb
2. My mother inherited a *surprisingly* old clock.   adverb modifying an adjective
3. She succeeded *quite* well.   adverb modifying an adverb

An adverb often indicates time (we must leave *now*), place (they stayed *over there*), manner (she walks *awkwardly*), or degree (all the relatives were *extraordinarily* kind). Some nouns function as adverbs and are called *adverbial nouns* (he left home *Monday*).

A special group of adverbs are the *conjunctive adverbs*. The primary conjunctive adverbs are:

accordingly	indeed
also	instead
anyhow	likewise
besides	meanwhile
consequently	nevertheless
furthermore	otherwise
hence	still
henceforth	then
however	therefore

When used to connect independent clauses, the conjunctive adverb is preceded by a semicolon:

1. We doubted their word; *nevertheless,* we went along with the plan.
2. Something about the garden pleased us; *however,* we did not wish to purchase the house.
3. The manager was harsh; *moreover,* he owed us our salaries.

When a conjunctive adverb is used parenthetically, it is set off by commas:

1. You can see, *moreover,* why this is important.
2. She, *however,* denied the truth.
3. This time, *furthermore,* he was forbidden to speak.

When the adverb *there* is used to introduce a sentence, it is called an *expletive: There* is a city in Algiers where bazaars appear everywhere.

Most adverbs end in *-ly.* The few that do not are called *flat* adverbs:

1. He walked *far.*
2. He walks too *fast.*
3. They work *hard.*

The Preposition

A preposition is used to show the relationship of a noun or pronoun to some other word in the sentence. For example, in "The airplane flew *above* the clouds," the preposition *above* shows the relationship between the clouds and the airplane. Anything else that an airplane can do in approaching clouds is likely to involve a preposition:

1. The airplane flew *into* the clouds.
2. The airplane flew *through* the clouds.
3. The airplane flew *across* the clouds.
4. The airplane flew *behind* the clouds.
5. The airplane flew *between* the clouds.
6. The airplane flew *after* the clouds.
7. The airplane flew *by* the clouds.
8. The airplane flew *over/under* the clouds.
9. The airplane flew *with* the clouds.
10. The airplane flew *out of* the clouds.
11. The airplane flew *near* the clouds.

A few prepositions, such as *for* and *of,* will not work in this example.

Some words like *off, on, out, in, over,* and *up* may be used as prepositions, adverbs, or verbs:

1. He climbed *up* the ladder.   preposition
2. All of us looked *up.*   adverb
3. When I arrived in New York, I *looked* him *up.*   verb
4. He ran *out* the door.   preposition
5. Reach *out* with your hand.   adverb
6. We must *watch out* for fires.   verb

The preposition and its object form a *prepositional phrase:*

1. The dog remained *inside his kennel.*
2. Every morning he looked *underneath the table.*
3. The thief lurked *near the car.*

The Conjunction

Conjunctions are connectors and can be classified into two types: *coordinating* conjunctions and *subordinating* conjunctions. Coordinating conjunctions (*and, or, nor, but, yet, for*) are used to connect words, phrases, and clauses that are of equal rank:

1. Apples *and* oranges.   words
2. With his lover, *but* not with his mother.   phrases
3. I love my son, *yet* he must obey me.   clauses

Subordinating conjunctions (*after, although, as, because, before, if, since, until, when, while, then*) are used to connect main clauses with subordinate clauses:

1. That man never looked us straight in the eye *when* he talked with us.
2. *If* you don't believe him, tell him so.
3. The bridge collapsed *because* it was so old.
4. She is stronger *than* any of the men are.

A special kind of conjunction is the *correlative* conjunction, which is used in pairs:

1. They were *not only* kind *but also* generous.
2. They *neither* complained *nor* cared.

The Interjection

Interjections are words or phrases used to express strong or sudden feelings that attract attention:

1. *Hurray!* They've won.
2. *Ouch!* The horse stepped on my foot.
3. *Whew!* That's hard work.

Context and the Parts of Speech

The role of the word in a sentence always determines the part of speech it is. Context may change the role of a word:

1. He must *round* the corner at top speed.   verb
2. The audience gave the orchestra a *round* of applause.   noun
3. The baby had a perfectly *round* face.   adjective
4. Her fiance lives *round* the corner.   preposition

Exercises

Identify the part of speech of each italicized word in the following paragraphs:

I[1] went back to the *Devon School*[2] not long ago, *and*[3] *found*[4] it looking *oddly*[5] newer than *when*[6] I was a student *there*[7] fifteen years before. It seemed *more*[8] sedate *than*[9] I remembered it, more *perpendicular*[10] and straitlaced, *with*[11] narrower[12] windows and shinier woodwork, *as though*[13] a coat *of*[14] varnish *had been put*[15] *over*[16] everything for better preservation. *But,*[17] of course, fifteen years *before*[18] there had been a war going on. Perhaps the school wasn't as *well*[19] kept up in those days; *perhaps*[20] varnish, *along with*[21] *everything*[22] else, had gone to war.

I didn't *entirely*[23] like this glossy new *surface,*[24] *because*[25] it made the school look *like*[26] a museum, and that's exactly *what*[27] it was to me, and what I did not want it to be. In the deep, tacit way in which *feeling*[28] becomes stronger than thought, I had always *felt*[29] *that*[30] the Devon School came *into*[31] existence the *day*[32] I entered it, was vibrantly *real*[33] *while*[34] I was a student there, and then blinked out like a candle *the*[35] day I left.

John Knowles, *A Separate Peace*

1. _____

2. _____

3. _____

4. _____

5. _____

6. _____

7. _____

8. _____

9. _____

10. _____

11. _____

12. _____

13. _____

14. _____

15. _____

16. _____

17. _____

18. _____

19. _____

20. _____

21. _____

22. _____

23. _____

24. _____

25. _____

26. _____

27. _____

28. _____

29. _____

30. _____

31. _____

32. _____

33. _____

34. _____

35. _____

14

Correcting
Common Errors

This unit presents the most common errors found in student essays. Most teachers use handwritten symbols to indicate student errors. For an explanation of your own errors and how to correct them, match the symbols in the margin of your paper with those provided in this unit.

frag   A sentence *fragment* results when a phrase or a dependent clause is treated as if it were a complete sentence. Correct a fragment either by attaching it to the previous sentence or by adding enough words to the fragment to make it a complete sentence:

Error: We thought about the weather. Decided to cancel the picnic.

Correction: We thought about the weather, and decided to cancel the picnic.

Error: Lonely house on the block.

Correction: There was a lonely house on the block.

Error: A man doesn't call a wall warped. Unless he knows what a straight wall is.

Correction: A man doesn't call a wall warped unless he knows what a straight wall is.

Error: Birds chirping, bees buzzing, the smell of honey in the air. I knew that spring was here.

Correction: Birds were chirping, bees were buzzing, and the smell of honey hung in the air. I knew that spring was here.

cs   A *comma splice* occurs when two independent clauses are separated by a comma instead of a period or a semicolon. There are four ways of correcting a comma splice:

1. Separate the independent clauses with a period.

Error: I was deeply shaken, my favorite cousin lay ill with cancer.

Correction: I was deeply shaken. My favorite cousin lay ill with cancer.

2. Separate the independent clauses with a semicolon.

Error: The backyard was full of plums, our family ate them all.

Correction: The backyard was full of plums; our family ate them all.

3. Join the independent clauses by a comma and a coordinating conjunction.

Error: Anyone can stick flowers in a vase, few can achieve an artistic arrangement.

Correction: Anyone can stick flowers in a vase, *but* few can achieve an artistic arrangement.

4. Subordinate one independent clause to the other.

Error: You failed to come to dinner, I ate alone.

Correction: Because you failed to come to dinner, I ate alone.

Don't let a conjunctive adverb trick you into a comma splice:

Error: I hate high altitude weather, however, the Rocky Mountains are good for my asthma.

Correction: I hate cold weather; however, the Rocky Mountains are good for my asthma.

rt A *run-together sentence* occurs when one sentence is piled on another without any kind of punctuation, often resulting in an incoherent passage. Correct a run-together sentence by placing a period or a conjunction between the two sentences.

Error: This map also predicts California's future the San Andreas fault, which underlies Los Angeles, is heading out to sea.

Correction: This map also predicts California's future. The San Andreas fault, which underlies Los Angeles, is heading out to sea.

Error: I like her attitude she is a solid person.

Correction: I like her attitude. She is a solid person.

Error: The first year of marriage is never easy I made it harder than need be.

Correction: The first year of marriage is never easy, but I made it harder than need be.

Exercises

In the blanks at the right, enter *C* if the sentence is correct, *frag* if it is a fragment, *cs* if it is a comma splice, and *rt* if it is a run-together sentence. Correct any sentence that is incorrect.

1. People must eat. _____

2. The countless women who need jobs. _____

3. Chicago being a city riddled with crime. _____

4. The rivers overflowed their banks the trees were swept away. _____

5. Houses were destroyed, and homes were burned. _____

6. Pet lovers in our country as well as abroad. _____

7. In particular the mayor, who had supported a transit system when he spoke to the legislature. _____

8. Irresistible also were the lovely orchards surrounding the swimming pool. _____

9. However, some crowds were vengeful. _____

10. "I cannot marry you," said the princess, "I am too ugly." _____

11. Every one of us felt the loss. _____

12. The Vietnam war was senseless it gained us nothing. _____

13. Run as fast as you can you need the practice. _____

14. Recalling his visit to Paris, my uncle smiled. _____

15. All of us visited the statue, few of us admired it. _____

16. Originally made in Taiwan but then transported to the United States. _____

17. I had no success. Soon giving up trying. _____

18. She was as delicate as a butterfly. With her iridescent eyes. _____

19. I want to excel not only as a musician, but also as a human being. _____

20. The car weighed a ton; they could not lift it. _____

agr An *error in agreement* occurs when the subject does not agree with the verb or when a pronoun does not agree with its antecedent. Avoid errors in subject-verb agreement by learning to recognize the subject of a sentence. To avoid errors in pronoun agreement, learn which pronouns are plural and which are singular.

Errors with Verbs

Error: My family, together with numerous other families, were checked for excess baggage.

Correction: My family, together with numerous other families, was checked for excess baggage.   The subject is *family*.

Error: The main issue are high taxes.

Correction: The main issue *is* high taxes. The subject is *issue*.

Error: My list of errors were so long that the teacher shook her head in despair.

Correction: My list of errors *was* so long that the teacher shook her head in despair. The subject is *list*.

Error: Either John alone or all of the boys together has to show up at the entrance.

Correction: Either John alone or all of the boys together *have* to show up at the entrance. The subject is *boys.* When two subjects, one singular and one plural, are connected by *or, nor* or *either,* the verb must agree with the nearer subject.

Error: Mary is among the girls who has collected funds to build a memorial hall.

Correction: Mary is among the girls who *have* collected funds to build a memorial hall. *Who,* subject of the dependent clause, refers back to girls, not Mary.

Error: Unemployment as well as inflation affect the voters.

Correction: Unemployment as well as inflation *affects* the voters. The addition of expressions such as *together with, along with, as well as, including, like,* does not alter the number of the subject.

Error: A pair of scissors and some thread is standard equipment for seamstresses.

Correction: A pair of scissors and some thread *are* standard equipment for seamstresses. Subjects joined by *and* require a plural verb. Exceptions are compound subjects referring to a single person, as "My lover and best *friend* has left me." Lover and friend are the same person.

Exercises

In the following sentences, change each verb that does not agree with its subject. Write the correct form in the blank, or if the sentence is correct, write *C.*

1. Neither storms nor illness delay our newspapers. _____

2. His five children and their education was his main worry. _____

3. There's much to be said for simplicity. _____

4. The importance of words are being stressed in all newspapers. _____

5. My chief concern this summer are my expenses. _____

6. Each member of the club, as well as all of the football players, were given free tickets. _____

7. Taste in books differs from student to student. _____

8. *The Three Stooges* are a wonderful movie. _____

9. Mathematics is one of my worst subjects. _____

10. Either you or I am mistaken. _____

11. My brothers as well as my sister is coming to visit me. _____

Errors with Pronouns

The following pronouns, when used as subjects, always require a singular verb: *each, either, neither, another, anyone, anybody, anything, someone, somebody, something, one, everyone, everybody, everything, nobody, nothing.*

Error: Each of the prizes were spectacular.

Correction: Each of the prizes *was* spectacular. Don't let prepositional phrases trick you into an agreement error. In the above case, *each* is the subject.

Error: Behind all the managers stand their president.

Correction: Behind all the managers *stands* their president.

Error: Everyone in that room care sincerely.

Correction: Everyone in that room *cares* sincerely.

Error: Neither of the twins plan to go to private school.

Correction: Neither of the twins *plans* to go to private school.

A pronoun must agree in number with its antecedent:

Error: Everyone who accepted the money knew that they would have to return it.

Correction: Everyone who accepted the money knew that *he* would have to return it.

Error: Anyone who visits the principal will find that they are welcome.

Correction: Anyone who visits the principal will find that *he* is welcome.

Error: Every woman who wrote demanding a ticket knew that they would get one.

Correction: Every woman who wrote demanding a ticket knew that *she* would get one.

Collective nouns are replaced by singular pronouns if they denote a single unit, but by plural pronouns if they denote a group acting separately and individually.

1. The jury rendered *its* verdict.   acting as a single unit
2. The jury could not reach an agreement; *they* argued all day.   acting individually
3. The whole family gave *its* view.   acting as a single unit
4. The family have gone their separate ways.   acting individually

Case *Case* errors most commonly occur when a student fails to distinguish between the subjective and objective cases. The subject is always a noun or pronoun that the predicate says something about. The subject answers who? or what? about the predicate. The object, on the other hand, receives the action of the verb and is not the same as the subject. Study the following diagrams:

subject   verb   object
The patient   watches   the sunset

The patient initiates the action of the verb *watched,* whereas the sunset being watched receives it. Two further examples will reinforce the difference between subject and object:

	subject	verb	object			subject	verb	object
	My brother	*hit*	*the dog*			*Americans*	*love*	*their country*

Problems in case arise when nouns are replaced by pronouns of the wrong case. The pronouns below are listed in the subjective case at left and in the objective case at right:

subjective	objective
I	me
you	you
he, she, it	him, her, it
we	us
they	them
who, whoever	whom, whomever

In the sentences,

1. John bit the dog.
2. The dog bit John.

a pronoun substituted for *John* must reflect in its case whether John is the subject or object of the verb *bit*—whether he initiates the action or receives it:

1. He bit the dog.
2. The dog bit him.

The subjective pronoun *he* is used in place of *John* when *John* functions in the sentence as a subject. The objective pronoun *him* is used in place of *John* when *John* functions in the sentence as an object.

Error: The coach called *he* and *I.*

Correction: The coach called *him* and *me.* *Him* and *me* are objects because they take the action from the verb *called.*

Error: Ellen and *me* decided to wear corsages.

Correction: *Ellen and I* decided to wear corsages. *Ellen and I* is a compound subject.

Prepositions always require the objective case.

Error: The teacher got a better understanding of him and *I.*

Correction: The teacher got a better understanding of him and *me.*

Error: Between you and *I,* the whole matter was a joke.

Correction: Between you and *me,* the whole matter was a joke.

Special care must be taken to use the right case with pronouns in apposition. An appositive must be in the same case as the noun or pronoun it qualifies.

Error: They told both of us—my mother and *I*—that the sale was over.

Correction: They told both of us—my mother and *me*—that the sale was over. *Me* is in the objective case since it is in apposition with *us.*

Error: Let's you and *I* make sure that the bill is paid.

Correction: Let's you and *me* make sure that the bill is paid.   Let us—you and *me*. *You* and *me* must be in the objective case since they are in apposition with *us*.

The case of pronouns used in clauses must be determined by treating each clause as a separate part.

Error: I shall vote for whoever I like.

Correction: I shall vote for whomever I like.   *Whomever I like* must be treated as a separate part. *Whomever* is the object of the verb *like*.

Error: Give the job to whomever is willing to work.

Correction: Give the job to whoever is willing to work.   *Whoever is willing to work* must be treated as a separate part. *Whoever* is the subject of the verb *is*.

Don't allow a parenthetical expression to trick you into a wrong pronoun case.

Error: The Smiths are people whom I think will make good neighbors.

Correction: The Smiths are people *who*, I think, will make good neighbors.   *Who* is the subject of *will make*.

Error: The Pennsylvania Dutch are people who, they say, we can trust.

Correction: The Pennsylvania Dutch are people whom, they say, we can trust.   *Whom* is object of verb *can trust*.

A pronoun following *than* or *as* is either subjective or objective depending on the implied verb:

1. He admires him more than (he admires) *her.*
2. He admires him more than *she* (admires him).
3. We are happier than *they* (are).

Use the subjective case when the pronoun follows the verb *to be:*

1. Answer the phone; it may be *she.*   not *her*
2. It was *they* who rang the bell.   not *them*

A pronoun used immediately in front of a gerund (noun used as a verb, such as *singing, talking, thinking*) requires the possessive case. The following pronouns are possessive:

my	our
your	their
his, her, its	whose

Error: *Him* lying is what tipped off the police.

Correction: *His* lying is what tipped off the police.

Error: *Us* checking the score helped.

Correction: *Our* checking the score helped.

Exercises

Underline the correct form of the pronoun in each of the following sentences:

1. I am more to be pitied than (he, him).

2. The saleslady (who, whom) they think stole the stockings lives next to us.

3. You must praise (whoever, whomever) does the best job.

4. During the Vietnam war some of (we, us) football players felt guilty.

5. Florence insists that I was later than (he, him).

6. Was it (she, her) that called you the other day?

7. The candidate made an excellent impression on us—my Dad and (I, me).

8. (Who, whom) do you think will set a better example?

9. We were relieved by (his, him) paying the bill.

10. Between you and (me, I), is she innocent or guilty?

11. The coach said that I swim better than (him, he).

12. (Him, his) daydreaming affected his work negatively.

13. Bud doesn't care (who, whom) he gives his cold to.

14. The pinecones were divided among the three of us—John, Bill, and (me, I).

15. (Our, us) leaving the inner city was a blessing in disguise.

16. Do you remember (me, my) telling you?

17. Can you tell me the rank of the general (who, whom) it is said, struck one of his soldiers?

18. (Whom, who) Ali will fight next is unknown.

19. Marilyn Monroe, (who, whom) most women envied, was unhappy.

20. Give the papers to (he and I, him and me).

pv Errors in *point of view* occur when the writer needlessly shifts person, tense, mood, voice, discourse, or key words.

Person

Error: We have come to the place where one should either fish or cut bait. shift from *we* to *one*.

Correction: We have come to the place where *we* should either fish or cut bait.

Error: If you turn right on LaFollet Street, one will see the sign on one's right. shift from *you* to *one*.

Correction: If you turn right on LaFollet Street, you will see the sign on your right.

Tense

Error: The weather suddenly turned windy, and clouds arise. shift from past to present.

Correction: The weather suddenly turned windy, and clouds *arose.*

Error: William Tell takes the apple, places it on his son's head, and shot an arrow right through the middle. shift from present to past

Correction: William Tell takes the apple, places it on his son's head, and *shoots* an arrow right through the middle.

Error: His face turned purple with rage and he would strike his friend. shift from past to conditional

Correction: His face turned purple with rage, and he struck his friend.

Mood

Error: People of America, why do you wait? Protect your environment and you should vote against nuclear plants. shift from imperative to indicative

Correction: People of America, why do you wait? Protect your environment. Vote against nuclear plants.

Voice

Error: John carried Mary's pack and her tent was also pitched by him. shift from active to passive voice

Correction: John carried Mary's pack and he also pitched her tent.

Discourse

Error: The minister asked Bill if he loved his fiancée and will he treat her with devotion. shift from indirect to direct discourse

Correction: The minister asked Bill if he loved his fiancée and if he would treat her with devotion.

or

The minister asked Bill, "Do you love your fiancée and will you treat her with devotion?"

Key Words

Error: Since everyone has a primary goal in life, I too have an outstanding goal. shift from *primary* to *outstanding*

Correction: Like everyone else, I too have a primary goal in life.

Error: I want to be a perfect human being. God made me, so why not be worthwhile? shift from *perfect* to *worthwhile*

Correction: I want to be a perfect human being. God made me, so why not be perfect?

Exercises

In the following sentences correct all shifts in (1) person, (2) tense, (3) mood, (4) discourse, (5) voice, or (6) key word. Identify the shift by placing the appropriate number in the blank at the right.

1. Everyone must live according to your conscience. _____

2. She insisted loudly that "I am opposed to abortions." _____

3. A good meal is enjoyed by all of us and we like fresh air, too. _____

4. She revealed that an unknown intruder is in the room. _____

5. So far we have not mentioned poverty. So let me discuss it now. _____

6. It is a principle everyone should cherish because you can be a better person when we adhere to it. _____

7. Lock the door and you should turn out the lights. _____

8. The robber stole her jewelry and she was mugged by him, too. _____

9. Slowly he crept toward me and grabs for my wallet. _____

10. A straightforward question to ask the salesman is, "Why people should buy his razors?" _____

11. He helped me out by pointing out where one could find an inexpensive hotel. _____

12. The doorman opened the door; then my baggage was picked up by a porter. _____

13. In his memory he heard the melody of that old song and knew that time is passing quickly. _____

14. She was a spoiled brat, it always seems to me. _____

15. If there is little wisdom around us, perhaps we should ask, "From whom this intelligence can be learned?" _____

 Reference errors occur with the use of pronouns that do not stand for anything specific. Every pronoun must have an unmistakable *antecedent*.

Error: No one is perfect, but that doesn't mean that I shouldn't try to be *one*. The pronoun *one* has no antecedent, no specific noun for which it stands.

Correction: No one is perfect, but that doesn't mean that I shouldn't try to be.

Error: She keeps her files well organized; she gets along well with her employers; and she has ethical integrity; however, this is not enough to convince us to hire her. The antecedent of *this* is too broad; it needs to be pinpointed.

Correction:	She keeps her files well organized; she gets along well with her employers; and she has ethical integrity; however, these qualities are not enough to convince us to hire her.
Error:	Our neighbor, Mrs. Irwin, told my mother that *she* had not chosen the proper dress. Who had not chosen the proper dress—Mrs. Irwin or the mother? The reference is unclear.
Correction:	Our neighbor, Mrs. Irwin, told my mother, "I have not chosen the proper dress." Turning the clause into direct address is the simplest way to correct this kind of reference error.
Error:	His clothes were scattered all across the room which needed folding. Confusion arises because the misplaced *which* makes it look as if the room needed folding.
Correction:	His clothes, which needed folding, were scattered all across the room.
Error:	In Europe they often claim that Americans eat too much ice cream. Avoid using *they* or *you* as a reference to people in general.
Correction:	Europeans often claim that Americans eat too much ice cream.
Error:	When the Godfather dies, it is due to a heart attack. *It* has only an implied reference.
Correction:	The Godfather's death is due to a heart attack.
Error:	Arthur Ash swung his racket hard, but it went into the net. *It* stands for ball, but the word *ball* never shows up.
Correction:	Arthur Ashe swung his racket hard, but the ball went into the net.
Error:	When Elmer Cole's restaurant was opened, he invited all the townspeople for a free meal. A pronoun in the subjective case must not refer to an antecedent in the possessive case.
Correction:	When Elmer Cole opened his restaurant, he invited all the townspeople for a free meal.

Exercises

Rewrite the following sentences to avoid confusing, implied, nonexistent, or vague pronoun references:

1. Many people are emotional but have difficulty showing them.

_____

_____

2. At the factory where I work at night, they say not to ask for salary advances.

_____

_____

3. My dad warned my brother that he would not get a promotion.

_____

_____

4. She sat by the window knitting, which was too small to let in any light.

_____

_____

5. The nuclear bomb was developed in the twentieth century; this completely changed man's approach to war.

_____

_____

6. The leading baritone didn't show up for the opening night, which caused all kinds of gossip.

_____

_____

7. In the South, you aren't understood if you have a New York accent.

_____

_____

8. Life is a cycle of happiness followed by misery, but I want to have them in equal portions.

_____

_____

9. Although it is muddy down by the river, it looks inviting.

_____

_____

10. The first chapter awakens the reader's interest in mining, which continues until the Camerons move to America.

_____

_____

11. The American colonists refused to pay taxes without being represented. This was the major cause of the 1776 revolution.

_____

_____

12. Tomorrow it may rain and damage our roof, and it should be protected.

_____

_____

13. The guests were perspiring and fanning themselves with the printed program; it really bothered them.

_____

_____

14. The rose garden in Hoover Park is spectacular. Some of them are deep purple, almost black.

_____

_____

15. I went over my checkstubs three times, but it never balanced properly.

_____

_____

dang   **Dangling** _modifiers_ occur when words or phrases are used that have no logical relaship to any other element in the sentence. These words simply "dangle" in front of the reader, causing mystification and mirth. The most frequent dangling errors are caused by (1) misused verbal phrases, and (2) misused subordinate clauses. To correct dangling elements, assign the logical subject to all verbal phrases or subornate clauses.

Dangling: Falling in love with Carole Lombard made me envy Clark Gable.   For this sentence to make sense, Clark Gable must be the subject of the phrase "falling in love with Carole Lombard."

Correct: I envied Clark Gable's falling in love with Carole Lombard.

Dangling: Upon reaching the age of six, my grandfather took me to school.   The sentence implies that the grandfather was six years old when he took his grandchild to school.

Correct: When I reached the age of six, my grandfather took me to school.

Dangling: To understand why fat people eat, a study of self-hatred is necessary. In this sentence, *a study* becomes the subject of the infinitive *to understand,* which is obviously silly since a study can't "understand."

Correct: To understand why fat people eat, we must study self-hatred.

Dangling: Although loved by Americans, historians deny the truth of many anecdotes involving Abraham Lincoln. This sentence implies that historians are loved by Americans.

Correct: Although loved by Americans, many anecdotes involving Abraham Lincoln have been labeled as historically untrue.

misp Misplaced modifiers occur when modifying words, phrases, or clauses are not placed as close as possible to the words they modify. Confusing, illogical, or awkward sentences are caused by misplaced modifiers.

Confusing: We looked inside the car with our friends for the package. Were the friends inside or outside the car?

Correct: With our friends we looked inside the car for the package.

Illogical: Visitors to France can see the Eiffel Tower floating down the Seine River on a barge. In this sentence, the Eiffel Tower is floating on a barge.

Correct: Floating down the Seine River on a barge, visitors to Paris can see the Eiffel Tower.

Awkward: My husband and I expect you to instantly pay for the damage to our car. It is best never to separate *to* from its verb.

Correct: My husband and I expect you to pay instantly for the damage to our car.

Exercises

Rewrite the following sentences to eliminate the dangling or misplaced modifiers. In the parentheses, write *dang* or *misp* to indicate the nature of your correction.

1. Looking down in horror the snake crawled away.

   _____

   _____ (_____)

2. To guarantee their rights, collective bargaining was organized by the teachers.

   _____

   _____ (_____)

3. She did not realize that she had had major surgery until Friday.

   _____

   _____ (_____)

266

4. John had looked forward to getting married for two weeks to Mary Ellen Davis.

_____

_____ (   )

5. Responding to consumer demands for better gasoline mileage, the Honda was promoted.

_____

_____ (   )

6. We bought ice cream cones at a small stand that cost ten cents.

_____

_____ (   )

7. We all agreed to instantly leave town.

_____

_____ (   )

8. Arriving at the pack station, our dried food had been stolen.

_____

_____ (   )

9. I held my breath as the car slid into the curb that had raced ahead suddenly.

_____

_____ (   )

10. While dreaming about the future, lightning flashed and the rain began to pour.

_____

_____ (   )

11. My mother promised again to let me use her car.

_____

_____ (   )

12. Continue to whip the cream until tired.

_____

_____ (   )

13. To understand T. S. Eliot, the classics must be read.

_____

_____ (   )

14. Drilling my teeth, I could tell he was an excellent dentist.

_____

_____ (   )

15. He was not willing to completely give up drinking.

_____

_____ (   )

16. Looking at the mountain range from the valley, a lovely rainbow could be seen.

_____

_____ (   )

17. My uncle had warned me never to leave a gun in my car that had not been unloaded.

_____

_____ (   )

18. Now is the time to, if you want a Democrat in the White House, vote for our governor.

_____

_____ (   )

19. At the shower delicious hors d'oeuvres were served to all of the guests on silver trays.

_____

_____ (   )

268

// Lack of *parallelism* occurs when similar grammatical constructions are not used to express parallel ideas. The result is a disruptive break in the rhythm of writing.

Not   I love swimming, hiking, and to ski.   The sentence starts with two
parallel: gerunds (ing words) but suddenly switches to an infinitive (to + a verb)

Parallel: I love swimming, hiking, and skiing.

Not   Community colleges are necessary because they give late bloomers a
parallel: second chance; they provide free tuition for the poor; and they have
      always encouraged the vocational trades.   The sentence starts with two
      verbs in the present tense, but suddenly switches to the past tense.

Parallel: Community colleges are necessary because they give late bloomers a second
      chance; they provide free tuition for the poor; and they encourage the
      vocational trades.

Not   For days the president of the club wondered whether he should pay the
parallel: bills or to resign.   "He should" is followed by "to resign."

Parallel: For days the president of the club wondered whether to pay the bills or
      to resign.

Exercises

Rewrite the following sentences to improve parallel structure. Join participles with participles, infinitives with infinitives, noun phrases with noun phrases, and so on.

1. She was a lovely blond-haired, blue-eyed, rosy china doll.

   _____

   _____

2. Bright sun gleams on the water, dark shadows across the cliffs, and the delicate flowers that blossomed in the desert created a memorable picture.

   _____

   _____

3. I prefer to attend small dinners than going to big banquets.

   _____

   _____

4. What we claim to believe and the things we actually do rarely agree.

   _____

   _____

5. The anthropologist traveled into heated jungles, along insect-infested trails, and he ventured up steep mountain trails.

_____

_____

6. I tried to explain that time was short, that the firm wanted an answer, and the importance of efficiency.

_____

_____

7. Most of our women's fashions come from Paris, Rome, and also from New York.

_____

_____

8. As we watched through the bars of the cage we could see the monkeys eating bananas, scratching their fur, and they swung on rails.

_____

_____

9. Most teachers try not only to engage the students' attention but they also want to say something important.

_____

_____

10. Victor Hugo was a statesman and who also wrote novels, including _Les Misérables._

_____

_____

11. Bigger social security checks would allow old people to pay for decent living quarters, to get proper medical help, and they could afford sound nutrition.

_____

_____

12. Basketball, football, and the game of baseball are favorite American spectator sports.

_____

_____

13. I admire the songs of Diana Ross, formerly a member of the Supremes, but who is now on her own.

_____

_____

14. Their divorce was due to his stressful job, his high temper, and because he hated her friends.

_____

_____

15. You have two choices: You must take either the exam or to write a research paper.

_____

_____

d   *Poor diction* (also called poor *word usage*) refers to the use of a word in a different sense than it is defined in the dictionary or the use of a word in a way unacceptable to standards of *ideal English*. In the use of words, ideal English should be distinguished from *real English*. Ideal English is language spoken or written according to educated and cultured standards. It is the language of good books, magazines, adn newspapers. Professors, lawyers, and others who arrange their English to follow precise standard usage rules are using ideal English. Real English, in contrast, is the language most Americans use to communicate their thoughts and to conduct their business. It is the language we hear most on the bus, in the laundromat, or at the supermarket.

Ideal and real English both have their places. One is the language of concentrated formality, the other of spontaneous relaxation. Dun J. Li, introducing a textbook on Chinese civilization, uses *ideal English* when he states: "Of all ideologies that influenced the thinking and life of traditional China none was more important than Confucianism." On the other hand, the irate factory worker, complaining about his wages uses real English when he writes, "If you wasn't so darn pig-headed, you'd raise our pay." Both messages are clear, but their differences reside in their levels of formality.

Use the Correct Word

Because it is more precise than *real English, ideal English* is generally required in student writing. Colloquialisms, slang, or substandard expressions are not acceptable in ideal English. Most dictionaries label words as colloquial, substandard, or slang. If you are unsure of a word, look it up. The following glossary will help you avoid expressions that are unacceptable in ideal English.

Glossary of Word Choice

ACCEPT, EXCEPT   To *accept* is to *receive;* to *except* is to *exclude.* (We *accepted* him into the group; we didn't let him in because C students were *excepted.* Everyone arrived on time *except* Jim.)

ACCIDENTLY.   No such word exists. The correct word is *accidentally.*

ADVICE, ADVISE.   *Advice* is a noun; *advise* is a verb. (A person receives *advice,* but he will *advise* another.)

AFFECT, EFFECT.   *Affect* means to *influence.* (It will *affect* my health.) *Effect* is both a verb and a noun. To *effect* is *to produce.* An *effect* is a *result.* (He *effected* a change. The *effect* of the paint was ugly.)

AGGRAVATE.   *Aggravate* means *to make worse.* It should not be used for *provoke* or *irritate.*

AGREE TO, AGREE WITH.   One agrees *to* a proposal but *with* a person. (I agreed *to* his plan. I agreed *with* Nancy.)

AIN'T.   Considered substandard.

ALLUSION, ILLUSION.   *Allusion* means *reference.* (The comment was an *allusion* to World War II.) *Illusion* means *false impression* or *belief.* (She is under the *illusion* that she is beautiful.)

ALL READY, ALREADY.   *All ready* means that all are ready. (The guests were *all ready.*) *Already* means *previously* or *before now.* (He had *already* moved away from town.)

ALL TOGETHER, ALTOGETHER.   *All together* means *all of a number* considered as a group. (She scolded them *all together.*) *Altogether* means *entirely, completely.* (The officer was *altogether* correct.)

AMONG, BETWEEN.   *Among* is used for more than two people or objects. (We searched *among* the many guests.) *Between* is used for two people or objects. (We found it *between* the table and the chair.)

AMOUNT, NUMBER.   *Amount* refers to uncountable things (a large *amount* of cement). *Number* refers to countable things (a large *number* of houses).

ANY PLACE, NO PLACE.   Corruptions of *anywhere, nowhere.*

ANYWHERES, NOWHERES, SOMEWHERES.   Corruptions of *anywhere, nowhere, somewhere.*

APPRAISE, APPRISE.   *Appraise* means to *estimate* (the *appraised* value of the car). *Apprise* means *to inform* (*apprise* me of your decision).

APT, LIABLE, LIKELY.   *Apt* means *suitable, qualified, expert* (an *apt* phrase, a man *apt* in his work). *Liable* means exposed to something undesirable (*liable* to be injured, *liable* for damages). *Likely* means *credible, probable, probably.* (He had a *likely* excuse. It is *likely* to rain.)

272

AWFUL. Colloquial when used for *disagreeable* or *very*.

BAD, BADLY. *Bad* is an adjective, *badly* an adverb. (He has a *bad* cold; he sings *badly*.)

BEING AS. Corruption of *since* or *inasmuch as*.

BESIDE, BESIDES. *Beside* is a preposition meaning *by the side of, in addition to,* or *aside from.* (He sat down *beside* her.) *Besides* is a preposition meaning *except* (He had much *besides* his good looks) and an adverb meaning *in addition, moreover.* (He received a trip and fifty dollars *besides*.)

BLAME ON. Correct idiom calls for the use of *to blame* with *for*, not *on*. (They *blamed* the driver *for* the accident, not They *blamed* the accident *on* the driver.) *Blame on* is colloquial.

BURST, BURSTED, BUST. The principal parts of the verb *burst* are *burst, burst, burst.* The use of *bursted* or *busted* for the past tense is incorrect. *Bust* is either sculpture or a part of the human body. *Bust* is a slang expression for *failure* and is sometimes incorrectly used instead of *burst* or *break.*

BUT WHAT. Use *that* instead of *but what*. (They had no doubt *that* he would win the New York primary.)

CANNOT HELP BUT. This is a mixed construction. *Cannot help* and *cannot but* are separate expressions, either of which is correct. (*He cannot but attempt it,* or *He cannot help attempting it.*) Do not write, "He *cannot help but* lose."

CAPITAL, CAPITOL. *Capital* is a city; *capitol* is a building. *Capital* is also an adjective, usually meaning *chief* or *excellent.* As a noun, *capital* means accumulated assets or wealth.

CENSOR, CENSURE. To *censor* means *to examine and prevent.* (The Vietnamese military *censored* his mail.) To *censure* means to *criticize severely.* (He was *censured* by the church.)

CHOOSE, CHOSE. *Choose* is the present tense. (Today I *choose* to stay.) *Chose* is past tense. (Yesterday I *chose* to stay.)

CITE, SITE. *Cite* means *to quote.* (He *cited* Abraham Lincoln.) Site means *place* or *plot* (It was a grassy, green *site*.)

COMPLEMENT, COMPLIMENT. In its usual sense, *complement* means *something that completes.* (His suggestion was a *complement* to the general plan.) A *compliment* is an expression of courtesy or praise. (My *compliments* to the chef.)

CONSIDERABLE. The word is an adjective meaning *worthy of consideration, important.* (The idea is at least *considerable*.) When used to denote a great deal or a great many, *considerable* is colloquial or informal.

CONTACT. Colloquial and sometimes vague when used for *see, meet, communicate with.* (I must *contact* my agent.)

CONTINUAL, CONTINUOUS. *Continual* means *repeated often.* (The interruptions were *continual*.) *Continuous* means *going on without interruption.* (For two days the pain was *continuous*.)

CONVINCE, PERSUADE. Do not use *convince* for *persuade*, as in "I *convinced* him to do it." *Convince* means to *overcome a doubt.* (I *convinced* him of the soundness of my plan.) *Persuade* means *to induce.* (I *persuaded* him to do it.)

COUNCIL, COUNSEL. *Council* means an *assembly.* (The *council* discussed taxes.) *Counsel* means *advice.* (The teacher gave him good *counsel*.)

CREDIBLE, CREDITABLE. *Credible* means *believable.* (His evidence was not *credible*.) *Creditable* means *deserving esteem* or *admiration.* (The male lead gave a *creditable* performance.)

DATA. *Data* is the plural of datum, something given or known. It usually refers to a body of facts or figures. It normally takes a plural verb. (These *data* are important.) At times, however, *data* may be considered a collective noun and used with a singular verb.

DIFFERENT THAN. Most good writers use *different from,* not *different than.*

DISINTERESTED. Often confused with *uninterested, disinterested* mean *unbiased, impartial.* (The judge was *disinterested.*) *Uninterested* means *bored with.* (She was *uninterested* in politics.)

DON'T. A contraction of *do not.* Do not write *he, she,* or *it don't.*

DUE TO. In formal usage, do not use *due to* for *because of* as in "Due to protracted illness, he left college." *Due to* is correctly used after a noun or a linking verb (His failure, *due to* laziness, was not surprising. The accident was *due to* carelessness). Oddly enough, *owing to,* which is grammatically parallel to *due to,* is used in all constructions.

EITHER. Used only with two items, not three or more. (*Either* the teacher or the book was wrong. *Not either* the teacher, the book, or I was wrong.)

EMIGRANT, IMMIGRANT. A person who moves from one country to another is both an *emigrant* and an *immigrant.* He *emigrates from* one place and *immigrates to* the other.

ENTHUSED. The word is colloquial, and almost always unacceptable.

EQUALLY AS. Do not use these words together; omit either *equally* or *as.* Do not write "Water is equally as necessary as air," but rather "Water is as necessary as air" or "Water and air are equally necessary."

ETC. An abbreviation of Latin *et* (and) and *cetera* (other things). It should not be preceded by *and,* nor should it be used to avoid a clear and exact ending of an idea or a sentence.

EXAM. Colloquial for examination. Compare *gym, lab, dorm, soph, prof.*

EVERYONE. A singular pronoun, takes singular verb forms. (Everyone *is* going.)

EXPECT. The word means *to look forward to* or foresee. Do not use it for *suspect* or *suppose.*

FEWER, LESS. Use *fewer* to refer to items that can be numbered, *less* to refer to amount. (Where there are *fewer* machines, there is *less* noise.)

FINE. Colloquial when used as a term of general approval.

FORMALLY, FORMERLY. *Formally* means *in a formal manner.* (He was *formally* initiated last night.) *Formerly* means *at a former time.* (They *formerly* lived in Ohio.)

FUNNY. When used to mean *strange* or *queer,* funny is colloquial.

FURTHER, FARTHER. *Further* is used for ideas. (We studied the question *further.*) *Farther* is used for geographical location (*farther* down the street).

GOT. This is a correct past tense and past participle of the verb *to get.* (He *got* three traffic tickets in two days.) *Gotten* is the alternative past participle of *get.* (He had *gotten* three tickets the week before.)

GUESS. Colloquial when used for *suppose* or *believe.*

GUY. Slang when used for *boy* or *man.*

HAD OUGHT, HADN'T OUGHT. Do not use for *ought* and *ought not.*

HARDLY, SCARCELY. Do not use with a negative. "I *can't hardly* see it" borders on the illiterate. Write "I *can hardly* see it" or (if you cannot see it all all) "I *can't* see it."

HEALTHFUL, HEALTHY.   Places are *healthful* (conducive to health) if persons living in them may be *healthy* (having good health).

IMPLY, INFER.   *Imply* means *to suggest.* (His girl *implied* that he was teasing.) *Infer* means *to conclude.* (I *inferred* from her look that she was teasing.)

INCIDENTLY.   There is no such word. The correct form is *incidentally,* which is derived from the adjective *incidental.*

INSIDE OF.   In expressions of time, *inside of* is colloquial for *within* (He will return *within* a week).

IRREGARDLESS.   No such word exists. Use *regardless.*

ITS, IT'S.   The form *its* is possessive. (*Its* cover is gray.) *It's* is a contraction of *it is.* (*It's* your fault.)

IT'S ME.   Formal English requires *It is I. It's me* is informal or colloquial.

KIND, SORT.   These are singular forms of nouns and should be modified accordingly (*this kind, that sort*). Do not write "*these kind.*"

KIND OF, SORT OF.   Do not use these to mean *rather* as in "He was *kind of* (or *sort of*) stupid."

LAST, LATEST.   *Last* implies that there will be no more. *Latest* does not preclude the appearance of another later. (After reading his *latest* book, I hope that it is his *last.*)

LEAVE, LET.   The use of *leave* for *let* in expressions like *leave him go* is incorrect.

LEND, LOAN.   *Lend* is a verb. *Loan* is a noun and its use as a verb is incorrect. (If you will *lend* me ten dollars, I will never ask you for another *loan.*)

LIKE, AS.   Confusion in the use of these words results from using *like* as a conjunction—"He walks *like* a gentlemen should." Use *as* instead. (He walks *as* a gentleman should.)

LOOSE, LOSE.   *Loose* means not attached. (The button is *loose.*) *Lose* means *to be unable to keep or find.* (Did she *lose* her diamond ring?)

LOT, LOTS.   Colloquial or informal when used to mean *many* or *much.*

MAD.   The meaning of *mad* is *insane.* Used to mean *angry,* it is informal.

MAY BE, MAYBE.   *May be* is a verb phrase. (They *may be* late.) *Maybe* used as an adverb means *perhaps.* (*Maybe* they will buy a boat.)

MEAN.   Used informally for *disagreeable.* (He has a *mean* face.) It is slang when used to mean skillful, expert. (He plays a *mean* tennis game.)

MEDIA.   Media is the plural of *medium*—a means, agency, or instrument. It is often used *incorrectly* as though it were singular, as in "The *media is* playing a big role in political races this year."

MOST.   Do not use for *almost.* "*Almost* all my friends appeared" is the correct form.

MYSELF.   Incorrect when used as a substitute for *I* or *me,* as in "He and *myself* did it." It is correctly used intensively (*I myself* shall do it) and reflexively (I blame only *myself*).

NICE.   Used as a term of approval, *nice* is overworked. It properly means *accurate, precise, exact* as in "a *nice* opinion," "a *nice* calculation."

NONE, NO ONE.   Singular pronouns taking irregular verb forms. (None of us *is* going. None of his reasons *is* valid.)

OF.   Unnecessary after such prepositions as off, inside, outside. (He fell *off* the chair. They waited *inside* the house.)

ON ACCOUNT OF.   Do not use as a conjunction. The phrase should be followed by an object of the preposition *of* (*on account of* his illness). "He was absent *on account of* he was sick" is poor English.

ORAL, VERBAL.   *Oral* means *spoken* rather than written; *verbal* means *associated with words*. When referring to an agreement or commitment that was not in writing, *oral* should be used.

OVER WITH.   The *with* is unnecessary in such expressions as "The concert was *over with* by five o'clock."

PAST, PASSED.   *Past* is a noun. (He remembers the *past*.) *Passed* is a verb. (She *passed* by his house.)

PEEVE.   Either as verb or noun *peeve* is informal.

PERSONAL, PERSONNEL.   Personal means *private*. (She expressed her *personal* view.) *Personnel* is a *body of employed people*. (The *personnel* demanded higher wages.)

PLAN ON.   Omit *on*. Standard practice calls for an infinitive or a direct object after *plan*. (They *planned to go*. They *planned a reception*.)

PRINCIPAL, PRINCIPLE.   Principal is both adjective and noun (*principal* parts, *principal* of the school, interest and *principal*). *Principle* is a noun only (*principles* of morality, a man of *principle*).

QUITE.   The word means *altogether, entirely*. (He was *quite* exhausted from his exertion.) It is colloquial when used for *moderately* or *very* and in expressions like *quite a few, quite a number*.

RAISE, RISE.   *Raise* requires an object. (She *raised* the cover.) *Rise* does not require an object. (Let us *rise* and sing.)

REASON IS BECAUSE, REASON WHY.   These are not correct forms in English. Examples of correct usage are "The *reason* I stayed home is *that* I was sick," "The *reason* (not *why*) they invited us is that. . . ."

RESPECTFULLY, RESPECTIVELY.   Respectfully means *with respect*. (The young used to act *respectfully* toward their elders.) *Respectively* is used to clarify antecedents in a sentence. (The *men and women* took their seats on the right and left, respectively.)

RIGHT.   In the sense of *very* or *extremely*, *right* is colloquial. Do not write, "I'm *right* glad to know you."

SAME.   The word is an adjective, not a pronoun. Do not use it as in "We received your order and shall give *same* our immediate attention." Substitute *it* for *same*.

SET, SIT.   *Set* requires an object. (She *set* the cup on the table.) *Sit* does not require an object. (You must *sit* in the chair.)

SHOULD OF, WOULD OF.   Do not use these forms for *should have, would have*.

SO, SUCH, TOO.   Avoid the use of *so, such*, and *too* for *very*, as in "Thank you *so* much," "He has *such* charming manners," "I do not know him *too* well."

SOME.   Do not use for *somewhat*, as in "She is *some* better after her illness."

SPRIGHTLY, SPRITELY.   *Sprightly* means *animated, vivacious, lively*. There is no such word as *spritely*, but may people use this term, probably because it suggests the word *sprite*, meaning *elf* or *fairy*.

STATIONARY, STATIONERY.   *Stationary* means *fixed, not moving*. *Stationery* means *paper* for writing letters.

STATUE, STATURE, STATUTE.   A *statue* is a piece of sculpture. *Stature* is bodily height, often used figuratively to mean *level of achievement, status,* or *importance.* A *statute* is a law or regulation.

STRATA. This word is the plural of the Latin *stratum.* One speaks of one *stratum* (layer) of rock but of several *strata* (layers).

SURE, SURELY. *Sure* is an adjective, and *surely* is an adverb. (I am *sure* that he will arrive, but he *surely* annoys me.)

SUSPICION. This word is a noun and should not be used for the verb *to suspect.* (His *suspicion* was right; they *suspected* the butler.)

SWELL. As a term of admiration, *swell* is slang.

THUSLY. No such word exists. The proper form is *thus.* "He did *thusly*" is just as absurd as "He went *hencely*." Some English adverbs do not end in *-ly.*

TRY AND. Use *try to,* not *try and,* in such expressions as "*Try to* be kind."

TYPE. Colloquial in expressions like "this *type* book." Write "this *type of* book."

UNIQUE. If referring to something as the *only* one of its kind, you may correctly use *unique.* (The Grand Canyon is *unique.*) The word does not mean *rare, strange,* or *remarkable,* and there are no degrees of uniqueness: Nothing can be *extremely* (almost, nearly, virtually) *unique.*

USE (USED) TO COULD. Do not use for *once could* or *used to be able.*

VERY. Do not use as a modifier of a past participle, as in *very burned.* English idiom calls for *badly burned* or *very badly burned.*

WAIT FOR, WAIT ON. *To wait for* means *to look forward to, to expect.* (For days I *have waited for* you.) *To wait on* means *to serve.* (The hostess *waited on* the guests.)

WANT IN, WANT OFF, WANT OUT. These forms are dialectal. Do not use them for *want to come in, want to get off, want to get out.*

WAY. Colloquial when used for *away,* as in "*way* out West."

WAYS. Colloquial when used for *way,* as in "a long *ways* to go."

WHOSE, WHO'S. The possessive form is *whose.* (*Whose* money is this?) *Who's* is a contraction of *who is.* (*Who's* there?)

WISE. Unacceptable when appended to a noun to convert it to an adverb as in *businesswise.*

WITHOUT. The word is an adverb and a preposition. Using it as a conjunction to mean *unless* is incorrect: "She could not go *unless* (not *without*) she bought some clothes."

YOU, YOU'RE. The possessive form is *your.* (Give me *your* address.) *You're* is a contraction of *you are.*

Exercises

Underline the correct term in each of the following sentences:

1. When they arrived at West Point, they received some practical (advise, advice) regarding the honor system.

2. During his lecture, the professor made an (allusion, illusion) to Abraham Lincoln.

3. The prime minister's illness was so (aggravated, irritated) by his drinking that he needed surgery.

4. My aunt does a (credible, creditable) job of sewing evening gowns.

5. In the past, interviewers were (disinterested, uninterested) when they interviewed candidates; now they are biased.

6. I was (enthusiastic, enthused) when they told me about the new director.

7. When we heard about the theft, we immediately (suspicioned, suspected) collusion within the company.

8. They received the news that he would return (within, inside of) a week.

9. Chris Evert's (latest, last) match gave the world of tennis something to rave about.

10. Please (loan, lend) them $5,000 for a down payment on a house.

11. We drank the spring water (as if, like) we would never drink water again in our lives.

12. When she gets home, she will find (lots, much) to do.

13. The agreement was (oral, verbal), so it will not hold up in court.

14. The reason grades are necessary (is that, is because) they are a point of reference for students.

15. If I had known you were coming, I (would of, would have) baked a cake.

16. Most people improve (somewhat, some) the moment they take one spoonful of Kay's cough syrup.

17. For Christmas, I sent mother some blue (stationary, stationery) so she could write to her friends.

18. The fight between Foreman and Frazier (surely, sure) evoked interest among boxing fans.

19. We still had a long (way, ways) to trudge uphill, but none of the students complained.

20. Will the person (who's, whose) wallet this is please claim it at the front ticket booth.

21. Before the tall buildings were built, we (used to, could, used to be able) to see the ocean.

22. That scandal in her (passed, past) may keep her from getting the promotion.

23. Many Americans want to return to old-fashioned, religious (principals, principles).

24. (Regardless, irregardless) of the consequences, the ambassador stood by his post.

25. The glint in her eye (implied, inferred) more clearly than words how she really felt.

Use Concrete Words

A word is *concrete* when it refers to a *specific* object, quality, or action. "He *limped* across the road" is more concrete than "He *went* across the road." "*One hundred women* attended the dinner" is more concrete than "*Quite a few people* attended the dinner." (See also Unit 1, the section on using details.)

Vague: I like her because she is such a *nice* girl.

Concrete: I like her because she is *witty* and *vivacious.*

Vague: The lyrics of Paul Simon are *relevant.*

Concrete: The lyrics of Paul Simon *expose many fears felt by our society.*

Vague: I dislike my teacher's *negative attitude* toward old people.

Concrete: I dislike my teacher's *contempt* for old people.

Exercises

Improve the following sentences by replacing the italicized vague words with more concrete words or phrases.

1. John *got* on his horse and quickly *went* away.

   _____

   _____

2. Eloise always wears such sloppy *apparel.*

   _____

   _____

3. The streets of Amsterdam are crowded with *vehicles.*

   _____

   _____

4. The lecturer was most *uninteresting.*

   _____

   _____

5. She *ate* her food *quickly.*

   _____

   _____

279

6. It was fascinating to watch the children *being active* on the school play-ground.

_____

_____

7. I was upset by this whole *business*.

_____

_____

8. What a *great* idea!

_____

_____

9. We expect to have a *wonderful* time in Palm Springs.

_____

_____

10. Eskimos are *unusual* in many *ways*.

_____

_____

11. I couldn't follow the complicated *setup* in his church.

_____

_____

12. My psychology class was one of the most *worthwhile* experiences of my college days.

_____

_____

13. Spanking is an important *element* of child rearing.

_____

_____

14. The *negative aspects* of driving huge cars outweigh the *positive aspects*.

_____

_____

15. "All the President's Men" is a *tremendous* movie.

_____

_____

16. Here are the *things* that bother me about assigning grades.

_____

_____

w   *Wordiness* results when writing is overly burdened with redundant or wasted expressions. Prune your rough draft of such redundancies.

Wordy: He spent *all of his entire* life in freezing temperatures.   *All* and *entire* are redundant.

Correct: He spent his entire life in freezing temperatures.

Wordy: After *the end of* the flood, Noah released the dove.   *The end of* is wasted.

Correct: After the flood, Noah released the dove.

Wordy: My dress was pink and yellow *in color*.   The term *in color* is wasted; pink and yellow are obviously colors.

Other redundancies of this kind are:

short *in length*	*necessary* requirements
circle *around*	*and* etc.
still persist	combined *together*
many *in number*	now *at this time*

Wordy: The Oldsmobile that was parked behind the supermarket was smeared with mud.

Correct: The Oldsmobile parked behind the supermarket was smeared with mud.

Often, relative clauses can be trimmed. Note the following:

the judge *who was* seated on the bench

the judge on the bench

the man *who was* accused

the accused man

Exercises

Revise the following sentences for economy by eliminating redundancies or wasted words.

1. The secretary who sat behind the big mahogany desk of wood seemed to be efficient.

_____

_____

2. Most people find it difficult to express the emotion of tenderness toward other people.

_____

_____

3. The winner was timid and reticent about accepting the trophy.

_____

_____

4. Her coat, which is of the fur type, cost $2,000.

_____

_____

5. Worshiping ancestors is a venerable, sacred, old religious tradition among the Chinese.

_____

_____

6. My study of history leads me to believe that the Danes were a militant people who loved war.

_____

_____

7. Probably paying decent wages is usually the right system in the majority of cases.

_____

_____

8. Workers who are employed shouldn't be allowed to collect food stamps.

_____

_____

9. If he wants to be President, he had better bring about new innovations in Congress.

_____

_____

10. Generally speaking, most of the time it is improper diet that causes gallstones.

_____

_____

11. All of the present clothing styles in our day and age reflect a taste for the bizarre.

_____

_____

12. At 10:00 P.M. at night a strange knock was heard.

_____

_____

13. The consensus of the majority in our class was that we should invite Dr. Boling as our keynote speaker.

_____

_____

14. The story dealt with a cruel murder and a tragic ending that was lamentable.

_____

_____

15. As a usual rule one should lock his car while shopping.

_____

_____

16. There were three women who decided to volunteer for the job without being forced.

_____

_____

17. Neil Simon writes humorous comedies.

_____

_____

18. If we don't cooperate together with the Russians, a nuclear war could annihilate the world.

_____

_____

19. Palestinians and Arabs are very different in various ways.

_____

_____

20. In this day and age it is difficult to find a musician in the entire field of music who gets at people's hearts the way Charles Witt does.

_____

_____

_____

𝒫   *Punctuation errors* occur with the omission or misuse of one of the following marks: period (.), comma (,), semicolon (;), colon (:), dash (—), question mark (?), exclamation point (!), apostrophe ('), parentheses (()), quotation marks ("...."), italics (underlining), and hyphen (-). The function of punctuation marks is to separate words and phrases within a sentence according to their meanings.

Frequently, meaning may be misinterpreted unless a punctuation mark is provided. Consider the following:

After we had finished the essays were read out loud.

The sentence must be reread with a pause inserted after *finished:*

After we had finished, the essays were read out loud.

The key to effective punctuation is to learn what each punctuation mark means and where it must be used.

The Period (.)

Periods are used after declarative or mildly imperative sentences, indirect questions, and abbreviations. (See also run-together sentences, p. 254.) Use ellipses—three spaced periods (. . .)—to indicate omissions from quoted material.

Declarative: We followed Mr. Smith upstairs to the conductor's room.

Imperative: Visit Old Amsterdam while you are in Holland.

Indirect question: The child asked if it was all right to pick an apple.

Abbreviation: Since we had so little money, we stayed at the Y.M.C.A.

                                       (good men)

Ellipses: Now is the time for all . . . to come to the aid of their country.

Current usage permits the omission of the period after these and other abbreviations: TV, CIA, FBI, UN, NBC, USN. If in doubt whether to omit the period after an abbreviation, consult the dictionary.

The Comma (,)

The comma is used and misused more than any other punctuation mark. (See also comma splice, p. 253.) A writer of factual prose must learn to master the use of the comma. While it is useful to equate commas with pauses, it is safer to follow the simple rules given below.

1. Use commas to set apart words that interrupt the flow of the sentence. In this use, the commas function as the equivalent of parentheses.

   a. Tatyana Grosman, as her first name suggests, is Russian by birth.
   b. Mrs. Jones, while charming in every way, held doggedly to her point.

2. Use a comma after a long introductory phrase or clause:

   a. Near the grove at the top of his block, someone was having a party.
   b. Since I meant my remark as a compliment, I was surprised when my boss became angry.

3. Use a comma to separate the main clause from a long clause or phrase that follows it, if the two are separated by a pause or break.

   a. Certainly no one has tried harder than Jane, although many of her ideas have proved to be disastrous when they have been put to practice.
   b. He awakened something new in me, a devotion I didn't know I was capable of.

4. Use a comma to separate long independent clauses joined by *and, but, or for, yet, nor:*

   a. The tunnel beside the house was very dark, but after school George used it as his imaginary fortress.
   b. If he uses three or four cans of balls, then that's it, and I don't want him to come to me begging for more.

5. Use commas to separate items in a series:

    a. I felt tired, cold, and discouraged.
    b. He raised his head, closed his eyes, and let out a deep moan.

If two adjectives in a series relate to the noun that follows, no comma is needed:

    My aunt lives in a big brown house.

6. Use a comma after words of address:

    a. Sir, that is not what I meant.
    b. Do you recall that night, Linda?

7. Use a comma to set off yes and no:

    a. Yes, the flight leaves at midnight.
    b. No, the letter has not arrived yet.

8. Use commas to set off dates and places:

    a. Miami, Florida, is humid in the summer.
    b. November 19, 1929, is my birthday.
    c. August, 1950, was a scorcher.

9. Use a comma to introduce quotations:

    a. Patrick Henry said, "Give me liberty or give me death!"
    b. The thief retorted, "You don't need the money."

10. Use commas to set off titles and degrees from preceding names:

    a. John Lawson, Jr., now runs the bank.
    b. Henry Knittle, M.D.
    c. Mark Hamilton, Ph.D.

The Semicolon (;)

The semicolon has three basic uses.

1. The semicolon is used to connect independent clauses that are so closely connected in their meaning that they do not need a full period:

    a. He was a wonderful chap; we all loved him dearly.
    b. Loraine left all her money to her stepson; in this respect, she showed considerable generosity.

2. A semicolon may be used to connect independent clauses when the second clause begins with a conjunctive adverb (for a list of conjunctive adverbs, see p. 249):

    a. Joe was not a candidate; nevertheless, the gang chose him as their captain.
    b. Following her to the kitchen, I found that she had made two sandwiches; however, I was not hungry, so I did not eat.

If the conjunctive adverb is not the first word in the second clause, the punctuation is as follows:

The fever had subsided; my mother felt, nevertheless, that a doctor should be called.

3. The semicolon is used to separate phrases or clauses in a series when commas appear within any one of those phrases or clauses:

   a. Her estate was divided as follows: Books, diaries, and notebooks went to her agent; jewelry, furs, and clothes went to her sister; and everything else went to charity.
   b. For three days we followed a strict diet: eggs, grapefruit, and coffee on the first day; lamb chops, toast, and tomatoes on the second day; and fruit with cottage cheese on the third day.

The Colon (:)

Do not confuse the colon with the semicolon. Colons are used in the following cases:

1. Use a colon when you introduce lengthy material or lists.

   a. The following quotation from Robert Frost will support my view:
   b. Here is a list of all the camping equipment necessary to climb Mt. Wilson:
   c. Literature can be divided into four types: short story, drama, poetry, and novel.

2. Use a colon after the salutation of a formal letter, between title and subtitle of a literary work, between chapter and verse of the Bible, and between hours and minutes in time:

   a. Dear Ms. Landeen:
   b. The Ethnic Cult: New Fashion Trends
   c. I. Corinthians 3:16
   d. 10:30 A.M.

The Dash (—)

On the typewriter, the dash is made by two hyphens without spacing before, between, or after. In handwriting, the dash is an unbroken line the length of two hyphens.

1. Use the dash to indicate a sudden break in thought.

   a. The clerk's illiteracy, his lack of judgment, his poor writing skills—all added up until the company fired him.
   b. The secret of the recipe is—oh, but I promised not to tell.

2. Use dashes to set off parenthetical material that needs to be emphasized:
   a. Every house in the neighborhood—from Kenneth Road to Russel Drive—was solicited.
   b. She stood there—tall, proud, and unrelenting—daring her accusers to speak.

The Question Mark (?)

Use a question mark after a direct question. Do not use it when the question is indirect.

Direct: He asked her, "Have you had lunch?"

Indirect: He asked her if she had had lunch.

Direct: Who am I? Where am I going? Why am I here?

Do not follow a question mark with a comma or a period:

Wrong: "When will you leave?," he asked.

Correct: "When will you leave?" he asked.

The Exclamation Point (!)

Exclamation points should be used only to express surprise, disbelief, anger, or other strong emotions:

1. What an adorable baby!
2. What a rat! He couldn't have been that evil!
3. "Jinxed, by God!"

The Apostrophe (')

Generally speaking, the apostrophe substitutes for the expression *of* to show possession: "John's book" rather than "the book of John." However, it is also used to form contractions (can't, don't) and certain plurals.

1. Use an apostrophe to indicate possession. Note that if the plural ends with an *s* or *z* sound, only the apostrophe is added:

   a. the attitude of the student
      the student's attitude
   b. the party of the girls
      the girls' party
   c. the home of the children
      the children's home

   Possessive pronouns do not require the apostrophe: "the book is theirs" *not* "the book is their's."

   For *inanimate* objects, *of* is preferable to the apostrophe: "The arm *of* the chair" *not* "the chair's arm."

2. Use an apostrophe to indicate an omission or abbreviation:

   a. He can't (cannot) make it.
   b. It's (it is) a perfect day.
   c. He graduated in '08.

   Caution: Place the apostrophe exactly where the omission occurs: isn't, doesn't—*not* is'nt, doe'snt.

3. Use an apostrophe to form the plural of letters, symbols, and words used as words:

   a. The English often do not pronounce their h's, and they place r's at the end of certain words.

   b. Instead of writing and's, you can write &'s.

4. An apostrophe is *not* needed for plurals of figures:

   a. Rock groups flourished during the 1960s.
   b. The temperature was in the 90s.

Parentheses (())

Parentheses always come in pairs. Use parentheses to enclose figures, illustrations, or incidental material:

1. To make good tennis volleys, follow three rules: (1) Use a punching motion with your racket, (2) volley off your front leg, and (3) get your body sideways to the flight of the oncoming ball.

2. The big stars of Hollywood's glamor days (Greta Garbo, Clark Gable, Marilyn Monroe) exuded an aura that was bigger than life.

3. Emily Dickinson (often called "the Nun of Amherst") lived a secluded life.

Quotation Marks (" ")

Quotation marks always come in pairs, with the final set indicating the end of the quotation. The most common use of quotation marks is to indicate the exact spoken or written words of someone else. There are several other uses of quotation marks as well.

1. Use quotation marks to enclose the words of someone else:

   a. Montesquieu has said: "The first motive which ought to impel us to study is the desire to augment the excellence of our nature, and to render an intelligent being yet more intelligent."

   b. With characteristic bluntness she turned to him and asked, "Are you as old as you look?"

If the passage being quoted is longer than five lines, indent it five spaces and single space without quotation marks:

In 1976, the *Los Angeles Times* indicated that actress Estelle Winwood was old but still remarkably spry:

> She plays bridge for six hours a night, smokes four packs of cigarettes a day, and at 93 Estelle Winwood is the oldest active member on the rolls of the Screen Actors' Guild.
>
> Although she professes to be through with acting, her close friends don't believe her. Only recently she joined the distinguished company of Columbia Pictures' "Murder by Death," Neil Simon's spoof of mystery films. And she held her own with the likes of Alec Guinness, Peter Sellers, Maggie Smith, Peter Falk, David Niven, and Nancy Walker.

2. A quotation within a quotation is enclosed by single quotation marks:

> According to Jefferson's biographer, "The celebrated equanimity of his temper, crystallized in his pronouncement 'Peace is our passion,' extended to his private as well as his public life; his daughter Martha described how he lost his temper in her presence only two times in his life."
>
> Fawn M. Brodie, *Thomas Jefferson*

3. Use quotation marks for titles of songs, paintings, and short literary works:
   a. My favorite Beatles song is "All the Lonely People."   song
   b. "The Guest" is a story written by Camus.   short story
   c. The "Mona Lisa" by DaVinci hangs in the Louvre museum.   painting

4. Use quotation marks to stress certain words:
   a. They killed her out of "mercy."   The author wants the reader to know that it was not genuine mercy.
   b. When we use the word "relevant," what do we mean?   Words used as words can be either placed inside quotation marks or underlined.

Italics (Underlining)

In longhand or typewritten material, italics are indicated by underlining; in print, italicized letters are slanted.

1. Use italics for titles of books, magazines, newspapers, and other long works:
   a. Most college students are required to read *Great Expectations* or *Oliver Twist*.
   b. *Harper's Bazaar* is a magazine about fashions.
   c. Although I live in California, I subscribe to the *Wall Street Journal* because it is an excellent newspaper.
   d. Mozart's *Magic Flute* is a long, tedious opera.

2. Use italics for foreign words:
   a. Everyone uses the word *détente*.
   b. I found her dress *très chic*.
   c. He gave an *apologia pro vita sua*.

3. Use italics for words, letters, and figures spoken of as such (see also quotation marks):
   a. Often the word *fortuitous* is misused.
   b. In the word *knight* only *n, i,* and *t* are actually pronounced.
   c. In the Bible, the number *7* represents perfection.

The Hyphen (-)

1. Use a hyphen for a syllable break at the end of a line:
   a. sac-ri-fi-cial
   b. nu-tri-tious
   c. lib-er-al

If in doubt about where to break a word, check with the dictionary.

2. Use a hyphen in some compound words:
   a. brother-in-law
   b. hanky-panky
   c. self-determination
   d. vice-president
   e. two-thirds

3. Use a hyphen in compound modifiers:
   a. well-known movie
   b. blond-haired, blue-eyed baby
   c. low-grade infection

4. The hyphen is omitted when the first word of the compound modifier is an adverb ending in *ly* or an adjective ending in *ish*, or when the compound modifier follows the noun:
   a. a deceptively sweet person
   b. a plainly good meal
   c. a bluish green material
   d. is well known

Exercises

Insert commas where they are needed. If the sentence is correct, write *C* in the space provided.

1. Professor Grover as all of his students agree is one of the most exciting history teachers on campus. _____

2. Madam I beg to differ with you; that is my purse. _____

3. We were asked to check with Mr. Weaver our head custodian. _____

4. Because the water was murky cold and swift we did not go swimming. _____

5. In denouncing the hypocritical Truman encouraged honest dealings. _____

6. Let's not give up until everyone agrees with us. _____

7. Since they belong to the neighborhood they should pay for part of the damage. _____

8. Address your letter to Mrs. Margerie Freedman 320 N. Lincoln Blvd. Reading Massachusetts. _____

9. So many memories are connected with the home of my grandparents a big red brick mansion surrounded by a white picket fence. _____

10. Twice the doctor asked "Have you ever had laryngitis before?" _____

11. Relaxed and happy Jim ignored the people who were angered by his decision. _____

12. July 4 1776 is an important date for patriotic Americans. _____

13. Glistening like a diamond in the sun the lake beckoned us. _____

14. Readers of the *Times* however were not all equally impressed with the editorial on abortions. _____

15. All together some ten thousand people filled out the questionnaire. _____

16. From the mountains, from the prairies, and from numerous villages came the good news about water. _____

17. "My most exquisite lady" he said gallantly "you deserve the Taj Mahal." _____

18. One of her sisters lives in Paris; the other, in London. _____

19. Pat Moynihan who was once the U.S. ambassador to the United Nations is a popular lecturer. _____

20. Well Mary are you satisfied with the result of your crass remark? _____

21. The laboratory technician has finished the gold tooth hasn't he? _____

22. Anyone who feels that this is a bad law should write to his congressman. _____

23. Outside a spectacular rainbow arched across the deep blue sky. _____

24. We walk down this street unafraid, not even thinking of fear. _____

25. Now his grandparents live in a condominium in Florida where they have no yard. _____

Punctuate the following sentences so that they read easily and clearly.

1. Shakespeare wrote many plays including the famous Hamlet

2. Listen he said if you want we can go to a movie any movie

3. The word renaissance literally means rebirth

4. We can have the party at Johns cabin or the Fieldings apartment

5. Its overtaxed heart failing the race horse collapsed before everyones eyes.

6. The most tragic poem I can imagine is Keats Ode to Melancholy

7. Get off my lawn you swine

8. The big bands of the 40s still sell millions of records

9. Last years flowers have wilted they have withered and died

10. As far as the committee is concerned you have lost the grant nevertheless you are to take the exam one more time

11. Just as the situation appeared hopeless a surprising thing happened A number of leading American artists became interested in making lithographic prints.

12. Then in the summer of 1976 the counterrevolutionary army took over

13. The word foolish used to mean simple.

14. Wonderful Here comes the beer Cheers

15. He entitled his paper June Wayne Profile of a California Artist

16. He lived a stones throw from Twin Lakes

17. This is what Bertrand Russell says Science from the dawn of history and probably longer has been intimately associated with war

18. Bertrand Russell has said that Science has been intimately associated with war. (*Refer to item 17.*)

19. He received his PhD at 9 am on Sunday June 6

20. My friend asked me Did you read Bill Shirleys article Worlds First Bionic Swim Team published in the Sports Section of the Los Angeles Times

21. The rule is that you must sign up two days in advance. See Section 25 paragraph 2

22. Dear Sir this is in answer to your letter of May 13

23. A slight tinge of embarrassment or was it pleasure crept across his face

24. The first day we studied later in the week however we relaxed

cap　*Capitalization errors* result when accepted conventions of capitalizing are not followed. Commonly capitalized are words at the beginning of a sentence and the pronoun *I*. Students tend to ignore rules of capitalization. The most important rules are given here.

1. Capitalize all proper names. The following belong to the group of proper names:

   a. specific persons, places, and things but not their general classes (Jefferson, Grand Junction, Eiffel Tower, Harvard University, and Hyde Park are capitalized, but people, cities, towers, universities, and parks are not)

   b. organizations and institutions (Rotary Club, Pentagon)

   c. historical periods and events (Middle Ages, World War II)

   d. members of national, political, racial, and religious groups (Mason, Republican, Negro, Methodist)

   e. special dates on the calendar (Veterans Day), days (Wednesday), months (July).

Freshman, sophomore, junior, and *senior* are not capitalized unless associated with a specific event: "The Junior Prom will take place next Saturday."

2. In titles of literary works, capitalize all words except articles, conjunctions, and prepositions: *All the King's Men,* "The Case against Welfare in Louisville," "The Man without a Country."

3. Capitalize titles associated with proper names: Mrs. Johnson, Ms. Mary Hanley, Judge Garcia, James R. Griedley, M.D., Henry Hadley, Jr.

4. Titles of relatives are capitalized only when they are not preceded by an article, when they are followed by a name, or in direct address:

   a. I gave the keys to Grandmother.
   b. My Grandmother Sitwell
   c. Could you help me, Grandmother?
   d. I was deeply influenced by my grandmother.

5. Unless a title is official, it is not capitalized:

   a. Peter Ferraro, President of the Valley National Bank
   b. Peter Ferraro is president of a bank.
   c. We shall appeal to the President (the top executive of a nation)

6. Capitalize specific courses offered in school, but not general subjects unless they contain a proper name:

   a. I enrolled in Biology 120.
   b. I am taking biology.
   c. I failed Intermediate French.

Exercises

In the following sentences, underline the letters that should be capitalized or made lower case. If the sentence is correct, write *C* in the space at the right.

1. Our memorial day picnic was cancelled due to rain. _____

2. The headline read: "U.S. agent Fired in Investigation of Missing Ammunition." _____

3. Any mayor of a city as large as Chicago should be on good terms with the President of the United States. _____

4. The democrats will doubtless hold their convention at the cow palace in san francisco. _____

5. The tennis courts at Nibley park are always busy. _____

6. If you have to take a psychology course, take psychology 101 from Dr. Pearson, a graduate of harvard. _____

7. There is something elegant about the name "Tryone Kelly, III, esq." _____

8. Until easter of 1949, they lived in a big white georgian home. _____

9. During the second world war, switzerland remained neutral. _____

10. I intend to exchange my capri for a toyota. _____

11. Socrates, the famous Greek philosopher, used Dialogue as a teaching method. _____

12. Some Socialists have joined the Republican Party. _____

13. She said, "the ticket entitles you to spend a night at the Holiday inn in Las Vegas." _____

14. The bible was not fully canonized until the council of Trent. _____

Write a brief sentence in which you use correctly each of the following words:

1. street _____

2. Street _____

3. Democratic _____

4. democratic _____

5. academy _____

6. Academy _____

7. biology _____

8. Biology _____

9. memorial _____

10. Memorial _____

11. father _____

12. Father _____

13. senior _____

14. Senior _____

15. against _____

16. Against _____

17. company _____

18. Company _____

sp *Misspelling* occurs when a word is written differently from the way it is listed in the dictionary (*recieve* instead of *receive*) or when the wrong word is used (*loose* instead of *lose*). The following list* of most commonly misspelled words will help the weak speller. Letters in italics are those that cause the most difficulty. For help in selecting the correct word, refer to the Glossary of Word Choice (p. 272).

Commonly Misspelled Words

1. accom*m*odate
2. achi*e*vement
3. a*c*quire
4. al*l* right
5. am*o*ng
6. ap*p*arent
7. arg*u*ment
8. arg*u*ing
9. bel*i*ef
10. bel*i*eve
11. ben*e*ficial
12. ben*e*fited
13. cat*e*gory
14. co*m*ing
15. compar*a*tive
16. con*scious*
17. cont*r*oversy
18. cont*r*oversi*a*l
19. de*f*ini*t*ely
20. de*f*ini*t*ion
21. de*f*ine
22. de*s*cribe
23. de*s*crip*t*ion
24. disa*s*trous
25. *e*ffect
26. embar*r*a*ss*
27. environ*m*ent
28. exa*gg*erate
29. ex*i*stence
30. ex*i*stent
31. experi*e*nce
32. expla*n*ation
33. fa*s*cinate
34. h*e*ight

35. interest
36. *its* (*it's*)
37. *led*
38. *lose*
39. *losing*
40. marri*a*ge
41. mer*e*
42. ne*c*essary
43. o*cc*asion
44. o*cc*urred
45. o*cc*urring
46. o*cc*urr*e*nce
47. o*p*inion
48. o*pp*ortunity
49. pa*i*d
50. *particular*
51. *performance*
52. person*a*l
53. person*nn*el
54. po*ss*e*ss*ion
55. po*ss*ible
56. practic*a*l
57. pre*cede*
58. prejudice
59. prepar*e*
60. *prevalent*
61. principal
62. principl*e*
63. privi*l*ege
64. proba*b*ly
65. proc*eed*
66. proc*ede*ure
67. pro*f*essor

68. pro*f*ession
69. promin*e*nt
70. p*u*rsue
71. qui*e*t
72. rec*e*ive
73. rec*e*iving
74. recommend
75. refe*rr*ing
76. repe*t*ition
77. r*h*ythm
78. sen*s*e
79. separate
80. separation
81. shi*n*ing
82. simil*a*r
83. stud*y*ing
84. su*cc*eed
85. su*cc*ession
86. su*r*prise
87. techniqu*e*
88. tha*n*
89. the*n*
90. the*i*r
91. there
92. the*y*'re
93. thor*o*ugh
94. *to* (*too*, *two*)
95. transfe*rr*ed
96. un*n*e*c*essary
97. vill*a*in
98. wom*a*n
99. *write*
100. *writing*

---

*From Thomas Clark Pollock, "Spelling Report," *College English*, XVI (November, 1954), 102–09.

Exercises

1. Some of the commonly misspelled words may not appear on either list supplied in this handbook section. If not, compile your own list of troublesome words. First, write the word correctly. Then, note the particular difficulty with it:

    bridle   I   always spell it bri*dal,* as if it came from *bride.*
    perspiration   I must be sure to pronounce it *per,* not *pre.*

2. Using the dictionary as a guide, study the list of 100 words until you know (1) what each word means, (2) how it is pronounced, and (3) how it is spelled. Study the words in groups of 20.

3. From each group of three, choose the misspelled word and write it correctly in the space provided. Check answers in the dictionary.

    a. existance, describe, personal   _____

    b. paid, particular, oportunity   _____

    c. benificial, apparent, experience   _____

    d. controversy, concious, occurred   _____

    e. preformance, similar, succeed   _____

    f. probably, marriage, predjudice   _____

    g. profession, persue, separate   _____

    h. catagory, paid, disastrous   _____

    i. effect, disasterous, mere   _____

    j. preceed, proceed, procedure   _____

    k. embarrass, exaggerate, envirement   _____

    l. prevailent, probably, existent   _____

    m. coming, heighth, professor   _____

    n. define, fascinate, posession   _____

    o. repetition, quiet, recieve   _____

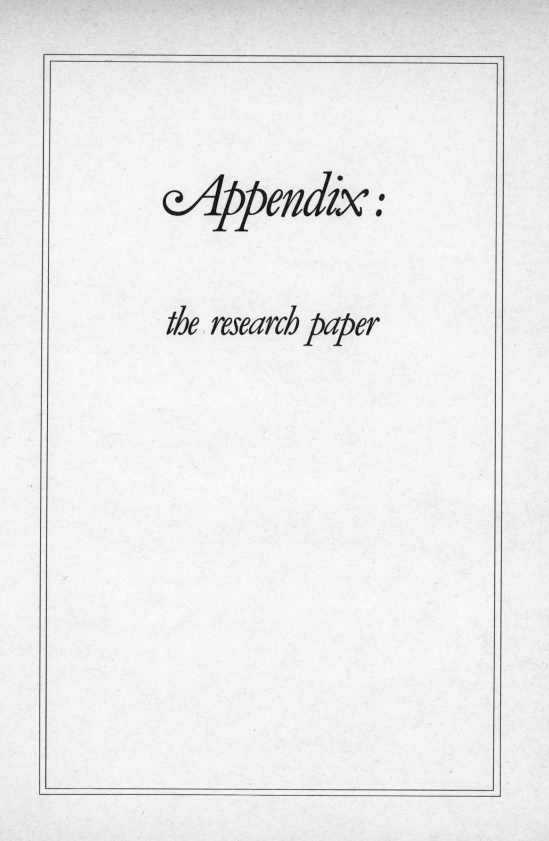

Appendix:

the research paper

the research paper

Students often anticipate the research paper with terror and dread, but for no good reason. From the French verb *rechercher,* meaning to seek, research requires a student to comb the library in an exhilarating and suspenseful search for information. The end product of this search is the research paper. Side benefits to the student include a mastery of the discipline involved in research and a familiarization with the library. Writing a research paper is very much a learning experience.

This appendix covers the principles of assembling library information into a research paper. The same principles, however, apply to other kinds of academic research. To begin with, we suggest the following steps in writing the research paper:

1. Choose the topic.
2. Get acquainted with the library.
3. Collect pertinent information.
4. Formulate a controlling idea and outline the paper.
5. Write the paper using proper documentation.

A. Choose the Topic

You may be assigned a specific research topic, such as a comparison of the social problems in *Oliver Twist* and *Great Expectations,* two novels by Charles Dickens. More often, however, the freshman term paper leaves the task of finding a workable topic to the student. Let us assume that your teacher has given a typical assignment—to write a ten-page research paper on a topic of your choice within the humanities or general sciences. The first problem is to find a specific topic that is challenging enough to support a ten-page research paper. Here are some topics to avoid:

1. TOPICS THAT ARE OVERLY BROAD.   A ten-page term paper, about the length of a short magazine article, cannot accommodate such massive topics as "The History of Painting," "Novels during the Victorian Age," or "The Life of Jesus Christ." To be properly covered, such topics would require an entire book.

2. TOPICS BASED ON PERSONAL OPINIONS.   Personal opinions are frequently not supportable by fact and are therefore seldom appropriate research paper topics. "Streaking Is Fun" or "Why the Counselors at Swanee College Are Stodgy Dressers" are not documentable enough to be usable topics.

3. TOPICS THAT ARE TOO CONTROVERSIAL.   A raging controversy is seldom a good topic for a term paper, because the writer frequently has a bias and is incapable of being objective. Moreover, it is easy for a writer to get bogged down in charges and countercharges and never come to a resolution. Topics such as "What Nixon Did Right in the Watergate Scandals" or "Marijuana Is No Worse than Booze" are best avoided.

4. TOPICS THAT ARE TRITE.   A trite topic will bore the reader to death and may also kill the writer's chances for a good grade. Avoid such topics as "The Advantages of a Supermarket over a Small Local Grocery," or "The Value of Motherhood to America." To spare yourself boredom, you also should avoid any topic on which you have already written another paper.

5. TOPICS THAT ARE TOO TECHNICAL.   Avoid topics involving technical terms and data that neither you nor your reader will completely understand. Papers on topics such as "Laser Geodynamic Satellites and Their Functions" or "Seismological Computations of Dilatancy in the Palmdale Bulge" generally end up as garbled horrors.

6. TOPICS THAT CAN BE DEVELOPED FROM A SINGLE SOURCE.   "How to Make Macramé Hangings" or "How to Use a Kiln" are examples of overly narrow topics that could be documented from a single accurate source. Such topics do not require enough research; moreover, they stultify a reader.

Choose a topic that generates wide-ranging research and requires documentation from several sources. Begin with some exploratory browsing through the library. Mammoth and unsuitable topics such as "Famine in Asia," "Prisons of the World," "Human Resources," "Tribes of Africa," might occur to you at first, but eventually an offhanded remark in the articles or book will trigger off a question in your mind. Properly worded as a controlling idea, the answer to that question, supported by researched information and data, will be the topic of your paper.

Let us, for instance, assume that your interest in the battered child leads you to ask, "When did violence against children begin and what can be done about it?" To answer that question, you begin to search through magazine articles and books.

B. Get Acquainted with the Library

Nothing teaches efficient use of the library better than the practical experience of actual research. The following is a review of the basic research tools available in the library.

1. THE CARD CATALOG. The card catalog is an alphabetical index of all books in the library, the starting point for any research. Ask a librarian to point out the location of the card catalog, which lists all library books on three separate cards, by author, title, and subject. The cards usually are stored in small, labeled drawers.

Following are three sample cards. Technical information, useful only to the librarian, is listed on the bottom half of the card. The top half of the card contains the book title, author's name, publication data, and the call number, which indicates the location of the book in the library.

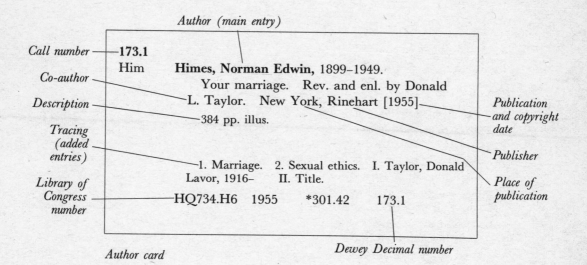

Author card

173.1	Your marriage.
Him	**Himes, Norman Edwin,** 1899–1949.
	Your marriage. Rev. and enl. by Donald
	L. Taylor. New York, Rinehart [1955]
	384 pp. illus.
	1. Marriage. 2. Sexual ethics. I. Taylor, Donald
	Lavor, 1916– II. Title.
	HQ734.H6 1955 *301.42 173.1

Title card

173.1 MARRIAGE
Him **Himes, Norman Edwin,** 1899–1949.
    Your marriage. Rev. and enl. by Donald
  L. Taylor. New York, Rinehart [1955]
    384 pp. illus.

    1. Marriage. 2. Sexual ethics. I. Taylor, Donald
  Lavor, 1916– II. Title.
  HQ734.H6 1955 *301.42 173.1

Subject card

2. THE STACKS. The stacks are the actual library shelves on which books, magazines, and other materials are stored. Some large universities do not permit undergraduate readers into the stacks, preferring instead to dispense requested books through a librarian. In some libraries, commonly used works are available in the main library area, with the remainder of the collection stored in stacks and available through the librarian. If your school library allows access into the stacks, be aware that important books missing from the shelves may be on loan, in a special collection, or on reserve.

Whether admitted into the stacks or not, every college student should know the systems by which library books are organized. Through these systems, a single title can be located among vast numbers of books. American libraries use two systems for organizing books: (a) the Dewey Decimal System, and (b) the Library of Congress System. Both systems assign each book a specific "call number," marked on its spine and listed on all catalog cards for that book.

Under the Dewey Decimal System, all knowledge is divided into ten general categories and indicated by decimal notation:

  000–099 General works
  100–199 Philosophy
  200–299 Religion
  300–399 Social Sciences
  400–499 Philology
  500–599 Pure Science
  600–699 Applied Arts and Sciences
  700–799 Fine Arts, Recreation
  800–899 Literature
  900–999 History, Geography, Travel

Every general area of knowledge is subdivided into tens. For example, Pure Science (500–599) is subdivided as follows:

  510–519 Mathematics
  520–529 Astronomy

530–539   Physics
540–549   Chemistry
550–559   Geology
560–569   Paleontology
570–579   Biology
580–589   Botany
590–599   Zoology

Additional subcategories are designated as in this example:

511   Arithmetic
511.1   Systems

   Invented in the 1870s, the Dewey Decimal System does not contain enough categories to adequately classify the knowledge that has accumulated since that time, especially in the sciences. Classifications are consequently often long and awkward. Most large libraries therefore use the Library of Congress System, which contains twenty-one major categories, broken down as follows:

A. General works, Polygraphy
B. Philosophy, Religion
C. History, Auxiliary sciences
D. History, Topography (except America)
E. America (general), United States (general)
F. United States (local), America (except the United States)
G. Geography, Anthropology
H. Social Sciences (general), Statistics, Economics, Sociology
J. Political Science
K. Law
L. Education
M. Music
N. Fine Arts
P. Language and Literature
Q. Science
R. Medicine
S. Agriculture
T. Technology
U. Military Science
V. Naval Science
Z. Bibliography, Library Science

Further subdivisions are created by the addition of a letter. For example, Agriculture (S) is subdivided as follows:

SB General plant culture, soils, fertilizers, implements
SD Forestry
SF Animal culture, veterinary medicine
SH Fish culture, fisheries
SK Hunting, game protection

3. THE REFERENCE ROOM.   Reference material consists of a variety of books and indexes that synopsize and classify information and its location. Usually stored on open shelves, reference material cannot be checked out and taken home.

Indexes: The *Reader's Guide to Periodical Literature,* issued monthly, is the most important and useful index in the reference room. It lists magazine and journal articles in specific subject areas according to author, title, and subject. The monthly indexes are bound into a hardcover volume at the end of each year and stored alongside other volumes, which go back to the nineteenth century. The facsimile of a page from *Reader's Guide* (opposite) will help you interpret its listings.

Following is a list of other useful indexes:

> *Applied Science and Technology Index*
> *Art Index*
> *Bibliographic Index*
> *Biography Index*
> *Book Review Digest*
> *Dramatic Index*
> *Education Index*
> *Index to the London Times*
> *Monthly Catalog of United States Government Publications*
> *Music Index*
> *New York Times Index*
> *Social Sciences and Humanities Index*

Bookseller's lists: Consult the following works for information about books currently in print:

> *Books in Print* (separate volumes for listings by author and by title)
> *Cumulative Book Index*
> *Paperbound Books in Print*
> *Subject Guide to Books in Print*

General encyclopedias: Encyclopedias can give a general overview of a subject. The best known encyclopedias are:

> *Chambers's Encyclopedia,* 15 vols.
> *Collier's Encyclopedia,* 24 vols.
> *Columbia Encyclopedia,* 1 vol.
> *Encyclopaedia Britannica,* 24 vols.
> *Encyclopedia Americana,* 30 vols.

Atlases and gazetteers: Atlases and gazetteers give information about places. An atlas is a collection of maps; a gazetteer is a dictionary of places. Be sure the atlas or gazetteer you use is up to date.

> *Columbia-Lippincott Gazetteer of the World.* 2d ed. New York: Columbia University Press, 1962.
> *Hammond Medallion World Atlas.* Maplewood, N.J.: C. S. Hammond, 1971.

CHILDREN, Adoption of. See Adoption
CHILDREN, Exceptional
    See also
Children, Handicapped
CHILDREN, Gifted

Education
Gifted programs for the culturally different. E. M. Bernal, Jr. Educ
    Digest 41:28–31 My '76
CHILDREN, Handicapped
    Thelma Boston. miracle worker. M. G. Crawford. il pors Good H
    182:40+ Je '76
    See also
Cerebral palsied children

Education
Education for all handicapped children. H. A. Williams, Jr. por
    Parents Mag 51:20 Je '76
Education of the handicapped today. il Am Educ 12:6–8 Je '76
CHILDREN, Psychotic. See Mentally ill children
CHILDREN and alcohol. See Alcohol and youth
CHILDREN and television. See Television and children
CHILDREN as stockholders
    Teaching children about stocks. C. Kirk. Parents Mag 51:14 Je '76
CHILDRENS art
Student art. See issues of School arts
    See also
Paperwork

Exhibitions
Art gallery in the lobby. K. Thompson. il Sch Arts 75:35 Je '76
CHILDRENS exhibitions
    See also
Childrens art—Exhibitions
CHILDRENS homes. See Homes, Institutional
CHILDRENS librarians
    Old strengths and new weaknesses. E. L. Heins. Horn Bk 52:250–1
    Je '76
    Skimming of memory; ed by M. Hodges. F. C. Sayers. il Horn Bk
    52:270–5 Je '76
CHILDRENS literature
    See also
Fairy tales

Authorship
Books that say yes. M. L'Engle. Writer 89:9–12 Je '76
Sprezzatura: a kind of excellence; excerpts from address. April 12,
    1975. E. L. Konigsburg. Horn Bk 52:253–61 Je '76

Awards, prizes, etc.
Memories of childhood; awarded to J. Reiss. A. Wolff. Sat R 3:8
    Je 12 '76

Bibliography
Books for the reluctant reader. A. R. Zinck and K. J. Hawkins. il
    Wilson Lib Bull 50:722–4 My '76
Children's books: the best of the season. W. Cole. il Sat R 3:36–9
    My 15 '76
CHILDRENS sayings. See Children—Sayings
CHILDRENS stories
    See name of author for full entry
Peachy pig. J. O'Reilly
CHILE

Commerce
Ray of hope from an export pickup. Bus W p48–9 My 24 '76

Economic conditions
Ray of hope from an export pickup. Bus W p48–9 My 24 '76

Politics and government
Protest in Chile. A. Bono. Commonweal 103:390–1 Je 18 '76
CHILEANS in the United States
    See also
California—Foreign population
CHIMERAS (biology) See Mosaics (biology)
CHIMES, Electric
Door chime. W. D. Leckey. il Pop Mech 145:107 My '76
CHINA (People's Republic)
    See also
Agriculture—China (People's Republic)
Education—China (People's Republic)

Subject

Title of article

Volume, pages, issue

Magazine

Cross-references

Cross-references subdividing a topic

National Atlas of the United States. Washington, D.C.: Government Printing Office, 1970.

Rand McNally Commercial Atlas and Marketing Guide. 1968–. (Annually.)

Shepherd, William R. *Historical Atlas.* 9th ed. New York: Barnes and Noble, 1964.

The Times Atlas of the World. 2d rev. ed. Boston: Houghton Mifflin, 1971.

Webster's New Geographical Dictionary. Rev. ed. Springfield, Mass.: G. & C. Merriam, 1972.

Biography: General information about well-known persons is listed in the following sources:

Biography Index. 1947–. Quarterly. Cumulated annually and every three years. An index to books and magazines.

Current Biography. 1940–. Monthly except August. Cumulated annually. Articles about living persons. Especially useful for current celebrities. See the index in each volume, which covers preceding years.

Dictionary of American Biography. 20 vols. New York: Scribner's, 1928–73. Index. Supplements. Authoritative articles on Americans no longer living who have made significant contributions to American life.

Dictionary of National Biography. 63 vols. London: Smith, Elder, 1885–1950. Supplements. The basic source of biographical information about Englishmen no longer living.

Webster's Biographical Dictionary. 2d ed. Springfield, Mass.: G. & C. Merriam, 1969.

Who's Who. London: Black, 1849–. Annually. *Who Was Who* reprints discontinued entries.

Who's Who in America. Chicago: Marquis Who's Who, Inc., 1899–. Biennially. *Who Was Who in America* reprints discontinued entries.

Dictionaries: Information about words, their meanings, and their histories, is found in one or more of the following dictionaries:

A Dictionary of American English on Historical Principles. 4 vols. Chicago: University of Chicago Press, 1936–44. An historical dictionary of American words and meanings, modeled after the NED.

Funk & Wagnalls New Practical Standard Dictionary of the English Language. New York: Funk & Wagnalls, 1964.

A New English Dictionary on Historical Principles. 10 vols. Oxford: Clarendon Press, 1884–1933. Reissued in 1933 as *The Oxford English Dictionary.* 13 vols. Dated illustrative quotations portray the history of a word's meaning. Three-volume supplement in progress.

Random House Dictionary of the English Language. New York: Random House, 1966.

Webster's New Dictionary of Synonyms. Springfield, Mass.: G. & C. Merriam, 1968.

Webster's Third New International Dictionary of the English Language. Springfield, Mass.: G. & C. Merriam, 1961. (Often referred to as W III.)

Quotations: To verify the source of a quotation, check one of the following dictionaries of quotations:

> Bartlett, John. *Familiar Quotations.* 14th ed. Boston: Little Brown, 1968. Arranged chronologically by author. Index.
>
> Evans, Bergen. *Dictionary of Quotations.* New York: Delacorte, 1968. Arranged alphabetically by subject.
>
> Hoyt, Jehiel K. *New Cyclopedia of Practical Quotations.* New York: Funk and Wagnalls, 1940. Arranged by subject. Index.
>
> Mencken, Henry L. *A New Dictionary of Quotations.* New York: Knopf, 1942. Arranged by subject. No index.
>
> *Oxford Dictionary of Quotations.* 2d ed. New York: Oxford University Press, 1953. Arranged alphabetically by author.
>
> Stevenson, Burton E. *The Home Book of Quotations, Classical and Modern.* 10th ed. New York: Dodd, Mead, 1967. Arranged by subject. Key-word index.

Reference works for special fields: A list of all the works that survey special fields would consume an entire volume. The following is a list, by subject area, of frequently used reference works:

Art

> *Art Index.* 1929–. Quarterly. Cumulated annually and biennially. An author-subject index to periodicals.
>
> Chamberlin, Mary W. *Guide to Art Reference Books.* Chicago: American Library Association, 1959.
>
> Cummings, Paul. *A Dictionary of Contemporary American Artists.* 2d ed. New York: St. Martin's Press, 1971.
>
> Gardner, Helen. *Art Through the Ages.* 5th ed. New York: Harcourt, Brace and World, 1970.
>
> Groce, George C., and David H. Wallace. *The New York Historical Society's Dictionary of Artists in America,* 1564–1860. New Haven, Conn.: Yale University Press, 1957.
>
> Lucas, E. Louise. *Art Books.* Greenwich, Conn.: New York Graphic Society, 1968.
>
> *McGraw-Hill Encyclopedia of World Art.* 15 vols. New York: McGraw-Hill, 1967.
>
> Mayer, Ralph. *A Dictionary of Art Terms and Techniques.* New York: Crowell, 1969.
>
> Robb, David M., and Jessie J. Garrison. *Art in the Western World.* 4th ed. New York: Harper, 1963.
>
> Sturgis, Russell. *Dictionary of Architecture and Building.* 3 vols. New York: Macmillan, 1901.

Biology

> *Biological Abstracts.* 1926–. Semimonthly. Annual cumulations.
>
> *Biological and Agricultural Index.* 1964–. Monthly except August. Annual cumulations.

Bottle, R. T. and H. V. Wyatt. *The Use of Biological Literature.* 2d ed. Hamden, Conn.: Archon, 1971.

Gray, Asa. *Gray's Manual of Botany.* New York: American Book Co., 1950.

Gray, Peter. *The Encyclopedia of the Biological Sciences.* 2d ed. New York: Van Nostrand Reinhold, 1970.

Henderson, Isabelle F. and William D. Henderson. *A Dictionary of Biological Terms.* 8th ed. Princeton, N.J.: Van Nostrand Reinhold, 1963.

Jaeger, Edmund C. *A Source-book of Biological Names and Terms.* 3d ed. Springfield, Ill.: Thomas, 1955.

Leftwich, A. W. *A Dictionary of Zoology.* 2d ed. New York: Van Nostrand Reinhold, 1967.

Walker, Ernest P. *Mammals of the World.* 3 vols. Baltimore: Johns Hopkins Press, 1964.

Willis, J. C. *A Dictionary of the Flowering Plants and Ferns.* 8th ed. New York: Cambridge University Press, 1973.

Business

Accountants' Index. 1921–. Biennially.

Bogen, Jules I. *Financial Handbook.* 4th ed. New York: Ronald, 1964.

Business Periodicals Index. 1958–. Formerly *Industrial Arts Index,* 1913–57. Subject index. Monthly except August. Annual cumulations.

Commodity Year Book. 1939–. Annual volumes except for 1943–47.

Johnson, H. Webster. *How to Use the Business Library.* 4th ed. Cincinnati: South-Western, 1972.

Munn, Glenn G. *Encyclopedia of Banking and Finance.* 6th ed. Boston: Bankers Publishing, 1962.

Poor's Register of Corporations, Directors and Executives. 1928–. Annually.

Chemistry

Chemical Abstracts. 1907–. Semimonthly. Indexed annually and every ten years.

Condensed Chemical Dictionary. 8th ed. New York: Van Nostrand Reinhold, 1971.

Crane, Evan Jay and others. *A Guide to the Literature of Chemistry.* 2d ed. New York: John Wiley, 1957.

Encyclopedia of Chemistry. 2d ed. New York: Reinhold, 1960.

Handbook of Chemistry and Physics. 1913–. Annual revisions.

Mellon, Melvin G. *Chemical Publications: Their Nature and Use.* 4th ed. New York: McGraw-Hill, 1965.

Thorpe, Jocelyn F., and M. A. Whiteley. *Thorpe's Dictionary of Applied Chemistry.* 12 vols. New York: Longman's, 1937–56.

Economics

Coman, Edwin T., Jr., *Sources of Business Information.* Rev. ed. Berkeley: University of California Press, 1964.

Economic Almanac. 1940–. Annually.

Economics Library Selections. 1954–. Quarterly.

Hanson, John L. *A Dictionary of Economics and Commerce.* 3d ed. London: MacDonald & Evans, 1969.

Journal of Economic Abstracts. 1963–. Quarterly.

McGraw-Hill Dictionary of Modern Economics. New York: McGraw-Hill, 1965.

Sloan, Harold S. and Arnold J. Zurcher. *Dictionary of Economics.* 5th ed. New York: Barnes and Noble, 1970.

Survey of Current Business. 1921–. Monthly.

Wall Street Journal. Five days a week.

Education

Burke, Arvid J., and Mary A. Burke. *Documentation in Education.* 5th ed. New York: Teachers College Press, 1967.

Current Index to Journals in Education. 1969–. Monthly. Semiannual and annual indexes.

Education Index. 1929–. Author-subject index. Monthly except July and August. Annual cumulations.

Encyclopedia of Education. 10 vols. New York: Macmillan, 1971.

Encyclopedia of Educational Research. 4th ed. New York: Macmillan, 1969.

Encyclopedia of Modern Education. New York: Philosophical Library, 1948.

Foskett, D. J. *How to Find Out: Educational Research.* Oxford, N.Y.: Pergamon, 1965.

Leaders in Education. 4th ed. New York: R. R. Bowker and Jacques Cattell Press, 1971.

NEA Journal. 1913–. Nine issues a year.

Research in Education. 1966–. Abstracts prepared by Educational Research

Research in Education. 1966–. Monthly. Abstracts prepared by Educational Research Information Center.

School and Society. 1915–. Weekly.

School Life. 1918–. Nine issues a year.

Engineering

Dalton, Blanche H. *Sources of Engineering Information.* Berkeley, Calif.: University of California Press, 1948.

Engineering Index Monthly, 1962–. Annual cumulations. Index to periodicals. Abstracts.

Jones, Franklin D., and Paul B. Schubert. *Engineering Encyclopedia.* 3d ed. 2 vols. New York: Industrial Press, 1963.

Perry, Robert H. *Engineering Manual.* 2d ed. New York: McGraw-Hill, 1967.

Souders, Mott. *The Engineer's Companion.* New York: Wiley, 1966.

Geology

Bibliography and Index of Geology. 1933–. Monthly. Annual indexes.

Dana, James D., and Edward S. Dana. *The System of Mineralogy.* 7th ed. 3 vols. New York: Wiley, 1944–62.

Geo-Science Abstracts. 1959–. Monthly. Annual index.

Loomis, Frederic B. *Field Book of Common Rocks and Minerals.* Rev. ed. New York: Putnam, 1948.

Minerals Year Book. 1933–. Annually.

Pough, Frederick H. *A Field Guide to Rocks and Minerals.* 3d ed. Boston: Houghton Mifflin, 1960.

History

Adams, James Truslow, ed. *Dictionary of American History*. 2d ed. 6 vols. New York: Scribner's, 1940–61.

America: History and Life. 1964–. Abstracts. Three issues a year.

American Historical Review. 1895–. Quarterly.

Barzun, Jacques and Henry F. Graf. *The Modern Researcher*. Rev. ed. New York: Harcourt Brace Jovanovich, 1970.

Beers, Henry P. *Bibliographies in American History*. New York: H. W. Wilson, 1942.

Cambridge Ancient History. 12 vols. New York: Cambridge University Press, 1923–29. Revision in progress.

Cambridge Medieval History. 8 vols. New York: Cambridge University Press, 1911–36. Revision in progress.

Cambridge Modern History. 13 vols. New York: Cambridge University Press, 1902–26. Revision in progress.

Commager, Henry S. *Documents of American History*. 2 vols. 7th ed. New York: Appleton-Century-Crofts, 1968.

Guide to Historical Literature. New York: Macmillan, 1961.

Historical Abstracts, 1775–1945. 1955–. Quarterly. Cumulative index every five years.

Journal of American History. 1914–. Quarterly. Formerly *Mississippi Valley Historical Review*.

Keller, Helen R. *Dictionary of Dates*. 2 vols. New York: Macmillan, 1934.

Morris, Richard B. *Encyclopedia of American History*. 4th ed. New York: Harper and Row, 1970.

Literature

Abstracts of English Studies. 1958–. Ten issues a year.

American Literature. 1929–. Quarterly. Bibliography in each number.

Benet, William R. *The Reader's Encyclopedia*. 2d ed. New York: Crowell, 1965.

Cambridge Bibliography of English Literature. 5 vols. New York: Cambridge University Press, 1940–57.

Cambridge History of American Literature. 4 vols. New York: Putnam, 1917–21. Bibliography in each volume.

Cambridge History of English Literature. 15 vols. New York: Putnam, 1907–33. Bibliography in each volume.

Columbia Dictionary of Modern European Literature. New York: Columbia University Press, 1947.

Gohdes, Clarence. *Bibliographical Guides to the Study of Literature of the U.S.A.* 3d ed. Durham, N.C.: Duke University Press, 1970.

Hart, James D. *The Oxford Companion to American Literature*. 4th ed. New York: Oxford University Press, 1965.

Harvey, Sir Paul. *The Oxford Companion to Classical Literature*. New York: Oxford University Press, 1937.

———. *The Oxford Companion to English Literature*. 4th ed. New York: Oxford University Press, 1967.

Holman, C. Hugh. *A Handbook to Literature.* 3d ed. Indianapolis: Odyssey Press, 1972. Thorough revision of a standard reference work with the same title by Thrall and Hibbard.

Leary, Lewis G. *Articles on American Literature, 1900–1950.* Durham, N. C.: Duke University Press, 1954. A second volume published in 1970 with the same editor, title and publisher covers 1950–67.

New Century Classical Handbook. New York: Appleton-Century-Crofts, 1962.

PMLA. 1884–. Quarterly. Annual Bibliographies since 1921. International coverage since 1956. Bibliography issue now entitled *MLA International Bibliography.*

Spiller, Robert E. and others. *Literary History of the United States.* 3d ed. 2 vols. New York: Macmillan, 1963. Bibliography in second volume.

Year's Work in English Studies. 1921–. Annual critical surveys.

Music

Apel, Willi. *Harvard Dictionary of Music.* 2d ed. Cambridge, Mass.: Harvard University Press, 1970.

Baker, Theodore. *Biographical Dictionary of Musicians.* 5th ed. New York: Schirmer, 1965.

Barlow, Harold and Sam Morganstern. *A Dictionary of Musical Themes.* New York: Crown. 1948.

Duckles, Vincent H. *Music Reference and Research Materials.* 2d ed. New York: Free Press, 1967.

Ewen, David. *The New Encyclopedia of the Opera.* Rev. ed. New York: Hill and Wang, 1971.

Grove, Sir George. *Dictionary of Music and Musicians.* 5th ed. 10 vols. New York: St. Martin's Press, 1970. The standard encyclopedia of music, first published in 1879.

Music Educator's Journal. 1914–. Bimonthly.

Music Index. 1949–. Monthly. Annual cumulations.

The Music Quarterly. 1915–. Quarterly.

Scholes, Percy A. *The Oxford Companion to Music.* 10th ed. New York: Oxford University Press, 1970.

World of Music. 4 vols. New York: Abradale Press, 1963.

Mythology and Folklore

Bulfinch's Mythology. New York: T. Y. Crowell, 1970. New issue of a standard work.

Diehl, Katherine S. *Religions, Mythologies, Folklores: An Annotated Bibliography.* 2d ed. Metuchen, N.J.: Scarecrow Press, 1962.

Frazer, Sir James. *The Golden Bough.* 3d ed. 12 vols. New York: St. Martin's Press, 1955. A one-volume abridgment, *The New Golden Bough,* was published in 1959.

Funk & Wagnalls Standard Dictionary of Folklore, Mythology, and Legend. New York: Funk & Wagnalls, 1972. Reissue of two-volume work published in 1949–50.

Hamilton, Edith. *Mythology.* Boston: Little, Brown, 1942. Published as a paperbound Mentor Book, 1953.

Mythology of All Races. 13 vols. Boston: Archaeological Institute, 1916–32.

Radford, Edwin and Mona Radford. *Encyclopedia of Superstitions.* Rev. ed. Chester Springs, Pa.: Dufour Editions, 1969.

Thompson, Stith. *Motif-Index of Folk-Literature.* 6 vols. Bloomington, Ind.: Indiana University Press, 1955–58.

Philosophy

The Encyclopedia of Philosophy. 8 vols. New York: Macmillan, 1967.

Journal of Philosophy. 1904–. Fortnightly.

Philosopher's Index. 1967–. Quarterly. Author-subject index to periodicals.

Philosophic Abstracts. 1939–54. No longer published.

Philosophical Review. 1892–. Quarterly.

Urmson, James O., ed. *The Concise Encyclopedia of Western Philosophy and Philosophers.* New York: Hawthorn Books, 1960.

Varet, Gilbert and Paul Kurtz. *International Directory of Philosophy and Philosophers.* New York: Humanities Press, 1966.

Wiener, Philip, ed. *Dictionary of the History of Ideas.* 4 vols. New York: Scribner's, 1973.

Physics

Besancon, Robert M. *The Encyclopedia of Physics.* New York: Van Nostrand Reinhold, 1966.

Encyclopaedic Dictionary of Physics. 9 vols. London: Pergamon, 1961–64. Supplements.

Handbook of Chemistry and Physics. 1913–. Annual revisions.

Parke, Nathan G. *Guide to the Literature of Mathematics and Physics.* 2d ed. New York: Dover, 1958.

Science Abstracts. 1898–. Monthly.

Whitford, R. H. *Physics Literature: A Reference Manual.* 2d ed. Metuchen, N. J.: Scarecrow Press, 1968.

Political Science

American Political Science Review. 1906–. Quarterly.

The Book of the States. Lexington, Ky.: Council of State Governments, 1935–. Biennially.

Congressional Record. 1873–. Daily. Cumulated for each session. Annual index.

Dictionary of American Politics. 2d ed. New York: Barnes and Noble, 1968.

Dunner, Joseph. *Dictionary of Political Science.* Totowa, N. J.: Littlefield, Adams, 1970.

Harmon, R. B. *Political Science: A Bibliographical Guide.* Metuchen, N. J.: Scarecrow Press, 1965. Supplements.

Holler, Frederick L. *The Information Sources of Political Science.* Santa Barbara, Calif.: ABC-Clio, 1971.

Plano, Jack C., and Milton Greenberg. *The American Political Dictionary.* Rev. ed. New York: Holt, Rinehart & Winston, 1967.

Political Handbook and Atlas of the World. New York: Simon and Schuster, 1927–. Annual revisions.

Public Affairs Information Service. 1915–. Weekly. Cumulated five times a year and annually.

Psychology

American Journal of Psychology. 1887–. Quarterly.

Drever, James. *A Dictionary of Psychology.* Rev. ed. Baltimore: Penguin Books, 1971.

Encyclopedia of Mental Health. 6 vols. New York: Franklin Watts, 1963.

Encyclopedia of Psychology. 3 vols. New York: McGraw-Hill, 1972.

Harvard List of Books in Psychology. 4th ed. Cambridge, Mass.: Harvard University Press, 1971.

Psychology Abstracts. 1927–. Monthly.

Psychological Bulletin. 1904–. Bimonthly.

Religion

Adams, Charles J. *A Reader's Guide to the Great Religions.* New York: Free Press, 1965.

Encyclopaedia Judaica. 16 vols. New York: Macmillan, 1972.

Hastings, James. *Encyclopaedia of Religion and Ethics.* 2d. ed. 12 vols. New York: Scribner's, 1907–27.

Index to Religious Periodical Literature. 1949–. Annually. Triennial cumulations.

Interpreter's Dictionary of the Bible. 4 vols. Nashville, Tenn.: Abingdon Press, 1962.

Mead, Frank S. *Handbook of Denominations in the United States.* 5th ed. Nashville, Tenn.: Abingdon Press, 1970.

Nelson's Complete Concordance. New York: Nelson, 1957.

New Catholic Encyclopedia. 15 vols. New York: McGraw-Hill, 1967.

New Schaff-Herzog Encyclopedia of Religious Knowledge. 13 vols. Grand Rapids, Mich.: Baker Book House, 1951–58.

Oxford Dictionary of the Christian Church. New York: Oxford University Press, 1960.

Religious and Theological Abstracts. 1958–. Quarterly.

Sociology

Abstracts for Social Workers. 1965–. Quarterly.

American Journal of Sociology. 1895–. Bimonthly.

American Sociological Review, 1936–. Bimonthly.

Encyclopedia of Social Work. 1965–. Annual volumes.

Fairchild, Henry P. *Dictionary of Sociology.* Totowa, N. J.: Littlefield, Adams, 1970. Paperbound reprint of a 1944 edition.

Mitchell, G. Duncan. *A Dictionary of Sociology.* Chicago: Aldine, 1968.

Reuter, E. B. *Handbook of Sociology.* New York: Dryden Press, 1946.

Social Forces. 1922–. Quarterly.

Sociological Abstracts. 1952–. Nine issues a year.

C. Collect Pertinent Information

1. COMPILE A BIBLIOGRAPHY.   You now have a research topic, and you know how and where to collect information on it. The next step is to compile a *bibliography,* a list of useful sources of information on the topic. Purposeful reading is now one of the most important skills you can develop. You must learn to separate useless from useful information without a wasteful and slow page-by-page analysis of the source.

Skim book chapters and magazine articles to see if they contain material relevant to the topic. Read tables of contents, index pages, and subtitles of books; read the topic sentences of paragraphs. Mark pertinent passages in pencil if the source belongs to you, or if it is a library source, place a paperclip on the page. When you are reasonably sure that the source will be useful, list it on a 3 × 5 bibliography card. A typical bibliography card looks like this:

Identifying name

Library call number

All information necessary for footnote or bibliography

Personal note about why the book may be useful

    364.15
    Gil

                                            Gil

Gil, David G.
Violence against Children.
Cambridge, Mass.: Harvard
University Press, 1968.

(contains numerous case
histories)

It will save you valuable time later if you note the call number of a book and the date and title of a magazine article on the bibliography card. Use a separate card for each source to simplify changes in your preliminary bibliography. To add a source, make a new card; to delete a source, remove the card on which it is entered.

2. TAKE NOTES.   By now, considerable skimming and reading should have given you an overall view of the topic. Quite likely, you have already formulated a controlling idea and are ready to begin taking notes from the sources you will use. The importance of careful note-taking cannot be overstated: accuracy and thoroughness at this stage will save literally hours of work in assembling the first draft of your paper.

Make notes on 4 x 6 cards. Any information, data, or quotation to be incorporated into the paper should be listed on the 4 x 6 note cards; call numbers and publication information on books or magazine articles should be listed on the bibliography cards. Therefore, there will be both a note card and a bibliography card for each source consulted.

The four primary forms of note-taking are: summarizing, paraphrasing, quoting, and a mixture of these.

a. *To summarize* means to condense. A condensation uses fewer words than the original. A book may be condensed into one paragraph; a paragraph may be condensed into one sentence. For example, a book citing numerous examples of child battering in the schools of Sumer, five thousand years ago, might be summarized like this on a notecard:

Key heading

Authors and page reference (the full bibliography information would be on the bibliography card)

Helfer and Kempe, p. 3

Battered child in early history

In the schools of Sumer, five thousand years ago, there was a man in charge of the whip. His special duty was to punish boys in order to maintain discipline and to please the gods. These boys were severely beaten as part of a routine approach to proper behavior.

b. *To paraphrase* means to restate an original source in your own words using nearly the same amount of space as the original. Here is an example of a paraphrase:

Original: The general public is not fully aware of the seriousness and prevalence of cruelty to children. The knowledge that babies suffer severe injury or death at the hands of their parents is repugnant and extremely hard to accept. Abuse of children, the greatest cause of death among children under the age of three, causes more deaths than auto accidents, leukemia, and muscular dystrophy.

Society's feelings
toward child
abuse

Paraphrase:

Because society feels repelled by the idea of child battering, it remains unaware of the extent and seriousness of the problem. Decent people tend to ignore the ugly truth that children are often seriously injured and even killed by their own parents. Few people realize that in fact child abuse is the greatest cause of death among children under the age of three, causing more deaths than car accidents or serious diseases like leukemia.

c. *To quote* means to use exactly the same words as the original. Many passages may be quoted in the notes, but as few quotations as possible should appear in the actual paper. A good research paper should reveal that the writer has assimilated and established information and data in his *own* flow of thought, and therefore need not rely on the words of others. Frequent quotations also give writing a choppy effect. Use quotations only when:

(1) You want authoritative support for a statement.
(2) Something is said with exceptional literary taste.
(3) The quotation is needed for accuracy.

Quotations must meticulously include every comma and every word in the original. Check quotations for accuracy. Oddities of spelling or phrasing in the original should be copied exactly and followed by a bracketed [*sic*], which indicates, "This is the way the text reads in the original." Any omitted portion of the original quotation is indicated by ellipses (. . .) as in this example:

It is thought that because of crowding in smaller quarters and because of having larger families, "the working-class parent uses . . . punishment more than the middle-class parent."

Ellipses are not used if the quotation is integrated into a sentence and the omission is made at the beginning or end of the original. Here is an example:

Quotation to be used: Many sociologists have noted that the working-class parent uses physical punishment more than the middle-class parent.

Quotation as it appears in the paper: It is thought that because of crowding in smaller quarters and because of having larger families, "the working-class parent uses physical punishment more than the middle-class parent."

Quotations in the final paper must fit coherently into the flow of writing. Transitional sentences, based on a thorough understanding of both the quotation and its context, should be used to introduce the quotation and move the reader on to succeeding material. A well-prepared notecard, with author and subject identified, will help you effectively use a quotation:

Neill, p. 102   An authority's
                                 view on
                                 punishment

A. S. Neill suggests that "Perhaps we punish because we are a Christian civilization. If you sin, punishment awaits you in the here and now, and Hell awaits you in the future."

Here are some additional suggestions for writing useful notecards:

a. Write in ink, not pencil, or the notecards will smudge when you shuffle them. Do not type notecards. Many libraries do not allow the use of typewriters on their premises; moreover, transcribing notes on a typewriter later wastes time and causes copying errors.

b. Use one card per idea. With one idea on each card, an outline can be created by shuffling the cards and arranging them in a logical sequence. To save money, cut your own note cards from regular paper.

c. In copying or paraphrasing material from more than one page in an original source, indicate all pages on the notecard. This information is needed for footnotes.

d. Write notes legibly or you may have to go back to an original source to decipher what you meant.

D. Formulate the Controlling Idea and Outline the Paper

1. THE CONTROLLING IDEA.   The controlling idea holds the research together and limits the paper's scope. Tinker with the wording of the controlling idea until it is abundantly clear. Acceptable controlling ideas for college papers are: (a) the *purpose* statement, and (b) the *thesis* statement.

a. The purpose statement is an initial statement of the paper's intent. It involves such phrases as "The purpose of this paper is . . . ," or "In this paper proof will be offered that . . . ," or "The intent of this paper is . . ." Here are some sample purpose statements, taken from student papers:

(1) The purpose of this paper is to prove that every major war in America has influenced women's fashions.

(2) This paper will relate certain aspects of Dietrich Bonhoeffer's life to his religious views expressed in his writings.

b. The standard *thesis statement* gets directly to the controlling idea and states it, as:

(1) Adolescence in American society today is characterized by the young adult's dependency on the family, his search for an identity, and the repression of his sexual drives.

(2) The Gods of the Greeks were human, with human appearances, human virtues, and human failings.

(3) We laugh at Charlie Chaplin's movies because they reflect the bumbling creature we all fear that we might be.

2. THE OUTLINE. The next step is to outline the paper. A simple procedure for creating an outline is to assemble the notecards according to the logical sequence of their major ideas. All information relating to one major idea is placed in the same stack. For example, in the paper on child abuse, perhaps the notecards could be logically grouped into three stacks based on the following major ideas:

I. Violence against children by adults has been practiced throughout history.

II. A wide variety of child abuse cases exist today and for numerous reasons.

III. Some effective action has been taken against child abuse, but more social cooperation and legal sanctions are needed to overcome the problem.

These three points could then be condensed into a controlling idea such as the following:

Adult violence against children, commonly practiced throughout history, occurs today for a variety of reasons in countless cases of child abuse, and can be corrected only through social cooperation and legal sanctions.

A controlling idea containing three major divisions is now established. Arrange the notecards within each division into a logical sequence of information, examples, and other data. If necessary, add or delete cards. Translate the logical arrangement of the cards into an outline as in this example:

Child Abuse

Thesis: Adult violence against children, commonly practiced throughout history, occurs today for a variety of reasons in countless cases of child abuse, and can be corrected only through social cooperation and legal sanctions.

I. Adult violence against children is common throughout history.
   A. The Sumerians beat children with whips to keep them disciplined.
   B. The Romans flogged boys before the altars of Diana as a religious practice.
   C. Early Christians whipped their children on Innocents Day in memory of King Herod's massacre.
   D. During the Middle Ages, children's eyes were gouged and their bodies mutilated to make them effective beggars.
   E. The factory system allowed foremen to beat children mercilessly if they didn't work hard enough.

II. Countless cases of child abuse exist today for a variety of reasons.
   A. Numerous child abuse cases have been recorded.
      1. On record are thousands of cases of planned falls, strangulations, and sex assaults.
      2. Parents have assaulted children with instruments ranging from plastic bags to baseball bats.
      3. Disciplinary measures may include cigarette burns, plunges into boiling water, or starvation.
   B. Child abuse cases exist for a variety of reasons.
      1. In a study of sixty families with beaten children, all the persecuting parents were beaten as children, indicating a revenge pattern.
      2. Some parents become abusive because they expect more love and affection from their child than the child is able to deliver.
      3. A frustrated parent will use the child's bad behavior to justify abuses.
      4. Unsatisfactory marital relationships are another frequent cause of child abuse.

III. Social cooperation and legal sanctions are needed to overcome the problem of child abuse.
   A. Although little was heard of the battered child syndrome before 1960, today all the states have adopted legislation governing reporting of battered children.
   B. But only two states, Maryland and New Jersey, have laws specifically prohibiting the use of physical force on children.
   C. Doctors and other people fear slander suits if they notify police of child abuse and an investigation does not support the charge.
   D. The other parent often protects the one inflicting the harm so that proof of battering is difficult to obtain.
   E. Society and its legal system must make further advances toward curbing child abuse.

Avoid an overly detailed outline. The rule of thumb is two pages of outline for every ten pages of writing.

E. Write and Document the Paper

With the outline completed, you are now ready to write the paper. Arrange the notecards in the sequence indicated by the outline. If properly assembled, the notecards can be expanded with transitions into a suitable first draft. Incorporate facts, opinions, data, and other information on the notecards into the first draft. Footnotes and bibliographic entries must be used to give credit to the authors of all material cited, quoted, or alluded to in the paper. You do not have to footnote your own ideas and insights, but you must acknowledge the contributions of others. This is the process of *documentation*.

Documentation for research writing became standardized with publication of the Modern Language Association's *Style Sheet* in 1951, which makes it easier for all readers to trace the source of researched information appearing in a paper. The most common kinds of documentation are illustrated below. If you have to refer to a source for which no footnote format is given here, either use the example most closely resembling the source, apply common sense, or check with the teacher. Bear in mind that the primary purpose of documentation is to indicate to the reader the original source of an idea.

1. Bibliography

The *bibliography* is a complete list of sources from which material or ideas were taken. The order and the punctuation of standard forms for a book and for a magazine are as follows:

Book: Author, *Title.* Volumes. Edition. Place: Publisher, Year.
Magazine: Author. "Title," *Magazine,* Volume (Issue), Pages.

STANDARD SOURCES

Book by a single author: Brodie, Fawn M. *Thomas Jefferson: An Intimate History.* New York: W. W. Norton & Company, Inc., 1974.

1. For easy alphabetizing, the author's surname comes first.
2. If the book is the work of an agency, a committee, or an organization, the name of that group replaces the name of the author.
3. If no author is given, begin the entry with the title.
4. In typing, the name of the book is underlined; in printing, it is italicized.
5. Facts of publication include: place of publication, name of publisher, and the date of publication. If more than one place is given, use only the first. Copy the publisher's name as it is listed on the title page of the book. If no date of publication is given, use the latest copyright date, or state "n.d."

Book by two authors: Hallberg, Edmond C., and William G. Thomas. *When I Was Your Age.* New York: The Free Press, 1974.

The names of second (and third) authors are not inverted. Use the same order of authors' names as found on the title page of the book.

Book by several authors:	Masotti, Louis H., *et al. A Time to Burn? An Evaluation of the Present Crisis in Race Relations.* Chicago: Rand McNally, 1969.

et al. may be replaced by the English "and others" if you prefer. This form for multiple authors should be used only for books by more than three authors.

Edition of an author's work:	Plath, Aurelia S., ed. *Letters Home by Sylvia Plath.* New York: Harper and Row, Publishers, 1975.
Edited work:	Arnold, Matthew. *Culture and Anarchy.* ed. J. Dover Wilson. Cambridge: University Press, 1961.
Edited collection:	Gordon, Walter K., ed. *Literature in Critical Perspectives: An Anthology.* New York: Appleton-Century-Crofts, 1968.
Translation:	Alighieri, Dante. *The Inferno,* trans. John Ciardi. New York: The New American Library of World Literature, Inc., 1954.
Edition other than the first:	McCrimmon, James M. *Writing with a Purpose.* 5th ed. Boston: Houghton Mifflin Company, 1974.

Other editions could be: Rev. ed. (Revised edition), 2d ed., rev. and enl. (revised and enlarged), and so on. Cite only the edition being used.

Work of more than one volume:	Harrison, G. B., *et al.*, eds., *Major British Writers.* 2 vols. New York: Harcourt, Brace and World, Inc., 1959.

If the volumes of a multivolume work were published over a period of years, the full period is cited: 1954–1960.

Title in an edited collection:	Thoreau, Henry David. "Observation." In *The Norton Reader.* 3d ed., ed. Arthur M. Eastman, *et al.* New York: W. W. Norton & Company, Inc., 1973.

1. This same form applies to short stories or poems.
2. The entry requires two titles, an author, and editor(s).
3. The title of the essay, short story, or poem is in quotation marks.
4. The title of the book is preceded by "In."

Article in a magazine:	Barthelme, Donald. "The Captured Woman." *The New Yorker,* 28 June 1976, pp. 22–25.
	Berger, Brigitte. "The Coming Age of People Work." *Change,* 8 (May 1976), 24–30.

1. The first entry shows an article in a magazine published weekly.
2. The second entry shows an article in a magazine published monthly, with volume number (8) cited. If the volume number is cited, then "p." or "pp." is deleted.

Newspaper article:	Shaw, Gaylord. "Goldwater Backs Ford—His Most Difficult Decision." *Los Angeles Times,* 1 July 1976, Part I, p. 1.

1. For news stories, simply cite the headline, newspaper title, section (if each section is paged separately), column (if helpful), and page.
2. The city is underlined if it appears as part of the newspaper title on the front page.

SPECIAL SOURCES

Article from an encyclopedia: Nicholas, Herbert George. "Churchill, Sir Winston Leonard Spencer." *Encyclopaedia Britannica* (1968), V, 747–51.

or more commonly

"Churchill, Sir Winston Leonard Spencer." *Encyclopaedia Britannica* (1969).

1. The authors of encyclopedia articles are usually listed by initials at the end of the articles; these initials are clarified in the index.
2. All facts of publication are not necessary; year and volume number suffice.
3. Watch the various spellings of encyclopedia.

Public document or pamphlet: U.S. Senate *Congressional Record.* 93d Congress. 10 June 1975.

Social Security Programs in the United States. U.S. Department of Health, Education, and Welfare, March 1968.

Kruger, Jane. *Teaching as an Art.* A Conference Syllabus published by Maryland University, 1970.

1976 Foreign Currency Converter, published by Deak and Co. of Los Angeles, 1976.

Because pamphlets are distributed by a variety of organizations in a variety of nonstandard forms, the best you can do is treat them as much like books as possible, supplying place of publication, publisher, and date.

Book review: Marcus, Greil. "Limits." Review of *Meridian* by Alice Walker. *The New Yorker,* 7 June 1976, pp. 133–36.

If the review is untitled, proceed directly with "Review of . . ."

Film: *Face to Face.* Film directed by Ingmar Bergman. Starring Liv Ullmann. A Paramount Release, 1976.

1. Film titles are underlined.
2. Supply name of director, star(s), and producer.

Recording or tape: Osborn, Alex. "Applied Imagination." Cassette, produced by Success Motivation Institute, Inc., 1972.

Roosevelt, Eleanor. "My Life with F.D.R." Cassette with regular library call number.

1. Copy all helpful information from tape or record.
2. The trend is to catalog tapes along with books.

Letter: Woolley, Morton. Personal letter. 12 Feb. 1976.

Interview: Hirshberg, Jennefer A. Personal Interview on College Grading Standards. Glendale, California, 19 Feb. 1976.

Manuscript: Zimmerman, Fred M. "Speculation: Los Angeles—1985." A working paper for the Los Angeles Goals Program. Los Angeles City Hall: Planning Department Library, 1967.

1. No specific rules exist for the documentation of manuscripts. When you use this kind of material, stick as closely as you can to the form for books or magazines.
2. The titles of unpublished works, no matter how long, are enclosed in quotation marks.

Radio or television program: Prokofiev, Sergei. "Romeo and Juliet" performed by the Bolshoi Ballet. Hosted by Mary Tyler Moore. CBS, 27 June 1976.

Include whatever information is needed to identify the program.

2. Footnotes

Footnotes have three uses:

1. To cite a specific source for borrowed material:

   [1]Jun J. Li, *The Essence of Chinese Civilization* (Princeton, New Jersey: D. Van Nostrand Company, Inc., 1967), p. 63.

2. To add an explanatory comment to the text without interrupting its main flow:

   [2]The "Cheng" referred to was later known as "Ch'in Shih Huang-ti," one of the greatest emperors of ancient China, who unified the country in 221 B.C. According to hearsay, his mother had been pregnant for twelve months before he was born; that was why, some people contended, his father never found out that he was not his true son.

3. To direct the reader to some additional source of information:

   [3]For further information on the May Fourth Movement, see Chow Tse-tung, *The May Fourth Movement* (Cambridge, Massachusetts: Harvard University Press, 1960), especially the introductory chapters.

Footnotes differ from bibliographic entries in supplying more specific information about exactly where in a work certain information was found. Primary footnotes have the following characteristics:

1. The first line is indented five spaces.
2. Authors' names are not inverted, but appear in regular order.
3. Commas separate the items of information.
4. Facts about publication are enclosed in parentheses.
5. The exact page reference is listed.
6. An elevated footnote number precedes the reference.
7. A footnote is single spaced, but separated from another footnote by a double space.

STANDARD FOOTNOTES.   The following footnotes illustrate the most common forms that occur. Refer to the section on bibliography to adapt any reference not given here.

Book with
one author: [4]Robert M. Pirsig, *Zen and the Art of Motorcycle Maintenance* (New York: William Morrow and Company, Inc., 1974), p. 49.

Subsequent reference: Pirsig, pp. 121–22.

Some teachers still insist on *ibid.,* meaning in the same place, for subsequent reference to an immediately preceding footnote, or "*Ibid.,* p. 10" if the source is the same but the page is different. However, the trend is away from Latin abbreviations.

Book with
two authors: [5]William H. Masters and Virginia E. Johnson, *Human Sexual Inadequacy* (Boston: Little, Brown and Company, 1970), p. 35.

Subsequent reference: Masters and Johnson, p. 50.

Essay in
an edited work: [6]Walter Lippmann, "Edison: Inventor of Invention," in *Modern Essays,* 3d ed., ed. Russell B. Nye and Arra M. Garab (Glenview, Ill.: Scott, Foresman and Company, 1963), p. 133.

Subsequent reference: Lippmann, p. 134.

Edited work: [7]William Wordsworth, *The Prelude,* ed. Ernest de Selincourt (Oxford: Clarendon Press), p. 55.

Subsequent reference: Wordsworth, p. 134.

Multivolume
work: [8]Le Roy Edwin Froom, *The Prophetic Faith of Our Fathers* (Washington, D.C.: Review and Herald Publishing Association, 1954), IV, 382.

Magazine
article: [9]George Leonard, "The Tattoo Taboo," *The Atlantic Monthly,* 238 (July 1976), 48.

Subsequent reference: Leonard, p. 49.

For a weekly magazine, the footnote would be as follows:

[10]Desmond King-Hele, "The Shape of the Earth," *Science,* 25 June 1976, p. 1293.

Subsequent reference: King-Hele, p. 1299.

Newspaper
article: [11]Alpheus T. Mason, "The Right to Revolt: A Last Resort in Pursuit of Happiness," *Los Angeles Times,* 4 July 1976, Part V, p. 1.

Subsequent reference: Mason, p. 4, col. 1.

Column numbers are cited only if the page in question is cluttered with articles:

[12]"No Greater Gift, No Greater Promise," *Los Angeles Times,* 4 July 1976, Part V, p. 2.

Subsequent reference: *Los Angeles Times,* p. 2.

FOOTNOTES FOR SPECIFIC ITEMS.   As in the case of bibliography entries, a chapter such as this cannot cover all the varied possibilities involved in footnoting. We offer the most common examples. For special cases, use the form closest to your specific example, follow your common sense, or ask your teacher how to footnote.

Famous play or poem: [13]William Shakespeare, *Macbeth*, III.ii.10.

       The reference is to Act Three, Scene Two, Line 10.

Subsequent reference: *Macbeth*, IV.iii.20.

       [14]John Milton, *Paradise Lost*, I.150.

       The reference is to Book One, line 150.

       Sometimes long poems also contain cantos, which are cited in small Roman numerals:

       [15]Edmund Spenser, *The Faerie Queene*, II.vi.26.

Bible passage: [16]John 3:16.

       [17]I Kings 2:12, Revised Standard Version.

       Translation is indicated only if not the King James Version.

Public document or pamphlet: [18]U.S., *Statutes at Large 1972*, Vol. 86, 1973, Public Law 92–347.

       Because public documents vary in format, you will need to improvise your own footnote, citing all information necessary for your reader to find the source.

       [19]George S. Duggar, *The Relation of Local Government Structure to Urban Renewal.* Bureau of Public Administration, University of California at Berkeley, 1961, p. 2.

Dissertation, thesis, or other manuscript material: [20]Joyce R. Cotton, "Evan Harrington: An Analysis of George Meredith's Revisions," Diss. University of Southern California, 1968, p. 25.

F. The Final Copy

The final copy should be clean and free of errors. Don't skimp on revising or proofreading time. If you do not type reasonably well, pay a good typist to type your paper, for the effort of a good paper is ruined by messy erasures or typographical errors.

    The body of the paper should be typed on 8 x 11 white bond (not erasable paper because it smudges), double spaced and properly footnoted, each footnote numbered consecutively and placed either at the bottom of the page where it occurs (see student sample paper), or accumulated in a "Notes" section at the end of the paper if your teacher stipulates this method. Remember that quotations of five or more lines are indented five spaces and single spaced without quotations marks. The margins of your paper should be 1 inch wide with the exception of the lefthand margin, which should be $1\frac{1}{2}$ inch.

Following is a checklist of what your paper must include:

1. A title page (see student sample paper)
2. A full outline of the paper (see student sample paper)
3. Body of the paper
4. An alphabetized bibliography
5. Notecards if your teacher requests them

Exercises

A. Unscramble the following bibliographical facts and arrange them in the proper bibliographical form.

1. A book by E. L. Doctorow, published by Random House of New York in 1975. The title of the book is *Ragtime*.
2. An article entitled "What Is the Federation Cup?" published in volume 23 of *World Tennis,* the August 1976 issue, covering pages 32–34.
3. "Good Country People," a story by Flannery O'Connor, taken from an anthology entitled *The Modern Tradition* (second edition), edited by Daniel F. Howard and published in 1972 by Little, Brown and Company of Boston.
4. Feodor Dostoevsky's famous novel *Crime and Punishment,* published by Oxford University Press, Inc. of New York (1953), in a translation by Jessie Coulson.
5. "The Dutiful Child's Promises," a selection from an old anthology entitled *Readings from American Literature,* edited by Mary Edwards Calhoun and Emma Lenore MacAlarney, published by Ginn and Company of Boston, 1915.
6. A two-volume work entitled *Civilization—Past and Present,* co-authored by T. Walter Wallbank and Alastair M. Taylor, published in 1949 by Scott, Foresman and Company of Chicago.
7. An unsigned encyclopedia article under the heading "Tiryns," found in volume 22 of the 1963 edition of the *Encyclopaedia Britannica,* pp. 247–48.
8. The sixth edition of Karl C. Garrison's book entitled *Psychology of Adolescence,* published in 1965 by Prentice-Hall, Inc. of Englewood Cliffs, New Jersey.
9. An article without author from the August 9, 1976, issue of *Time.* The article appears on pages 16 and 19 and is entitled "To Plains with the Boys in the Bus."
10. A feature article by Jim Murray, entitled "The Real Olympian," which appeared in Part III of the *Los Angeles Times,* pp. 1 and 7 (Wednesday, August 4, 1976).

B. Using the biographical information provided in exercise A, convert the items below into a proper sequence of footnotes.

1. Page 25 of the book by Karl C. Garrison.
2. Page 50 of that same book.
3. Page 30 of Volume One of the book by T. Walter Wallbank and Alastair M. Taylor.
4. Page 31 of that same book.
5. Page 90 of the book edited by Mary Edwards Calhoun and Emma Lenore MacAlarney.
6. Page 1 of the *Los Angeles Times* article.
7. Page 248 of the encyclopedia article.

8. Page 48 of Feodor Dostoevsky's novel.
9. Page 507 of Flannery O'Connor's story.
10. Page 46 of *Ragtime*.

C. From the works mentioned in this appendix, compile a list of sources that you would consult if you were to write on one of the following topics:

1. The last year of Thomas Jefferson's life
2. Research regarding the education of blind children
3. The novels of William Makepeace Thackeray
4. The myth of Europa
5. The rise of Mao Tse-tung
6. Safety in nuclear plants
7. The art of Jacques Louis David
8. Famous quotations about the value of education
9. The murder of Stanford White by Harry K. Thaw
10. The philosophy of Bertrand Russell

D. Summarize the following paragraph into one sentence:

Those who are awed by their surroundings do not think of change, no matter how miserable their condition. When our mode of life is so precarious as to make it patent that we cannot control the circumstances of our existence, we tend to stick to the proven and the familiar. We counteract a deep feeling of insecurity by making of our existence a fixed routine. We hereby acquire the illusion that we have tamed the unpredictable. Fisherfolk, nomads and farmers who have to contend with the willful elements, the creative worker who depends on inspiration, the savage awed by his surroundings—they all fear change. They face the world as they would an all-powerful jury. The abjectly poor, too, stand in awe of the world around them and are not hospitable to change. It is a dangerous life we live when hunger and cold are at our heels. There is thus a conservatism of the destitute as profound as the conservatism of the privileged, and the former is as much a factor in the perpetuation of a social order as the latter.

Eric Hoffer, The True Believer

E. Paraphrase the following paragraph so that it sounds like you.

The urge for a touch of class, for something better than others have, has put new pressure on that classic Russian institution—the queue. Customers the world-over wait in lines, but Soviet queues have a dimension all their own, like the Egyptian pyramids. They reveal a lot about the Russian predicament and the Russian psyche. And their operation is far more intricate than first meets the eye. To the passerby they look like nearly motionless files of mortals doomed to some commercial purgatory for their humble purchases. But what the outsider misses is the hidden magnetism of lines for Russians, their inner dynamics, their special etiquette.

Hedrick Smith, The Russians

G. Sample Student Paper

A student research paper is included on the following pages to give you an idea of what a good student paper looks like. It was written by a college freshman and demonstrates what any conscientious student can achieve when he or she tries.

THE INTERNMENT OF JAPANESE AMERICANS DURING WORLD WAR II

by

Diane L. Thomas

English 101
Glendale Community College
May 28, 1976

THE INTERNMENT OF JAPANESE AMERICANS DURING WORLD WAR II

Thesis: The internment of Japanese Americans during World War II was an
         abominable violation of American ideals.

I. The United States government abused the rights of an entire group.
    A. Guaranteed Constitutional rights were suspended.
    B. The Japanese Americans were judged by their ancestry rather than
        by individual acts.
        1. German and Italian aliens suspected of disloyalty were
            treated more fairly than were the Japanese Americans.
        2. Efforts on the part of Japanese Americans to demonstrate
            loyalty and patriotism were futile.

II. In a land where "all men are created equal," the underlying force
     behind the internment was extreme racial prejudice.
     A. There was a history of anti-Japanese feelings and actions in the
         United States prior to World War II.
         1. The stereotyped Japanese were viewed as a threat to Americans.
         2. Anti-Japanese legislation was already in existence.
     B. With racism to back it up, the hysteria that pervaded after Pearl
         Harbor was aggravated by politicians, anti-Japanese groups, and
         the press.

III. The unjust suffering that faced Japanese Americans seems a paradox in
      a country where "justice for all" is loudly proclaimed.
      A. Japanese Americans suffered severe economic losses as a result of
          the relocation.
      B. The camps themselves were inadequate.
      C. While Japanese Americans were living in internment camps, Japanese
          American soldiers were serving the United States in the war effort.
      D. The psychological and emotional suffering was perhaps the most
          tragic.

THE INTERNMENT OF JAPANESE AMERICANS DURING WORLD WAR II

On February 19, 1942, President Franklin D. Roosevelt signed an executive order that allowed the United States government to begin the evacuation and incarceration of 110,000 Japanese Americans. The order for relocation applied to "all persons of Japanese ancestry" and, of the total number of evacuees, 70,000 were American-born citizens. Forced to leave behind their homes, lands, and businesses, they were herded off to ten desolate camps scattered throughout the United States, surrounded by barbed-wire and under military guard, where they made their homes for nearly three years. The possibility of sabotage or espionage from among these people was the primary rationale behind this mass removal of the entire Japanese American population in California, western Washington, Oregon, and Arizona.[1] It is difficult to imagine how this unhappy event could have happened in these United States, but it did happen. Our history books often seem to imply that we are the heroes without guilt and the protectors of freedom carried on by the democratic principles for which we stand. The mass incarceration of Japanese Americans during World War II, however, is a part of our history that Americans cannot be proud of. Without a doubt, at that point in our history democracy was operating at its worst. Racial prejudice, wartime hysteria, fear, and outrage made the evacuation decision a popular one that caused us to commit "our worst wartime mistake."[2] The internment of Japanese Americans during World War II was an abominable violation of American ideals.

---

[1]Dillion S. Myer, Uprooted Americans (Tucson: University of Arizona Press, 1971), p. xiii.

[2]Roger Daniels, Concentration Camps U.S.A. (New York: Holt, Rinehart and Winston, Inc., 1972), pp. xi-xii.

By allowing the evacuation, the United States government abused the rights of an entire group. There is no question that the evacuation of men, women, and children from their homes without being charged with any crime, without trails or hearings, was a drastic invasion of the Constitutional rights of citizens.[3] Guarantees covered under the fourteenth amendment were ignored, depriving Japanese Americans of liberty and property without due process and the "equal protection of the laws" afforded other citizens.[4] All of this was done out of "military necessity" because the Japanese Americans were thought to be potentially disloyal. Even if there were saboteurs among them, such a fact does not justify suspending the rights of an entire group because of the possible guilt of a few.[5] There was not, however, one actual case of any act of sabotage or disloyalty by Japanese Americans during the entire war.

The government further abused the rights of Japanese Americans by judging them by their ancestry rather than by individual acts. Aliens and citizens alike were lumped together as a racial group whereas German and Italian aliens suspected of sabotage or espionage were handled on an individual basis. It is worth noting that, with few exceptions, the Japanese alien residents that were interned had lived in the United States from twenty to thirty years, having arrived prior to the Japanese Exclusion Act of 1924. Amazingly, the discriminating laws that were in effect made Japanese immigrants ineligible for citizenship, whereas a large percentage of German and Italian immigrants had become naturalized American citizens and, therefore, exempt from the "enemy alien"

---

[3]William Petersen, "Incarceration of Japanese Americans," National Review, 8 Dec. 1972, p. 69.

[4]Janet Stevenson, "Before the Colors Fade: The Return of the Exiles," American Heritage, 20 (June 1969), 24.

[5]Carey McWilliams, Prejudice (Boston: Little, Brown and Company, 1944) pp. 109-110.

classification.[6] Army General John L. DeWitt had said, "a Jap's a Jap"[7] and
it appears that this was the policy that was followed.

Despite numerous efforts, Japanese Americans found that attempts to prove
their loyalty and patriotism were futile. For example, immediately following
Pearl Harbor, the Japanese American Citizens League wired President Roosevelt
pledging their cooperation: "...We, in our hearts are Americans--loyal to
America. We must prove that to all of you."[8] Other Japanese Americans bought
defense bonds, donated to the Red Cross, and volunteered for civil defense
and intelligence work in an effort to prove their loyalty.[9] These patriotic
actions were apparently meaningless because these same people would soon find
themselves identified as the enemy and placed in barbed-wire enclosures.

In a land where "all men are created equal," the underlying force behind
the internment was extreme racial prejudice. Even prior to the evacuation in
1942 the Japanese had been the victims of racism in America, particularly
on the West Coast where their population was most concentrated. When immigrants from Japan began to arrive in the United States after 1890, they were
stereotyped, along with other Orientals, and viewed as a threat to Americans.
There was a general feeling that the Japanese would eventually overpopulate
the country and conquer the Caucasians.[10] Economically, they were resented
because of competition in agriculture, business, and labor. The development

---

[6]Dorothy S. Thomas, The Spoilage (Los Angeles: University of California
Press), p. 5.

[7]Ronald O. Haak, "Co-opting the Oppressors: The Case of the Japanese
Americans," Transaction, 12 (Oct. 1970), 23.

[8]Maisie Conrat, Executive Order 9066 (Los Angeles: California Historical
Society, 1972), p. 57.

[9]Audrie Girdner and Anne Loftis, The Great Betrayal (London: The Macmillan
Company, 1969), p. 11.

[10]Daniels, p. 2.

of Japan as a world power also contributed to this irrational fear and hatred of the Japanese, who were described as the "yellow peril."[11]

The anti-Japanese movement in America goes back to the turn of the century when the United States Industrial Commission claimed that the Japanese "are more servile than the Chinese, but less obedient and far less desirable. They have most of the vices of the Chinese with none of the virtues. They underbid the Chinese in everything and are as a class tricky, unreliable and dishonest."[12] At about the same time, the slogan of politician and labor leader Dennis Kearney was "The Japs must go!" while the mayor of San Francisco insisted that it was impossible for the Japanese to assimilate into our culture and that they were "not the stuff of which American citizens can be made."[13] Appropriately, the Japanese and Korean Exclusion League was formed in 1905 and a number of other anti-Japanese societies followed. There were scattered cases of individual and mob violence directed against the Japanese, the press made verbal racist attacks, and the yellow peril continued to gain credibility.[14]

With the agitation against the Japanese came continual proposals of anti-Japanese legislation. Indeed, every session of the California legislature between 1905 and 1945 attempted to pass at least one piece of anti-Japanese legislation.[15] They were successful in 1913 when the Alien Land Law was passed, preventing Japanese from purchasing or leasing land for more than three years. In most of the western states, residence choices were restricted by covenants, intermarriage with Caucasians was forbidden and free access to certain public

[11]Myer, pp. 11-12.

[12]Conrat, p. 18.

[13]Daniels, pp. 9-10.

[14]Myer, pp. 11-14.

[15]Daniels, p. 11.

places was forbidden.[16] Finally, in 1924 the agitation subsided temporarily
when an exclusion act was passed specifically preventing further Japanese
immigration.

With years of racism to back it up, the hysteria that pervaded after
Pearl Harbor was aggravated by politicians, anti-Japanese groups, and the
press. Newspapers led the already-frightened public to believe that Japanese
saboteurs were lurking everywhere, by publishing headlines like "JAP BOAT
FLASHES MESSAGE ASHORE," "JAPANESE HERE SENT VITAL DATA TO TOKYO" and "JAPS
PLAN COAST ATTACK IN APRIL WARNS CHIEF OF KOREAN SPY BAND."[17] The stories,
of course, were totally unfounded. To add to the panic, former Supreme Court
Justice Earl Warren, then attorney general, testified that American-born
Japanese were even more dangerous to the security of the United States than
alien Japanese.[18] Emotional demands for action by leaders like Congressman
John Rankin helped make up the minds of the public: "I'm for catching every
Japanese in American, Alaska, and Hawaii now and putting them in concentration
camps. Damn them! Let's get rid of them now!"[19] The pressure increased, more
unfounded rumors were spread, and the fear of invasion and suspicion of sabotage eventually led to the imprisonment of 110,000 Japanese Americans.

Considering the unjust suffering that Japanese Americans faced, it seems
a paradox that it took place in a country where there is "justice for all."
The economic losses suffered by Japanese Americans as a result of the internment has been nearly impossible to calculate. Given only a matter of days
or a few weeks between notification and evacuation, they were forced to sell

---

[16]Thomas, p. 2.

[17]Daniels, p. 33.

[18]Haak, p. 23.

[19]Conrat, p. 21.

their property at prices far below its real value. Far away at relocation centers and unable to protect their interests back home, their property that had been stored or left to trustees was often stolen, vandalized, or sold.[20] It is impossible to calculate the lost wages, income, and interest; but the property losses have been estimated to be worth $400,000,000. The United States government has repaid Japanese Americans a portion of this amount, and in 1967 the Supreme Court ruled that an additional $10,000,000 was owed to Japanese Americans whose dollar savings had been confiscated during the internment.[21]

To add to the miserable plight of the internees, the camps themselves were inadequate. Small, semi-private barracks were hastily built with wood and tar paper and often located in desolate, out-of-the-way deserts and waste-lands. There were no cooking or plumbing facilities in the barracks, but each block had a mess hall and a building with latrines, showers, and laundry facilities.[22] Protection from the elements and sanitation was simply not adequate.[23] In spite of these obstacles, cooperating communities were established in the camps and, through a lot of hard work and determination, they led a reasonably comfortable existence.

It is ironic that while the internees were overcoming these conditions within their barbed-wire enclosures, Japanese American soldiers were serving the United States in the war effort. The 442nd Combat Team, an all-Japanese volunteer unit, distinguished themselves on the battle front in Italy with more casualties and decorations than any other unit of similar size and length

---

[20]Conrat, p. 22.

[21]"Tule Lake Thirty Years Later," Time, 10 June 1974, p. 31.

[22]Myer, pp. 30-32.

[23]Conrat, p. 22.

of service in the history of the army.[24] It seems incredible that while Japanese soldiers were being injured and killed overseas, their brothers, sisters, mothers and fathers were back in the states imprisoned by the very country they were fighting for. Knowing this, it must have been frustrating for many members of the 442nd Combat Team when, at an honorary citation ceremony, President Truman said to them: "You are to be congratulated for what you have done for this great country of ours. I think it was my predecessor who said that Americanism is not a matter of race or creed, it is a matter of the heart...."[25]

Perhaps the most tragic of the injustices inflicted upon Japanese Americans was the psychological and emotional suffering they experienced. The internment was morale-killing, humiliating, and frustrating. The internees had to live with the knowledge that they were being regarded as traitors to their country and that they would always be judged by their ancestry rather than their actions. For those Americans, it is fair to conclude, the imprisonment represents a very bad memory that is permanently engraved in their minds.

Today the internment of 110,000 Japanese Americans in the United States is difficult to imagine, but thirty years ago it was a cold reality. Every aspect of it was diametrically opposed to the treasured ideals of America. That such a tragedy could have taken place in this country illustrates that prejudice, hate, and fear can cause us to ignore completely the rights and freedoms of which we are so proud. It should also serve as a ghastly reminder that such a tragedy should never be allowed to happen again.

---

[24]Conrat, p. 23.

[25]Myer, p. 148.

BIBLIOGRAPHY

Conrat, Maisie. _Executive Order 9066_. Los Angeles: California Historical Society, 1972.

Daniels, Roger. _Concentration Camps U.S.A._ New York: Holt Rinehart and Winston, Inc., 1972.

Girdner, Audrie, and Anne Loftis. _The Great Betrayal_. London: The Macmillan Company, 1969.

Haak, Ronald O. "Co-opting the Oppressors: The Case of the Japanese Americans." _Transaction_, 12 (Oct. 1970), 23-31.

McWilliams, Carey. _Prejudice_. Boston: Little, Brown and Company, 1944.

Myer, Dillion S. _Uprooted Americans_. Tucson: The University of Arizona Press, 1971.

Petersen, William. "Incarceration of Japanese Americans." _National Review_, 8 Dec. 1972, pp. 49-50.

Stevenson, Janet. "Before the Colors Fade: The Return of the Exiles." _American Heritage_, 20 (June 1969), 22-25.

Thomas, Dorothy Swaine. _The Spoilage_. Los Angeles: University of California Press, 1946.

"Tule Lake Thirty Years Later." _Time_, 10 June 1974, p. 31.

Index

The text of this book is set in 10-point Baskerville; the readings, in 9-point Vega Light. The display type is Garamond Italic. The book was set by Applied Typographic Systems, Mountain View, California, and printed and bound by R. R. Donnelley, Crawfordsville, Indiana.

Acquisition Editor: Gerald Richardson

Project Editor: Ronald Q. Lewton

Designer: Naomi Takigawa

890/65